The Orton Diaries

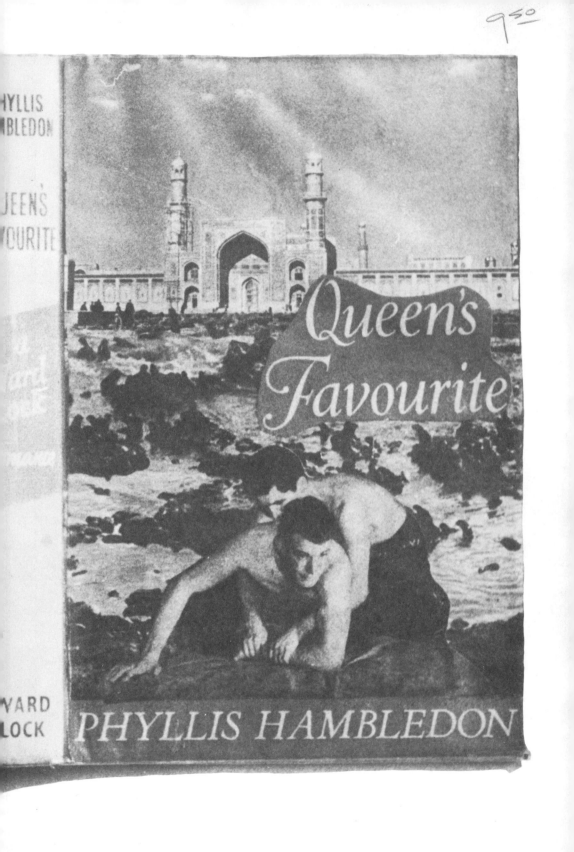

Queen's
Favourite

PHYLLIS HAMBLEDON

THE
ORTON
DIARIES

including the correspondence of Edna Welthorpe and others

EDITED BY JOHN LAHR

Methuen · London

First published in Great Britain in 1986
by Methuen London Ltd, 11 New Fetter Lane, London EC4P 4EE
Copyright © 1986 by the Estate of Joe Orton, deceased
Introduction copyright © 1986 by John Lahr

Printed in Great Britain

British Library Cataloguing in Publication Data

Orton, Joe
The Orton diaries: including
the correspondence of Edna Welthorpe and others.
1. Orton, Joe – Biography   2. Dramatists,
English – 20th century – Biography
I. Title   II. Lahr, John
822'.914   PR6065.R7Z/

ISBN 0-413-349660-0

Contents

List of Illustrations

End papers: Orton's defaced library books.

Frontispiece: Joc Orton opposite 25 Noel Road, 1964. (Associated Newspaper Group Ltd.)

Part Title page 33: Orton in his bedsitter, 1966. (Daily Mirror)

Between pages 64 and 65:

Joe Orton, 1967. (Douglas Jeffery)
Leonie and George Barnett, 1966.
Elsie Orton.
Orton asleep in Leicester backyard.
Peggy Ramsay and Bill Roderick.
Oscar Lewenstein, 1967.
Peter Willes, *c.* 1967.
Orton's scrapbook collage of *Entertaining Mr. Sloane's* West End transfer.
Orton with Dudley Sutton and Madge Ryan, 1964.
Orton with Geraldine McEwan and Kenneth Williams, 1965. (Donald Southern)
Kenneth Cranham, the corpse of Mrs. McLeavy, and Simon Ward in the successful West End production of *Loot*, 1966. (John Haynes)
Michael Bates and Sheila Ballantine in funeral fiasco in *Loot*, 1966. (Romano Cagnoni – Report London)
Orton receives *Evening Standard* Award for Best Play, 1966. (BBC Hulton Picture Library)

Between pages 128 and 129:

Orton, 1965.
Orton at desk, 1966. (BBC Hulton Picture Library)
Peter Gill discusses the set of *Crimes of Passion*. (Douglas Jeffery)
Donald Pleasence and Hermione Baddeley in *The Good and Faithful Servant*, 1967. (Rediffusion Television)
Orton outside 25 Noel Road. (Associated Newspaper Group Ltd.)
Orton, drawn by Patrick Procktor.

Orton, 1964. (Associated Newspaper Group Ltd.)
'The most perfectly developed playwright'.
Orton, 1967. (Douglas Jeffery)
The successful playwright. (Associated Newspaper Group Ltd.)

Part title on page 155: Moroccan boy. (Photo: Orton)

Between pages 192 and 193:

Orton in Tangier flat, 1965. (Edward Quinn)
Orton on patio terrace, 1967.
Orton eating hash cake, 1967.
Orton and Friend, 1965.
Kenneth Halliwell, 1967.
Orton, Kenneth Williams and Halliwell in Tangier, 1965.
Halliwell, 1967; Orton sunbathes in background.
Tangier from their balcony, 1965.
Halliwell and Orton go native, 1965.
Avril Elgar and Michael Standing in *The Ruffian on the Stair*, 1967. (Douglas
    Jeffery)
Stanley Baxter, Sir Ralph Richardson and Julia Foster in *What the Butler Saw*,
    1969. (Douglas Jeffery)
Bill Fraser in *Funeral Games*, 1968. (Yorkshire Television)
Orton, 1966. (John Haynes)
Exterior of 25 Noel Road, 9 August 1967. (BBC Hulton Picture Library)

Part title on page 227: Orton on steps of 25 Noel Road, 1964. (Associated
    Newspaper Group Ltd.)

Editor's Note

Except to avoid libel, I have kept the cutting of Orton's London diaries to the minimum. The Tangier diary has been trimmed of some of its repetition. A few names have been changed for legal reasons. Otherwise, the diaries are as, we assume, the police found them on top of Orton's desk on the day he was murdered.

In the footnotes and the introduction, I have used, where at all possible, new material culled from Orton's correspondence and from the people – many now dead – whom I originally interviewed for *Prick Up Your Ears* (1978), my biography of Orton. In a few instances, for professional reasons, theatre people have requested their dates of birth not be published. Future Orton scholars interested in reading the hundreds of hours of this biographical testimony, plus Orton's prison letters, can find it on file at the 'John Lahr Collection', Mugar Memorial Library, Boston University.

Some mystery still surrounds the diaries. Halliwell's suicide note says that the diaries – especially the latter part – will explain everything. They don't, at least not definitively. As Orton wrote them, the diaries end with a hyphen: cut off, like Orton himself, in full flow. This seems to me improbable for someone as consistent and meticulous about his writing as Orton. The diaries end on 1 August 1967, and he died on 9 August. In the Coroner's Report, the entries for May 1–3 are cited. But what happened to the last pages? The mystery in some way adds to Orton's myth. History can never know what exactly sparked off the murder. For dramatic symmetry, I have ended the *Diaries* on Orton's and Halliwell's last exchange. The diaries' final paragraph about Orton's return to Leicester to see his sister's new-born daughter and a local production of *Entertaining Mr. Sloane* follows:

I caught the 11.05 train. Uneventful journey. It was raining in Leicester. I caught the bus outside the station. Went straight to Leonie's house. Leonie, George and my father were there. My father was staring at the cricket on the television. 'Hello', he said, stumbling to his feet. 'The baby's called Lois,' Leonie said. She went into the kitchen and brought me a plate of food. As I ate it the rain started. George went back to work. Leonie said she'd had a bad time with the baby. 'I don't want any more,' she said. 'George does, though,' my father said. 'He can bloody well want then,'

Leonie said. 'I was on pethidine. And they put it into my hand wrong. Did I write and tell you?' 'No,' I said. She told me how she'd been taken to hospital two weeks before the baby was born. 'High blood pressure,' she said. 'I was in labour and the doctor gave me saline drips in my hand. Only he didn't put it in my vein. He put it in the actual tissue.' She switched off the television which had just been calling for blood donors. 'I didn't know what was happening. I was on the pethidine. And then the sister came and nearly died. She screamed, "What's happened to this patient's hand!" And, you know, it was unbelievable. I've never seen anything like it. I had to laugh. My hand was like a balloon. Right up it was. "What've you done!" she said to the doctor – he was supposed to be a specialist. "I know what I've done," he said. "You put it in the tissue," she said – and what

'Ever since they've been courtin',' wrote a friend in an anniversary poem, 'he's been workin' on Orton.' Well, not quite. But my work on Orton, which began back in 1970, is now over. It has been an exciting enterprise made possible by substantial encouragement and help from others: The Orton Estate, especially Leonie Orton Barnett; Peggy Ramsay; Kenneth Williams, Oscar Lewenstein; Richard Simon; Paul Sidey; Geoffrey Strachan; and Nick Hern. A special acknowledgement must go to the editorial skills of my wife Anthea Lahr who wants everything shorter but her encomium. I end this project as I began it so long ago – dazzled by Orton's theatrical audacity, his candour, and his ability to corrupt an audience with pleasure.

Introduction

On 30 April 1967, the comedian Kenneth Williams strolled in Hyde Park with Joe Orton and Kenneth Halliwell, Orton's companion for sixteen years. Williams had starred in the first disastrous production of Orton's *Loot* (1965), which Halliwell had titled and which, revised and remounted, was now the West End comedy hit of the year. In his radio and screen performances in the 'Carry On' films, Williams affected outrageousness; but Orton lived it. Williams was always a good audience for the boundless irreverence which distinguished Orton's life and his laughter. On this occasion, Orton was recounting the picking up of a man near a public loo. Williams recorded the conversation in his diary:

> 'We'd been eyeing each other warily – and this fellow asked, "You got a place we can go?"' Joe said (in front of Halliwell), 'I told him that I lived with someone, and it wasn't convenient. The man replied, "I often get picked up by queers 'round here. Some of them have very nice places. They must be on quite good money. I've had as much as thirty shillings from some of them. They're not all effeminate either, some of them are really manly and you'd never dream they were queer. Not from the look of them. But I can always tell 'cos they've *all* got LPs of Judy Garland. That's the big give-away."' I told Joe, 'It's marvellous the way you remember dialogue as well as the accents! You really capture the flavour of the personality you're describing.' Joe said, 'Yes, I've started a diary.' I said, 'Pepys put all his references to sexual matters in code so that no one would know'. Joe said, 'I don't care who knows.'

'The whole trouble with Western Society today is the lack of anything worth concealing,' Orton wrote in his diary[1], which covered the last eight eventful months of his life. Orton had willed himself into the role of rebel outcast: beyond guilt or shame. At thirty-four, already with a criminal record for comically defacing public library books, Orton had rejected the world of conventional work, conventional sex, and conventional wisdom. He was an iconoclast who believed there was no sense being a rebel without applause.

Orton loved to shock. *Loot*'s success emboldened him. 'Well, the sound and fury is over,' Orton wrote to a friend on 4 October 1966, sending press clippings

[1] *Diaries*, 24 June 1967.

which compared him to Ben Jonson, G. B. Shaw and – the soubriquet that stuck – 'the Oscar Wilde of Welfare State gentility'[1]. '*Loot* and *Joe Orton* are a great success. I feel exhausted. 18 months of struggling to vindicate the honour of my play (my own is beyond vindication) has left me weak at the knees.' But with acclaim, Orton's literary style and his life acquired a new swagger. Orton's journal, which he began two months later, was called *Diary of a Somebody*.[2]

The idea of a diary was first suggested by Orton's agent, Peggy Ramsay in 1965. 'I didn't write the Morocco diary as you wanted,' Orton wrote her on 30 August 1965. 'I thought there might be difficulties in getting it published.' Ramsay continued to press for an account of their Tangier adventures, if not from Orton then from Kenneth Halliwell whose literary ambitions Orton had inherited and then surpassed. 'I urge *one* of you, at least to start a journal à la Gide[3] ... I'm sure it would be a good idea and the publishers would snap at it,' she wrote, prematurely as it turned out. 'Why not talk this over with Ken, who has real writing talent, but finds stage plots so difficult.'[4]

But Halliwell was fast losing what literary confidence he had left. His latest rejection had come the day after *Loot* opened to phenomenal reviews, and was from Orton's agent. 'What I've read,' Peggy Ramsay wrote, too bored to finish Halliwell's *The Facts of Life*, 'reads like an adaptation from a novel, because the first speech, for instance, is so damned *literary* and the speeches are nearly always written beyond their "holding" capacity.' Before he finally gave up writing, Halliwell sent the play to a few more agents and to Peter Willes, who produced Orton's television plays. 'I'd had several plays sent me by Ken,' Peter Willes recalled. 'They were not like Joe's whatsoever. They were like very pseudo-Ronald Firbank.'

Halliwell, who never found himself, had also never found his literary voice. Orton had. Orton's unrelenting display of verbal prowess was a terrific offence that masked his own defensiveness; but Halliwell's literary archness only made his insecurity more transparent. Between October and December when the diary began, Halliwell abdicated the literary obsession that had dominated their adult lives and turned to his collages. 'Does my real talent if any lie in this direction?' he wrote to Peggy Ramsay on 30 October 1966. Orton was now the writer; and

1 Ronald Bryden, *The Observer*, 2 October 1966.
2 Listed as the title of the Diaries in the Coroner's Report; but the title page was not returned with the Diaries to the Estate after the inquest.
3 André Gide (1860–1951) French writer whose books focus on his sexual, moral, religious, and literary problems. In 1893, convalescing from tuberculosis in Algeria and after meeting Oscar Wilde, Gide discovered he was homosexual. His *Journals* (first published in 1939 and continued in 1951, 1952 and 1960) chronicle his feelings and attitudes as well as personalities and his wide-ranging reading. Received the Nobel Prize for Literature in 1947.
4 Peggy Ramsay to Orton, 7 June 1966.

Halliwell, who had nurtured Orton's skills and ambitions, was increasingly a factotum. Inevitably, the idea of a journal became Orton's project.

'I'm keeping a journal,' Orton wrote to Peggy Ramsay from Tangier on 30 May 1967, five months after he'd begun it, 'to be published long after my death.' To Orton, the value of a diary was its frankness. Reality, as his plays insisted, was the ultimate outrage. Orton despised the bogus propriety – the 'verbal asterisks' – with which public figures doctored the picture of their life. 'It's extraordinary,' he complained to Peggy Ramsay, 'how, as people grow older and they have less to lose by telling the truth, they grow more discreet, not less.'[1] To Orton, indiscretion was the better part of valour. 'He thought he was a very important writer,' said Kenneth Cranham, Orton's friend, who played Hal in the first London production of *Loot*. 'He'd talk to you about his diary. He had a vision of this diary . . .'

'I'm going up, up, up,' Orton wrote a friend in March 1967; and the diary was a symbol of Orton's confidence in his new-found momentum. He was going to have an interesting life after all. For a while, even after he'd broken through, he wasn't sure. '*Sloane* wasn't easy. It wasn't the overall critical success people think it was,' Orton said. 'I had to hack my way in.'[2] Although *Entertaining Mr Sloane* (1964) had succeeded in London, it had failed miserably on Broadway. 'I must close now because I'm tearful and I must go out,' Orton wrote to his American director Alan Schneider at the news the show was coming off after only thirteen performances, typically hiding his sadness behind a joke. 'The air around Islington is like wine.'[3] The débâcle of the first production of Orton's second full-length play, *Loot*, had left his career and his self-confidence in shambles. Orton stopped writing for a while. He threatened to quit the theatre. 'I'm really quite capable of carrying this out,' Orton warned Peggy Ramsay, just four months before Orton's play and his reputation were reborn. 'I've always admired Congreve who, after the absolute failure of *Way of the World*, just stopped writing. And Rimbaud who turned his back on the literary world after writing a few volumes.' But *Loot*'s success liberated Orton. Before it, he had been promising; now suddenly he was major. His literary style and his life acquired a new amperage. He was on the top of his form, full of fun and writing like the young master he knew himself to be. The buoyant outrageousness of Orton's comic style evolved mostly in the last fecund eight months of his life. In that time, besides the diaries, Orton wrote the ghoulish capriccio about faith and justice, *Funeral Games*; rewrote his first play *The Ruffian on the Stair* (1963) and *The Erpingham Camp* (1965) for their stage premieres under the collective title *Crimes of Passion*; completed the screenplay *Up Against It*; and wrote his farce masterpiece *What the Butler Saw*.

1 *Diaries*, 27 July 1967.
2 Barry Hanson interview for the programme of *Crimes of Passion* (Royal Court, June 1967).
3 Orton to Alan Schneider, 21 October 1965.

Orton's plays caught the era's psychopathic mood, that restless, ruthless pursuit of sensation whose manic frivolity announced a refusal to suffer. The diaries are a chronicle not only of a unique comic imagination but of the cock-eyed liberty of the time – a time before the failure of radical politics, before mass unemployment, before AIDS.

Orton had long harboured fantasies of omnipotence. As late as 1961, in his novel *Head to Toe*,[1] Orton contemplated a new kind of writing 'that would create a seismic disturbance' whose 'shock waves were capable of killing centuries afterwards'.[2] In farce, Orton found a way of turning his aggression into glory. 'To be destructive,' he wrote, 'words have to be irrefutable.'[3] And Orton's hard-won epigrammatic style achieved just that: 'With madness as with vomit, it is the passer-by who receives the inconvenience.' Orton's diaries make explicit his desire to drive an audience crazy with pleasure. 'Much more fucking,' he writes on 26 March 1967, making a note to hot-up *What the Butler Saw*, 'and they'll be screaming hysterics in next to no time.' To be a 'panic' is the aspiration of all great comedians, an encounter that exhilarates as it infantilises an audience, Orton's comedy personified this instinct for anarchy and, in *What the Butler Saw*, even invoked the traditional jester's symbol for it: the penis.[4] Farce plays on a common recognition of insecurity and creates the illusion of mastery. Orton's obsession with the penis, on and off stage, tried to turn his fears of inadequacy into a spectacle of potency and control.

'"I'm from the gutter", I said, "And don't you ever forget it because I won't."'[5] Orton saw himself as a mixture of 'truculence and charm' and recorded the impact of his studied toughness. He had lived through a lot and came across as a cool customer. On her first meeting with Orton, Peggy Ramsay recalls, 'I was very hard on him because he was talented. He had this lovely detachment.' And in her letter to Harold Hobson a few months later, urging him to attend the opening of *Entertaining Mr Sloane*, Ramsay's admiration for Orton's toughness comes through:

> This play came to me in January and I thought it extremely talented and asked to meet the author. A young man called and I was much struck with him. I frankly told him that I was uncertain about the advisability of selling this play in case the critics might label it 'Pinterish'. He replied that I must

1 Originally titled *The Vision of Gombold Proval*; posthumously published as *Head to Toe*.
2 *Head to Toe* (Anthony Blond, 1971), p. 149.
3 *Ibid.*
4 In *What the Butler Saw*, 'the missing part of Sir Winston Churchill' is produced and waved like a wand over the mayhem. 'How much more inspiring,' says Dr Rance, 'if, in those dark days, we'd seen what we see now. Instead we had to be content with the cigar – the symbol falling far short, as we all realise, of the object itself.'
5 *Diaries*, 9 January 1967.

do anything I wished and that he could easily manage if I didn't sell it, because he was living on £3. 10s. p.w. National Assistance[1], and had been doing so 'ever since he came out'. He then went on to tell me that he had been six months in Wormwood Scrubs for a series of minor thefts and that it had been remarkably good for him. When I asked if he intended going back to crime, he said certainly not, if it was possible to earn a living in any other way.

Finally, I decided to get the play done quickly at the Arts ... In the meantime, I've been trying to help the author with money, but he firmly and tactfully says it's quite unnecessary and that he 'can manage'. I even offered him a TV set as a present, but he said he was quite all right without one!

I'm much struck with a young man who doesn't want to exploit people, who is prepared to live on £3. 10 p.w., who doesn't whine, or tell a hard luck tale.[2]

With success, Orton continued to build up his reputation for hardness. To the *Evening Standard*, Orton drew another comparison between himself and Oscar Wilde besides wit: 'I didn't suffer the way Oscar Wilde suffered from being in prison. But then Wilde was flabby and self-indulgent. There is this complete myth about writers being sensitive plants. They're not. It's a silly, 19th-century idea. I'm sure Aristophanes was not sensitive.'[3] He had himself photographed bare-chested with arms akimbo in stark and shadowy angles, glowering into the camera with a hard man's steely gaze. Orton worked at not only being well-built ('I shall be the most perfectly developed of modern playwrights if nothing else') but also well-hung. In the famous photo of Orton reclining in a deckchair with his crotch looming up in the foreground, Orton had stuffed his swimming trunks with toilet paper.[4] 'He looked tight and tough,' the actor Simon Ward recalled. 'Joe's hair was like a little tight skull-cap. He walked very erect, his buttocks clenched, the pelvis thrust forward. There's only one way you can walk when you carry yourself like that – a cross between an automaton and a sailor's roll.'

Orton's swagger, like his characters' strutting dialogue, presented an image of power that betrayed inadequacy. Says Detective Truscott in *Loot*, for instance: 'How dare you involve me in a situation for which no memo has been issued.' As the diaries show, when faced with situations which made him feel 'weak' or out of control – the enervating rows with Halliwell, the depressing opening of *Crimes of Passion*, his mother's funeral – Orton sought to test and to confirm his strength in the anonymous dangers of the public lavatories. The tongue-in-cheek title of

---

1 In 1963, Orton was living on £161 a year. In 1983, his Estate earned £74,294.
2 Peggy Ramsay to Harold Hobson, 1 May 1964.
3 *Evening Standard*, 3 October 1966.
4 Information provided by Henry Budgen, who took the photo.

the diaries[1] suggests that Orton was aware, on some level, of the comic strain of always having to appear big. The diaries contain many examples of Orton's detached amusement at himself. 'Perhaps you better find yourself a different writer,' he tells the Beatles' management brazenly, when the Fab Four stand him up at a meeting to discuss the possibility of writing their next film. But Orton spoils the startling hard-nose effect with a slapstick exit. 'Left almost tripping over the carpet and crashing into the secretary who gave a squeal of surprise as I hurried past her. This I never mention when retelling the story. I always end on a note of hurt dignity.'

Orton's celebrity protected him from feeling humiliation. Every failure – his day trip to Libya, the Beatles' rejection of his screenplay, the fiasco of *The Evening Standard* Award – could be turned to his advantage. But his search for invulnerabilty dominates his life as well as his stage laughter. Orton's notorious practical jokes – the defacement of 'dull, badly written books'[2] and letters written in the spirit of oafish English middle classery and signed under the name of 'Edna Welthorpe (Mrs)' – are defensive, albeit hilarious, pranks. The mischief is aggressive, but the culprit is invisible, the work of a trickster with a strong rage and a weak ego. Orton pasted an anonymous quotation on the back page of his *Loot* scrapbook: 'I was not nearly so sure of myself as I should have liked, and this made me present a brassy face to the world and pretend to be more hard-boiled than I was ... I developed a mocking, cynical way of treating events because it prevented them from being too painful ...'

The landscape of Orton's London is bleak: a soiled world of loss, isolation, ignorance, and bright decline. 'I'm a believer in Original Sin,' Orton said. 'I find people profoundly bad and irresistibly funny.' Public lavatories were often the setting where his point was proved most outrageously. 'No more than two feet away,' Orton writes in the diaries,[3] as seven men grope each other, including him, in a loo, 'the citizens of Holloway moved about their ordinary business.'

But if Orton relished the humour, his sense of sadness at his incidental encounters also comes through strongly in the diaries. He records the poignance of a derelict singing 'Once I had a secret love'. And two aged, out-of-work actresses touch him with buoyant small talk about their decrepitude. 'It was a very sad scene,' Orton writes, of a tactic he himself used in his plays, 'because it was played in such a cheerful way.'[4] Likewise, the diaries sparkle with fun during a time when his mother dies, his father is hit by a car and goes blind, and his relationship with Halliwell (and Halliwell himself) is cracking up. 'He thought,

1 Echoes George and Weedon Grossmith's *Diary of a Nobody*, the ludicrous chronicles of the suburban misadventures of the prim, social-climbing fictional diarist Charles Pooter.
2 *Daily Sketch*, 30 November 1966.
3 *Diaries*, 4 March 1967.
4 *Diaries*, 3 July 1967

planned, waited, and waiting, plunged into dreams,' Orton wrote, summarising his life before success so accurately that he'd repeated it both in *Head to Toe* and *The Boy Hairdresser* (1960). Now that the dreams had come true, Orton still couldn't banish his sense of foreboding. Happiness was rare enough in their life for Orton and Halliwell to have little faith in it. As he wrote in his Tangier diary:

> Kenneth and I sat talking of how happy we both felt. We'd have to pay for it. Or we'd be struck down from afar by disaster because we were, perhaps, too happy. To be young, good-looking, healthy, famous, comparatively rich *and* happy is surely going against nature . . . I hope no doom strikes.[1]

'Outcasts always mourn,' Wilde wrote for his epitaph, and Orton's furious hilarity always contains a sense of loss. 'I'm not in favour of private grief,' says Fay in *Loot*, which mocks the rituals around death. 'Show your emotions in public or not at all.' In Orton, grief translates as aggression; and sadness is never far beneath the lethal wit he showed both on stage and off it. 'Joe had those absolutely black eyes with no expression in them at all,' says Peter Willes. 'They were pretty nearly dead eyes. I attribute it to unhappiness.'

Orton had a long history of regrets. In *Head to Toe* he dramatised his condition as lost in an alien world, imprisoned in a country that confounds him and where his survival is uncertain. 'I feel a great need of knowledge,' says Gombold, Orton's fictional spokesman. And later: 'He passed through each degree of despair that prisoners suffer.' Orton was trapped by the deprivations of his working-class Leicester background, the first of four children in a family where there was never enough money or attention to go around. He had failed his eleven-plus; failed as an actor after RADA; failed for a decade as a writer; failed in the eyes of society to be a responsible, even normal, citizen. His laughter got even for these sources of humiliation: his credulous parents, sexual guilt, social stereotyping, the double-binds of authority in which his identity was discounted. 'He'd suffered an awful lot from people's ribaldry about camp,' says the novelist Penelope Gilliatt, who befriended Orton in 1965 when she was the drama critic of the *Observer*. 'He was furious. He lived a lot of his life in a state of cold, marvellous, funny fury.'

The diaries are full of Orton's percolating rage. 'There's no such thing as a joke,' Orton says, in one particularly instructive passage of the Tangier diary, on 25 May 1967, after he faced down the judgemental glare of a heterosexual couple with a bravura display of outrageousness. ('We've got a leopard-skin rug in the flat and he wanted me to fuck him on that, only I'm afraid of the spunk you see, it might adversely affect the spots of the leopard.') On stage, Orton deployed his wit to the same end: to put distance between himself and the things that

1 *Diaries*, 25 May 1967.

oppressed him. 'If you could lock the enemy in the room and fire sentences at them ...' Orton wrote in 1961. By 1967, his salvoes were disarming the public, and the enemy was within.

'When Joe sent me *Sloane*, he spoke of it as "our play",' says Peggy Ramsay. 'The first time he came to see me, Joe didn't produce Kenneth. But the second time he said "Can I bring my friend?" And never at any stage was Kenneth not there.' Orton dedicated *Entertaining Mr Sloane* to Halliwell, and Halliwell too talked of 'a genius like us'. This continued to be the pattern through Orton's struggles of 1965 and 1966. Orton wrote to Halliwell from New York, nervous about the Broadway reception of *Sloane*: 'I'm not hopeful of success. But we never were, were we.'[1] And when the original production of *Loot* faced its first audiences, Orton's distraught letters home to Halliwell register a tone of dependence and concern that are not in the diaries. 'The play is a disaster,' Orton wrote Halliwell on 9 February 1965, from its first try-out in Cambridge. 'There were hardly any laughs for Truscott. The audience seemed to take the most extraordinary lines with dead seriousness ... I shall have to do some surgery. I can't come back Wednesday. Can't you ring me? It's all so dreadful. I've already had two rows of nerve-wracking proportions. I've said to [Peter] Wood that I'm not a commercial writer and perhaps he understands now why it's impossible that I should ever be a "national humourist" ... I'm going to try and get back before the weekend, but I can't leave with it in this state.' And from Oxford, the news was no better, but Orton's tone had the same solicitousness. 'Do try and hang on doing something if you get too fed up without me,' Orton wrote, signing off 'Love, Joe'. 'I'll get back as soon as humanly possible. I'm not gallivanting about down here. It's the most depressing few weeks I've ever lived through.'[2]

But when Orton's luck changed, so did his relationship with Halliwell. 'Joe had only one overwhelming relationship allied to loyalty, and that was Ken,' said Peggy Ramsay. 'He didn't care a damn about anybody else.'[3] Orton remained loyal in his fashion to Halliwell; but once in the public gaze, he couldn't bring himself to acknowledge the collaboration that made his success possible. Orton had cured himself of many of the culture's deliriums, but not its romance of self.

History is not kind to those sacrificed to someone else's art. Emma Hardy was seen as a vituperative, no-talent ninny; Vivienne Eliot as the loony baggage the great poet was lumbered with, and Halliwell as 'a middle-aged nonentity'. They were all silent partners to admired artists and they all had literary ambitions of their own. They stuck with their literary marriages in part because the other

1 Orton to Kenneth Halliwell, 2 October 1965.
2 Orton to Kenneth Halliwell, undated February 1965.
3 Peggy Ramsay to John Lahr, 5 June 1970.

partner fulfilled a dream and in part because they had helped fulfil it. But their collaboration became an alienation. This was especially true of Halliwell, who had worked a lifetime to create art and whose great creation was Orton. Halliwell supposed that with Orton's success some residual kudos would come to him. But Halliwell had to share Orton with a new lover – the public. 'If he belongs to the public,' Emma Hardy wrote to a friend about marriage, counselling not to expect gratitude, attention or justice, 'years of devotion count for nothing.' Halliwell found himself forced into a position of being at once invisible and unwanted. 'I hated Halliwell. No, I disliked him, he wasn't important enough to hate,' says Peter Willes. 'I put up with Halliwell the way one does with authors' wives if you want their work . . .'

Halliwell was experiencing the desperation of many partners of the famous: discounted in public, they go quietly mad in private. 'Everyone wanted to meet Joe – Emlyn Williams, Pinter, Rattigan,' says Peter Willes. 'I introduced Harold to Joe. Harold said "I couldn't believe he was so young." Joe looked much younger than he was.' But Halliwell looked old, and irrelevant. 'They treated me like shit,' Halliwell shouts in the diaries, hammering the wall after an evening with a new couple dazzled by Orton's name. 'I won't be treated like this.'[1] Celebrity widened the scope of Orton's charm, which Halliwell had always envied. 'God is on his side and fights for him and all people like him,' says Halliwell's spokesman in *The Boy Hairdresser*, of the way Orton attracted people. Orton's celebrity blinded people to Halliwell. 'With Halliwell one always had to make such an effort,' says Peter Willes. 'He was just unsympathetic. It took enormous tact not to leave him out altogether.' To get attention, Halliwell exaggerated both his importance and his actions; and made large and startling gestures, like Vivienne Eliot who appeared at the first night of *The Rock* holding a placard that read: 'I am the woman he abandoned.' Halliwell didn't display a placard; but he did wear an Old Etonian tie to a swank cocktail party given by Peter Willes. Orton was that night delivering *What the Butler Saw* for Willes to read. If Halliwell couldn't win the approval of Orton's admirers, then hostility was something to build on:

> Went to Peter Willes' for dinner. When we got there he stared at Kenneth in horror. 'That's an Old Etonian tie!' he screeched. 'Yes,' Kenneth said. 'It's a joke.' Willes looked staggered and wrinkled up his face in an evil sort of way. 'Well, I'm afraid it's a joke against you then. People will imagine you're passing yourself off as an Old Etonian. They'll laugh at you.' 'I'm sending up Eton,' Kenneth said. 'Oh no!' Willes cackled with a sort of eldritch shriek. 'You're pathetic! I mean it's disgraceful wearing that tie.'

1 *Diaries*, 2 May 1967

'It's a joke!' Kenneth said, looking tight-lipped, a little embarrassed and angry. 'People will know.' 'Not the people I meet,' Kenneth said, 'They'll think it's funny.' 'You're making people angry,' Willes said. 'I don't care,' Kenneth said, laughing a little too readily, 'I want to make them angry . . .'[1]

While in private he always acknowledged Halliwell's importance to his work, Orton completely edited Halliwell out of the public story of his success. 'All you people who are mad on Joe really have no idea of what he's like,' Halliwell said that same evening. But people weren't interested in Halliwell's version of events, only Orton's. Halliwell usually absented himself from the flat when Orton was interviewed. He was absent on the day Orton explained the origins of his mandarin style to *The Transatlantic Review*. 'I like Lucian and the classical writers,' Orton said, never mentioning how he'd come by such tastes. 'I suppose that's what gives my writing a difference, an old-fashioned classical education! Which I never received, but I gave myself one.' Orton also portrayed himself to the press as having been married and divorced. His comments about marriage were a disturbing projection of his fraught relationship with Halliwell. 'It just didn't work out. I mean, I was too young,' said Orton, who'd moved in with Halliwell as a teenager. 'We drifted apart. Those kinds of marriages never last.'[2] And as late as 9 June 1967, two months to the day before he was murdered, Orton was insisting to the *Evening News* on a writer's need for freedom as the reason he'd never remarry: 'That's tied up with the possession thing, too. Even in a very liberal marriage, a wife and children are your possessions. They have to be your responsibilities . . .'[3]

Scrupulously excluded from Orton's public world, Halliwell was beginning also to be excluded from Orton's social world. 'Joe was very protective of Halliwell,' says Peter Willes. 'He wouldn't go anywhere without him. He didn't care if he gave a bad impression. It was "take me as you find me".' But in the last weeks of his life, Orton had agreed to come without Halliwell to a party of showbiz luminaries given by Dorothy Dickson. Orton was killed within a week of the party, but Halliwell's distress was apparent before it. 'Ken came to see me while waiting to get a prescription of tranquillizers from Dr Ismay filled,' says Peter Willes, who helped organise the party, when Halliwell landed on his doorstep on 7 August 1967. '"You don't realise how Joe carries on at the thought of separating. You don't realise how dependent he is on me." I couldn't wait to get Halliwell out of the flat. I felt I wanted to disinfect the place. I telephoned Joe and said, "Listen, you can't leave Kenneth and come to the party." It was quite a big decision because it was a grand party. That was the first time I knew for sure

1 *Diaries*, 22 July 1967.
2 Barry Hanson interview. Not printed in programme.
3 'Money and Mr Orton' by Patricia Johnson.

that I was talking to Joe on the telephone because Kenneth had just left my flat. Ken imitated Joe's voice on the phone – they sounded just alike – and you had to be careful. He wanted to find out what people were saying to Joe – anything that might possibly affect their life together.'

The famous leave around them shattered lives which are either overlooked or underplayed by biographers, or rewritten by the celebrities themselves. After Emma Hardy's death, Thomas Hardy burned her diary testimony entitled 'What I think of my husband', ghosted his biography and recast the barbarity of their relationship into fine poetry. Eliot sealed his past in silence by stipulating no biography in his will, while the Estate continues to buy up and keep under wraps Vivienne Eliot's correspondence. Orton never had time to rewrite his history. The diaries offer a rare, if unwitting, glimpse into the punishing dynamic of celebrity's self-aggrandisement. As Halliwell's suicide note implies ('If you read his diary all will be explained'), the diaries were both an explanation *and* a provocation. Orton owned the future, the past, and now even Halliwell's suffering.

The diaries are not just a chronicle of the drama between them, but a prop in it. Orton and Halliwell lived in extraordinary physical proximity to each other. Their room was sixteen by twelve. The space was so small that two people could not easily move about in it at once. The bulk of the diaries were written virtually under Halliwell's nose. They were kept in a red-grained leather binder in the writing desk where Halliwell could – and did – read their punishing contents. Everything about the diaries was provocative, a symbol of Orton's retreat into himself and away from Halliwell. The title, which emphasised Orton's singularity, was also a reminder that if Orton was somebody, by implication, Halliwell was nobody. Orton was the centre of Halliwell's life; but, as he could read, Halliwell was an increasingly minor – and frequently irritating – extra in the drama of Orton's eventful life.

Inevitably, Orton's memory is selective. Orton's accounts of Halliwell's depression – the rows, the nagging, the brittle *hauteur* – are well documented; but the issues behind these scenes are kept very much off-stage. 'Halliwell felt he was excluded somehow and not valued,' says Dr Douglas Ismay, a GP with an interest in psychology to whom Peter Willes had sent Halliwell for help, and who gave Halliwell tophrynil and sympathy. 'People didn't know he helped to write and edit some of the plays. He said that Orton was a much less well-educated person than he was and Orton drew on his know-how and grasp of English. He felt frustrated.' Although Orton acknowledges Halliwell's critical acumen in the diaries, none of Halliwell's claims come into the debate between them. In Orton's version of his daily life, Halliwell is shown merely as an accoutrement. And by then, he was. But the Beatles' screenplay was based, in part, on their first novel (1953), when the only thing Orton could contribute to the collaboration was his typing. *The Ruffian on the Stair* which Orton polished for the Royal Court was adapted from their novel *The Boy Hairdresser*. *Sloane* was, according to Orton, 'our play'. Even Orton's wonderful gift for dialogue owed its power to collage which was originally Halliwell's fascination. Halliwell had been completely taken over by the imperialism of Orton's fame. ('Must make it plain,' Halliwell wrote to Peggy Ramsay, asking her to assess his collage murals, 'this invite is not from J or anything to do with him or his Works . . .'') On that painful issue Orton in the diaries remains mum. According to Dr Ismay, Halliwell 'said that Orton thought he was a pain in his side, a nuisance who was interfering with Orton's success.' Orton rarely states his feelings in the diaries. Instead, he signals his disaffection in small asides ('Kenneth quel moan') and throw-away snatches of sour conversation. 'You look like a zombie,' the diary reports Orton saying to Halliwell on 23 April, never in print probing Halliwell's complaints too deeply. 'He replied, heavily, "And so I should. I lead the life of a zombie."' Crying on the terrace of a Tangier restaurant, creating a scene at Peter Willes's home, threatening suicide, Halliwell's emotional pressure on Orton is as apparent as Orton's refusal to be moved by it. 'The tranquillisers worked against too much yapping,' Orton writes on the day of the 'zombie' exchange.

But the diaries are also an extraordinary record of Orton's sexual adventures: his way not just of keeping count but of recapturing desire. 'At one moment,' Orton writes on 11 June, 'with my cock in his arse, the image was, and as I write still is, overpoweringly erotic . . .' Halliwell hated Orton's promiscuity. 'Halliwell was disgusted more and more with Orton's promiscuity,' says Dr Ismay. 'The public lavatory theme was the thing that bothered him most.' Orton insisted the trolling fed his work; but it also fed Halliwell's rage. 'I'm disgusted by all this immorality!' Halliwell shouts at Orton, after the anti-climactic dinner on 4 May with Clive and Tom. 'Homosexuals disgust me!' Promiscuity not only exacerbated Halliwell's sense of sexual guilt, but his sense of sexual inadequacy. Halliwell may have been the focus of Orton's affections, but never his sexual desire. 'Kenneth knew that Joe didn't reciprocate his romantic attachment in any way,' says Peter Willes. 'Joe had no feeling for him except protection and loyalty.' But the issue of sexual prowess became an in-fighting point between them. When Halliwell loudly claims in front of the *Loot* cast that Orton isn't over-sexed, Orton takes umbrage; likewise, Orton is angered by Halliwell's bravado on the subject of Tangier rent boys:

> Kenneth said 'Oh, all the boys will do anything.' 'They won't,' I said. 'There's a lot of things they won't do.' It was irritating to be told by someone who likes being masturbated that the boys 'will do anything' . . .²

1 Halliwell to Peggy Ramsay, 3 October 1966.
2 *Diaries*, 27 June 1967.

The jibe about Halliwell's prowess precipitates the first of Halliwell's violent attacks on Orton.

Orton instinctively taunted the bogus; and promiscuity was, on some level, a way of taunting and testing what he saw as Halliwell's illusion of their family unit. 'The household they had was a fake household and Joe knew this,' says Penelope Gilliatt. 'Joe knew the fakery well enough to kick it about and endanger it as much as possible by staying out late, by promiscuity, by every means he could. To see how far he could drive Halliwell. I think Joe hated himself for accepting domesticity and carrying on with it.' The diaries brought Orton's promiscuity off the streets and under their roof. The fact that Orton described these scenes with such humour and insight only compounded the problem. Orton was making a legend of something profoundly undermining to Halliwell. Orton was writing down these scenes – and relishing them in set pieces of conversation – while Halliwell was at the same time acting out his desperation to be loved. It was a dangerous game. Orton was not only flirting with death in the public lavatories, but with Halliwell at home. He and Halliwell had already explored the murderous parameters of Halliwell's self-loathing and possessiveness in *The Boy Hairdresser*. They had already imagined their deaths in print: Orton's 'beauty smashed forever'; Halliwell dreaming of one crazy act of revenge before killing himself – 'When he went, he'd take others with him . . . the last laugh had to be played correctly.'

In their novel, the revenge is botched; in life, it wasn't. The diaries were the focus of both attacks on Orton. The first, in Tangier, took place while Orton was writing the diary, with Halliwell 'hitting me about the head and knocking the pen from my hand'. In the second attack, Halliwell's suicide note was placed directly on top of the diaries, directing police to them as an explanation for the bludgeoning and his own suicide.

The diaries pick up Orton's story just after the power in Orton's and Halliwell's relationship had shifted irrevocably in Orton's favour. Orton had the big bank balance, the big name and the big future. All the calls and letters were for him. Halliwell, who had been Orton's mentor, was now his employee. 'When I said, "What's your job?",' recalls Dr Ismay of his first meeting with Halliwell, 'he said, "I'm a secretary." Later it transpired that he was a writer.' By the time of the diaries, Halliwell's resentments and frustrations had changed Orton's tone from one of comradely dependence to forbearance ('We got home, had a cup of tea, and it was smiles until bedtime'). In the diaries, Orton continually looks at Halliwell and finds him lacking. Halliwell's whining, his prissiness, his self-consciousness, his bombast are all noted in Orton's asides. And when Orton forthrightly defends Halliwell against the slander of being a 'middle-aged nonentity', he is compelled to add: 'Kenneth has more talent, although hidden . . .'

There was nothing hidden about Halliwell's talent to Orton when they first met at RADA in 1951. Halliwell was twenty-five, imposing in his bravado and his baldness. Orton was seventeen, a raw kid who'd never spent two weeks away from Leicester. To him, Halliwell was promise incarnate. Halliwell had everything Orton envied and lacked: his own flat, a car, a library, an education. He also had a good line in literary chat. Halliwell spouted the kind of romantic idealism he put into his play about Edmund Kean, *The Protagonist*: 'This is the end to which my being has been directed: the acclamation of the world and nothing else.' Halliwell preached the gospel of Art, at least until he became its victim. 'He was an artist,' he wrote in *The Protagonist* of Kean. 'If a man must, by the very nature of his work, live more intensely than others, may not extravagances be forgiven in him, which would be blameworthy in others?' Orton became Halliwell's acolyte. 'When I spotted Orton in the RADA canteen queue, I'd been at the academy about three weeks,' recalls Frank Whitby who had met Orton and his mother the previous year at a try-out for the Old Vic Theatre School. 'I went across and reminded him of our meeting and congratulated him on getting into RADA. He immediately flashed a look over his shoulder, and there, looking at me with malevolence, was Kenneth Halliwell. Already, after one full term, Orton had exchanged maternal possessiveness for something that was to be lethal.'

Halliwell's possessiveness and desire to control were the result of the traumatic abandonments of his childhood. Halliwell's mother died in 1937, when he was eleven, of a wasp sting on her finger while making breakfast. Up to then, according to J.P. Howarth, who was the Halliwell's lodger from 1933–7, Kenneth had been a 'mother's boy' whose mother wouldn't let her taciturn husband touch him. 'She pampered him. They talk of the silver chord – well, it would never have been severed between them.' With her death, Halliwell 'became introvert and very difficult to talk to.' He and his father had little to say to each other. They lived as strangers under the same roof. In this sad atmosphere, Halliwell studied hard at the Wirral Grammar School and did well, earning Higher School Certificates in Ancient History, Greek, Latin and German. And then in 1949, Halliwell came downstairs one morning to find his father lying dead with his head in the oven. With typical reticence, the father had left no note. Inevitably, after such overwhelming rejection, Halliwell, whose mother had expected great things from him, found refuge in grandiose fantasy. His mother had wanted him to be a doctor. His father quarrelled with him about his decision not to follow the academic path. But Halliwell had his heart set on the glory road, which would lead him nowhere.

'"Tight" is the word that comes to mind for Halliwell,' said Charles Marowitz, the director of the first London production of *Loot*. 'He was organising his social persona so vigorously, so forcefully that I never once saw him in repose. He could never unclench.' Even as a teenager, Halliwell was grave. By the time he'd got to RADA, as his teachers' comments indicated, the strain of his defensiveness was already visible in the tension in his body, his voice and his personality. On stage, Halliwell was all perspiration and no inspiration. What came across the footlights was not strength but self-consciousness.

—I think a little more divine discontent with his own work might be welcome . . .

—Seems to be unconvinced that acting is the expression of *emotion*. The result is that his approach is all mental – giving a tight, almost prim aspect to his work . . .

—a strangely set and rigid student . . .

—sound work but really too boxed up . . .

Halliwell was older than most of the students, and his high-handed manner kept them at a distance. What Orton saw as intellectual authority came across to more sophisticated students as hapless insecurity. 'He was a very affected little man,' said Margaret Whiting who won the Bancroft Medal for the outstanding performer of their year. 'He had visions of grandeur. He was always in his little world of creative fantasy. He was so selfish and preoccupied about himself. Constant talking of self, ego, ambition. He was a great egotist.' 'Artistic temperament', Chesterton wrote, 'is a disease that afflicts amateurs'. Halliwell's tantrums, his conceit, his high-falutin' pronouncements about art and other actors would in time be an example of Chesterton's point: 'There are many real tragedies of the artistic temperament, tragedies of vanity or violence or fear. But the great tragedy of the artistic temperament is that it cannot produce any art.'

All too aware of his threadbare resources, Orton saw Halliwell as a teacher, a father and a friend. And Halliwell, an orphan, found in Orton someone willing to share his life and his dreams of glory. Orton was vivacious and charming; and, so they wrote in *The Boy Hairdresser* reconstructing the origins of their relationship, Orton 'made him feel young'. He also made Halliwell feel powerful: 'he was in need of protection'. Orton, as depicted in *The Boy Hairdresser*, 'was half-educated, half-baked, half-cut'. And to educate Orton gave them both a mission and a bond. They were united in their desire to be special.

'I never was able to imagine myself as ordinary,' said Orton.[1] Orton got this idea from his mother Elsie, who looked upon 'her John' as the most gifted of her children. Elsie refused to admit the ordinariness of her life or her children. She

1 *Evening News*, 'Money and Mr Orton'.

was always in search of some indication of status: Players not Woodbines, ham not Spam, opera not Gilbert and Sullivan. She wanted the best; but she had been short-changed in life. Her family had no money, no education, no prospects. When Orton failed his eleven-plus, Elsie pawned her wedding ring so that Orton was the only boy on his Leicester estate of 1,500 to attend a fee-paying school. Typically, Elsie chose Clark's College, which offered a commercial curriculum, not the academic course she'd intended. In his plays, Orton mocked his mother's pretentions to propriety; but Orton worked to fulfil the generalised ambition he'd absorbed from her. At fifteen, before he'd even appeared in a play, Orton had dedicated his life, so he wrote in his teenage diary, to the theatre. 'He seemed a child that had missed out on a lot of love,' said Joanne Runswick, who directed Orton in one of his early amateur theatricals. 'I used to want to draw him to me because he used to go away, always apart. He was so apart.' While at RADA, Orton came back to see Joanne Runswick, already fired with Halliwell's ambition to write. 'He said, "I want to write plays,"' she recalls. 'I wanted him to make good, but I was a little worried. He was so tense about it, about becoming somebody.' And so too was Elsie, who accompanied Orton to his audition at the Old Vic Theatre School in 1950. 'After Orton had gone off to do his prepared pieces she began to talk to me,' says Frank Whitby. 'She babbled on about him. With her strong accent, one that I was not used to, and her old-fashioned clothes, she looked and sounded like a character out of an Ealing comedy. I remember her constant falling inflexions at the end of each sentence. This "dying fall" certainly had a depressing effect on me . . .'

Although Orton came home for two weeks each summer, Elsie only started to correspond with Orton after his success. 'You will be surprised to hear from your mother,' she wrote, after *Entertaining Mr Sloane*'s reviews at the end of May 1964. 'First of all I am very happy for you had a little weep to think you had done it at last . . . God bless you John look after yourself you have had your troubles now look forward and not back any more.' Elsie was bowled over by Orton's celebrity and wasted no time in pressing its advantage. 'It gave me great pleasure to brag about one of my sons my boss ask me if you belong to me since then they treat me very good can't do nothing wrong . . .' Always in debt, Elsie frequently asked Orton to get her out of hock. He paid, and she made a show of looking out for his economic interests: 'I can't believe months ago you were broke now you are better off than any one in all the family both sides . . . several people want to borrow your book but I won't let them have it let them buy one.' Elsie waited eagerly to see her son on television and sent him clippings about himself from the *Leicester Mercury*. 'People want to know,' she wrote on 10 September 1964, 'why there is never any mention of your parents.'

The reason was simple: home was with Halliwell. Orton's family had nothing to do with the bright talent being praised in the press. Orton not only glossed over his family in interviews, he left them out of his will, which named Halliwell as the sole beneficiary. Although Orton had been living with Halliwell since 1951, the family didn't clap eyes on him until 1964, when Halliwell, standing in for Orton who was nervous of his mother seeing her pretensions lampooned on stage, escorted them to *Entertaining Mr Sloane*. 'Ken we all thought was a very nice chap,' Elsie wrote Orton.

'If we could pool our resources, we could help each other,' says Halliwell's spokesman in *The Boy Hairdresser*. Orton's contribution, at first, was enthusiasm and attention. Halliwell exerted almost complete control over the relationship. Halliwell cooked and provided the food. And more than that, as Laurence Griffin, who shared their first flat at 161 West End Lane, recalls, 'Halliwell showed Orton what to wear, what to read, where to go.' The price Orton paid for this largesse was loyalty. Halliwell, who called him 'my pussycat', kept Orton on a tight leash. 'Kenneth Halliwell didn't like John being away,' Griffin says. 'You could see Halliwell was jealous. John didn't bridle. It was useful. It was a base to go back to. He was like Sloane, a tease.' Griffin was not the only one of Orton's acquaintances who saw the connection. 'Joe was Sloane,' says Peter Willes. 'Ruthless, not immoral but amoral, and pragmatic.' Orton followed the line of least resistance; and, like Sloane, was manoeuvred into a situation he'd never bargained for.

'They had the idea they were going to be brilliant actors,' says Griffin. 'Sometimes I used to feel the odd one out because they practically convinced me they were so good. They looked upon themselves as very special.' But when their acting dreams collapsed, Orton and Halliwell fixed on writing. Cocooned in their room and their dream of literary success, they began to write and make a study of literature. Orton projected their relationship into *Head to Toe*, with Orton as the lost wayfarer Gombold and Halliwell as Doktor Von Pregnant who offers Gombold knowledge as a means of escape.

> The Doktor talked constantly, continuing Gombold's education.
> 'What's the abiding value?' he said one evening.
> 'Truth', Gombold replied.
> 'I have taught you nothing then,' the Doktor said. 'The rulers of whatever country you choose will designate as true that which is useful to them. Truth is relative, and always behind it stands some interest, furthering its own end.'

'To escape unaided,' wrote Orton, 'had never occurred to Gombold.' Nor had it occurred to Orton. After a while, their regimen of writing and reading became habit; and Orton, like Gombold, 'never now mentioned escape. Study took the place of liberty; absorbed in acquiring knowledge, days, months, and years passed in rapid and instructive course.' Orton's fictional characters 'slithered to what they hoped was freedom'. They didn't find it; and neither did Orton and Halliwell. For them success was freedom; and it completely eluded them. Nothing was published. Their hostility – in the form of the defaced books – landed them in an actual, not an imagined cell. In 1962, they were sent to separate prisons for six months. It was the first time Orton had been away from Halliwell for a sustained period of time. On summer holidays, Orton never stayed away longer than a fortnight. 'I must get back to Ken', according to Orton's sister Leonie Barnett, was always his explanation. Ken was also the reason Orton never returned at Christmas. 'I can't leave Ken on his own.' In jail, on his own, Halliwell grew depressed; and soon after his release attempted suicide. But Orton learned something about himself that brought detachment and boldness to his writings: 'Before, I had been vaguely conscious of something rotten some-where; prison crystallised this. The old whore society really lifted up her skirts, and the stench was pretty foul.'[1] For Orton, the experience was a liberation. 'Being in the nick brought detachment to my writing,' he told the *Leicester Mercury*. 'I wasn't involved any more and suddenly it worked.'[2] Orton had passed beyond suffering. He now had nothing to lose. His laughter became dangerous. He had at last found a way to 'rage correctly'.[3]

'I don't write fantasy,' Orton said. 'People think I do, but I don't.'[4] The diaries confirm this. Orton's comic world, with its monsters of power and propriety, was all around him. He heard his brand of daft pretension in passing street talk; and he lived the truth of farce's momentum. 'My life is beginning to run to a timetable no member of the royal family would tolerate,'[5] he writes, as the traffic plan for his liaisons with Moroccan boys assumes farcical complications. Orton's complaint about traditional farce was that it was 'still based on the preconceptions of half a century ago, particularly the preconceptions about sex. But we must now accept that, for instance, people *do* have sexual relations outside marriage . . .'[6] On stage and off it, Orton practised an unbuttoned liberty.

But it was not just the rapacity of his farces that mirrored Orton's life. Farce is ruled by the law of momentum: at a certain speed all things disintegrate. At speed, panic substitutes for reason, and characters are pushed beyond guilt and beyond their connection to each other. So it was with Orton and Halliwell. In the momentum of Orton's new celebrity, he could not properly register Halliwell's disintegration. In any case, neither of them probably had the inner resources to cope with such drastic changes in their relationship. Halliwell's persistent

1 *Plays and Players*, August 1964.
2 *Leicester Mercury*, 22 June 1964.
3 In *Head to Toe*, Gombold prays: 'Cleanse my heart, give me the ability to rage correctly.'
4 Barry Hanson interview.
5 *Diaries*, 19 May 1967.
6 *Plays and Players*, June 1966.

psychosomatic complaints – the tightness in his chest, the constipation – broadcast his sense of being trapped. Orton, on the other hand, was feeling the heady rush of his new freedom. 'Kenneth v. depressed,' he writes on 10 March, contemplating writing a joke play under an assumed name. 'I was feeling merry.' Orton was unprepared to concede anything to Halliwell's signs of unhappiness. In Tangier, desperate to win Orton's approval, Halliwell makes the mistake of posing as Orton's Pandarus:

> We were hailed with 'Hallo' from a very beautiful sixteen-year-old boy whom I knew (but had never had) from last year. Kenneth wanted him. We talked for about five minutes and finally I said, 'Come to our apartment for tea this afternoon.' He was very eager. We arranged that he should meet us at The Windmill beach place. As we left the boy, Kenneth said 'Wasn't I good at arranging it?' This astounded me. 'I arranged it,' I said. 'You would have been standing there talking about the weather forever.' K. didn't reply.[1]

Often their bickering takes on the crazy symmetry of Orton's farce double-binds:

> 'Are you going to wear your blue suit for the summer?' he said. 'No,' I said. 'Then why did you have the trousers altered?' he said. 'If you hadn't had them altered, I could've worn them.' 'But if you could wear them,' I said, 'they wouldn't've fitted me. That's why I had them altered.' 'And now they don't fit me,' he said. 'No,' I said. 'But if they'd've fitted you they wouldn't've fitted me. And as they didn't fit me I had them altered. And now I've had them altered they don't fit you.'[2]

The joke at the heart of Orton's farce mayhem is that people state their needs, but the other characters, in their spectacular self-absorption, don't listen. 'Hum to yourself if you're sad,' says the nurse in *Funeral Games*, taking leave of the defrocked priest who is her patient. Orton's laughter invokes a world of no consolation; and in private, Orton could give little to Halliwell. He was incensed on Halliwell's behalf over the 'middle-aged nonentity' slur. He continued to try to get Halliwell's collages exhibited. And in the last week of his life, with Halliwell sinking into his final, fatal depression, he offered to take him to Leicester, a strange suggestion since Halliwell had never visited Orton's family and would again find himself only an appendage. As the diaries show, nothing, not even Halliwell's veiled threats of violence, could make Orton attend properly to Halliwell's anguish. On 9 March, Orton writes: 'Kenneth said, "You're turning into a real bully, do you know that. You'd better be careful. You'll get your just deserts!" Went to sleep.'

1 *Diaries*, 9 May 1967.
2 *Diaries*, 3 April 1967.

'You're a quite different person, you know, since you've had your success,' Halliwell tells Orton in the diaries. And he was. Orton was more confident. Halliwell, as they'd written in *The Boy Hairdresser*, 'preferred him wracked with hesitation, only at ease in a conspiratorial way'. But now Orton's conspiracy for high jinks was with the public. It made him bolder, and, to Halliwell, more threatening. 'Arguing about a polaroid camera,' writes Orton on 26 July. 'Kenneth says it's a waste of money. I want one. Conspicuous wealth, I suppose.' Orton had his own money now, and, with it, the freedom to do what he liked. Their old style of making-do didn't fit his new life. Their room was no longer the haven it once had been. Orton was increasingly lured away into the world where there were other people to listen to him and to laugh with him. 'When I've taught you a little,' says Dr Von Pregnant in *Head to Toe*, 'You'll know as much as I do myself.' That day had come. Halliwell had invented his Perfect Friend, only to watch his efforts win from the world an admiration he himself could never earn. In *The Boy Hairdresser*, they'd imagined Orton's 'charm become sinister'. And from Halliwell's point of view, it had. Orton sneered at Halliwell's attempts to stand out (the Old Etonian tie, his safari suit); he mocked Halliwell's sexual passivity, and, more hurtful, he disrespected Halliwell's 'wifely' role:

> Kenneth's nerves are on edge. Hay fever. He had a row this morning. Trembling with rage. About my nastiness when I said, 'Are you going to stand in front of the mirror all day?' He said, 'I've been washing your fucking underpants! That's why I've been at the sink!' He shouted it out loudly and I said, 'Please don't let the whole neighbourhood know you're a queen.' 'You know I have hay fever and you deliberately get on my nerves,' he said. 'I'm going out today,' I said, 'I can't stand much more of it.' 'Go out then,' he said, 'I don't want you in here . . .'[1]

'The *Daily Express* telephoned me and said "Have you heard the news about Joe Orton?"' Peter Willes recalls, of how he learned of the death. 'I thought Joe had been up to no good at the King's Cross cottages. My first thought was to ring Ken at the flat. I called. The police answered. That's when I learned Halliwell had killed him.' Orton was a voluptuary of fiasco; and his death seemed a macabre echo of his plays. (Even Peggy Ramsay, terrified at having to identify the bodies, made a farce entrance: walking backwards into their room.) Nobody, certainly not Orton, expected Halliwell capable of such an act of will. Orton had long ago begun to discount Halliwell's threats as yet another indication of his hectoring impotence. '"When we get back to London we're finished!"' Halliwell snarls at Orton, in their bitter quarrel on 27 June, a few days before leaving Tangier. '"This is the end!" I had heard this so often. "I wonder you didn't add

1 *Diaries*, 17 July 1967

'I'm going back to Mother'" . . . It went on and on until I put out the light. He slammed the door and went to bed.'

When he wasn't writing, Orton increasingly found ways to stay away from their flat. But he was adamant to Kenneth Williams that he'd never forsake Halliwell. And Peter Willes concurs: 'Kenneth thought he was losing Joe, but he never would have.' In one sense, as the diaries show, Orton had already made an imaginative separation from Halliwell. Orton certainly couldn't continue to cohabit long in the atmosphere of cramped desperation and envy which Halliwell created around them. But Halliwell was the entire creative environment of Orton's adult life. Orton, like so many literary figures with unhappy silent partners, had persisted so long in the relationship not only out of loyalty to his partner, but also because it was advantageous to his craft. Halliwell was not only Orton's editor and sounding board; he was his subject matter. Out of their melodramatic and tortured arguments about personal needs Orton got *What the Butler Saw*. Orton was prepared to buy Halliwell off with a house. He encouraged Halliwell to take up other people and other interests. The only way to change Halliwell was to change his situation. But Halliwell wanted only Orton and their old world back. And that was lost.

'Events move in one direction and are cumulative,' they wrote in *The Boy Hairdresser*. From their calendar in mid-August, it was clear in just what direction their destinies were going. On the day they died, a chauffeur was set to take Orton to Twickenham Studios to discuss *Up Against It* with Richard Lester. The following day Halliwell was scheduled to see a bona fide psychiatrist at St Bernard's Hospital. When Dr Ismay called in the psychiatrist, Halliwell told him he was 'taking the matter far too seriously'. But in the early hours of 9 August, the prospect of Halliwell's left-over life drove him crazy. Halliwell beat out the brains that poked such wicked fun at the world, then took his own life. In murder, Halliwell was imitating *their* art. 'Which is worse?' asks Halliwell's alter ego in *The Boy Hairdresser*, before he attempts murder. 'Evil to look back on, nothing to look forward to, and pain in the present.' Death made them equal again, linking Halliwell finally and forever to Orton. In the anarchy of his farces, Orton took revenge for the fretfulness of his desires and disillusion. Now Halliwell did the same. What is left to the world is Orton's evergreen laughter, and the last testament of the fierce, sad kingdom of self from which it came: his diaries.

London
December 1966–May 1967

Tuesday 20 December

I went to the Cochrane Theatre[1] to meet Charles Marowitz[2]. Discussed excerpt from *Loot* to be televised. We're doing the confession scene. It seems that our excerpt is to be on first in the programme – originally titled *Accolade*, now called *Darling, You Were Wonderful*. I don't quite see why we should be on first. We won the prize.[3] I'd've thought the runners-up should be on first . . .

Peter Willes[4] rang this evening. He's had a letter from Pinter[5] in Boston where *The Homecoming*[6] has opened. One of the first things they saw on arriving at their hotel was a large poster of five men cycing a big, beefy woman in a grass skirt. This to advertise the Royal Shakespeare Company's production of the play.

Wednesday 21 December

Foul weather. Bleak. Rain late in the morning. I find, after paying the income tax, that my current account is reduced to £199. I have £2,500 in a deposit account, though.

I did nothing today except write. I've begun the second half of *What the*

---

1 *Loot* opened at the Jeannetta Cochrane Theatre, 27 September 1966. Transferred to the Criterion Theatre, 1 November 1966.
2 Charles Marowitz (1934–). American-born director of *Loot*. Also founder of the Open Space Theatre (1968) and author of *Confessions of a Counterfeit Critic*. His own dramatic writing includes *Artaud at Rodez; Marowitz Shakespeare; Sex Wars: Free Adaptations of Ibsen and Strindberg*.
3 *Evening Standard* Drama Award for Best Play, 1966, given to *Loot*.
4 Peter Willes (1913–). Former Hollywood actor turned television producer. Orton's champion in television as head of drama at Rediffusion Television and later Yorkshire Television (1968–78). Orton dedicated *Crimes of Passion* to Willes. In his introduction to Orton's *Funeral Games*, Willes wrote: 'Joe was very puritanical; he did not smoke and drank very little; just to be social at parties. He did not have a heart – but I loved what was there instead, which was infinite kindness and good manners. . . . His complete originality is what I miss most of all.' Willes also produced for TV Harold Pinter's *The Lover, The Connection* and *The Caretaker*.
5 Harold Pinter (1930–). Actor, playwright and director. The only contemporary English playwright besides himself that Orton admired. 'When I look back on what I've written,' Orton wrote in production notes for the American version of *Loot*, insisting on the play's seriousness, 'I think it would be safer to say ideally I'd like an amalgam of *Black Comedy* and *The Homecoming* . . .'
6 By Harold Pinter, 1965. 'Very brilliant play,' Orton wrote to Glenn Loney, 25 March 1966. 'The best he's written. Sexual sharing. A girl though. Makes it more wholesome.'

Butler Saw.[1] Successful at the moment. Likely to raise eyebrows in the Lord Chamberlain's office, I should think. I hope I'm inspired to complete the play. It's a hard grind ahead.

Peter Willes told me that when he was young in the thirties he stayed for the weekend at a house where Churchill[2] was a guest. During the visit Churchill suggested that he do a painting of Willes. Willes said he agreed. Reluctantly, because he thought it rather a bore. At the end of the visit Churchill presented him with some dreadful daub and Willes threw it out of the train going home. Now Churchill's paintings sell for thousands of pounds. Willes is awfully cross.

Sheila Ballantine[3] said she heard a conversation between two women in a bus. One woman said, 'There's a lot of blue about lately.' After a pause the other woman said, 'Yes. And there's a lot of green about too.' There was another pause and the first woman said, 'And there's a lot of red. Have you noticed?' Sheila said they didn't mention purple which is quite in evidence.

I told Sheila of a woman I'd seen on television. She was at a caged bird exhibition. She had an enormous parrot-like creature on her shoulder which she insisted could speak 'Or at least,' she said, 'he doesn't speak. He reasons.' After five minutes trying to get the wretched thing to say something the woman said, 'Isn't it funny how silent he is. It's because there's company. When we're at home on our own he's quite garrulous.'

Thursday 22 December

Mild morning. Cold later. Kenneth and I went down to Bloomsbury to get a pig made of china for Peter Willes. It's enormous. When we bought one two years ago it cost twenty-five shillings. Today they cost forty-six. The woman packed it in a cardboard box that had originally held three dozen Bronco toilet rolls. A more sensible present in many ways.

Traffic absurd on the way back. Roads choked with cars. The streets thronged with gay, fat women spending money like water. We counted five with bunches of plastic holly. On the bus was an old man and woman. They were talking to the bus conductress. Everything the conductress said the old woman repeated to her husband. 'It's taken us forty minutes to get from Vic to here,' the conductress said. The old woman leaned across to her husband and said, 'It's taken her forty

---

1 Produced posthumously by Lewenstein-Delfont Productions Ltd. and H.M. Tennent Ltd. at the Queen's Theatre, 5 March 1969. With Stanley Baxter, Coral Browne and Sir Ralph Richardson.
2 Sir Winston Churchill (1874–1965). British prime minister and war leader.
3 Sheila Ballantine. Actress and good friend of Orton's. Played Fay in the first London production of *Loot*. 'I see bright eyes and warmth. Marvellous embracing warmth. He used to pick me up and whirl me around the dressing-room. You just had to love him. Everybody did. Joe made life very exciting. He became very important in my life. We were going to go on vacations. We were going to have adventures. He loved being alive. He enjoyed everything.'

minutes to get from Vic to here.' A little while later the conductress said she was working on Christmas Day. 'She's working on Christmas Day,' the old woman shouted. 'Isn't it a shame for her?' 'Oh, I don't mind,' the bus conductress said. 'She doesn't mind, though,' the old woman said. 'That nice for her, isn't it?'

I saw Mrs Corden[1] from Flat One today. I said how much I admired her evening dress which I'd seen on the night she went to Mr Corden's firm's get-together. 'It came from Africa the material. All the way from Africa,' she said. I wasn't too surprised. She looked like a fucking hottentot in it.[2]

Friday 23 December

I had to go down to Holborn to give P. Willes his pig. West End v. awful. Drunken people behaving in a foolish way. Singing and shouting. What for, I'd like to know. They've nothing to celebrate.

I went on to Peggy's[3] to give her Kenneth's present of two Al Bowlly LPs[4]. She said that the *Late Show* had asked if I'd do a sketch. She sent them her copy of *An Unsavoury Interlude*. It's really a two-minute version of *The Ruffian on the Stair*.[5] Just the essentials of plot retained. I did it two years ago. It was supposed

1 Hilda Corden (1915–1981), who with her husband Ernest (1910–1977), lived in the basement flat of 25 Noel Road. Mrs Corden's pretensions to refinement were a source of constant amusement and inspiration to Orton, who used the clutter of her apartment and the sludge of her speech in *Entertaining Mr Sloane* and *The Good and Faithful Servant*. 'My vagina has come up the size of a football,' she once told Orton, visiting her in hospital after a cup of tea had spilled in her lap. 'The matron of the hospital said to me that in all her years of medical experience she'd seen nothing like it. But I've no complaints. I've been given top-class penicillin.'
2 Orton used the notion of the company dance in the bitter finale of *The Good and Faithful Servant* (Scene 19). Doris Boynes, Orton's neighbour: 'Mr Corden was a commissionaire at a firm of chartered accountants who did the accounts of the Savoy Hotel in the Strand. So I suppose they got a reduction at the Savoy where they had the staff dinner. For this occasion, Mrs Corden would take days to get herself done up. It was extraordinary to see this woman emerge. Normally she wore no make-up, no camouflage whatsoever. She looked very ordinary, dirty. Quite incredible. She'd got very poor skin, almost pock-marked, but obviously with layers of make-up she could look entirely different. John and Kenneth were intrigued by this; and they deliberately went out to meet her – casually – in the hall. Her hair had been tinted and she looked quite different. John was dumbfounded. He couldn't believe it. "You're quite unrecognisable," he said.'
3 Margaret (Peggy) Ramsay. Theatrical agent. Took Orton on her books in December 1963, and by the end of January 1964 had sold *Entertaining Mr Sloane* to Michael Codron. The show was mounted five months later at the New Arts Theatre Club. Ramsay wired Orton on opening night: 'WISHING YOU ENORMOUS SUCCESS NOW AND IN THE FUTURE'. She backed her taste with more than rhetoric, investing £250 in the show.
4 Al Bowlly (1906–1941). Popular English band singer of the thirties, considered 'the English Bing Crosby'. Killed in the Blitz.
5 Orton's first professional play. Broadcast as a radio play on BBC Third Programme, 31 August 1964. First stage production without decor by the English Stage Company at the Royal Court Theatre, 21 August 1966. First staged with *The Erpingham Camp* as *Crimes of Passion* by the English Stage Company at the Royal Court, 6–17 June 1967. Directed by Peter Gill.

to be for a film with Vanessa Redgrave[1] and David Warner[2]. It didn't come to anything. I said that the *Late Show* could have it if they wanted. I'm not writing anything fresh. I'm too involved at the moment with *What the Butler Saw*. I've got to the second half. It's largely unmapped territory. Hope to have it finished (with luck) by the spring.

On the way home I met an ugly Scotsman who said he liked being fucked. He took me somewhere in his car and I fucked him up against a wall. The sleeve of my rainmac is covered in whitewash from the wall. It won't come off.

I hate Christmas.

Saturday 24 December

Rained most of the day. I haven't been out. Hard at work on *What the Butler Saw*. I've reached the point where Dr Rance certifies Geraldine and Nick and relieves Dr Prentice of his post. I've had an excellent idea for continuing: Nick disguises himself as a policeman *and* Geraldine's father. Her real father will turn up. I hope I can keep up a sufficient frenzy to the end of the play. Kenneth H. said today that the first half (32 pages of single spacing) surely wasn't long enough. This depressed me. I shall have to add earlier. Of course if the whole structure was finished I wouldn't mind. I enjoy adding to something that's already there.

Mr and Mrs Corden have left in their car for Holland-on-Sea. A dreadful semi-detached called 'Hilearn'. They call it 'Hilearn' because her name is Hilda and his is Ernest. They've taken their two dogs, Candy and Sukey, with them. And Mrs Corden has had her hair dyed ginger to celebrate the event. Her bald patch is even more prominent now.

Kenneth said when he went out he saw an old woman in Marks and Spencer's. She was very poor. And she'd bought herself a packet of jam tarts and a half of chicken. Obviously she couldn't afford anything else. How awful to be trying to celebrate when you're old and lonely. I wish there was something to be done. We're not taking any notice of Christmas.

It's a hateful time.

One of the dogs bit Mrs Corden as she was getting in the car. The whole street must've heard the frightful row as Mrs Corden screamed and began belting the animal.

Sunday 25 December

Usual messages from the heads of the establishment. The Queen from Windsor, the Pope from Rome: Pilate and Caiaphas celebrating the birth of Christ.

Ninety-nine idiots dead on the roads. We've had the transport minister Mrs

1 Vanessa Redgrave (1939–). Actress.
2 David Warner (1941–). Actor.

Castle[1] asking why. And a general shaking of heads all round. A BBC pantomime in which every single effect was muffed. Genies kept appearing in front of the magic smoke instead of from behind it. Shots of the audience – they'd combed the mental homes from the look of it. In *TV Times* Cliff Richard[2] announces that 'Christmas celebrates one of the happiest events in history – the birth of Christ.' He's going to be singing his heart out in his own little church.

Miss Boynes,[3] full of the Christmas spirit, said, when I met her on the stairs that 'the Cordens are the filthiest people' she'd ever met. She said, 'I had to do Mrs Corden's hair for her appearance at the Savoy. And you know I can't stand touching other people's hair. But I did it for the goodwill. And I pressed her dress because my board is more suitable. But when she hinted that I do Mr Corden's suit as well, I nearly took off.' She said the Cordens had gone down to spend Christmas with friends. 'What a sight that woman looked,' Miss Boynes said. 'She'd bought herself a type of fur hat.' She gave a toss of her head. 'I was quite put out by it.' I said, 'Was it out of her box?' Because Mrs C. has boxes and cupboards full of rubbish. 'Oh, no!' said Miss Boynes. 'It was the latest thing. But really, you know, she looked a sight. I had a little laugh to myself as she drove off. If only she could see herself as others see her.'

Kenneth and I went for a walk through the City. And came home. We had bacon and cauliflower for lunch. Feeling grandly nonconformist. Only because the chicken hasn't thawed out. We're having that tomorrow.

Monday 26 December

I began writing *What the Butler Saw* at eleven o'clock this morning. At twenty past, the telephone rang.[4] It was from a call-box and the caller had difficulty

---

1 The Rt Hon. Barbara Castle (1910–   ). Politician. Then Labour MP. Minister of Transport from 1965–68.

2 Cliff Richard (1940–   ). Durable English pop star and actor.

3 Doris Boynes (1907–   ). Lived on the first floor below the Orton and Halliwell flat at 25 Noel Road. 'One knew that John was becoming well-known and achieving some kind of fame. Kenneth was very much left behind, which was unusual because at the beginning they were never apart. But increasingly John was invited out without Ken. Ken used to wander around really just to find someone to talk to. I used to think it was odd that Kenneth was at home. It was like a housewife would be. It looks strange for a man, doesn't it? He used to say: "I like doing it. I don't want to go out to a job. I like being at home." I think Kenneth had a lot more to say than John. I think John did the listening. I could tell when sometimes Ken would use an odd expression that John was listening. Ken would be very pleasant when he entertained us. He would make odd looking sandwiches which he joked about.'

4 Eleanor Salvoni (1920–   ), next door neighbour, popular Maitre D. of L'Escargot, then of Bianchi's: 'They didn't have a phone for a long time. They used to come here and use the phone. "If you're not here, Eleanor, I can't waste all my time in a phone-box," Joe said. They had the money, but I think they were waiting to see if Joe's success was going to carry on. If it didn't, then they didn't want a phone.'

Peggy Ramsay, *Evening News*, 3 March 1967: 'We had to force him to buy a telephone because I was so bored sending him wires.'

getting through. When they did it was George.[1] He said, 'I've rung to tell you that your mum[2] died this morning. It was very quick. She had a heart attack.' He didn't say anything else.[3]

My father,[4] who has just come out of hospital having been run over by a car, is staying with Leonie[5]. The funeral is on Friday.

I went down to the Criterion to see the cast.[6]

Sheila Ballantine has been invited to the *Evening Standard* luncheon. Nobody else in the cast has.

On our way home we passed the Palace Theatre where *The Sound of Music* is playing.[7] I heard a woman saying, 'I've seen that show three times. A lovely evening out. I'd go through it again only they're bringing it off.'

While we were waiting for the bus an old man, thin, ragged and shaking with the cold came up and began to play an accordion. After a few moments he started to sing, 'Once I had a secret love'.

Tuesday 27 December

Last night I heard Feydeau's *Occupe-toi d'Amélie* on the wireless.[8] Surprisingly good. Better, by far, than that nauseating production of *A Flea in Her Ear* at the National. It had speed and managed to capture the style. At the National they gabbled the lines. Everything was taken at breakneck pace with the result that it seemed to drag. Of course the advantage of sound radio was that no idiot designer got in the way. In *A Flea in Her Ear* the sets and costumes appeared to be the fantasies of a demented pervert.

Today I did nothing but write *What the Butler Saw*. Met Miss Boynes on the

1 George Barnett (1938–   ). Engineer and husband of Orton's youngest sister, Leonie.

2 Elsie Orton (1904–1966). Orton's mother. A hosiery worker and char.

3 In the last months of her life, Elsie Orton was admitted to the Leicester General Hospital twice with high blood pressure and pains in her chest. Orton kept all her letters and dated them. One of her last, written from the hospital ward, was on 20 September 1966: 'The nurses want to know when you will visit me but I know you can't dear with your play so near at hand you see John I'm ill any fool knows that with heart trouble if I was serious I would tell the hospital staff to let you know but your grandma's heart they said hung on a thread for years and she lived to be 84 Margaret next door said I was the talk of The Tiger [pub] also Trenant Road. When the ambnleance [sic] came to fetch me they saw the specialist come and the doctor so I caused a little exsiment [sic] one thing john they have told me here I shall never be 100 per cent better again I am not to do my own washing and only very light cleaning such has [sic] dusting won't it be awful it's like a death sentence well any way cheerio all my love mum write back soon.'

4 William Orton (1903–1978). Orton's father. A gardener.

5 Leonie Orton (1944–   ). Orton's youngest sister and closest family connection. Library assistant.

6 *Loot* was still playing at the Criterion Theatre.

7 *The Sound of Music* (1959). Book by Howard Lindsay and Russell Crouse. Music by Richard Rodgers. Lyrics by Oscar Hammerstein II. (Performances: 1,925 USA; 2,385 UK.)

8 Georges Feydeau (1862–1921). Master French farceur. Plays include *A Flea in Her Ear* (1910); *Occupe-toi d'Amélie* (1908).

stairs with an expression of misery on her face. 'Jenny's passed away,' she said. Jenny is a foul, fat, moulting budgerigar. Miss Boynes has three in all. 'Of course,' she said, 'I knew Jen-Jen wasn't a young bird when I bought her. And she was delicate. That's why she never got on with Sweep.' 'Sweep never liked her, did he?' I said. 'No. They never got on,' she said. 'I shall wait until I'm at Holland before I have another one. I don't think the climate agrees with them up here.' She went on to tell that long story of hers, how she brought a sick budgerigar across London in a shoe-box. She claimed to understand their thought. 'And now I'm on my own with Sweep and Miss Clark's[1] bird,' she said, as a parting shot.

Leonie hasn't rung. I'll have to send a telegram to find out details of my mother's funeral. I can't go home if there's nowhere to sleep.

And I don't fancy spending the night in the house with the corpse. A little too near the Freudian bone for comfort.

Dreary weather. Pissing continually with rain.

Wednesday 28 December

Letter this morning from the editor of the *Evening Standard* inviting me to the lunch at Quaglino's on the eleventh of January. The invitation said 'and guest'. I asked Kenneth. He said nothing on earth would get him to such a macabre affair. He suggested I ask Peggy. So I did. She seemed thrilled by the idea.

Hard at work on *What the Butler Saw* all day. I wrote a scene where Geraldine disguises herself as an Indian nurse. Cut it though after laughing a lot. Held up the action. And whenever anything makes me roar with laughter it's a sure sign it must be cut.

Leonie rang at about six. I'd sent a telegram earlier today. She'd just got in from work. She said that Dad has gone back home. Sleeps in my mother's bed downstairs with the corpse. After his accident he can't piss straight and floods the lavatory with it whenever he goes. She said, 'Well, I'm shocked by our Marilyn,[2] you know.' I said, 'Why, what's she done?' Leonie said, 'Oh, you know, she behaves very ignorantly all round. And when I told her Mum was dead all she said was – "I'm not surprised". Well, you know, what kind of remark is that?' Dougie[3] was upset. Remarkable how those without hearts when young suddenly develop them in later life.

I promised to go home tomorrow. Leonie and George will come round in the evening. As the corpse is downstairs in the main living-room it means going out

1 Miss Helen Clark (Mrs Ditchburn) (1904–   ). Lived in the ground floor apartment at 25 Noel Road.
2 Marilyn Lock *née* Orton (1939–   ). Orton's sister. Hosiery worker.
3 Douglas Orton (1935–   ). Orton's brother. Plumber.

or watching television with death at one's elbow. My father, fumbling out of bed in the middle of the night, bumped into the coffin and almost had the corpse on the floor.

Peggy said how dreadfully reminiscent of *Loot* it all was.

Thursday 29 December

I arrived in Leicester at 4.30. I had a bit of quick sex in a derelict house with a labourer I picked up. He wore a navy-blue coat with leather across the shoulders. He carried a sort of satchel. Some kind of roadmender, I thought. The house was large. Windy because the doors were off. We went in the hall. He took his pants down. He wouldn't let me fuck him. I put it between his legs. He sucked my cock after I'd come. He didn't come himself. It was pissing with rain when we left the house. Mud all over the place.

I got home at 5.30. Nobody in the house. My father was across the road with friends. He can't see now. The accident has affected his walking. He trembles all the time. I said I'd take him to the doctor's tomorrow. He should be in hospital. Later on George and Leonie came round. We went to see Mum's body. It isn't at home as I'd supposed. It's laid out in a Chapel of Rest. Betty[1] came round with Susan[2] and Sharon[3]. Both very giggly. Dougie also with them. He wasn't coming to see the body. He said he'd lifted Mum from the chair where she died and put her into the bed. He didn't want to see her again.

We all went to the Chapel of Rest. It's a room, bare, white-washed. Muted organ music from a speaker in the corner. The coffin lid propped up against the wall. It said 'Elsie Mary Orton, aged 62 years'. Betty said, 'They've got her age wrong, see. Your mum was 63. You should tell them about that. Put in a complaint.' I said, 'Why? It doesn't matter now.' 'Well,' said Betty, 'you want it done right, don't you? It's what you pay for.'

Mum quite unrecognisable without her glasses. And they'd scraped her hair back from her forehead. She looked fat, old and dead. They'd made up her face. When I asked about this the mortician said, 'Would you say it wasn't discreet then, sir?' I said, 'No. It seems all right to me.' 'We try to give a lifelike impression,' he said. Which seems to be a contradiction in terms somehow. I've never seen a corpse before. How cold they are. I felt Mum's hand. Like marble. One hand was pink, the other white. I suppose that was the disease of which she died. The death certificate said, 'Coronary thrombosis, arteriosclerosis and hypertension'.

Great argument as we left. The undertaker gave Marilyn a small parcel

---

1 Elizabeth Orton (1934–   ). Douglas Orton's wife. Canteen assistant.
2 Susan Orton (1956–   ). Orton's niece. The daughter of Douglas and Elizabeth Orton.
3 Sharon Orton (1959–   ). Orton's niece. The daughter of Douglas and Elizabeth Orton.

containing the night-gown Mum was wearing when she died. Nobody wanted it. So the undertaker kept it. Not for himself. 'We pass it on to the old folks,' he said. 'Many are grateful, you know.'

Didn't sleep much. Awful bed. Damp. And cold. House without Mum seems to have died.[1]

Friday 30 December

I got up at eight o'clock. I went downstairs to the kitchen. My father appeared in the doorway of the living-room dressed only in a shirt. He looks thin and old. Hardly more than a skeleton. He weighs six stone four. I said, 'Hallo.' He peered blindly for a second and said, 'Hallo.' After a pause he said, 'Who are you?' 'Joe,' I said. He couldn't remember I'd come last night. Then he said, 'D'you know where my slippers are?' I said, 'What do you mean – where are your slippers?' He got down on his knees and began feeling around. 'I can't find my slippers,' he said. 'They're on your feet,' I said. And they were. He'd been wearing them all the time.

I made a cup of tea and shaved. Then I went out to try and buy some flowers. I had no intention of getting a wreath. Putting money in some ignorant florist's pocket. I couldn't get flowers. The shop said they didn't deliver until 10.30. The funeral is at ten. So I didn't give Mum any flowers. Actually, when I read the dreadful, sickening wording on the other wreaths: 'To a dear Mum. At peace at last with little Tony'[2] from Marilyn and Pete,[3] I was glad not to be involved.

When I got back home Leonie and George had arrived. Also Dougie and Betty. My father was in such a state that he had to be dressed. I took him to the bathroom and shaved him. At ten the undertaker arrived, 'What about the flowers?' he said. I said I'd no idea what to do with the flowers. 'Where's father's tribute?' he said. 'I think just father's tribute on the coffin.' He found my father's wreath and put it on the coffin. Then we all got into the cars. My Aunt Lucy[4] was upset because strict protocol wasn't observed. 'They're all walking wrong,' she said. 'They shouldn't be with husbands and wives. Just immediate circle should be in the first car.' Several women were at their garden gates as the cortège passed. I noticed two old women weeping on each other's shoulders.

At the chapel in the cemetery they held a brief burial service. They didn't carry

---

1 In *Loot*, Detective Truscott sees the wrapped corpse of Mrs McLeavy.

TRUSCOTT: . . . The theft of a Pharaoh is something which hadn't crossed my mind.

He folds the screen revealing the corpse, swathed in the mattress cover and tied with bandages.

Whose mummy is this?

HAL: Mine.

2 Anthony Lock (1958–1965). Orton's nephew. The son of Marilyn and Peter Lock.

3 Peter Lock (1940–   ). Orton's brother-in-law. Engineer.

4 Lucy Cox (1906–   ). Housewife.

the coffin into the chapel. They wheeled it in on a trolley. The vicar, very young and hearty, read the service in a droning voice. And then the coffin was wheeled out and to the graveside. It was a cold, bright morning. My mother's grave was a new one. Her last wish was to be buried with Tony, my nephew who was drowned, aged seven, eighteen months ago,[1] but Pete and Marilyn refused to have the grave reopened and so my mother's last wish was ignored. Leonie said, 'They've caused a lot of bad feeling all round. But she's hard. I can't understand her at all.'

The coffin was lowered. The vicar said his piece. The earth was sprinkled over the coffin. My father began to cry. And we walked back to the waiting cars. Immediately the mourners left the graveside, a flock of old women descended on the grave, picking over the wreaths and shaking their heads.

We got back home at half-past ten. Sandwiches and tea had been prepared by a neighbour. The party got rather jolly later. My Aunt Olive[2] wanted to know what was being done for Dad. I said I was going to take him to the doctor's. 'That's right,' she said, 'he wants a doctor. I'll come over tonight with Charlie[3].' My father sat through the party looking very woebegone. The only person who seemed to be at a funeral. Mrs Riley, Mum's lifelong friend, was crying quietly in a corner and drinking endless cups of tea. 'I don't expect I'll see you again,' she said, as she left. 'Your mother was very dear to me. I've known her all my life. I shan't come up here now she's gone. Goodbye,' she said, kissing my cheek. 'I hope you have a happier life than your mum did.'

Leonie and I spent part of the afternoon throwing out cupboardsful of junk collected over the years: magazines, photographs, Christmas cards. We burnt eight pairs of shoes. I found a cup containing a pair of false teeth and threw it in the dustbin. Then I discovered that they belonged to my father. I had to rescue them. I found my mother's teeth in a drawer.[4] I kept them. To amaze the cast of *Loot*. Later in the afternoon Leonie went into the town to put an acknowledgement of floral tributes and kind cash gifts in the *Leicester Mercury*. I telephoned Kenneth to say that I wouldn't be coming home until tomorrow.

After I left Leonie, I picked up an Irishman. Pretty baggy. I wasn't going to

1 Orton to Marilyn Lock, 31 March 1965: 'I arrived back at the flat tonight to hear the news from home. There's nothing I can write that will make any difference. I know how you must be feeling. Do understand that I would've come home if I'd known, and if there was anything I could've done. I haven't been told when the funeral is and I suppose it's over. I wouldn't send a wreath. I don't begrudge the money, but it seems a lot of show. Nothing can bring the kid back . . .'
2 Olive Orton (1909–   ). Orton's aunt. Housewife.
3 Charlie Orton (1909–72). Orton's uncle, the brother of William Orton. Mechanic.
4 In *Loot*, the dead mother's teeth are used as castanets. Dentures had also played a part in *Entertaining Mr Sloane*.
   KATH: 'My teeth, since you mentioned the subject, Mr Sloane, are in the kitchen in Stergene. Usually I allow a good soak overnight . . . I hate people who are careless with their dentures.'

bother but he had a place so I said 'OK.' It was an empty house. Not derelict. Just unoccupied. He had a room on the ground floor of a large house. The place was damp, not lived in. A smell of dust. He didn't live there. He rented it for sex. There was a table covered in grime. Bits of furniture. A huge mantlepiece with broken glass ornaments on it. All dusty. There was a double bed with greyish sheets. A torn eiderdown. He pulled the curtains which seemed unnecessary because the windows were so dirty.

He had a white body. Not in good condition. Going to fat. Very good sex, though, surprisingly. The bed had springs which creaked. First time I've experienced that. He sucked my cock. Afterwards I fucked him. It was difficult to get in. He had a very tight arse. A Catholic upbringing, I expect. He wanted to fuck me when I'd finished. It seemed unfair to refuse after I'd fucked him. So I let him. We lay in bed and talked for a while. He showed me a photograph of his fiancée. Not a particularly attractive piece. As I lay on the bed looking upwards, I noticed what an amazing ceiling it was. Heavy moulding, a centrepiece of acorns and birds painted blue. All cracked now. Must've been rather a fine room once.

Marilyn, my Aunt Olive and Uncle Charlie, Leonie and George came round later to our house. Dismal sort of evening. We burnt a lot more of Mum's clothes. The best ones Leonie is taking to the WVS[1] for old people. I gave my father supper and went to bed.

We'd been to the 'doctor's with my father. We said he should be in hospital. Very obtuse doctor. Said he'd try. We should come back tomorrow morning at ten o'clock. Said there was little he could promise.

Saturday 31 December

Leonie and I went round to the doctor's at ten o'clock. We had to wait till the end. The receptionist said, 'Why can't you have Mr Orton to live with you?' I said, 'I live in London.' She said, 'But surely someone in the family could help?' Leonie said, 'Well, I'm out at work all day. So we wouldn't be much further forward. He'd still be on his own.' The receptionist, who was making coffee, tossed her head, 'Ever since I can remember,' she said, 'I've had a horror of abandoning old people. Well, I've nothing on my conscience. My poor dear mother, bless her, lived with me for years. And she was no trouble. And my husband and I had to change her bedclothes to prevent sores. She's been gone now for eight years, but if she could come back I'd willingly have her.' She went into the dispensary with the coffee. 'Silly moo,' Leonie said.

The doctor said that he hadn't been able to get in touch with any hospital. It was Saturday morning. So we came away. Leonie has to ring him at eleven on Monday.

---

1 Women's Voluntary Service.

I prepared a dinner for Dad for tomorrow, showed him where everything was and left for London on the 5.30 train. When I got in, Kenneth was watching a film about the French Resistance in the last war. I went to bed pretty soon afterwards.

Sunday 1 January 1967.[1]

Fine weather. I slept most of the day. Didn't go out.

Monday 2 January

Spent the day working on *What the Butler Saw*. In the evening P. Willes rang. He's off to New York to see *The Homecoming*. Don't envy him. All that way. What a journey. I told him about the funeral. And the frenzied way my family behave. He seemed shocked. But then he thinks my plays are fantasies. He suddenly caught a glimpse of the fact that I write the truth. I told him to tell Peter Hall[2] about *The Ruffian on the Stair* and *The Erpingham Camp*[3]. He said he would.

A man called Lewis Gilbert[4] rang. Said would I meet him at the RAC Club at one o'clock on Thursday. He wants me to do a film. Says I'll be very excited when I know what it is. Bet I shan't. I'd like to do a film of something interesting. Or I'd like to ask a ridiculous price in the hope that I'd be turned down.

Wednesday 4 January

Cold, grey morning. Went into town. Bought a single of Donovan[5] singing 'Sunshine Superman'. An obsessive tune. George calls him 'Dirty Donovan'. Because of the drugs scandal. On the bus coming home I heard a woman behind me say, 'I come in here 'cause I see you were on your own.' And a second woman replied, 'Yes, I come inside now my feet are bad. Well, I 'as to, see. Since my feet got worse.' The other woman, after a long silence, said, 'My mum laughed over your Doll. Your Doll give me a ring for Christmas. And my mum says to her, "She's got a handful of rings." I'll let you see what she bought me some other time, Gloria. I haven't got it on, see. I'll put it on tomorrow and show you. I'm a

---

1 Orton's birthday. Born John Kingsley Orton in 1933.

2 Sir Peter Hall (1930–   ). Aristic Director of the National Theatre. In his *Diaries*, Hall writes: 'Orton was a miraculous writer. I still remember the sheer breathless pleasure I had when I first read *What the Butler Saw*. The play is surely one of the comic masterpieces of the century. Has to be.'

3 Produced in an early version by Rediffusion Television, 27 June 1966. First staged with *The Ruffian on the Stair* as *Crimes of Passion* by the English Stage Company at the Royal Court Theatre, 6–17 June 1967. Directed by Peter Gill.

4 Lewis Gilbert (1920–   ). Producer, director and screenwriter. Directed *Alfie, You Only Live Twice*. Produced and directed such films as *Educating Rita, Not Quite Jerusalem*.

5 Donovan (Donovan Leitch) (1946–   ). Singer and songwriter. In the sixties linked rock with hippie mysticism in such songs as 'Catch the Wind', 'Sunshine Superman', 'Mellow Yellow'.

bugger for the jewellery, see. And they know that.' The other woman said, 'Did you have a nice time over the holidays?' And the second woman said, 'No.' And then she got off the bus.

Peggy rang me at 1.45. She said that a man called Freddie Bartman, who had an antique shop in the King's Road called Anno Domini, had seen Kenneth's screen in her flat.[1] He was so impressed he said he'd like to see more of Kenneth's work. So Kenneth is to take some of his collages to him on Friday. It would be nice if he could sell some of them.

I went down to the Criterion tonight. We were having a rehearsal of the excerpt for television. On the bus I saw the man next door. He works in a club from six in the evening till three in the morning. 'I generally catch the three o'clock bus home. I'm in bed by three-thirty,' he said. His brother-in-law has had mental troubles for three years. 'He can't sort his life out,' he said. He told me he'd played tennis yesterday. 'I'm perfectly mad,' he said as he left me at Piccadilly Circus.

I'd taken my mother's false teeth down to the theatre. I said to Kenneth Cranham[2], 'Here, I thought you'd like the originals.' He said 'What?' 'Teeth,' I said. 'Whose?' he said. 'My mum's,' I said. He looked very sick. 'You see,' I said, 'it's obvious that you're not thinking of the events of the play in terms of reality, if a thing affects you like that.'[3] Simon Ward[4] shook like a jelly when I gave them to him.

---

1 Kenneth Halliwell to Peggy Ramsay, 2 October 1966: 'I should like your opinion of my collage murals. Does my real talent if any lie in this direction etc . . . For instance, the woman who came to interview J from The *Evening Standard* this afternoon spent her time admiring my murals and saying did they cost a terrific lot of money and how professional they were, etc. This has happened before with all sorts of people. However . . .' The *Evening Standard* (3 October 1966) mentions: 'the spotless flat in Islington with yellow walls, three complicated collages and rows of books, records and framed posters neatly juxtaposed'. There is no mention of Halliwell. Of Orton, the story says: 'His marriage has been dissolved.'

    Peggy Ramsay to Kenneth Halliwell, 15 November 1966: 'I hadn't realised that you had started on a screen and I must say I am terribly excited as I think your screens are marvellous . . .'

2 Kenneth Cranham (1944–). Actor. Played Hal in the first London production of *Loot*, and on Broadway. One of Orton's favourite actors who embodied his own truculence and charm. 'I was very right for Orton's plays physically. I'm also genuinely working-class London, which he liked too. I'm very proud of my working-class background. You're allowed to be much more defiant.'

3 Orton told *Plays and Players*, June 1966: 'I have great reverence for death but no particular feeling for the dust of a corpse.'

4 Simon Ward (1941–). Actor. Played Dennis in the first London production of *Loot*. 'Sometimes we'd sit around in the dressing-room with Joe before the show. I'd come out of that dressing-room clutching my heart. Cranham and I used to reel down the corridor together. I was shocked by the boys in Tangier. I felt as if Joe was doing it to take himself out to the very edges. . . . It came out in an urbane, pedestrian, downbeat sort of way. He didn't appear to be taking any pleasure out of it . . . I never felt when Joe was being casual that he was casual. That's one of the reasons I couldn't get to know him. With Joe, his tales – everything he said – was just an act. . . .'

Unpleasantness over rehearsals. They're paid two guineas for each television rehearsal. They've only contracted for one on the day of recording. Rediffusion want three. Sulks all round. I'm angry because there seems to be a sinister suggestion that *Staircase* [1] (a runner up) is having more time than we are. I've told the management to look into it. I don't trust the television company not to slant the programme to give the impression that *Staircase* is at least equal with *Loot*. [2]

Simon Ward says a man keeps ringing him up and writing evil-sounding letters wanting him to be in a film of *Giovanni's Room*, the homosexual novel by James Baldwin [3]. Simon said that the writing is illiterate. And the man over the phone has a thick Glasgow accent. 'Of course, laddie,' he said, last time he rang, 'we'll be having extensive rehearsals. In depth.'

Thursday 5 January

Spent the morning, until 12.15 writing *What the Butler Saw*: scene where Nick, disguised as the policeman, tells Dr Rance that he has arrested himself. At 12.15 I took the 19 bus to St James's Palace and walked to St James's Street. I was to meet Lewis Gilbert at a restaurant called Overton's at 1 pm. I was early. It was cold. So I walked to Duke Street and called on Michael White [4]. He had the original of the caricature of the cast in *Loot* on his wall. He said, 'I was going to give it to you.' I said, 'But, of course, you're too mean.' He said, 'Yes. And, in any case, you're too spoilt as it is.' We talked of the play. He showed me a review in *Queen* magazine that I hadn't seen. The takings went up again last night. Good news which brought a smile to everybody's face. He said Jennie Lee [5] and Michael Foot [6] had been to see the play. I said, 'What a pity Michael Foot didn't take Hugh [7]. Then I could tell everyone that the Feet had seen the play.' He then had to go because he said he was lunching with Kenneth. 'Kenneth McKellar [8] or

1 By Charles Dyer (1928–   ), 1966.
2 Charles Marowitz: 'The contradictory part of Joe's nature was that he was very charming, very boyish, and jolly; but he also had a convict mentality. Having been a convict, his attitude towards the outside world was always that of the convict to the screws. There was a built-in antagonism between him and people in authority ... Whenever there was a difference of opinion either between him and me, between him and the others, it was always as if something more was at stake. The screws were out to get him, or the authorities were out to get him. There was this long-standing antagonism between them and us ...'
3 James Baldwin (1924–   ). Black American novelist and essayist. His books include *Notes of a Native Son, The Fire Next Time, Go Tell It on a Mountain.*
4 Michael White (1936–   ). Theatrical impresario and co-producer of *Loot*. Collaborated again with Oscar Lewenstein in the Joe Orton season at the Royal Court, 1975.
5 Jennie Lee (Baroness Lee of Asheridge) (1904–   ). Politician and wife of Aneurin Bevan (1897–1960). Labour MP, 1929–31. Since 1945, she was responsible for the Arts as a member of the Department of Education and Science, 1965–7. Made life peer in 1970.
6 Michael Foot (1913–   ). Labour MP. Leader of the Opposition, 1980–83.
7 Hugh Foot (Baron Caradon) (1907–   ). Diplomat.
8 Kenneth McKellar (1927–   ). Scottish singer.

Kenneth Williams[1].' I said. He said, 'Kenneth Tynan.'[2] I peed in his lavatory and went to my lunch at Overton's.

When I got into the restaurant I looked around and a man of medium height, thin-faced and middle-aged came towards me. He was Lewis Gilbert. He's a bit suburban. Well meaning, though. I met his son and partner. Lewis G. said, 'We were in Paris yesterday. We were talking to a lot of Americans. I love Paris.' After a pause he said, 'I was going to make *Oliver*[3] you know.' I thought of repeating the joke I'd made in Michael W's office and saying, 'I thought he was dead.' Or 'Wouldn't Stan Laurel[4] object?' But I said nothing. 'Yes,' he went on rather boringly, 'I was all set to make it and then I had to drop everything and make six films for Paramount. Couldn't turn the offer down. Wait till I tell you what I want you to do.'

Halfway through the meal Lewis G. said he wanted me to do a film with him based on the life of Alfie Hinds, who escaped several times from gaol to prove his innocence. He finally won his case. 'I thought of you for the job instantly,' Lewis G. said. 'Your attitude to authority in *Loot* is exactly Alfie Hinds's. You see,' he said, 'in a way it's similar to *Loot* – an ordinary man fighting the might of the law. And winning.' 'Except that in *Loot* he doesn't win,' I said. 'Ah, well,' Lewis G. said, looking a bit put out, 'we wouldn't expect you to write *Loot* all over again.'

I promised to read the book, *Contempt of Court*. But I'm sure it isn't the kind of thing I'd want to do.[5]

1 Kenneth Williams (1926–). Popular comedian and actor. Played Truscott in the original production of *Loot*. A good friend of Orton's and Halliwell's. 'What is heart? If we're talking about compassion and sympathy, I'd say Joe had it. He showed tremendous loyalty to Halliwell. He showed it to me. I went to Joe Orton when I was suicidally depressed about my unshared life, my living alone. When I got to the flat, Halliwell answered the door. He hadn't got his toupé on and this great boiled egg answered the door. "Yes," he said, in a prissy voice. And I said "Hello." "Joe isn't here," he said. And I said "Well, I'll come and see you." "But he's not here. You don't want to see me," Halliwell said. His terrible inferiority always came to the surface. He always believed he was only wanted because Joe was wanted. "Nonsense," I said. "I'd love to see you. And I can smell something cooking." "Oh, it's a bit of haddock I'm doing for him." "I love haddock," I said and walked into the kitchen. He said, "There's only enough for two." "Rubbish," I said, "Split the two bits and put an egg on top. We'll have it!" I sat down in the kitchen. There were only two stools – everything was arranged for two in that flat. Two easy-chairs and two stools. Then Joe came in. He said, "What made you come up here?" I said I was at a loose end. Then I dropped my façade. Up to that point I'd been brittle and arch with Halliwell because I sensed his inwardness and his desire not to talk. Joe said, "Anytime you feel like this always come here . . ." He made me talk. He was the most marvellous counsellor. He actually got the adrenalin going, forced the pendulum, which had almost stopped, to swing again. He was a great *activator* . . ."

2 Kenneth Tynan (1927–80). Drama critic and producer.

3 *Oliver* (1968). Adapted from the stage version of *Oliver Twist* by Lionel Bart. Directed by Carol Reed.

4 Oliver Hardy (1892–1957). Film comedian. Stan Laurel (Arthur Stanley Jefferson) (1890–1965), Film comedian and Hardy's comedy partner.

5 Orton to Lewis Gilbert, 8 January 1967: 'I've now had the opportunity of reading the Alfie Hinds book. And I must agree that it could make a very good film. However, I am not the man to write it.

I went down to the Criterion to meet Peter Moffat[2], who is directing the television excerpt from *Loot*.

Kenneth Cranham said, 'What happened about your lunch?' I said, 'He wanted me to do a life of Alfie Hinds, but I want to make a film called *Fifteen Nights in a Girl's School.*' 'Really,' K. said. 'I'd like to be in that.' 'The film or the school?' I said. 'Which pays better?' he said.[3]

Marowitz was there. I told him of the man who'd written up to *Penthouse* magazine. 'He said he'd decided to see whether spanking wouldn't improve his marriage,' I said. 'And he'd talked it over with his wife. He said, "We'd decided that I would spank her should occasion arise, but that there must be a genuine occasion. Next day she came to me with a gleam in her eye holding up one of my best shirts which she'd scorched whilst ironing." So,' I said to Marowitz, 'he belted her. And apparently the sex was marvellous. And now they do it all the time. Only it comes expensive on shirts.' 'What a morbid mind this character has,' Marowitz said, addressing everybody present. 'I didn't invent it,' I said. 'What about the other one?' Kenneth Cranham said. 'Where she takes his thin pyjamas down and whips him savagely on the bare buttocks.' 'Oh, yes,' I said to Marowitz, 'only he found that it hurt him. And now he wants to stop. Only his wife has developed a taste for it. And she won't let him fuck her without first he has his bottom spanked.' Marowitz snickered to himself and said I'd made it all up.

Friday 6 January

I helped Kenneth to carry his collages (five in all) down to Chelsea. A man called Freddie had seen Peggy's screen and wondered if Kenneth had anything else. We took the five pictures to his shop called Anno Domini in the King's Road. The shop smelt of damp. It had natural-coloured hessian on the walls. In the back was a room the size of a cupboard. Freddie was crouching in there among old playbills and books on antiques. Stuck all over the walls were cards saying 'H. Wallace – Picture framer', 'Coral Williams – miniatures'. And one largish card

---

I'm sorry to have to say "no". Especially as it would be a wonderful opportunity for me. I'll try and explain why I'm turning it down. I'm prepared to accept that the man is innocent – though only because it seems inconceivable that anyone would fight so hard to prove his innocence if he were guilty. Though this isn't, *ipso facto*, proof. I don't believe that Hinds, in the early part of the book, is telling the whole story. I may be wrong. It may be the unfortunate effects of a ghost writer. But there it is. The way the story should go, it seems to me, is that a petty criminal, committing crimes for which he is never convicted, is framed by the police for a crime of which he had no knowledge. An ironic story, but I'm sure, not one which you or your backers (or Mr Hinds) would welcome ...'
2 Peter Moffat (1925–). TV director.
3 Kenneth Cranham: 'Joe seemed to be very sensual. He had this very innocent-looking thing of cocking his head to the side like an animal when it's contemplating something. He was very amused and titillated by the rubbish around him.'

which simply read: 'Refectory Tables. Cheap' and a telephone number. Freddie got up when we entered. He was a youngish, middle-aged man with glasses. 'What have we here?' he said, with a certain eagerness, as Kenneth placed the first of the pictures against the wall. It was a macabre Venus made of bits of fingers and mouths on a background which looked like a crumbling tube station wall. 'Well!' said Freddie, looking impressed. 'You've certainly got something here.' The next picture seemed to be of eggs bursting over a suburban landscape. A negress, cut from a book on African art, lifted up her hands and screamed. Freddie examined it and went on to the three I had brought: a hideous youth sitting in the foreground with a nightmare scene going on behind, a cadaverous monk and a wraith-like nun standing either side of a small picture which was captioned 'Rosencrantz was Jesus CHRIST?' and, lastly, a bull made of human hair leaping around in a sandpit and charging three human eyes. Freddie turned the pictures around and said, 'I think they'd have to be dolled up a bit. Don't you?' He looked beadily around for confirmation. 'I think they ought to be mounted nicely. Don't you?' 'They should be framed,' I said. 'Oh, yes,' he said. 'They'd want nicely framing. What do you think?' he said, turning to Kenneth. 'They want putting under glass,' Kenneth said. 'It'll bring out the colours.' 'Definitely,' Freddie said, 'I quite agree with you. And what about a dab of varnish? Do you think that'd help? Because, quite obviously, we've got to find a way of presenting them, Don't you agree?' 'Yes,' Kenneth said. 'Let me show you my intentions,' Freddie said, leading the way into the cellar.

'I'd put them in this room,' he showed us into an underground cavern.

'I'd take those mirrors down.' He'd led us into another room, musty and evil-smelling. 'I'd make a show of it for you.' He took us back upstairs. 'Can I use your lavatory?' I said. 'I want to pee.' 'In the corner,' he said, with a light laugh. He opened the door of what I'd taken to be a cupboard. Inside was a lavatory. 'My time machine,' Freddie said, with another laugh. Whilst I was in the lavatory, Freddie prepared a cup of tea. 'You want a nice framer,' I heard him saying to Kenneth. 'I'll look out for one. Let you know. And what are you thinking of asking for them?' Kenneth looked vague.

'Let's leave that till they're framed and ready,' I said, emerging from the lavatory. 'Right you are,' said Freddie. 'We'll leave it to fate then, shall we?'

He promised to ring Kenneth with the name of a picture framer. Kenneth said he'd have fifteen framed to start with. 'Just to start with,' Freddie cackled to himself. 'After all,' he said, 'we don't know whether they're going to bite, do we?'[1]

---

1 Halliwell didn't sell any.

Saturday 7 January

Very sick last night. Must've been something I ate. I was up three or four times vomiting. Felt well enough, though, to write further on *What the Butler Saw*.

Miss Boynes appeared at the door at 11.30 this morning. 'I wondered,' she said, 'did you hear a noise in the night?' 'About two?' I said. 'Yes,' she said. 'I heard a bang,' I said. 'It was those wretched kids in Mrs Ditchburn's flat. They were late home. They slammed the door. It broke my window. Well, I've complained to Madam Ditchburn. I'm having it stopped. You've no idea of the racket they kick up. I can hear them giggling till four in the morning. Well, I mean to say, is that right?' 'Did they break the window?' I said. 'I'd say they did, wouldn't you?' She backed away from our door and halfway down the stairs. 'I said there'd be complaints. I included you.' She was on the landing by now. 'I'm taking out an injunction,' she shrieked up from her door on the floor below. 'Such noise! I've heard nothing like it!'[1]

Monday 9 January

The alarm woke me at 8 o'clock. I got up at 8.30. Had a cup of tea. Was down at the Criterion by 9.30. The televisation of the excerpt from *Loot* was scheduled to begin at 10 o'clock. Sat in Sheila Ballantine's dressing-room talking. She said William Gaskill[2] had loved *Loot*. 'I hadn't expected to,' he said, kissing her on her cheek, 'but I thoroughly enjoyed it.' 'He kissed me too,' Kenneth Cranham said. 'Well, that's more in character for him, isn't it?' I said. 'Bernard Braden[3] walked out,' Sheila said. 'After the interval there was an empty space.' 'I wouldn't've thought one more would be noticeable, the houses we're getting lately,' I said. 'Is it bad?' she said, looking severe in her nurse's uniform. 'We're not getting the stalls trade,' I said. 'I wonder why?' Sheila said. 'It'll be a pity if we come off.'

Simon Ward came in later, looking pale. He'd had his nose glued to Kenneth Cranham's copy of *Penthouse*. 'The candle and the ebony ruler was much in evidence,' he read out, settling down in a comfy chair. 'What's that?' Sheila hurried over, her eyes popping. 'Lesbianism,' Kenneth Cranham rolled over on the couch. 'Really?' Sheila picked up the hairbrush and spanked him. 'No, but at our school nothing went on like that.' 'Perhaps you went to the wrong school,' Simon said. 'Must've done,' Sheila said. 'I was ever so innocent, though. I remember two girls being told off for doing something in the loo.' 'Perhaps it was

---

1 Miss Boynes: 'There were a lot of arguments between Ken and John at the end. I bought earplugs, being absolutely underneath.'
2 William Gaskill (1930–   ). Director. Then artistic director of the English Stage Company (the Royal Court), 1965–72. Peggy Ramsay to Orton, June 1966: 'Bill Gaskill obviously decided not to do *Loot* because of the dislike of the play by Desmond O'Donovan . . . Oscar is furious. The Court will definitely do *Ruffian* and I feel this will endear Orton to them.'
3 Bernard Braden (1916–   ). Actor and media personality.

smoking,' I said. 'No. I think, now I look back on it, that they must've been having each other.' She gave a sort of terrified giggle. 'I wouldn't've known then what was going on.'

The recording seemed to go quite well. The set looked better on the screen. Black and white imposed a harsh style which suited the play. Peter Moffat said he'd love to do *Sloane* on television. I don't see why they shouldn't.

I was told by Mark Linford[1] that the WVS had refused to either hire or sell us a uniform for the play. We'd had to have one specially made.

Oscar[2] said that David Merrick[3] had asked Marowitz to direct the play in New York. Did I object? 'It's a bit late to ask me,' I said.[4] Oscar had asked Marowitz to lunch to discuss New York. I agreed to go as well. The televising finished at twelve.

Over lunch Oscar said that *The Homecoming* had received a poor showing in New York. 'They said it was in bad taste,' Marowitz said. 'Well, what are they going to say to *Loot*?' I said. 'Well, I think *Loot* could go very well in America. It has just the right elements to delight them over there. After all, American society is obsessed by money and authority.' 'They're obsessed by nymphomania and homosexuality,' I said, 'and *Sloane* lasted for thirteen performances.' 'I don't think we should be drawn into a discussion of *Sloane*,' Oscar said. 'No,' I said. 'It's my obsession.'[5]

There were a number of suggestions made for casting the part of Truscott. All more or less unworkable. And Fay was the second part under discussion. Marowitz keen on Fenella Fielding[6]. I think she's very camp. But since Broadway

1 Mark Linford. Stage manager of *Loot*.
2 Oscar Lewenstein (1917–). Co-producer of *Loot*. Lewenstein remained loyal to Orton's work. Buying the screenplay *Up Against It*; co-producing *What the Butler Saw* in 1969; and as Artistic Director of the Royal Court (1972–75), mounting a Joe Orton season of full-length plays.
3 David Merrick (1917–). The most powerful and successful Broadway producer of the post-war period. Among his hits are *Fanny; Hello, Dolly; Gypsy; Jamaica.*
4 Orton to Michael White, 14 July 1967, about Marowitz: 'God knows I'm not a fan of his. I think a lot of the direction in *Loot* is atrocious. But on the principle of "Better the Devil you know than the Devil you don't", I'd think about it. With a stronger cast his direction wouldn't stick out much. And it's a success in London!! Remember that.'
5 Orton to Glenn Loney, 17 November 1965, about the failure of *Entertaining Mr Sloane* on Broadway: 'It's the character of Eddie which got under their skin. We know over here that there are two American neuroses – Communism and Homosexuality. We believe Americans (in general, not you or the people I met when I was in NYC) aren't sane on those subjects. I touched off number one neurosis. It'd be interesting to put out a questionnaire – "Would you rather your son grew up to be a Communist or a Homosexual?". In the South you could add "Would you rather your son grew up to be a Communist or a Homosexual or a Negro?"'
6 Fenella Fielding (1934–). Actress. Orton to Michael White about casting *Loot* on Broadway: 'None of your Tennessee Williams drag queens. Having said all this I am probably going to undo it by saying that I wouldn't object to Fenella Fielding. I don't like her – she's a camp lady – but if she could be controlled I wouldn't say no. And I'm sure she'd be v. popular in New York (for so many reasons).'

is already, in my mind, a dead duck, I let them talk on.[1] The food was gone. 'What about Michael Redgrave[2] for Truscott?' Michael White said. 'I thought he made a poor caterpillar in *Alice*,' I said. 'However, he might be better at portraying human beings.' 'Take the case of Gielgud[3],' Oscar said, spooning something white and frothy into his mouth. 'He made a superb Mock Turtle, yet I'm sure he'd be uninteresting as a man.'

We parted having agreed to make a list of possibles for all parts. 'Like a nice afternoon, gents?' a tout outside a strip-club said, as we passed, 'Naked ladies. All alive.'

'You look very pretty in that fur coat you're wearing,' Oscar said, as we stood on the corner before going our separate ways. I said, 'Peggy bought it me. It was thirteen pounds nineteen.' 'Very cheap,' Michael White said. 'Yes, I've discovered that I look better in cheap clothes.' 'I wonder what the significance of that is,' Oscar said. 'I'm from the gutter,' I said. 'And don't you ever forget it because I won't.'

Tuesday 10 January

Cold, rainy day. I went out early to post a couple of letters and to buy a loaf. As I came down the stairs I heard Mrs Corden saying, 'It was originally done out in rich ruby, but of course, with the passing years, the colour has faded. It's more of a deep shell now. And dirty too.' The man with her was a salesman from a soft furnishings store. Mrs Corden was having a chair re-covered. 'Is that the pattern you'd like, madam?' His voice was low, as though they were bent over a book. 'Yes,' Mrs Corden said. 'I'd be happy with that.' It seemed odd to carry out the whole operation on the stairs outside the flat. But then, the Cordens' flat is so choked with rubbish that it isn't possible to have anyone inside.[4] 'I'll be expecting to see you *and* the chair within a fortnight,' Mrs Corden said, as though the salesman was going to materialise on the chair outside her grubby front door in exactly fourteen days. 'And, please remember, I don't wish to have the fringing.' 'No, madam,' the salesman said, and followed me out of the front door.

When I got back Kenneth was on the telephone. It was Henry Budgen[5]. Kenneth passed the phone over to me.

1 Orton to Glenn Loney, undated 1967: '*Loot* will be on Broadway sometime next year (for about three days I'd say).' *Loot* ran 22 performances on Broadway.
2 Sir Michael Redgrave (1908–1985). Actor, director, author. Father of Vanessa Redgrave and Lynn Redgrave (1943–).
3 Sir John Gielgud (1904–). Distinguished actor and director.
4 Miss Boynes: 'I was never admitted to the Cordens' flat, thank goodness, as I didn't want to go in. But once I did go in. The Cordens were passing between them a bag, a paper bag. With biscuits in it. Of course, John noticed that. When I saw *Entertaining Mr Sloane*, there was the bag. Kath had a bag of sweets. That's what the Cordens would do. They wouldn't dream of putting them in a dish. They were always left in a paper bag.'
5 Henry Budgen (1912–1979). Journalist and friend of Orton and Halliwell.

'How are you?' Budgen said, sounding nasal and flat over the phone. Even more nasal and flat than in reality. 'Are you well?' 'Yes,' I said. He told me that Hubert[1] had rung to say he'd seen *Loot*. 'He said you were a very clever boy,' Budgen said. 'I had a telephone call from Kenneth Williams yesterday. He said he'd seen Bernard in Biagi's last night. He was wearing a smart suit. Very different from Tangier.' 'He always dressed smartly in Tangier,' I said. 'Only he wore less.'

Budgen said someone he knew had been to Libya. 'I have to be discreet over the phone,' he said, dropping his voice to a whisper. 'Only this friend of mine says it's marvellous. They're queueing up outside your hotel door.' 'Oh,' I said, having already decided months ago to go to Libya in the spring. 'Yes.' There was a pause. 'Have you been having any little adventures lately?' He sounded as though he were panting. 'I can't tell you over the phone,' I said. 'No.' Another long pause. 'You must come and have lunch with me sometime and then you can tell me everything.' 'I'd like to,' I said. 'I can't wait.' Budgen coughed. 'Are you dressed?' 'Yes,' I said, 'Why.' 'Nothing.' Pause. 'I just thought you might be in your pyjamas.'

'Tell the fat fool you've won the *Evening Standard* Drama Award,' Kenneth hissed at my elbow. 'Was that Kenneth?' Budgen asked. 'Yes.' 'What did he say?' 'He said for me to tell you that I'd won the *Evening Standard* Drama Award for *Loot*.' A stunned silence and then he said, 'For the best play of the year?' 'Yes,' I said. 'Will you be going to the luncheon?' 'Yes.' 'How nice. Well, I'm going. I'm going with David Tomlinson[2]. If you see me you will be discreet.' 'What do you mean?' I said. 'You won't say anything?' Pause. 'You know what I'm talking about.' A nervous laugh. 'He's always asking about me. And he's very anti-. You won't shock him, will you?' 'What do you mean?' I said. 'Well,' he somehow, even over the phone, managed to give an impression of pop-eyes and a toothbrush moustache. 'I've got to be so careful. Anyway I can trust you not to misbehave.' He gave a sort of breathless laugh. I agreed to see him tomorrow and rang off.

Wednesday 11 January

I rang Michael White before eleven. He said that Monday and Tuesday night this week were a disaster. If the award doesn't bring some people in we're sunk. The *Standard* came out at ten-thirtyish. The copy I got was splendid. A banner headline: "SCANDAL. BUT LOOT HAS IT." There was no runner-up. It was four to one. Penelope Mortimer[3] thought *Loot* simply nasty. The three men over-ruled her, though.[4]

1 Sir Hubert Pitman (1901–1986) Member of Lloyds since 1929. Chairman of H. Pitman & Co.
2 David Tomlinson (1917–   ). Actor.
3 Penelope Mortimer (1918–   ). Author. Among her best known books: *The Pumpkin Eater, About Time* (Whitbread Prize, 1979).
4 Hugh Cruttwell, Principal of RADA; Philip Hope-Wallace, drama critic of the *Financial Times*; Milton Shulman, drama critic of the *Evening Standard*.

I tried to do some work on *What the Butler Saw* and gave up. Too difficult to concentrate. I left home at twelve. I'd borrowed Kenneth's striped suit. I wore a wide, flowered tie, a high-collared, striped shirt and boots (suede). I arrived at Peggy's office. There were three letters. One for me from Grove Press giving me a review of the book of *Entertaining Mr Sloane*. One from The Writer's Guild in America (this went straight into the wastepaper basket). And one from the editor of *Plays and Players* telling me that the critics, in their annual poll, had voted *Loot* the best play of 1966.[1] So I've got a bonus.

Peggy and I decided to walk to Bury Street to Quaglino's where the luncheon was being held. On the way I told Peggy of the girl who'd written up to *Penthouse* magazine saying that her boyfriend had objected to her wearing ordinary knickers under a mini-skirt. So he'd bought her a G-string. And she wears it all the time now, she finds it so delightful. The funny thing is that her boyfriend wears one under his jeans. 'But, darling,' Peggy said, wide-eyed, 'I mean – wire – isn't it desperately uncomfortable?' I couldn't believe that she was seriously pretending not to know what a G-string was. I was going to tell her that it was a brief pair of panties when we arrived at Quaglino's. Sheila Ballantine was just going in. We greeted each other in a conspiratorial whisper. It was so grand inside. I left my coat, and Peggy and I appeared at the top of a staircase. The toastmaster, in a sort of hunting-pink coat, asked our names. We gave them and he boomed them out over the crowd below. It was like a thirties film of *Lady Windermere's Fan*[2].

Quite crowded. Bill Gaskill came up. Very bright-eyed. 'Loved *Loot*,' he said. 'I'm so glad,' I said. 'It's always nice to convert somebody.' Spoke to Oscar for a while. Peggy saying how brave he was to have taken up an option. True in a way, I suppose. Though she has a convenient lapse of memory about the period (ten days before rehearsals were due to begin) when Oscar, dissatisfied with the casting, asked me if I wanted to cancel the production. 'If we cancel,' I said, 'when will we remount it?' 'I can't guarantee when we'll do that,' Oscar said. This is the play's last chance, I thought. If it comes to grief now plus the original tour, the dubiety as to *Loot* will harden into certainty. Everyone will be sure that the play is no good. 'It must go on,' I said. 'With this cast. I must let the London critics see the play. After that I'll shut up about *Loot* and write another play.' All this, naturally, wasn't mentioned, or even thought of, probably, except by me.

Peggy introduced me to Ted (Lord) Willis[3]. Surprisingly he turned out to be a fan. 'I loved *Sloane*,' he said, 'and I love *Loot*. I'd give anything to have a play as brilliant as *Loot* on at the Criterion.' 'Oh, but surely, Ted,' Peggy said, with a

---

1 For *Entertaining Mr Sloane* Orton had come second in the London Critics' Poll (1 July 1964) for most promising playwright; and *Sloane* had come second behind *Alfie* for best play.
2 By Oscar Wilde (1854–1900), 1892.
3 Lord (Ted) Willis (Baron Willis) (1918–   ). Playwright, screenwriter and novelist.

flashing smile, 'you've had plays on at other theatres.' 'No,' he put his hand on my shoulder, 'I'm a hack. Just a hack, Peggy. This boy has real talent. He's something special. I'm a hack.'

The lunch was announced. On the board it said "Mr and Mrs Orton". Peggy laughed. 'I'll be your wife for the afternoon,' she said. All I could think of was how embarassing if, as I'd originally planned, I'd taken Kenneth.

In the doorway of the dining-room I spotted Michael Codron[1]. Dark-suited and a little po-faced. Though as this is natural with him I thought it was nature, not the occasion. 'Congratulations, Joe,' he said. 'You can imagine what I must be feeling.' 'No, I can't,' I said. 'I haven't got that strong an imagination.' All done with a merry sort of twinkle, but it had the effect of a knee in the groin.

I saw Budgen. Briefly. He grinned, sheepish. Even more sheepish when he realised that he was on table six and David Tomlinson on table five sitting next to me. Throughout the meal he kept looking round, anxious, his eyes popping almost onto his cheeks. Each time he saw me laughing at something D. Tomlinson had said. 'Have you won anything?' Tomlinson said, as he sat down. 'Yes. *Loot* has won the "Best Play".' 'Good gracious. Congratulations.' During the meal he said, 'I want you to promise me something. I want you to promise, when you accept the award, to say, "Ladies and Gentlemen, I'm not surprised to be here. I'm only surprised that I haven't been here before." Will you say that?'

'No,' I said.

'Why not?'

'Because I haven't your talent for comedy,' I said. 'It sounds witty and urbane when you say it. Listen to what it's like when I say it.' I said it. He said, 'Yes.' 'It sounds arrogant, conceited, would-be funny and gutter when I say it.' I began to eat ice cream very fast because the coffee was coming round. It was extra-cold ice-cream and my teeth started to hurt. 'I feel as though I ought to have a brandy before I go on,' I said. 'Drink some wine,' said the girl next to me. She was called Susan Engel[2] and had played Lady MacDuff in the Gaskill *Macbeth*. She was receiving the Best Actress Award on behalf of Irene Worth[3], who was in New York.

After coffee the toastmaster announced that the meal had ended. Rather surprisingly, I thought. The lights for the television cameras came on. And the business of speeches began. And then, after Frank Marcus[4] had made a long

---

1 Michael Codron (1930–). Producer. Co-produced with Donald Albery *Entertaining Mr Sloane*; and the first abortive production of *Loot* starring Kenneth Williams which closed at Wimbledon the week of 15 March 1965. Codron introduced Kenneth Williams to Orton.

2 Susan Engel (1938–). Actress.

3 Irene Worth (1916–). American leading actress in recent years on British stage.

4 Frank Marcus (1928–). Playwright and critic. Marcus's play *The Killing of Sister George* had won the *Evening Standard* Award for Best Play, 1965. Marcus heralded *What the Butler Saw* as a

speech about me, I went up on the platform. I was very nervous. Drinking the wine hadn't helped much. I didn't say much. I said, as near as I can remember, 'In the early days we used to give complimentary tickets to various organisations. We sent a few to Scotland Yard. And the police loved the play so much that they rang up asking for more tickets. Everyone else thinks the play is a fantasy. Of course the police know that it's true.' And then I said that I hoped to get another award in about two years' time. Robert Morley[2], later on, said that it was no good having one. You had to have two for bookends.

A lot of funny speeches. One wonderful one from Frankie Howerd[3]. Only I can't remember what it was now. 'I adore him,' David Tomlinson said, 'he is a real artist.'

And then the toastmaster said that was all. The lights were switched out and people started going home. It was over.

I was on the front of the *Evening Standard* receiving the award.[4] And I'm very happy. Pleased though that I've almost finished the first draft of *What the Butler Saw*. It'd be difficult to have to begin a play from scratch.

I didn't want to go to the theatre for the drinks etc. tonight. So I made some excuse. We invited Mr and Mrs Corden up from the basement. Also Miss Boynes. We watched the programme called *Accolade*. Before we did this we had a sandwich or two. I showed Mrs Corden the menu for the lunch. 'How lovely,' she said. 'It looks like a skilled printing job to me. But, of course, the actual luncheon isn't as good as Mr Corden's firm's annual get-together's dinner. It was at the Savoy. And we had a sweet which was like straw. I have never, in the whole of my life, tasted anything so scruptious. That is the only word to describe it.

---

masterpiece and also wrote enthusiastically about *Loot*. 'Thank you for your review of *Loot* in the *London Magazine*,' Orton wrote Marcus on 7 February 1967. 'Very interesting. I mean, quite apart from it being a good notice of the play. I'd just been having a long argument with Simon Ward about tragedy today. He argued and argued. I wish I'd read your review and then I'd've been able to quote George Steiner . . . My third play (at present tucked away in a bottom drawer to marinate) has, as its leading characters, a foolish old man and a near certifiable doctor. I can't see any sign of the Captain, though there is a (uniformed) police sergeant. As I've already written the play no one can say I've done this to fit in with your theories.'

2 Robert Morley (1908–). Popular West End actor and playwright, famous for *Edward My Son* which he co-authored. Entered films in 1937, among them the title role in *Oscar Wilde; Major Barbara; The African Queen; The Loved Ones*.

3 Frankie Howerd (1921–). Comedian.

4 *Evening Standard* editorial, 'Glowing Theatre', 11 January 1967: 'Among the fashionable nonsense talked about Swinging London, one truth stands out: the drama in London is in one of the most vigorous and exciting phases of its history. Probably not since the Elizabethans has it displayed so much richness, colour, depth and imagination. . . . Above all this resurgence of the drama is due to the new writers who have sprung up since the end of the war. They are the ultimate source of vitality. Osborne, Pinter, Wesker, Arden, Orton: these are the names who stimulate our minds, invigorate our culture, and irritate our conscience.'

Scrumptious,' she said, saying the word twice and hoping that nobody would notice she'd made a mistake the first time.[1]

Miss Boynes said, 'I had a bite yesterday. From a businessman.' She was talking about her flat. 'Only he told the agent that he wasn't prepared to pay more than £3,000 for it. Cheek!' Kenneth and I exchanged looks. I'd been thinking of offering her £2,500. And Kenneth said £2,000.[2] 'Cheek!' Miss Boynes said again. 'Why if I took £3,000 I'd escape with only £2,800 after the agent's commission and other expenses have been paid. Oh, no! I'm not doing that. Not on your life, I'm not! The cheek!'

Mr Corden, after examining the award statuette, suddenly said, 'Under the green baize bottom is a bolt which bolts the actual object to the marble plinth. If you were to strip the baize away you'd see the workmanship beneath.' Like turning round the Rokeby Venus to see how the frame was made.

The programme called *Accolade* was a disappointment. The excerpt from *Loot* was good. The set seemed to have more style on film than in reality. The performances were excellent. Then we had a long excerpt from *Staircase*. For no good reason. It wasn't a runner-up. As had been suggested (by inference) in the *TV Times*. The real blow fell when, after excerpts from Finney's[3] new film, *Two for the Road*, and a long piece from *Little Malcolm and His Struggle Against the Eunuchs*[4], we came to the luncheon. But, by this time, the programme was over. When Frank Marcus announced me as award winner, the sound was off. I appeared briefly with the sound still off and the captions and credits coming over my face. Then the sound came on for the other winners. The whole had the effect of the man with the bladder hitting the emperor on the head as he rode in triumph. Just to take him down a peg or two and remind him that he wasn't a god. Only I don't think this could've been intentional.

Went to bed very disgruntled.

Thursday 12 January

Wrote angry letter to Rediffusion about the programme, spurred on by Peggy, who agreed that the whole thing was deliberately done.[5] Told Peter Willes, who

1 Miss Boynes: 'Mrs Corden was quite ordinary but she made out she was quite an elegant woman with a good background. She had such bad grammar but she spoke in a high-falutin' voice.'

2 Eleanor Salvoni: 'Joe was very happy that things were happening. He wanted to expand but not move. He didn't know whether he should buy Miss Boynes's flat. Joe said, "We could take the flat underneath: one to live in, one to work in." Ken said, "Yes, I know Joe, but one of these days you may dry up. Then what?." Joe was baffled by this attitude. "Don't think of it like that," he said. They asked us for a lot of advice.'

3 Albert Finney (1936–). Actor. His films include *Saturday Night and Sunday Morning*, *Tom Jones*, *Charlie Bubbles*, *Gumshoe*. Directed *Loot* in the 1975 Royal Court revival.

4 By David Halliwell (1936–), 1964.

5 'I had up to this time been kindly disposed toward Associated Rediffusion,' Orton wrote to Cyril Bennett. 'I might add that among serious playwrights I'm in the minority. You can be sure that after this treatment I've joined the majority.'

rang up having returned from New York. He most upset at what he said was 'Hysterical and childish behaviour on my part.' 'Fuck off,' I shouted down the telephone. 'I'm not hysterical!!' 'Well, I think you are,' he said. 'And further more if you don't want to write any plays for Rediffusion there are many other writers who will.' I put the telephone down, but before I did so he said, 'Go and run your wrists in luke-warm water. It will calm your nerves.' Very irritated by this remark as I suspect it wasn't unkindly meant.

A man called Walter Shenson[1] called Peggy. He is the man who produced the first two Beatles films. He had a script, written by somebody else – it isn't quite good enough. 'Dull,' he said. 'Would you like to see it with a view to working on the film script?' I was very impressed by this, but I put on a nonchalant manner. 'Well, I'm frightfully up to my eyes in it at the moment,' I said. 'I'm writing my third play.' 'I'd certainly love to have you take a look at this draft,' he said. 'I've discussed it with the boys. I mean I mentioned your name to them. They've heard of you. They didn't react too much, I must say. But I think I can persuade them to have you.' By this time I was feeling foolish and not at all nonchalant. 'Yes,' I said. 'Please send the script over and I'll read it.'

Kenneth and I went down to the Criterion to show the cast the award. Everybody came into Sheila's dressing-room. They'd heard about the programme. 'But surely,' Michael Bates[2] said, 'it was just inefficiency.' 'No,' I said, 'it was deliberate.' 'Really?' Michael looked most upset. 'How disgraceful. I thought it was just the usual badly put-together programme. I'd no idea it was deliberate. How shocking. Something should be done about it. Really it should. Disgraceful.' He went away shaking his head, looking more like McLeavy than Truscott.

From the theatre we went on to Adrienne Corri's[3]. She was giving dinner to Madge Ryan[4] who is off to America tomorrow on a tour with the Bristol Old Vic. We expected just dinner, but upon going in we were given champagne. Tiresome because it meant that I had to drink. And, somehow, ended up very drunk talking to a roomful of people until two in the morning. I enjoyed it. So did Kenneth, but next day was hell.

---

1 Walter Shenson (1919–). American film producer.
2 Michael Bates (1920–1978). Actor. Played Truscott in the London production of *Loot* and listed the role as his favourite part in *Who's Who in the Theatre*. Bates found Orton and Halliwell 'both absolutely weird'. Orton sent him a postcard from Tangier: 'Just a line to let you know that I'm having a total experience (as Charles M. might say). I wouldn't sit under one of these umbrellas for all the tea in China – but I believe the deckchair-loungettes are très comfy.'
3 Adrienne Corri (1933–). Actress and author. 'The evening with them was terribly uncomfortable. It was just small bickering the whole time. Their roles had become reversed. Joe was protecting Ken, instead of Ken protecting Joe. I had some champagne because Madge was leaving; and Ken drank a hell of a lot, then disappeared upstairs and passed out.'
4 Madge Ryan (1919–). Actress. Played Kath in the original production of *Entertaining Mr Sloane* (1964). Introduced Orton and Halliwell to Adrienne Corri.

Talked, at first to Fanny Carby[1], a rather fat, plain woman with buck teeth. Very good and funny actress. I'd originally wanted her to play Lou in *The Erpingham Camp*. She was one of the few people, as far as I could tell, who'd seen *The Erpingham Camp* and, not knowing who wrote it, had loved it. Next I found myself talking to Julian Holloway[2]. He used to be a great friend of Ian McShane's[3]. He told me of a waiter in a Chelsea bistro who, whilst serving him, murmured 'There's something wrong with my tits.' He was three-parts of the way through a sex-change. His name was Rex Poynter.[4] Julian said that a few months later he met him in the King's Road in drag. 'Why are you dressed as a woman, Rex?' he said, half-expecting the police to arrest them. 'I am a woman,' he said. 'And don't call me Rex. My name is Lorraine Poynter-Smith.' Julian said he invited him up to his flat. 'He'd turned into a whore,' Julian said. 'Well,' Rex had told him, 'I decided I'd sooner be a rich whore than a poor queen. So I went to this psychiatrist. I went in drag, you see. And this psychiatrist fella said "Why are you dressed like that?" "Like what?" I said. "As a woman," the psychiatrist said.' 'I am a woman, doc,' Rex had pleaded. 'What do you do for sexual intercourse – er Miss Poynter-Smith?' 'How can I have sexual intercourse, doctor,' Rex said, 'with this terrible growth?'

Julian said that he saw a letter from a client of Rex's (or Lorraine's). It said, 'Dear Lorraine, I'm looking forward to seeing you on Saturday. When you arrive at my house I'd like you to first assault me violently and then take over the running of my home. At some time during the evening I'd like to be undressed, forcibly, and tied to my bed. I'd like you to smack my buttocks with a riding crop (provided) and then go and watch television. During the rest of the evening you may do what you wish – either knitting, reading or watching television. From time to time I'd like you to come into my bedroom and hit me, making ungrateful comments. In the middle of the night I want you to rise from your bed and lock me in the coal cellar. For this you will be paid £25.'

When we left it was two in the morning. One of Adrienne's friends dropped us off at Baker Street. We got a taxi home.

Friday 13 January

Terrible day. I was sick – because of drinking too much last night. And Kenneth was sick – with the same thing, plus a touch of gastric flu. I went out at eleven o'clock and bought a packet of Alka-Seltzer. Took two. Felt dreadful and went back to bed. When I woke up I felt better. We both stayed in bed though, for the

1 Fanny Carby (1931–). Actress.
2 Julian Holloway (1944–). Actor, director, producer. Son of Stanley Holloway.
3 Ian McShane (1942–). Played Hal in the original production of *Loot*.
4 Rex Poynter (1938–81). Escort.

day. I got up at five and went to shave. Peter Willes had invited me to dinner. Peggy rang at six. She said, 'Your letter to Rediffusion was super. You're going to receive an apology.' 'Apologies cost nothing,' I said. 'Still, it's nice to know we were right, isn't it?' Peggy said.

When I got to P. Willes's flat I expected anything but what happened. He came to the door with a worried look on his face. 'Are you still crawss?' he said. 'No, of course not,' I said. 'I've taken up the whole matter with Cyril Bennett[1]. And he agrees that it was disgraceful. He's going to write to you.'

Later, after dinner, he told me that *The Homecoming* had been disaster in New York.[2] There is now only one critic of any consequence – Walter Kerr[3]. He hadn't liked *The Homecoming*. They had played to empty houses. It bodes ill for *Loot*. Kerr is a pretty conventional Catholic.

Peter Willes said, later, that he'd give Cyril Bennett a copy of *Sloane* on Monday. 'Of course,' he said, 'we won't be able to do it. But we can have a try.' Now is the psychological time. After all, they'll be wanting to do something to placate me after Wednesday.

On the way home a man behind me on the bus sat next to a young woman and said, 'It's sevenpence to where I'm going, my dear. I remember when it was twopence.' 'Do you really?' she said, looking most unimpressed. 'You don't mind my speaking to you without your permission, do you?' The man seemed extremely nervous. 'No,' the girl said. 'I usually travel by underground. I'm a railway official. We travel free of charge. As I expect you've read.' Pause, and then, heavily, 'When I get in my four-footed friend will run to greet me.' He added, 'My dog' as though she might imagine he meant his donkey.

Saturday 14 January

Felt better today. Spent this morning writing up the events of the last few days. The afternoon completing the first draft of *What the Butler Saw*. It is too long. So I shall be able to cut. Yesterday Peter Willes said that Pinter was starting a new play. He had just finished the fourth page. Felt very smug to say I'd almost completed a whole draft.

1 Cyril Bennett (1928–1976). Then Controller of Programmes for London Weekend Television.
2 Orton to Glenn Loney, undated 1966: 'After the virtual rejection by New York of *The Homecoming*, I feel the sooner England and America declare war on each other the better. I certainly think that we are talking a different language. It bears superficial resemblances but the resemblances are accidental and have no real significance.'
3 Walter Kerr (1913–   ). Critic and author. Then the drama critic for the *Sunday New York Times*. Orton to Glenn Loney, 15 April 1966: 'I received a curiously worded letter (printed) from Jean Kerr asking for money for New Authors. I was on the point of replying that if her husband had been a little fairer in his criticism of my first play I might not now be refusing her request for aid for authors of first plays. But then I thought . . . I might just be in the position of wanting W. Kerr's notice for another play. So I just thought a lot and didn't write at all.'

Manuscript came by post of the Beatles script. I have to start reading it in a minute. Then I shall go to the Criterion to fetch my trophy, which I left there in Sheila's dressing-room on Thursday.

Photographs of the Berlin production of *Sloane* arrived today. Not good photographs, but interesting to have.

Sunday 15 January

Last night I went to the Criterion. Showed the cast the book of *Loot*[1]. Sheila and Michael delighted to have their photographs on the jacket. Remembered to tell the story of how Madge Ryan had overheard a fattish, middle-aged woman saying, in the hairdressers' 'There's simply nothing for it. You must eat French, fuck Italian and be British.' 'Fuck Italian,' Sheila said, wonderingly. 'Oh, I don't fancy that much.' 'Peter Willes told me a very interesting thing yesterday,' I said. 'He went to Cartier's in New York and said "I want to speak to someone in authority". "Yes, sir," the receptionist said. "There's Mr Van Eisen or Mr Bergman." "I'll speak to Mr Van Eisen," Peter Willes said. He was ushered into a vast room. A tall, bald man was sitting behind a desk. "I'm an Englishman," Peter said, shaking his hand, "My name is Willes. I want to give a present to a friend. Cuff-links would be nice. Of course, you realise I can't pay for them?" Mr Van Eisen looked a little put out. "The squeeze, you know," Peter said. "What have you to show me?" He flashed his own cuff-links which were Cartier's and looked at his watch – also Cartier's. Mr Van Eisen brought out a tray of cuff-links. "How about these, sir?" "Oh, good gracious me, Mr Van Eisen. These are as light as thistle-down. They might have come out of a Christmas cracker. Take them away. I couldn't possibly give my friend such trash." Mr Van Eisen brought out another pair and Willes examined them. They cost about £30. "I'll take these. Have them gift-wrapped, will you?" he said. "You do realise that we have no connection with Cartier's in London, sir?" Mr Van Eisen said. "Of course," Peter said. "Well, sir, would you object to our having your home address?" Willes gave it. "Now please, let me have those cuff-links at once. I'm extremely busy." They were given to him in a gift-wrapped box and he left the shop.' 'He could've been a confidence trickster,' Sheila said. 'I wouldn't've got inside the door,' I said. 'Not if I had a million. And Willes has no money at all.'

Later Mark (Michael White's manager) said to me, 'Joe, come and see something. It's what you've been waiting for.' We went into the corridor by the stalls entrance. The stalls were packed. He took me up upstairs to the circle. The circle was packed. And in the gallery they were standing. 'I hope it builds from this,' I said. 'It mustn't just be tonight. It must go on. We're not out of the wood yet.' 'We've not lost a single customer since the award was announced,' Mark

1 Published by Methuen.

said. 'No one has complained since Wednesday. Now they've been told they can enjoy it, they do.'

Came home by bus. Outside the Globe, the 'HOUSE FULL' notices were up. I hope to see them up at the Criterion soon.

Today (Sunday), I read through the first draft of *What the Butler Saw*.[1] Pleased, but still work to be done. Also read the Beatles' script. Like the idea. Basically it is that there aren't four young men. Just four aspects of one man. Sounds dreary, but as I thought about it I realised what wonderful opportunities it would give. The end in the present script is the girl advancing on the four to accept a proposal of marriage from one of them. (Which, the script coyly says, we shall never know.) Already have the idea that the end should be a church with four bridegrooms and one bride. *The Homecoming*, in fact, but alibied in such a way that no one could object.[2] Lots of opportunities for sexual ambiguities – a woman's bedroom at night, her husband outside, and four men inside. I also would like to incorporate a lot of material from the first novel Kenneth and I ever wrote called *The Silver Bucket*.[3] In it a young girl is expelled from her native village for some unnamed offence. Already see how it could be one boy expelled from some great industrial metropolis accompanied by a ceremony of mammoth proportions. Could be funny. As long as I wasn't expected to write a naturalistic script. Rang Walter Shenson, who made the first two Beatles' films, *A Hard Day's Night* and *Help!* Arranged to meet him tomorrow.

Basically the Beatles are getting fed up with the Dick Lester[4] type of direction. They want dialogue to speak. Also they are tired of actors like Leo McKern[5] stealing scenes. Difficult this, as I don't think any of the Beatles can act in any accepted sense. As Marilyn Monroe couldn't act. Hope to discuss the problem in detail tomorrow.

1 Orton to *The Evening Standard*, 12 January 1967, about *What the Butler Saw*: 'I think it will have another offensive theme. I don't do it on purpose. It just comes out like that.'
2 Orton began by imitating Pinter (his radio version of *The Ruffian on the Stair* echoes *The Birthday Party*), and ended by parodying him. Orton's characters state their needs, Pinter's obfuscate them. Orton's comic characters are images of action, Pinter's of entropy. By 1967, in his production notes to the Royal Court for *Crimes of Passion*, Orton wrote: 'Everything the character says is true. The play mustn't be presented as an example of the new outdated "mystery" school – *vide* early Pinter. Everything is as clear as the most reactionary *Telegraph* reader could wish. There is a beginning, a middle and an end ... I hope these notes are helpful. They're rather obvious, but I've learned from experience how strangely people will set about putting on my plays if they're not watched.'
  For a detailed analysis of Orton's parody of the implications of Pinter's style see *Prick Up Your Ears*, pp. 130–2.
3 1953.
4 Richard Lester (1932–). Director. Films include *A Hard Day's Night*, *Help!*, *A Funny Thing Happened on the Way to the Forum*, *Superman I & II*. Orton was scheduled to see Lester about *Up Against It* on the day he was killed.
5 Leo McKern (1920–) had played one of the character parts in *Help!*.

Above left:
Peggy Ramsay and Bill
Roderick, 1967

Above right:
Oscar Lewenstein, 1967

Right:
Peter Willes, c. 1967

Overleaf:
Orton's scrapbook collage of
Entertaining Mr. Sloane's
West End transfer

KINKY...THE FLOGGING OF SHOWGIRLS...NYMPHOMANIACS IN BOOTS AND MACKINTOSHES...

Right:
Orton goes over the
script of first
production of
*Entertaining Mr.
Sloane* with Dudley
Sutton (Sloane) and
Madge Ryan (Kath),
1964

Below:
Orton with
Geraldine McEwan
(Fay) and Kenneth
Williams (Truscott)
at rehearsals of the
first botched
production of *Loot*,
1965

Opposite:
Kenneth Cranham
(Hal), the corpse of
Mrs. McLeavy, and
Simon Ward
(Dennis) in the
successful West End
production of *Loot*,
1966

Above: Michael Bates (Truscott), right, sifts the evidence. Sheila Ballantine (Fay) and Kenneth Cranham (Hal) look on as McLeavy (Gerry Duggan) explains the funeral fiasco in *Loot*, 1966
Below: Orton receives the *Evening Standard* Award for Best Play, 1966

Monday 16 January

Saw Peggy for half an hour this morning before my lunch appointment with Walter Shenson. Told her that Willes had sounded out Peter Hall as to the possibility of doing *The Ruffian on the Stair* and *The Erpingham Camp* on a double-bill. Peggy said that P. Hall was v. busy at the moment. Would he read the scripts if they were sent to him? She finally said she'd write to Peter Hall and see what happens. 'Anyway,' she said, 'he'd probably read a script by you. He's very snobbish about "names".'

Discussed the coming lunch. 'Ask who is directing, darling, and don't move without a director.' She went on to talk about money. 'We'll ask for ten thousand. Not a hope of getting it, of course. They certainly won't pay that much. But we'll allow ourselves to be beaten down. And, you know, don't you, that if you prepare a first draft it becomes their property? They can buy it and put someone else to work on it.' 'What about my lines and dialogue?' I said. 'Well, if they use a lot of it you must be given a credit. But films are difficult. Anyway see this man and if you feel like doing it, tell him to ring your agent.' With that I went to the lunch.

Walter Shenson (Films) Inc was the plaque on the door of an eighteenth-century house just off Hyde Park. It was next door to the larger house with a blue LCC plaque which stated that Sheridan (politician and playwright) had once lived there. Both houses were now turned into offices. A very old lift took me up to the second floor. Silence. Thick carpeting. I went into a door with a sheet of paper pinned onto it saying 'With the compliments of Walter Shenson (Films) Inc'. Inside was a small office. Empty. I looked into a further office. In it was a man about thirty-five, pinkish face, rather a bright, cringing air. 'Are you for Walter?' he said. 'Yes,' I said. 'My name is Joe Orton.' I said this in a bold, confident tone. He squeezed past me in the doorway. 'Walter!' he gave a quick, sharp call. A man appeared in a far doorway. Middle-aged. Short hair going grey. A bald patch. He started towards me, his hand outstretched. In fact he'd begun the motion of shaking hands before his hand touched mine. 'Come into my office,' he said. 'That's the wrong door.' 'I thought it was a bit crummy,' I said. 'For a film producer.' 'Heh, heh, heh,' laughed Walter Shenson. 'Throw your coat over there, heh, heh, heh.' I put down my coat and he disappeared into another office. It was like a set of chinese boxes. While he was gone I looked around. It was a big, long room. On the shelf over the fireplace was a cube with the faces of the four Beatles on each side of the cube. I picked it up and opened the lid, inside was a card saying "Horse shit". 'Heh, heh, heh,' said Walter Shenson, appearing behind me, 'that's a joke thing some guy sent me from back home. They're quite a thing over there now, heh, heh, heh.'

We talked for a while about the script. I gave away a few of my ideas. Enough to whet his appetite. Then we went to lunch. Over lunch he said that one of the ideas for a new Beatles' film was *The Three Musketeers*. 'Oh, no!' I said. 'That's been done to death.' 'Brigitte Bardot wanted to play Lady de Winter,' he said. 'She's been done to death as well,' I said. 'Oh, heh, heh, heh, boy!' he said. 'You certainly are quick.' He said that the Beatles had turned that idea down. He told me that the scene where George[1] had been interviewed by Kenneth Haigh[2] on trendy clothes in *A Hard Day's Night* had been written the night before shooting. And that another scene where George was shaving and John[3] was in the bath beside him was also a spur-of-the-moment idea. I was interested to find out from him that *Some Like it Hot* (film with Monroe, Tony Curtis and Jack Lemmon) had been plagiarised. Billy Wilder[4], he said, had seen a bad German B-film in which two musicians, in order to get a job, had dressed in drag and taken jobs in a ladies' orchestra. The film wasn't well-known and it was easy to buy up all copies. Then they set about re-doing it. And one of the first things they had to settle was why the two men remained dressed as women. In the end they found the perfect solution by making them witness the St Valentine's Day Massacre in Chicago and, in order to escape from the gangsters, dress in drag.

On the whole a dull lunch. I'm interested in doing the film. He's going to contact Karel Reisz[5] about directing. Also contact the Beatles to fix a meeting.

P. Willes rang to say that Cyril Bennett had said, 'Of course we can do *Entertaining Mr Sloane* on television.' Willes, in a fit, has given a copy of the play to Joan Elman the legal woman. 'I mean,' Willes said, 'I don't believe a play in which a lady and a gentleman share a young boy sexually can be called "family viewing".'

I began the first page or two of the film which I'm calling *Up Against It*. Mrs Drumgoole and Father Brodie have come to life as interesting characters. Which should delight the Beatles. I'm not bothering to write a character for them. I shall just do all my box of tricks – Sloane and Hal on them. After all if I repeat myself in this film it doesn't matter. Nobody who sees the film will have seen *Sloane* or *Loot*.

Tuesday 17 January

In the post this morning was a clipping from some paper which said I'd written the best play of 1966 called '*Loo*'.

Spent the afternoon roughing the first scenes in *Up Against It*. I'm pleased with

---

1 George Harrison (1943–). Beatles' guitarist, songwriter, now film producer. (HandMade Films).
2 Kenneth Haigh (1932–). Actor.
3 John Lennon (1940–1980). Lead singer and founder of the Beatles, songwriter, author.
4 Billy Wilder (1906–). Director, writer, producer. His films include: *Double Indemnity*, *Stalag 17*, *The Apartment*, *Sunset Boulevard*, and *Some Like it Hot*.
5 Karel Reisz (1926–). Director. Among his outstanding films are *Saturday Night and Sunday Morning*, *Morgan*, *The French Lieutenant's Woman*.

them. So far. Difficult setting up the fact that only one person exists. Not four. When I've finished the setting up I shall treat them as four.

Man from the BBC rang this afternoon to say that Kenneth Williams had suggested me for a curious panel game called *Call My Bluff*. I said I couldn't do it because I wasn't good at inventing things on the spur of the moment. 'Oh,' he said, 'don't let that worry you. The programme is scripted.' So I said I'd do it. 'You'll get seventy five,' the man said. What I wonder? Pounds or guineas.

Walter Shenson rang. He said he'd been having a talk with Brian Epstein[1], the Beatles' manager. He was delighted that I'd like to do the film. 'So,' W. Shenson said, 'you'll be hearing either from Brian or Paul McCartney[2] in the near future. So don't be surprised if a Beatle rings you up.' 'What an experience,' I said. 'I shall feel as nervous as I would if St Michael or God were on the line.' 'Oh, there's not any need to be worried, Joe,' Shenson said. 'I can say, from my heart, that the boys are very respectful of talent. I mean, most respectful of anyone they feel has talent. I can really say that, Joe.'

Wednesday 18 January

Went to a gathering of London booksellers tonight. I had hoped to get a meal. Instead there were plates of horrible mini-sandwiches and glass cups full of shrimpy things. I was v. disappointed as I was hungry. My publisher said, 'Are you hungry?' 'Yes,' I said. 'Good. There'll be something hot in a minute.' I imagined he meant a decent trolley full of beef and Yorkshire pudding. Instead two or three greasy-looking waiters came round with trays of minute chicken legs covered in some foul concoction. I took one bite and threw mine away. V. depressed. Then we went to see *Loot*. Patchy performances and, as I thought then, not a particularly good house. (Actually £263.)

'How did we do last night?' I asked Charles Marowitz. 'Very good,' he said. 'A most intelligent audience.' 'I don't give a fuck for their intelligence,' I said 'how many of them were there?' He blinked. 'I see you've been corrupted already.' 'Any intelligent person should've seen the play weeks ago,' I said; 'All I'm interested in now is their money.'

The party of booksellers appeared to be composed of grossly fat youngish men, teenage girls and a female dwarf. In the interval, one of the theatre ushers came up to me and asked if I would speak to a young lady. 'I'm from Minnesota,' she said. 'I'm a student. And I'm here with twenty-five other students from the USA. And, well, Mr Orton, we go to the theatre every night. And afterwards we have a discussion on the play at our hotel, at the Royal Hotel, and well, we'd just love to

---

1 Brian Epstein (1934–1967). Beatles' manager and musical impresario.
2 Paul McCartney (1942–   ). Musician, composer, lead singer of the Beatles. Founded the band Wings, 1971.

have you come and discuss your play with us tonight.' I made some excuse for not going. And she looked disappointed but said, 'Well, that's too bad, Mr Orton. But, well, I'm just loving your play. I can't quite understand it. I'm tremendously involved, though. I mean, now, what are you trying to show us? I mean, well, what about this mummy? What does it mean? I'm sure my fellow students would be delighted to hear what you mean by the play. We're all wild in the gallery talking about it.' She took herself off at last, much to my relief. Silly American cow.

On the bus going home I heard a most fascinating conversation between an old man and woman. 'What a thing, though,' the old woman said. 'You'd hardly credit it.' 'She's always made a fuss of the whole family, but never me,' the old man said. 'Does she have a fire when the young people go to see her?' 'Fire?' 'She won't get people seeing her without warmth.' 'I know why she's doing it. Don't think I don't,' the old man said. 'My sister she said to me, "I wish I had your easy life." Now that upset me. I was upset by the way she phrased herself. "Don't talk to me like that," I said. "I've only got to get on the phone and ring a certain number," I said, "to have you stopped."' 'Yes,' the old woman said. 'And you can, can't you?' 'Were they always the same?' she said. 'When you was a child? Can you throw yourself back? How was they years ago?' 'The same,' the old man said. 'Wicked, isn't it?' the old woman said. 'Take care now,' she said, as the old man left her. He didn't say a word but got off the bus looking disgruntled.

Friday 20 January

Went down to Peggy's to collect my six copies of *Loot*. As I came back along Charing Cross Road I heard a loud voice say: 'Don't try and pretend you haven't seen me!' It was Kenneth Williams, smiling and looking old in the bright sunlight. We talked of the programme I've agreed to be on with him. It's called *Call My Bluff*. It's a quiz programme where people have to guess if the story you tell is true or false. Rubbish, of course. 'We wanted Robert Bolt[1],' Kenneth said, 'and we rang Peggy, who said, "Oh, I couldn't possibly ask Bob to appear on a quiz."' Kenneth sniffed and his nose appeared to be about a foot long. 'Silly cow your agent is, isn't she? Don't you think so? That Peggy Ramsay? Silly cow.' I told him of Budgen and the luncheon. He avoided mentioning *Loot*.[2]

When I got back, the phone was just ringing. It was a man called Peter

---

1 Robert Bolt (1924–). Playwright and screenwriter. Among his films are *A Man for All Seasons* (from his play), *Lawrence of Arabia*, *Doctor Zhivago*.

2 Orton wrote Williams, 16 October 1966: 'As you know by now, *Loot* has had an unqualified success. I hope this won't affect our friendship.

Brown.[1] He's Brian Epstein's personal assistant. He wanted to know if I could meet the Beatles at 5.30. I said 'Yes'. Then I had some lunch and went off to the first reading of *The Good and Faithful Servant*[2]. On a church nearby (at the Oval) I saw a poster which said 'He who has the Son has perfect happiness.' And, in large red letters, 'Life Without Christ Isn't.' It took me a few minutes to work out what it meant. The church aren't good at selling their product.

Gave Peter Willes his copy of Albee's *A Delicate Balance*[3]. I thought it a pretentious work. By T.S. (*Cocktail Party*) Eliot[4], out of Henry (*The Heiress*) James[5]. Twenty years out of date. Willes said, 'Well, of course, if it were played English it *would* be twenty years out of date. But it's American.' 'And they are twenty years out of date,' I said, 'and so it's excusable.'

The reading promises well. Patricia Routledge[6] excellent as the personnel officer. Pleasence[7] gave a weird reading. The two youngsters very good. A girl called Sheila White[8] and a boy called Richard O'Callaghan.[9] Both very sweet. Exactly right. Hermione Baddeley[10] a bit worrying. It's not that she's bad. Just doing a different style of acting. Her old char is straight out of a thirties revue. Not right. She will characterise. Not realising that as she is the same age as the woman she's playing there is no need to put on a quavering voice.

Talking to the boy afterwards he said that when Donovan was arrested for smoking marijuana two of the Beatles were in the house with him. The police waited outside until the Beatles left. Because international stars of their magnitude couldn't be involved in a drugs scandal.

He said that he was in *Ubu Roi*[11] with Kenneth Cranham. I think he's softer,

1 Peter Brown (1938–). Film producer, former Executive Director of Apple Corporation. Best man at marriage of John Lennon and Yoko Ono. Author (with Steve Gaines) of *The Love You Make: The Inside Story of the Beatles*.

2 Written 1964. Produced Rediffusion Television, 6 April 1967.

3 By Edward Albee (1928–), 1966. Albee's telegram to Orton at the Broadway opening of *Entertaining Mr Sloane* read: 'MAKE THE BRIGHT CRITICS STAY AWAKE AND THE OTHERS GO TO SLEEP'. Orton wrote to Alan Schneider, 21 October 1965: 'Thank Edward Albee for the first night telegram. Tell him that too many of the critics stayed awake unfortunately.'

4 Thomas Stearns Eliot (1888–1965). American/British poet, critic and playwright. Author of the poetic drama *The Cocktail Party*, 1930.

5 Henry James (1843–1916). American/British novelist and critic. Author of *Washington Square* adapted for the movies as *The Heiress* (1949).

6 Patricia Routledge (1929–). Actress. Played Mrs Vealfoy in *The Good and Faithful Servant*.

7 Donald Pleasence (1919–). Actor. Played Buchanan in *The Good and Faithful Servant*. He read his own poem at Orton's funeral, 'Hilarium Memoriam, J.O.': 'Some met together when he died/ Not in the name of any god/But in his name/Whom they lost to the coffin,/The box which caused him endless mirth,/His lesson – which he could not read again – Hilarity in death.'

8 Sheila White (1950–). Actress. Played Debbie in *The Good and Faithful Servant*.

9 Richard O'Callaghan (1940–). Actor. Played Ray in *The Good and Faithful Servant*.

10 Hermione Baddeley (1906–). Actress. Played Edith in *The Good and Faithful Servant*.

11 By Alfred Jarry (1873–1907), 1896.

sweeter than Kenneth. He isn't going to be as brilliant, I don't think, as K.C. But he's better for this part.

Before I left the rehearsal I had a message from Peter Brown. Could I make the meeting on Monday? The Beatles won't be able to make it today.

Monday 23 January

On Saturday I went down to the theatre to give the actors copies of the play. Outside the London Pavilion was a long queue. The film was Genet's[1] *Mademoiselle* with Moreau[2], directed by Tony Richardson[3]. A middle-aged man moved up and down the queue carrying a large banner. On one side was printed 'THE END IS NIGH' and on the other, 'GOD WANTS YOU'. An old man was following the man with the banner and saying in a loud voice 'How can I find him then? Eh? How can I find him?' The man carrying the banner was trying to avoid the old man. He was clearly embarrassed by his attentions. 'Has he got a telephone number? Eh? What's his telephone number then? Hah, hah, hah, hah.' Finally the man with the banner ducked up a side street away from the crowds to escape the old man. The old man looked around at the crowd and wandered away.

I watched a bit of the play from the OP box[4]. Very good reception from a full house. Came home after talking to Michael Bates who said, 'I'm just reading Trollope[5]. *Dr Thorne*. I find it very restful, you know, when I have to do two performances. I like to browse through something with a bit of class.'

Sunday was dull but pleasant. I read Genet's *Querelle of Brest*. An interesting book, but unformed. A first draft or rough jottings for a masterpiece. Undoubtedly Jean Genet is the most perfect example of an unconscious humourist at work since Marie Corelli[6]. I find a sentence like 'They (homosexuals in Brest) are peace-loving citizens of irreproachable outward appearance, even though, the long day through, they may perhaps suffer from a rather timid itch for a bit of cock' irresistibly funny. A combination of elegance and crudity is always ridiculous. All the same Genet is compulsive reading though, as Kenneth Halliwell said when I made that statement, it may just be the subject which is attractive. I had the idea that the play I intend to write set in prison, *Where Love Lies Bleeding*, should be, in the main, a satire on Genet using much of the story of *Querelle of*

---

1 Jean Genet (1910–1986). French criminal and homosexual turned playwright and novelist.
2 Jeanne Moreau (1928–   ). Actress. Among her films: *Jules et Jim, Les Liaisons Dangeureuses, Chimes at Midnight.*
3 Tony Richardson (1928–   ). Director. Films include: *Tom Jones, Look Back in Anger.*
4 OP Box. The box on the Opposite Prompt (or stage right) side of the theatre.
5 Anthony Trollope (1815–82). Novelist. *Dr Thorne* (1858) is one of his 'Barsetshire' novels of English provincial life.
6 Marie Corelli, pen-name for Mary Mackay (1855–1924), popular English novelist.

Brest. K.H. said, 'You must use all Genet's subjects – beautiful young murderers, buggery, treachery, bent and brutal policemen and theft.' I had originally intended to make *Where Love Lies Bleeding* a parody on Brecht[1]. This worried me slightly because I've already parodied Brecht in *The Erpingham Camp.* But Genet is a much richer field for a prison play.

Monday. I spent the morning writing *Up Against It.* The afternoon K.H. and I went down to the record shop and bought some records. Old ones. For the collection. A Jessie Matthews[2], a Carl Brisson[3], the Boswell Sisters[4] and an original recording of *Band Wagon*[5] with Fred and Adele Astaire[6] from 1931. Disappointing, this last, in a way. Rather a dismal show, but worth getting for the original rendering of 'Night and Day' and *The Gold Diggers*[7] song 'We're in the money'. P. Willes rang me up to say that he'd got three tickets, as arranged for *The Soldier's Fortune*[8] at the Court. 'What are you doing about dinner?' he said. 'Well, Ken and I shall have ours before we arrive. After all we'll be meeting you at 7.15 and that's much too early for you to have dinner.' 'It's most unsociable of you not to have it after the show,' he said, rather petulantly. 'But I don't want a meal so late,' I said. 'If I wait until after ten I shan't want a meal at all.' 'Very well. I shan't ask you again, though. I've never met such an extraordinary pair as you and Kenneth Halliwell.' He's so thirtyish about 'dining out'. 'A man rang up and asked me to give my views on comedy,' I said. 'Why don't you and Kenneth

---

1 Bertolt Brecht (1898–1956). German poet and playwright.

2 Jessie Matthews (1907–1981). Vivacious British singing and dancing star of the thirties. Later Mrs Dale of *Mrs Dale's Diary*.

3 Carl Brisson (1895–1958). Danish leading man who made films in England. Orton: 'I collect old records. I like popular songs right through from the very earliest. I collect records on the basis of whether they'll be part of the history of popular song. That's all I'm interested in. I can't understand classical music, I just think it's noise. There was a time when I tried to educate myself into liking classical music. I think it's a terrible racket, probably because I'm tone-deaf. I love all those stupid songs like 'Marta, rambling rose of the wildwood'. I've just bought a record of Carl Brisson when he does a scene from *The Merry Widow*. It's utterly absurd and ludicrous, but he does it in a style – the scene where he's telling the girl off because she doesn't love him – it's all done in a sort of absurd style, but it works and it's very moving . . .'

4 The Boswell Sisters. Led by Conee (1907–76) with her sisters Vet and Martha, they revolutionised close harmony singing. Between 1931–36, they appeared and recorded with Benny Goodman, Artie Shaw, Glenn Miller. In 1936, Conee went solo.

5 *The Band Wagon*, a revue considered one of the best of its genre. Music by Arthur Schwartz. Book and lyrics by Howard Dietz. Twice filmed, the last and best a vehicle for Fred and Adele Astaire, 1931.

6 Fred (1899–) and Adele (1897–) Astaire. Famous brother and sister song and dance act. Adele retired from theatre in 1932. She married Lord Charles Cavendish, second son of the Duke of Devonshire.

7 *The Gold Diggers of 1933.* The first of five Warner musicals featuring loose plots and Busby Berkeley's tight choreography.

8 By Thomas Otway (1652–85), 1681.

get up an act and go busking?' he said. He's cross because he thinks a 'serious playwright' shouldn't accept offers to appear on TV and in newspapers. 'I turned down the offer,' I said. 'Because the other people who were going to give their views on comedy were shitty hacks. And anyway I've no theories about comedy. I've no theories at all. I dislike theories.' 'What are you doing about this Beatles film?' he said, not really changing the subject because, although he hasn't said this in so many words, he thinks that a film for the Beatles isn't the kind of thing 'a serious playwright' should do. He thinks that failures, like Pinter has with *The Servant*[1] and, although it isn't out yet, *Accident*[2], more worthwhile. 'I was supposed to be seeing them today,' I said. 'But they haven't rung.' He gave me another lecture on my lack of social grace in not having a meal with him after the show on Wednesday and rang off.

Brian Epstein's adviser rang while I was eating a meal of mashed potatoes, tinned salmon and beetroot. He asked if I could meet 'the boys' on Wednesday. Said I'd ring him back tomorrow to confirm.

Wednesday 24 January

I went to meet Cyril Bennett at one o'clock at the White Elephant in Curzon Street. I arrived much too early and walked past the place. I went for a stroll and got back at the restaurant at 12.55. The man on the door seemed surprised to see me going in. I was wearing a huge tie which I'd bought yesterday. It's white with enormous black leaves over it. And I was also wearing it with a high-collared shirt. Felt rather self-conscious sitting in the bar. Waiters kept coming up to me and saying 'Can I get you a drink, sir?' and looking supercilious when I said 'No, thank you'. Cyril Bennett came in at ten past one. I'd got pretty hot and bothered by this time. I hate restaurants like that. I feel out of place waiting. C.B. brought along Peter Willes. So the dinner went rather well. C.B. said he knew Brian Epstein. 'What are you going to ask?' he said. 'Ten thousand,' I said. 'Ask fifteen. If he doesn't pay, you can go lower. If you ask for ten they'll get you down to five.' 'Very true,' Peter Willes said, nodding sagely. 'What do you mean by opening your big mouth to the *Evening Standard*,' he said over the coffee. 'Is there anything in about me?' I said. 'Yes.' Willes said. 'And a photograph.' The edition of the *Standard* I got hadn't got a photograph, though. Must've been an earlier one.

Went home after the lunch. 'We'll do *Entertaining Mr Sloane*,' Cyril Bennett said as a parting shot.

1 Screenplay by Harold Pinter, directed by Joseph Losey, 1963. With Dirk Bogarde, James Fox, Sarah Miles.
2 Screenplay by Harold Pinter, directed by Joseph Losey, 1967. With Stanley Baker, Dirk Bogarde, Michael York.

I got to Brian Epstein's office at 4.45. I looked through *The New Yorker*. How dead and professional it all is. Calculated. Not an unexpected line. Unfunny and dead. The epitaph of America. After about five minutes or so a youngish man with a hair-style which was way out in 1958, short, college-boy, came up and said, 'I'm Peter Brown, Brian Epstein's personal assistant. I'm afraid there's been a most awful mix-up. And all the boys' appointments have been put on an hour and a half.' I was a bit chilly in my manner after that. 'Do you want me to come back at six?' I said. 'Well, no. Couldn't we make another appointment?' 'What guarantee is there that you won't break that?' I said. 'I think you'd better find yourself a different writer.' This said with indifferent success, though the effect was startling. He asked me to wait a minute and went away to return with Brian Epstein himself. Somehow I'd expected something like Michael Codron. I'd imagined Epstein to be florid, Jewish, dark-haired and over-bearing. Instead I was face to face with a mousey-haired, slight young man. Washed-out in a way. He had a suburban accent. I went into his office. 'Could you meet Paul and me for dinner tonight?' he said. 'We do want to have the pleasure of talking to you.' 'I've a theatre engagement tonight,' I replied, by now sulky and unhelpful. 'Could I send the car to fetch you after the show?' I didn't much relish the idea but agreed and, after a lot of polite flim-flammery, left almost tripping over the carpet and crashing into the secretary who gave a squeal of surprise as I hurtled past her. This I never mention when re-telling the story. I always end on a note of hurt dignity.

When I got back home, Kenneth, all dressed up to go, announced that Peter Willes had rung up to say he wasn't coming to the theatre. 'I've a high funeral Mass tomorrow and I really can't,' he'd said. Kenneth said he was a fucking pest. 'Well, Kenneth,' Willes replied, mournfully, 'I'm afraid I can't help my relatives passing away.' Kenneth suggested that I rang Brian Epstein and agreed to meet him and Paul McCartney for dinner after all. So I did. And said I'd meet them at eight at Epstein's house in Belgravia. Chapel Street. I told P. Willes about this. He seemed as relieved as I was not to be going to the Royal Court to see that wretched Otway.

Arrived in Belgravia at ten minutes to eight having caught a 19 bus which dropped me at Hyde Park Corner. I found Chapel Street easily. I didn't want to get there too early so I walked around for a while and came back through a nearby mews. When I got back to the house it was nearly eight o'clock. I rang the bell and an old man opened the door. He seemed surprised to see me. 'Is this Brian Epstein's house?' I said. 'Yes, sir,' he said, and led the way into the hall. I suddenly realised that the man was the butler. I've never seen one before. He took my coat and I went to the lavatory. When I came out he'd gone. There was nobody about. I wandered around a large dining-room which was laid for dinner. And then I got to feel strange. The house appeared to be empty. So I went upstairs to the first floor. I heard music, only I couldn't decide where it came from. So I went up a further flight of stairs. I found myself in a bedroom. I came down again and found the butler. He took me into a room and said in a loud voice, 'Mr Orton'. Everybody looked up and stood to their feet. I was introduced to one or two people. And Paul McCartney. He was just as the photographs. Only he'd grown a moustache. His hair was shorter too. He was playing the latest Beatles recording, 'Penny Lane'. I liked it very much. Then he played the other side – Strawberry something. I didn't like this as much. We talked intermittently. Before we went out to dinner we'd agreed to throw out the idea of setting the film in the thirties. We went down to dinner. The crusted old retainer – looking too much like a butler to be good casting – busied himself in the corner. 'The only thing I get from the theatre,' Paul M. said, 'is a sore arse.' He said *Loot* was the only play he hadn't wanted to leave before the end. 'I'd've liked a bit more,' he said. We talked of the theatre. I said that compared with the pop scene the theatre was square. 'The theatre started going downhill when Queen Victoria knighted Henry Irving[1],' I said. 'Too fucking respectable.' We talked of drugs, of mushrooms which give hallucinations – like LSD. 'The drug not the money,' I said. We talked of tattoos. And, after one or two veiled references, marijuana. I said I'd smoked it in Morocco. The atmosphere relaxed a little. Dinner ended and we went upstairs again. We watched a programme on TV. It had phrases in it like 'the in-crowd', and 'swinging London'. There was a little scratching at the door. I thought it was the old retainer, but someone got up to open the door and about five very young and pretty boys trooped in. I rather hoped this was the evening's entertainments. It wasn't, though. It was a pop group called The Easybeats[2]. I'd seen them on TV. I liked them very much then. In a way they were better (or prettier) offstage than on. After a while Paul McCartney said 'Let's go upstairs'. So he and I and Peter Brown went upstairs to a room also fitted with a TV ... A French photographer arrived with two beautiful youths and a girl. He'd taken a set of new photographs of The Beatles. They wanted one to use on the record sleeve. Excellent photograph. And the four Beatles look different with their moustaches. Like anarchists in the early years of the century. After a while we went downstairs. The Easybeats still there. The girl went away. I talked to the leading Easybeat. Feeling slightly like an Edwardian masher with a Gaiety Girl[3]. And then I came over tired and decided to go home. I had a last word with Paul M. 'Well,' I said, 'I'd like to do the film. There's only one thing we've got to fix up.' 'You mean the bread?' 'Yes.' We smiled and parted. I got a cab home. It was pissing down.

1 Sir Henry Irving (1838–1905). English actor-manager.
2 The Easybeats. Formed in Australia in the early 1960s.
3 Gaiety Girl. A chorus girl at the Gaiety Theatre in the 1890s, famous for burlesques.

Told Kenneth all about it. We talked for an hour or so. Then he got up to make a cup of tea. And we talked a little more. And went to sleep.

Thursday 26 January

I decided to buy a suit. Kenneth and I went to look for one. Went to Carnaby Street. I didn't like them much. Cut very good. But the material is poor. Went to John Michael's and tried on a brown suit. Bought it but left it to be altered. In Carnaby Street I bought a purple velvet tie. Very wide. And in Austin Reed's I found a high-collared shirt with brown stripes. When I got back I spoke to Peggy on the phone. 'We should ask for 15,000 pounds,' I said. 'And then, if they beat us down, remember no lower than 10,000. After all, whether I do it or not is a matter of indifference to me.' Peggy agreed. She said she'd ask for fifteen and try to get twelve and a percentage. 'If they won't pay us ten they can fuck themselves,' I said. 'Of course, darling,' Peggy said.

Friday 27 January

Went to a rehearsal of *The Good and Faithful Servant*. Pleasence has decided to play the part of Buchanan wearing a ghastly pair of false teeth. Quite macabre. Surprising how stars add to a play. I'd never realised quite what real stars did. They light up lines and situations in an uncanny way. There's no question of a real star doing a line wrong. One accepts the most lurid interpretation of a role when a great star plays it well. Hope it all records OK.

Walter Shenson rang as I was about to have tea. He seemed pleased that I'd seen Paul M. He said he'd ring Peggy to discuss money. I hope it's not too much of a shock.

Sunday 29 January

Last night Kenneth and I went down to the theatre.[1] I wanted to see the play with a full house. Before curtain up I spoke to Michael White's business manager. We've done rather well again this week. It will be over £2,000 in spite of the fact that we were £65 down on Monday and Tuesday because of the rain. We watched the play from the back stalls. Disappointing really. They just aren't getting things that are there in the lines.[2] Except Kenneth Cranham who is splendid. In the interval I heard a man saying 'How many more acts are there in

---

1 Kenneth Cranham: 'Ken and Joe used to come to the theatre a lot. It was quite a strain. If you lost a line or didn't pick up a cue, they'd come down pretty heavily. They used to give me a hard time . . .'

2 Orton to Michael White, 14 July 1967: 'In general the tone of the London production is OK. Of course a lot of lines are muffed. This is the fault of having inexperienced actors in the parts. If we replaced Fay, McLeavy and (possibly) Dennis by more experienced actors (not necessarily better – just more experienced in comedy), the play would be a lot better . . .'

this bit of rubbish?' A number of people clearly hate the play and have only come because it won the award.

Today I've been writing *Up Against It*. I had an inspiration. I'd already written the beginning of the script up to where McTurk is thrown out of the town. And then I remembered that in the cupboard somewhere was the manuscript of a novel I'd written in 1961 called *The Vision of Gombold Proval*.[1] It had always been my intention some day to rewrite it. I decided to get it down and see if there was anything I could use. I found, to my surprise, that it was excellent. It had great faults as a novel, but as the basis for a film it was more than adequate. So I'm rewriting the whole thing. Miraculously, towards the middle of the novel four young men appear. Might have been designed with the Beatles in mind.

In any case I shall enjoy writing the film.

Monday 30 January

Kenneth had made an appointment late last week to take several of his collages to be framed. The framers is in Lamb's Conduit Street. He was going by bus, but with nineteen pictures to carry, some of them large, we decided to go by taxi. It cost only five shillings. The picture framer very interested in the pictures. When we came out we noticed a shop next door. It was a superior junk shop. Full of chi-chi odds and ends like Victorian dolls' prams and stuffed birds, a full-sized china aspidistra and a glass dome with a top hat under it. In the front of the window were several heads (or rather wig-stands with painted faces on them). Kenneth thought they looked rather good and he tried to open the door of the shop. It was locked. He said that when he was last by the shop it had been locked. He went back into the framers who said that the shop was never open, but they knew the man who owned it. They rang him at his private address and asked what the wig-stands cost. 'Oh,' the man said, 'I'm not selling them.' Kenneth asked when the shop was open. 'I never open,' the man said. 'I'm not interested in selling.' So we went away.

We next walked to Sicilian Arcade to the record shop. Kenneth bought an LP of Sophie Tucker[2] (reduced to 12*s*. 6*d*. and, as we later found, expensive at half the price). I ordered the new Beatles single which is being issued on 20 February. The first quarter of a million have the photograph I saw them choosing.

In the afternoon I went to Rediffusion studios at Wembley to watch the recording of the first scene in *The Good and Faithful Servant* plus the small scene in the clothing store. I arrived to find Jimmy Ormerod[3], who is directing, talking to Pat Routledge. She was pleased with the new line I'd written for the end: 'I'm

1 Posthumously published as *Head to Toe* (Anthony Blond, 1971 and reissued by Methuen, 1986).
2 Sophie Tucker (1884–1966). Rumanian-born American singer. 'The red hot momma' of vaudeville.
3 James Ormerod (1923–   ). Director. Also directed the TV version of *The Erpingham Camp*.

sure we have many happy negatives up our sleeves.' 'I like the idea of that,' she said. Next I met Donald Pleasence all got up as Buchanan, looking splendid in a commissionaire's uniform complete with hearing-aid and false teeth. 'You're growing a moustache!' he said. (I've let it grow since Friday.) 'How brave of you. Oh, I do admire people who strike out into new frontiers.'

I think the direction could be a little more exciting. I notice all the time that the interesting and unusual angles are always on the cameras that Jimmy isn't using. The shot he does use is conventional.

The overall that the wardrobe had got for Hermione Baddeley to use wasn't very good so they gave her one that the canteen staff have at the studio. It was perfect. Very appropriate. Exactly right.

Tuesday 31 January

Rather a nasty day out (so Kenneth tells me, I haven't put my nose beyond the door), windy and dusty. I've spent the whole day writing *Up Against It*. I've got as far as the scene where McTurk (Ringo¹ if they buy the script) arrives home from the revolutionary meeting to find Connie giving a party. Peggy rang to say that Walter S. had been in touch. After a bit of preliminary skirmishing, she'd said, 'Well, we'd normally ask between fifteen and twenty thousand for a script by Joe.' Walter S. had gasped 'My God!' and asked to be excused whilst he talked with Brian Epstein. Peggy says she doesn't think that we will get that much, but it's fun asking. I want it put in the contract that I can buy my script back wholesale if they don't want it. I don't like the idea of them being able to bugger about with the idea if I'm not on it.

Peggy agrees that we could say perhaps 5,000 for the first draft. If they don't like it we have the right to buy it back wholesale. Lock stock and barrel. It means, I suppose, in effect, that I'm writing a first draft for nothing, but I do want it back if they're not interested. To sell to Oscar or someone else.

Wednesday 1 February

Miss Boynes has sold her flat for £3,150. She is leaving the house on the 21st to take up residence at Holland-on-Sea. 'I've asked Mr Corden to take me and the birds down to Holland,' she said. 'Well, there it is. Just one of those things. Quite, quite,' she seemed to be talking nonsense most of the time out of relief. She came out with the information that her new bungalow will be 'centrally heated throughout' and, a little while later, 'every room heated from all points.' She said she was worried about the light switch in the hall. I told her that Miss Clark had broken the switch fiddling with it. 'Oh,' she blinked, 'I see. Yes, I see. Very well then. I shall have to pay for it to be done myself,' she said, pursing her

---

1 Ringo Starr (1940–   ). Actor, performer, composer. The Beatles' drummer.

lips. She's become neurotic about any 'last minute hitch'. As though the man taking over her flat won't buy because of the light switch being broken in the hall. 'And there's sand outside,' she said. 'What's to be done about that? I've rung the police, you know. They said they'll send someone round to see about it. Only they haven't come.' She asked if I would ring the police. I said I would. To get rid of her. Later Mrs Corden told me she'd heard Miss Boynes talking to the electrician about the switch. 'I have to pay for it myself,' she said. 'And there's Joe Orton upstairs. The playwright. With plenty of money. Really, the more people have the meaner they get.'[1]

Thursday 2 February

I went to see the rehearsals of *The Good and Faithful Servant*. Seemed rather good. Pleasence especially. Though it's all so difficult. I remember *The Erpingham Camp* being well received by the technicians in the studio.

Sunday 5 February

Very badly kept journal of the last few days. *The Good and Faithful Servant* has been recorded.[2] I believe it to be one of the best things of mine I've seen.[3] This mainly due to the fact that Rediffusion have dipped deeply into their pockets and got actors of the calibre of Donald Pleasence, Hermione Baddeley and Patricia Routledge.

Peter Willes said that Joan Elman (their legal woman) has now had the opportunity of reading *Entertaining Mr Sloane*. 'And what did she say?' I asked. 'Well,' Peter said, 'I've never seen anything like it. She came up to me and flung the book on my desk. "I think this a perfectly disgusting play," she said. "Joan," I said, "I'm not interested in your views on the play. What is the legal position?" "Disgusting," she said. "Horrible." And she went on and on. "Perfectly horrible and filthy. I don't know why we want to consider such a play." So I told her she'd better go and see Cyril (Bennett). And he's mad about you. I can't imagine why because you're so ungrateful. So Joan Elman went to him and he said, "What's

---

1 Miss Boynes preferred Halliwell to Orton. 'Kenneth would never dream of sitting down if I was looking after the birds. His manner. His ways. He would treat you so gently and pleasantly. He would never take advantage of your phone and your flat the way John did, sprawling and putting his feet on the chair. Kenneth would offer to help, to carry or do anything. And he would be flattering too somehow . . . I liked him because he was pleasant. He had a very good voice.'

2 Transmitted by Rediffusion Television, 6 April 1967.

3 Orton to Glenn Loney, 25 March 1967: 'I've now just finished writing (and filming) a television play (no, that sounds second-rate to begin with – a play which they are putting on television). I'm very pleased with it. It's been directed and acted absolutely *real*. With astonishing results. H. Pinter says it's like *The Battleship Potempkin*. I won't go as far as this, but it's very good. As I said in my last note, nobody has seen it yet – only me, H. Pinter and assorted weirdies at the Television Centre. I don't know what the average member of the public (if he exists) is going to say' . . .'

the legal position with regard to this play?" "What a vile play it is," Joan had said, "I was shocked and disgusted by it." Anyway he told her to fuck off and he's going ahead with doing the play. Most unwisely in my opinion. But, there you are. Don't say people aren't nice to you.' A little while later we were watching Routledge being particularly good in the scene with Ray. Willes came over and offered me a toffee from a large bag on the desk. 'What do you think of Routledge for Kathy?' he said. 'She'd be very good,' I said. He looked pleased. 'And I'd like Robert Stephens¹ for Eddie,' I said. 'What a good idea,' he said. He went away very pleased. Later I talked to Muriel Cole (the casting woman) and said I wanted a really young boy for Sloane. 'None of these aged juveniles,' I said. 'A very young boy.' I nearly said, someone you'd love to fuck silly, but I didn't think she'd understand.

On Saturday I was watching an episode of *Dr Who* and spotted a little boy in that called Frazer Hines.² So I rang Willes up and told him. He said, 'My word you are going to enjoy yourself on this production, aren't you?' He said he's spoken to Routledge. And he thought he'd probably get on to Bob Stephens as well. They are going to record in August. 'And I simply won't do it without your being at hand to keep an eye on things,' he said. 'If you're in Morocco or somewhere, I shan't do it.'

On Thursday night I got home to find that Peggy had rung. Kenneth said I was to phone her. When I did she said that W. Shenson said he and Epstein would go as high as ten thousand. 'I said I thought you'd accept that, darling,' Peggy said. 'Oh, yes,' I said. 'That's what I wanted after all.' She said that there was a difficulty about owning the copyright. So I shall just have to do a first draft and hope they like it enough to continue.

Yesterday (Saturday) I went for a long walk in the morning with Kenneth. We went to the *Daily Mirror* building to get a copy of yesterday's *Daily Mirror*. The vicar of the church where a scene of *The Good and Faithful Servant* was filmed is objecting to a scene where the pregnant bride faints on the church steps and a baby is heard wailing. Great fuss at Rediffusion. P. Willes nearly frantic. In the end they agreed to cut the wail. When we got back from a fruitless journey (I got the wrong edition), we had bacon and egg for luncheon and I fell asleep. So I didn't do any work on *Up Against It*.

Today I worked hard on *Up Against It*. I've got up to the parody on the Sydney Street siege³. Then we watched *Shanghai Express*⁴ with Marlene Dietrich. Made in 1932. Very ridiculous. Well-worn cliches all the way. And no inkling that they

1 Robert Stephens (1931–). Actor.
2 Frazer Hines. Actor.
3 3 January 1911. Winston Churchill, then Home Secretary, deployed a detachment of Scots Guards to the East End of London where two armed anarchists were firing on police.
4 *Shanghai Express* (1932). Directed by Josef von Sternberg.

were using them. Dietrich looked wonderful and strange. Photographed in exotic gowns. As a Shanghai prostitute (called in the *Radio Times* 'an adventuress' and in the film 'a coaster' – apparently that meant she lived by her wits on the Chinese coast. Coasting between Peking and Shanghai). A most foolish story which I fully intend to pinch at some time in the future. It was the full Tosca/ Scarpia bit at one point except that another tart (Chinese) got in between. We cannot have the honour of a white Aryan tart soiled by a Chinaman. So a Chinese tart got stuffed instead.

Monday 6 February

Last night Kenneth and I watched, with increasing aggravation, Zeffirelli's[1] National Theatre production of Shakespeare's *Much Ado About Nothing*. Maggie Smith[2] as Beatrice. Robert Stephens as Benedick. Dressed early twentieth century and set (one supposes) in Sicily. This to be guessed at since most of the settings were composed of tulle rosebushes, draperies and irrelevant bits of architecture. Living statues looking like some set-piece in a pre-war follies. Occasionally they came to life and winked or even shook hands with the characters. Most of the cast had Italian accents except Beatrice and Benedick. Dogberry and the watch had such ludicrous accents that of course, all the malapropisms were lost. The play mangled, the verse butchered. The cold, calculated line of Don John, 'Your Hero, My Hero, any man's Hero,' ended in Don John sticking out his tongue. 'Sigh No More Ladies' – sung by a fat queeny ice-cream vendor – was camped unmercifully. The play disappeared under a welter of tricks. God's curse light upon all directors!

I did like the Italian moustaches, though. And have decided to have mine cut in that style as soon as it is long enough. Also I saw another boy suitable for Sloane. His name is Barry Evans.[3] I saw him in *Spring Awakening*[4]. I wanted him to play Hal when we were casting *Loot*. He was at the National. 'Olivier[5] collects young actors like butterflies' someone once said. He doesn't give them parts, though. He has them playing the set.

I did a little work on *Up Against It*. I've now got McTurk into prison. Realise that, of course, the whole script is about schizophrenia. At half-past one I met Peter Willes outside the Royal Academy. We went to see the Millais[6] exhibition.

---

1 Franco Zeffirelli (1923–). Director and designer.
2 Maggie Smith (1934–). Actress.
3 Barry Evans (1943–). Actor.
4 By Frank Wedekind (1864–1918), 1907.
5 Sir Laurence Olivier (1907–). Pre-eminent English actor and then artistic director of the National Theatre which he was instrumental in founding (1963–73).
6 Sir John Everett Millais (1829–96). Artist. With Holman Hunt and D.G. Rosetti founded the pre-Raphaelite Brotherhood.

Five shillings entrance and 7s. 6d. for the catalogue. Rather steep. To cool my anger at the price charged for admission, Willes said, 'I've arranged to buy *Sloane.* I'm paying you £250 for adapting it. And £850 for the play. So that's eleven hundred pounds. Ridiculous really, but there it is. Now shut up about five shillings for seeing these beautiful pictures.'

A lot of them were wonderful. The famous ones mostly. The *Ophelia,* drowning, like a weird nightmare. Every detail painted in with the most meticulous care. Surprisingly this piling on of detail didn't result in naturalism, but in a dream-like atmosphere. 'Drugged' K. H. said later when I told him. 'But then they were all on laudanum, weren't they?' Odd though how much anger a picture like *Ophelia* caused when it was painted. The *Times* notice was printed in the catalogue. I liked *The Woodman's Daughter.* And the *Marianne.* But, oh, how Millais sold out later on. Those dreary later pictures. Endless simpering children. He could've been a great genius instead of merely promising well.[1]

When I got back (one of P. Willes's last remarks before he got a taxi was: 'How your moustache has grown in the past few days. It must be the excitement'), Kenneth Williams and Henry Budgen were at the flat. Pleased to see them. 'Oh, how fab!' Kenneth W. said, looking at my moustache. 'It's given you a look of mystery. Don't you think so, Henrietta?' Henry Budgen, looking most stuffy and RAC Club pretended not to have heard. Kenneth W. said: 'Well, I told Codron all about this experience Henrietta here had. You know she came back from Amsterdam having had a really lovely time in a brothel. "I was the set-piece," she said. "Up the bum, in the mouth, everywhere."' He flashed looks at H. Budgen, who coloured and said, 'Now Kenneth really! It's all quite untrue, you know that.' 'There were lights trained on me,' K. W. said. '" And," she said, "I was the set-piece."' He relapsed into his natural voice, 'Like a fucking plum pudding.' H. Budgen changed the subject. 'Hubert won't like your moustache,' he said to me. 'He'll be most upset when I tell him.' 'Oh, stuff Hubert,' Kenneth W. said. 'Mouldy old queens you go around with. Here,' he said to me, 'I'm awfully fond of you, you know. I'm glad you're going to be on my programme.'

Thursday 9 February

Kenneth bought me a pink-striped shirt with white collar and cuffs. We went, yesterday, into the West End to buy cuff-links. He bought himself a pair (triangular ones) and I bought a pair of round ones with a bit of stone in the middle. Both pairs cost 30s. and are supposed to have been made in Mexico. We

---

1 Peter Willes, in his Introduction to *Funeral Games*: 'We went to the Millais exhibition at Burlington House. I bought the catalogue and we stared at some of the earlier paintings. They published in the catalogue the press comments of the day about the pictures: "His notices were as bad as mine," said Joe. Then we went on and had tea at Fortnum and Mason; he loved all the ladies' hats . . .'

then went round to the Prince Charles Cinema to see a double feature of Roman Polanski's[1] *Repulsion* and *Cul-de-Sac*. I mainly went to see Donald Pleasence in *Cul-de-Sac*. *Repulsion* was on first. For the first half-an-hour of the film I thought it was good. Then it went on and on and on. The story didn't convince, the climax was absurd. These wretched directors. A mess of director's tricks. No script at all. The second film came on and it soon became apparent that what Polanski had directed seriously in *Repulsion* he'd decided to send up in *Cul-de-Sac*. After half-an-hour or so of it Kenneth and I both left the cinema in a rage.

Today I did nothing but write *Up Against It*. Peggy rang to ask if W. Shenson had got in touch with me. When she realised that he hadn't she said she'd write him a letter to ginger him up. Michael White rang. The takings for *Loot* are down. And David Merrick isn't now presenting the play in New York. I said 'Why?' and Michael said 'Well, he wanted to offer us so little that we told him he couldn't really be keen. So he dropped out. However, another management are very interested. Friends of Charles's.' 'Well,' I said, 'I think all Americans are cunts.' And left him to it.

Friday 10 February

Have a headache. Feel tired. Very weary. Am looking forward to a holiday which I hope to take in Libya at the end of the month. Kenneth and I both got up early today. Rather unexpectedly at ten o'clock Kenneth suddenly decided to cook a breakfast. Haven't had breakfast for ages. Bacon and eggs. Sat talking till elevenish and then we went down to Peggy's. She'd written a letter asking me to pick up some books from Germany. *Sloane* and *Loot* in German. They'd sent me twenty copies. Whatever for? I gave Peggy ten. Though she won't be able to get rid of them. She was rather wary about my moustache. It seemed to fascinate and repel her. I tried to explain that it hasn't been trimmed into shape yet. 'It looks rather like a Renaissance portrait,' she said. She'd had a telephone call from Shenson in answer to a curt note she'd written to him asking about the *Beatles III* contract. I'm expecting a call from him tomorrow morning. Peggy lent me her ms. of *A Flea in Her Ear*. 'He's[2] translating another one for Binkie[3],' she said. 'I suggested he call it *By the Short Hairs*.' 'What a marvellous title,' I said. 'Do you like it?' she seemed pleased. 'Mortimer wasn't keen. He isn't going to use it.' 'I'm going to steal it off you,' I said. 'Do,' she laughed. 'I'll give it to you.' Kenneth

---

1 Roman Polanski (1933–). Film director and writer. His controversial films include *Knife in the Water*, *Repulsion*, *Cul de Sac*, *Rosemary's Baby*, *Chinatown*.

2 John Mortimer (1923–). Barrister and playwright. Best known for *Voyage Round My Father*, his adaptations of Feydeau, and *Rumpole of the Bailey*.

3 Sir Hugh ('Binkie') Beaumont (1908–1973). Theatrical impresario and managing director of H.M. Tennent Limited.

said, 'He'll call the Beatles' film *By the Short Hairs* now.' 'No,' I said, 'it's much too good for a film.'

Came home. Began writing more of *Up Against It*. I've found it difficult to get them off the wretched yacht. But I've managed it now. I'm having them blown (like Odysseus) off course when they escape from the yacht in the lifeboat. Then, of course, I can go into the war scenes from Gombold. After that I'm almost home and dry.

Miss Boynes came up. 'As you know, I'm leaving on the twenty-first,' she said. 'And I wondered if I could leave the birds with you when I travelled down to Holland to finalise arrangements.' Kenneth said, 'Yes.' And Miss Boynes spent the next twenty minutes telling him that M. and Mme Corden have sold their flat for £3,500. 'Isn't it ridiculous?' she said. 'But there it is. Just one of those things, I suppose.' She went away looking most disgruntled.

'Do you think the Cordens have sold that pokey little hell-hole for £3,500?' I said to Ken. 'No,' Kenneth said. 'They've told Doris they've sold it for that price to depress her.'

Saturday 11 February

After a morning spent reading what I'd already written of *Up Against It*, I went this afternoon to see W. Shenson. His flat – in Chesham Close, off Lyall Street – is in Chesham House. Until 1917 it was the Imperial Russian Embassy. It remained empty for years after the Revolution. The Bolsheviks moved their embassy to another part (and a richer part) of London. 'This place wasn't good enough for them,' Shenson said, waving his hand benignly around what could only be described as a small palace. Outside his kitchen window was a view of rooftops and a mews, 'where they kept the horses, I guess,' W.S. said. Below was a paved courtyard now full of cars but presumably in the past it was a garden. Enormous rooms. A sad house, but better a block of flats than pulled down.

Shenson lit a cigar when I was settled. 'You haven't seen my moustache?' I said. He peered rather puzzled at my face. 'You haven't got one,' he said. 'No,' I said. 'I've shaved it off. But I had one yesterday.' 'You didn't have one when I last saw you.' 'No, but I grew one for a fortnight and then I shaved it off.' He shook his head and offerred me an After Eight wafer-thin mint.

He was most concerned to impress upon me that 'the boys' shouldn't be made to do anything in the film that would reflect badly upon them. 'You see,' he said, 'the kids will all imitate whatever the boys do.' I hadn't the heart to tell him that the boys, in my script, have been caught *in flagrante*, become involved in dubious political activity, dressed as women, committed murder, been put in prison and committed adultery. And the script isn't finished yet. I thought it best to say nothing of my plans for the Beatles until he had had a chance of reading the script. We parted at five o'clock amicably. With the contract, according to him, as good as signed. And, on my part, the film almost written.

Kenneth and I went down to the Cri to see the cast of *Loot*. We were down a little this week, so Mark says. But not under £2,000. Several shows coming off. I mentioned that the *Loot* poster was mysteriously placed in all sorts of out of the way places in the agency windows. Behind pillars, round corners, partly covered by other posters. Mark agreed, but said there was little one could do against such anti-*Loot* practices on the part of the big agencies. 'After all,' he said, 'Prowse[1] and Peter Cadbury[2] are declared enemies of yours.'

Sunday 12 February

I left home at 4.15 pm today to go to the BBC Television Centre at White City. Kenneth was with me. We travelled by tube. I wore a brown suit, with hipster pants, a pink-striped shirt with white collar and cuffs and a black-and-white flowered tie. Very smart and *outré*. I rather regretted not having the moustache. We arrived at the television centre on time. A doorman directed us to the section in which *Call My Bluff* was to be recorded. We wandered around for a long time in the semi-darkness of partly-lit studios looking for someone in authority. Our voices echoed, lights saying 'To the Red Assembly Area', 'To the Blue Assembly Area', 'To the Green Assembly Area', flashed on and off. We finally found someone who told us to go to reception. Reception was in a great glass bowl-like building. A vast area of parquet flooring with a desk in one corner. We were crossing the courtyard when we met Kenneth Williams with an actor called Gordon Jackson[3] who was also appearing on the programme. Kenneth told me to get the key to my dressing-room. I did this and followed him to the Red Assembly Area. 'A man was absolutely furious last week,' Kenneth W. said. 'Furious she was. Came up to me and said, "I expected to see a decent programme. But it's all a *fake*." Shouted it out, she did, bellowed it. "A fake"!' Kenneth whisked us all into our separate dressing-rooms. 'You get these silly queens carrying on though, don't you?'

1 Keith Prowse. The ticket agency.
2 Peter Cadbury (1918–   ). Chairman and managing director of the Keith Prowse Group. Cadbury had been caught up in 'the dirty plays controversy' in 1964, sparked off, in large part, by the West End run of *Entertaining Mr Sloane*. Cadbury argued for a 'clean-up' of West End theatre and an 'x' certificate for plays of questionable taste. When *Loot* was reportedly sold for £100,000, Orton told the *Sun*, 3 March 1967: 'For four years I unloaded chocolate at Cadbury's. And one of the strongest critics of the alleged obscenity in my plays is Peter Cadbury. I put in a lot of hard graft for Cadbury's. He might have done the same.' On reading this, Cadbury invited Orton to lunch. Orton to Peter Cadbury, 16 March 1967: 'It's nice to know that I've one enemy less in the world. I based my remarks in the *Sun* on your (reported) 1964 attitude to *Entertaining Mr Sloane*. I'm sorry if you were misrepresented. I'd like to meet you. When? Do give me a ring. I don't think we'll see eye to eye on Drama. We might talk about less dangerous subjects: religion and politics.'
3 Gordon Jackson (1923–   ). Actor. Best known to TV audiences as the butler in *Upstairs, Downstairs*.

We were introduced to the producer of the programme, who explained how the game was to be played. 'Maxine Audley's[1] not here,' Kenneth said. 'Where is she then?' We were taken down to Kenneth's dressing-room and our cards allotted. Maxine Audley turned up at last in a sort of glittering siren suit. We then went into a lounge and had what Kenneth called 'drinkies'.

The programme was due to begin recording at eight. The game consisted of two teams, one led by Kenneth and one by Patrick Campbell[2]. A word was read out and then Team A gave (individual) definitions of the word. One member of the team gave the correct definition. The object was to bluff the opposite team into thinking an incorrect definition was the correct one. I quite enjoyed playing the game. I got £75 for so doing.

Afterwards I went out to dinner with Kenneth and Gordon Jackson. 'That Maxine Audley!' Kenneth said, 'What a dead loss she turned out to be.' She'd bluffed so badly on the last word of the series that the opposing team guessed that she had the correct definition. We lost the game. During an after-the-show chat with a very BBC-ish company, Kenneth astounded everyone by giving an imitation of a fat, black woman singer. 'She was got up in all this flowered rubbish. Like a Nigerian priestess or something. And she couldn't tell sharps from flats. Well, you should've heard the dizzy cow. Moaning away "bout mah chains".'

Monday 13 February

Kenneth Halliwell and I went to Freddie Bartman's this morning. We took Kenneth's collages which have been framed. Freddie very impressed. He's going to hold an exhibition for Kenneth, though whether anybody will come is the problem.[3] In the afternoon we went to see the playback of *The Good and Faithful Servant*, which was impressive. Seemed to go down well with everybody. Though since it was mainly actors, their agents, the author and director and friends, this doesn't give one any real indication of how it will fare with the public. A letter from Kenneth Williams to say he'd received the tie I'd sent him as a present. It was a Dior one. The irony of it is that it was given to me by Peter Wood[4] during the tour of *Loot*. I never liked it and never wore it. So I gave it to Kenneth

---

1 Maxine Audley (1923–). Actress.

2 Patrick Campbell (Lord Glenavy) (1913–1980). Humorist and raconteur.

3 Peggy Ramsay: 'Kenneth's pictures were very talented and very unpleasant. Joe and I both tried to get him an exhibition, and although we got an antique dealer to show some, nobody bought anything. Joe was worried that maybe Kenneth ought to have an outlet. He was a talented man who didn't really know in what to pour his talent.'

4 Peter Wood (1927–). Director. Mounted the original production of *Loot* in which Kenneth Williams starred. Also directed the premiere productions of Harold Pinter's *The Birthday Party* and Tom Stoppard's *Jumpers* and *Travesties*.

knowing that it was more his cup of tea than mine. I wrote an Edna Welthorpe letter to the Ritz¹ because Kenneth is always asking how Edna is doing. I sent him a copy.

Tuesday 14 February

A knock came at the door at 10 o'clock this morning. It was Miss Boynes wreathed in smiles. 'My carpet's just arrived,' she said. 'I wondered if you'd help me into my flat with it. Later on. When you're ready.' I said I'd come down when I'd had breakfast. 'It looks as though I'm finally going,' she said. 'I've had the forms through, you know. I've to be out by the twenty-first. I'm really moving, I think.' She then said that the man who'd built the bungalow had put the wrong door-handle on the front door. 'He's put a blue handle on my front door,' Miss Boynes said, looking over her shoulder as though she expected the man to be coming up the stairs. 'It's a yellow front door as well. Looked most out of place. Very common. Still, there it is. I'll soon have that altered. And the builder is most pleased with everything.' The builder told her that 'there's plenty of whist drives and bridge. We're a merry community.' Miss Boynes gave a smirk. 'He seemed to think I was the artistic type. Well, I let him think so. It's not lies, is it?' She went away. At eleven she was back. 'I'm going out,' she said, 'so if you would come and give me a hand.' She had on a green overall. Her hair was standing on end. I went down and helped her into the flat with the carpet. She stood at her door, breathless. 'I've told the gentleman who is taking the flat that I've left the keys with you.' She lowered her voice and smirked. 'I don't want him to get onto the Cordens. My word he'd have a shock.'

Kenneth went to Freddie Bartman's this afternoon to fix up about titling the pictures. I wrote more of *Up Against It.*

Wednesday 15 February

Went for a walk this morning. Weather cold, bright. A wind blew grit about. Spent most of the time wiping running eyes with my handkerchief. Kenneth went to have his passport photograph taken. He had it done by polaroid camera. It cost 7s. 6d. for two. No negatives. I'd like a polaroid camera. Most useful for taking pornographic pictures, I should say. We went then to the record shop to enquire whether the new Beatles' single is out. It won't be on sale till Friday. Then we walked to Bloomsbury to look into the university bookshop at the copies of *Loot* which they have on their counter and in their window. We asked for a paperback

---

1 See pp. 281–2. In his covering letter to Williams, Orton wrote: 'Edna has written the following letter to the Ritz. I shouldn't really let you see such personal correspondence, but there it is – I know you follow all her activities, even the minor ones, avidly.'

edition of *Gentlemen Prefer Blondes*[1]. It's out of print. I looked at, and thought of buying, *Little Malcolm and His Struggle Against the Eunuchs*[2]. But really it's written in some stupid northern dialect and so I didn't bother. I'm not going to read a play that practically requires a translation. Looked at, and also thought of getting, a play by Fielding called *The Author's Farce*[3]. Dipped into it and got the impression that it was rubbish. Like most classical drama. Not worth the paper it was printed on. I'd like to have a burning of the books.

Came home. Had lunch and began work on *Up Against It*. Kenneth engaged in making a poster for his exhibition of collage-pictures which Bartman is (supposed) to be organising.

Watched a programme called *Three After Six* on television. It's just three middle-class people discussing 'problems' posed in the newspapers. Words like 'psychological aspects' and 'social workers' and 'the social and legal aspects of the case' and 'this poses great problems for the sociologist' abound in the programme. They discussed the proposed amendments to the abortion laws. Kept saying what is best for the 'mother' and 'of course, for the unborn child'. As though anyone in their right minds would consider the unborn child. Any more than one would consider the feeling of a tumour or cancer. How I hate the liberal-minded, smooth, middle-class, 'broadminded', 'with-it' woman.

Friday 17 February

I went to see a man in Brook Street about making a film of *Loot*. He was very keen. He said he wanted to film it with the colours very bright and glittering. He suggested Bardot for Fay. Extraordinary idea. Was cool in accordance with Peggy's instructions.

Saturday 18 February

Met Miss Boynes on the stairs. She said, 'Well, I'm off on Tuesday.' She gave me ninepence to get her copy of the *Sunday Times*. 'I shan't be requiring that little service any more,' she said, nodding her head. She's rinsed her hair again. It's a sort of weird silvery-blue. Or rather it is in certain lights. In others it looks ashen. 'The men will be in at eight o'clock,' she said. 'So I'd be grateful if you'd have my birds – because they'll be frightened by the noise, I suppose.' Started typing up my final version (of the first draft) of *Up Against It*. Kenneth suggested

1 By Anita Loos (1893–1981), 1925.
   TRUSCOTT: What an amazing woman McMahon is. She's got away with it again. She must have influence in heaven.
   HAL. God is a gentleman. He prefers blondes.
2 By David Halliwell (1937–), 1965.
3 By Henry Fielding (1707–54), 1730.

that I call it *Prick Up Your Ears*[1]. But this is much too good a title to waste on a film. My visas came today from the Libyan Embassy. In answer to my enquiry as to whether I needed references actually in Libya – the visa form stresses that references in Libya are necessary – I received a note saying 'References are *not* necessary'. Can't understand why the visa should say 'Libyan references'. Went to the Criterion tonight. Gloom, gloom. The takings here dropped by about £300. We clearly aren't going to have a long run. About another month and we'll be off. This may be because there are no names in the cast. Much of the play's lack of success must be put down to the theme and to the undoubted fact that the general public are, where plays are concerned, ignorant shits.

Sunday 19 February

Watched an old film on television called *My Favourite Blonde* with Bob Hope.[2] This had sentimental overtones for me. It was at the companion picture, *My Favourite Brunette* (also with Bob Hope), some time in the early forties that I was first interfered with. A man took me into the lavatory of the Odeon and gave me a wank. I re-lived those happy moments as I sat watching the picture today. I remember coming down his mac. I must've been about fourteen.

Monday 20 February

Wrote a little this morning. In the afternoon Kenneth and I went to BOAC[3] to find out about flights to Libya. There seems to be very little choice as to a direct flight. It must be to Tripoli (no one flies direct to Benghazi) and (as far as time of day goes) it must be on a Thursday. Fare is £75 pounds return. It's impossible for us to find out what the weather is like in Tripoli at this time of the year. We shall just have to go and hope for the best. Possible date seems to be a week on Thursday.

Peggy rang and said Michael White has asked if I'll take no percentage for the past week (the takings have slipped down to below £2,000). Said yes. What else could I say? Peggy says it will enable them to carry on a few more weeks and that any extra time is (from our point of view) good.

Miss Boynes said, when I went down to the dustbin, 'Is it all right if I bring my birds up tomorrow morning then?' I said, 'Yes.' She was fiddling about with her shed. 'I've left the door of my cupboard in here,' she said. 'I took it off to make room for my fridge. Which I'm leaving behind.' She seemed very giggly about

---

1 The title is a triple-pun, 'ears' being an anagram of 'arse'. Orton intended using it as the title for a farce about the backstage goings-on prior to a coronation. Used by John Lahr as the title for Orton's biography, published 1978.

2 Bob Hope (1903–). English-born American comedian.

3 British Overseas Airways Corporation, now merged into British Airways.

going tomorrow. Kenneth said she told him that the builder had said, 'I'll switch the heater on for you.' 'Central heating, you know,' she said.

We watched a programme of old newsreels from the war. We watched hoping there would be shots of Rommel[1] in Libya which happened 25 years ago this week. But there was nothing except shots of the fall of Singapore (also 25 years ago this week). So we still don't know what the weather is like in Libya.

Tuesday 21 February

Miss Boynes, after eight years, left our block of flats today. During the night Kenneth heard a shrieking outside the window. Miss Boynes was having a furious row with the man who lives two doors away in the house down the street. He'd parked his car outside our block. 'You must move it,' Miss Boynes was crying. 'Move it or I'll ring the police!' I was asleep and didn't hear any of this. Kenneth said it went on for about fifteen minutes. Shrieking like a banshee, Miss Boynes finally ran into the house and slammed the door.

The furniture van came at eight. The next minute Miss Boynes was outside our door with a bird cage and a rather depressed-looking blue budgerigar. She handed it to me and went away. She returned almost at once with another cage and in it a fat yellow budgerigar. 'My goodness,' she said, breathless, 'these men don't waste time, do they?' She hurried downstairs to supervise the removal of her furniture. I put the two cages in our living-room and went to make a cup of tea. Kenneth was in bed. When I got back with the tea, he said, 'I don't know what she's been doing to the blue one. It hasn't made a sound. The yellow one has been twittering most neurotically ever since you brought it in.'

Miss Boynes kept coming back with various bags she wanted me to look after until 10.30 when she was packed into Mr Corden's car and driven away to her bungalow at Holland-on-Sea. She was wearing a black coat and a black toque-like hat. It's strange to watch someone leave whom you've known, however distantly, for a number of years, with the certain knowledge that you'll never see them again.

Wednesday 22 February

Kenneth and I made a trip to South Kensington to apply for visas for Libya. The man at the consular section looked at my application form and said, 'One pound please.' I gave him a pound and he asked me to call back on Monday. When Kenneth gave in his form and his passport he looked oddly at him and said, 'You may have to see the consul. Will you call tomorrow morning?' He gave Kenneth the telephone number. We went away. Kenneth making a great fuss. 'I always knew we shouldn't try to go to a country with visas! I don't believe in going where

1 Erwin Rommel (1891–1944). German field marshall.

I'm not wanted.' 'Why should they want me?' I said. We came to the conclusion that it must be because of the passport photograph. On the passport Kenneth was shown with a shaven head. Since then he has bought his wig.[1] The photographs for the visas show him with hair. This seems the only explanation.

P. Willes came for dinner. He said, 'Aren't you excited by the prospect of going away?' 'Yes,' I said. 'Well, I must say, you both looked plunged in gloom,' he said.

Thursday 23 February

Telephoned the Libyan Embassy for Kenneth, who is in such a rage that it isn't possible to get him to do anything. He has to go and see the consul tomorrow. 'I can't get the photographs changed in time,' Kenneth said. 'It's just not possible.' 'Wait and see if that's what they want. They may just wish to check that you're not your own brother,' I said.

Went down to Criterion for the matinee because the understudy – a girl called Lisa – is to play Fay this afternoon. Went determined to come away if it was too awful. Stayed in fascination. Lisa is a very beautiful, blonde girl. She has an overblown rose kind of figure. She'll go to fat when she's older, but at about 23 she's very sexy. The effect of playing Fay like this is unbelievable. Suddenly I saw what is missing from Sheila's performance. Gloom, gloom from the other actors who say, 'She can't act' and 'We had to carry her all the way'. True, but it's the first time for a long while that I've been able to sit through more than ten minutes of the play.

Friday 24 February

Kenneth went to the Libyan Embassy, very unwillingly and with a long face. I typed up a sketch for a sort of revue which Michael White is putting on. Kenneth Tynan is involved in it in some obscure way. I was asked for a sketch 'to do with sex'. As I think that this revue is doomed from the start I wasn't going to put myself out. So I typed up a pornographic sketch which I wrote long before *Sloane* or *The Ruffian* to amuse Kenneth. It was called *The Patient Dowager*. I retitled it *Until She Screams* and slightly altered some of the more deliberately pornographic

---

1 Peggy Ramsay to John Lahr, 29 May 1970: 'Joe's extraordinary charm captured everyone, whereas Kenneth's rather brittle, sharp manner didn't. Certainly Kenneth improved when he began wearing a wig. He was quite bald, and was very ashamed of his baldness, and kept his hat on everywhere, including the theatre. The first money Joe earned was spent on a couple of wigs for Kenneth, and he chose a style with a rather endearing forelock. I think that by looking at himself in the mirror and seeing someone rather charming and sincere, it actually altered his personality, and he became rather charming and sincere, so that indeed I quite forgot my first alarmed reaction to his personality.'

element. I posted it off to Michael White. Kenneth Tynan apparently said the revue was to be straight-forward, and no phoney 'artistic' shit. Since the revue is called *Oh, Calcutta!* it begins with an artistic title. Anyway they can have the sketch. If they dare do it.[1]

Kenneth arrived back wreathed in smiles. The consul had wanted to see him because on his passport it says he is a 'freelance writer'. The consul wanted to assure himself that there was no suggestion of 'writing anything about Libya'. Kenneth said that of course there was not. Privately we are both intrigued. If the Libyan authorities are so anxious that the country shouldn't be written about – what on earth is it like? 'Perhaps it's hashish and bum all the way,' I said, open-mouthed. Kenneth more sceptical. 'I wouldn't write about them,' I said. 'I disapprove of these evil journalists who go to places and spoil them. I wouldn't expose them whatever they did. Look at how Tangier has been ruined by nosey journalists and United Nations beagles.' So we're probably leaving on Thursday.

Early this week (I forgot to note it down) I finished *Up Against It*. Kenneth was impressed. Hope W. Shenson is. This evening we went to Peggy's to watch my appearance on *Call My Bluff* and to let her have *Up Against It* to read.

On the way we saw headlines saying, 'MARTINE CAROL'S[2] GRAVE – ROBBED' and 'THE BOSTON STRANGLER – ESCAPES' and 'SS MEN GAOLED FOR ANNIE FRANK[3] KILLING'.

When we got to Peggy's, Oscar L. was there, also a man who is going to buy *Loot* for a film. This afternoon he rang Peggy and asked if he could buy the option. Peggy said that if he came round with a cheque for £20,000 he could have it. He rushed round. Oscar then said to Peggy, 'See what happens if you ask for 25.' So she did. He signed a cheque for £18,000 with another £7,000 when the contract is signed. When the man had gone (he's in with Bernard Delfont[4]), Oscar said 'Only this afternoon I was saying to Michael, "I expect about £5,000 is all we'll get for *Loot* now."' Remarkable the man must be. Especially as *Loot* is quite unsuitable for filming.[5] Watched the TV programme on which I appeared. I thought I looked like a younger Robert Mitchum.[6]

---

1 They did. *Oh, Calcutta!*, with contributions from, among others, Samuel Beckett, Jules Feiffer, Sam Shepard and John Lennon, ran for over thirteen years on both sides of the Atlantic, recording over 80 million admissions. It was still running on Broadway in 1986.

2 Martine Carol (1922–1967). Popular French leading lady.

3 Anne Frank (1929–1945). Jewish concentration camp victim whose *Diary* became world famous.

4 Bernard Delfont (Lord Delfont) (1909–). Chairman and chief executive of First Leisure Corp. Since his first London production in 1942, he has presented over two hundred shows.

5 Orton was right, although *Loot* did get made into a film, directed by Silvio Narizzano; screenplay by Alan Simpson and Ray Galton. Starring Richard Attenborough, Lee Remick, Hywell Bennett, Milo O'Shea. An Arthur Lewis Production for British Lion (1970).

6 Robert Mitchum (1917–). Actor. Among his films are *Night of the Hunter*, *Ryan's Daughter*.

Saturday 25 February

Oscar Lewenstein rang up about 7.15 as I was getting ready to go to the Criterion. He'd read *Up Against It* and liked it very much. He thought it had a poetic quality. This is because I used all the romantic clichés – moonlight, roses, unrequited love and the Cinderella figure of the poor girl who loves him and finally is rewarded by his love in the last reel. O.L. said he liked least the scenes in the Albert Hall (with the shooting down of the woman prime minister, Lillian Corbett). This clearly because, the parody on the Kennedy assassination, he doesn't think that Epstein, the Beatles, or W. Shenson will opt for.

Went down to the Criterion. Not a full house. I took heart from the fact that outside the Globe, where usually the 'HOUSE FULL' sign is up for *A Girl in My Soup*¹, was no sign at all of the sign. I wore a leather jacket (which I'd found at the bottom of a suitcase, put away from 1964 when leather jackets went out of date) and my cap from Hamburg. As uniforms are now 'in' it looked very way out. 'Oh,' Sheila Ballantine said, 'how trendy.' Stayed until the rise of the curtain and then left. In Piccadilly a rather slant-eyed and pissed (or drugged) poove sidled past me and said in a low, hot tone, 'I say, how camp'. But, as Kenneth Halliwell said, it's rather pointless making to pick-up when the object of your desires is clearly with someone else.

Sunday 26 February

Dreary day. Watched *The Outlaw*², a boring film, on TV. Made in the heyday of Hollywood. Pornography with the pornography left out. And pretentious at that. Went for a long walk – about three miles – and came back to watch another rubbishy film on TV, this time Hollywood in decline. Made, I'd guess, during the mid-fifties. *23 Paces to Baker Street*. Van Johnson³ as a blind playwright. More pretention. This was soap opera with the soap left out.

Monday 27 February

Went to the Libyan Embassy to collect our visas. The idiots have dated the visas as from last Thursday when we applied for them. We couldn't face more arguments and so we're going to take the chance. We'll probably have to come back after three weeks if the worst happens. Got our plane tickets from BOAC. In South Kensington, admired the architectural splendours of the Science Museum and the V. and A. Came home in a howling gale. Peggy said that *Up Against It* was splendid. She was worried by the way what she called 'your dubious morality' showed through. Especially the killing of the prime minister.

1 By Terence Frisby (1932–   ), 1966.
2 *The Outlaw* directed by Howard Hughes, 1944.
3 Van Johnson (1916–   ). Actor. Film leading man since 1941.

Anyway she said that we mustn't proceed any further without a director. I said she must give Shenson the script in about three weeks' time.

Coming away from the Libyan Embassy Kenneth v. depressed over the inefficiency of the Libyans in dating our visas wrongly. 'I had a dream last night,' he said, in a mournful voice, 'that we went to get our tickets and the plane was full.' 'I wonder you don't start chewing laurel leaves like the Delphic Oracle,' I said. He stamped along in a grim mood until we got to Piccadilly, when he brightened up considerably.

In the evening it poured with rain. I'd intended going to Golders Green to see Hermione Baddeley in *The Killing of Sister George*, but was put off by the weather. Watched various lousy programmes on the TV until 7.30, when there came a gentle scratching at the door. It was Mr Corden. He held a letter in his hand. 'I found this for you in the hall,' he said, rocking backwards and forwards on his feet. I took the letter. It was from Kenneth Williams. I'd written (or rather Edna Welthorpe had written) to congratulate him on his performance in the panel game, *Call My Bluff*. He said he thought I looked very good and that a lady with him asked 'if there was any chance of a fuck.' He went on to say, 'I soon disabused her of that idea.' Reading the letter I came to the end and decided to shatter Mr Corden by allowing him to read it. 'I've a letter here from Kenneth Williams (the star, you know),' I said. 'Would you like to read it?' Mr Corden was very eager, but Kenneth H. who'd already got a glance at what the letter contained said 'Oh, he doesn't want to read that rubbish.' So Mr Corden had to pretend that he wasn't particularly interested. 'Why did you want to let him read Kenny's letter?' K.H. said, later. 'He'd've shit himself.'

Mr Corden stayed on and on. 'Miss Boynes is well settled-in,' he said. 'She's feeling much better. And, fair's fair, she's behaving herself.' 'Is she getting a dog?' I said. 'Well, that depends on many factors,' Daddy Corden said. 'She's got a new carpet to think of. And as we all know, she's a most houseproud woman.' He gave us the address of Hilearn. 'In case you should wish to come and stay with us.²' He said they didn't want to lose touch. And that they'd continue to write. Which I thought was nice of them. 'Miss Boynes went without even the suggestion of meeting again,' I said. 'Well, Joe, you've got to look at it like this,' Mr Corden said. 'She is a woman who likes to have her own way in everything. And we must allow her to. As far as it's conducive.' He went in the end, having

1 See pp. 287–8.
2 Mrs Corden: 'They came for a weekend. Joe bought a postcard of Clacton, and put on it that he was staying with people of "independent means". We're just ordinary people and that was sort of a joke between us over the years.' But the joke was lost on William Orton to whom the postcard was sent. William Orton to Joe Orton, undated: '. . . we received your p.c. from Clacton and hope you are still acquainted with your friends of independent means and that you have also found some sort of a situation to help you through the winter months . . .'

spent an hour or more in the flat and saying nothing of any interest. He'd tried to explain to me, on the stairs, how I should fiddle the income tax. 'You want to ring for a taxi. Go to the West End. Note carefully the fare and, when you come home, double it. And if anybody says anything, you swear blind that you came home by taxi when, in reality, you came home by bus. Oh, there are many little fiddles that the ordinary person simply will not take the trouble to learn.' 'That's quite right,' Mrs Corden called up the stairs, 'Mr Corden was in the accounting.' She climbed the stairs and stood breathless, telling me how he was in a firm of accountants. (He was a commissionaire.[1]) They both went away in the end, after many protestations of goodwill and a determination to 'keep in touch'. They're leaving on Thursday.

Tuesday 28 February

Went to tea at Simon Ward's house.[2] It's an 1830 period house. Simon and his wife have redecorated the place. It had been split up into separate 'rooms'. On the second floor an old woman with heart condition had rotted with nobody to look after her. She'd been cooking a pan of bacon and sausages for her tea when she'd collapsed and died. The fat from the pan had spilled over the wall and caught fire, burning a large patch. How awful to be alone in a house knowing that no one cared when you died.

We talked of slavery and masturbation during tea. Kenneth Cranham and Sheila Ballatine arrived later. We talked of Madeleine Smith[3] after tea. Simon's wife said she'd read somewhere that Madeleine and her lover used to strip off and cover themselves with arsenic, which she'd then lick clean. I'm not sure how this killed him. We talked of murder until half-past five, and fat children until I left at six. Rather a pleasant afternoon.[4]

---

1 Eleanor Salvoni: 'John wrote a television play about the Cordens. Mr Corden was a commissionaire. John asked me if I'd seen the play. "No", I said. "But Aldo saw it and says it's about the Cordens." John said, "They haven't got a television and I'm glad that they showed it while the Cordens were down in the country." I said, "You villain". John laughed.'

2 Orton and Halliwell had previously invited Ward to tea at Noel Road. Simon Ward: 'We had this extraordinary tea party. I thought I might get to know Ken well; but I never, ever, thought I'd get to know Joe well. Joe was very loyal to Halliwell when Ken wasn't there, but when they were together, they bickered the whole time. At first, they used to laugh about it with you – either partner being such a fool, completely incompetent. At the tea party, I got an incredible headache after an hour and a half. I've been with some dodgy couples who really know how to fight, but nothing like that. I was in a terrible state. The claustrophobia of their room coupled with the killing claustrophobia of their marriage was more than I could take. It was quite remarkable for its incessant quality.'

3 Madeleine Smith (1835–1928). Scottish defendant in one of the most baffling murder trials in modern times. Stood trial in Edinburgh (1851) for the alleged murder by poison of her former lover. Although she'd purchased arsenic three times, there was no evidence of any meeting between them in the last three days of the dead man's life.

4 Mrs Simon (Alexandra) Ward: 'I thought Joe was quite bored with Kenneth.'

Kenneth Halliwell and I arrived at Peter Willes's at about seven. He opened the door and drew himself up in a proud way, 'I thought you were arriving at half-past five! Really, you're so inconsiderate. I could've had tea with my mother!' I said we'd had tea with Simon Ward and his wife. 'I've bought a bottle of champagne,' he said, leading us into his bedroom and taking our coats. 'Will you have a glass now?' Both Kenneth and I said we didn't want champagne. 'Oh, really! How annoying. I was hoping you'd be in a mood to celebrate. You're both so dull!'

He gave me a large soda with a dash of whisky, and Kenneth a sherry. 'Guess who's coming round on her broomstick?' he said, settling himself into an armchair. 'The Queen,' I said. Peter gave an impatient twitch, 'Really, what a perfectly stupid remark! No. Margaret Rawlings[1] is coming over. Well, Vivien Leigh[2] was coming but, in a way, I'm rather glad she's not. She'd be frightfully grand. You see, Dorothy's coming (Dorothy Dickson[3]) and Margaret and we'll all be able to go home to our beds well before eleven. But if Lady Olivier came we'd be still talking at four in the morning. She's frightfully frisky.' Margaret Rawlings arrived and told a few stories about shit. She said she never mentioned the word except when telling these stories. Then Dorothy Dickson came. She was a famous musical comedy star in her youth. Now she's seventy, but there a sort of faded glamour about her. You can see she was a star once. Peter said that the whole stage used to light up when she appeared. She talked about Dame Marie Tempest[4] and how terrible she was to young actresses. 'My dear, she was an absolute horror,' Margaret Rawlings said. 'In *The First Mrs Frazer*[5], she used to do actual bodily harm to poor Isabel (Isabel Jeans[6]),' Dorothy Dickson said. 'Well, I acted with the creature,' Margaret Rawlings said, 'and in one scene she used to get hold of my hand in some way and jab one of her rings into the palm. And after several weeks, do you know, there was an actual hole in my hand. Oh, it was perfectly monstrous.' She went on to tell a story of how Dame Marie had Isabel Jeans's chair actually screwed down on the stage to prevent her moving it into a different position in *The First Mrs Frazer*. 'Because it distracts the audience so' was her excuse. She told another story of how during a scene with Dame Marie she suddenly realised that the audience wasn't listening to a word she was

---

1 Margaret Rawlings (1906–   ). Actress.

2 Vivien Leigh (1913–1967). Actress. For many years wife of Laurence Olivier. Best known for her film roles in *A Streetcar Named Desire* and *Gone with the Wind*.

3 Dorothy Dickson (1894–   ). American musical comedy star who spent most of her career in Britain.

4 Dame Marie Tempest (1864–1942). Singer and actress who acquired in later years a gift for comedy. Played Judith Bliss in the original production of Noël Coward's *Hay Fever* and the title role in *The First Mrs Fraser*.

5 By St John Ervine (1883–1971), 1929.

6 Isabel Jeans (1891–1985). British stage actress in aristocratic roles.

saying and couldn't understand why this was. And then she found Dame Marie was waving to imaginary people in the garden beyond the French windows. Dorothy Dickson said that Mrs Patrick Campbell¹ was 'even worse'. 'When I was very young I went to a dinner party at which Mrs Pat was one of the guests. After dinner she said to me, "You're so young. So beautiful. You've the world at your feet" (she was appearing in *Sunny*²). "Everybody loves you. They've forgotten me completely. I'm old. Lonely." And then, without a word of warning, she lowered her voice and hissed, "Can you lend me half-a-crown?"'

During dinner we talked of the war. Dorothy Dickson said she stayed in Libya. 'There were enormous cockroaches in the hotels,' she said.

Wednesday 1 March

Whole day spent packing and arranging for holiday tomorrow. This evening the news broke that *Loot* had been sold for £100,000. Absolutely ridiculous.³ How this is, I can't tell. I suppose they've added on the amount I'd get if the play ran for two years on Broadway. Anyway the phone rang three times and a photographer from the *Daily Mail* called round and spent three quarters of an hour taking photographs. We can buy copies of the papers at the airport tomorrow. On the tube today I listened to a conversation about a 'lovely girl' called Rosalind. An elderly man leaned across to a woman and said, 'My last memory connected with her was when she was home from college and she took a job in a nursery.' The woman with him smiled and said, 'That's why they had such lovely bulbs in their beds.'

Thursday 2 March

Bright sunny day. Great activity in the block. K.H. and I were packing. M. and Mme Corden's removal van arrived at 8.30. We left at 9.30. 'And don't forget we shall want a postcard,' Mrs Corden said. I kissed her goodbye. They won't be here when we get back.

We got to the Victoria air terminal, checked our baggage. BOAC issue absurd stick-on labels for luggage. Guaranteed to peel off. I tried to get tie-on labels without any success. I bought a copy of the *Mail* and the *Sun*. In both were small announcements of £100,000 paid for the film rights of *Loot*. No pictures. We sat drinking orangeade until time to board the coach to London Airport. I heard a

1 Mrs Patrick Campbell (1868–1940). Actress whom G. B. Shaw called 'perilously bewitching', and for whom he wrote the role of Eliza Doolittle in *Pygmalion*, which she played in the original 1914 production.

2 Music by Jerome Kern. Lyrics and book by Oscar Hammerstein II and Otto Harbach, 1925. Post-World War I romance between an ex-soldier and a circus performer.

3 Orton told the BBC about his money: 'I put it in the bank. I don't expect to be a playwright all my life.'

woman saying to her companion, 'Well, Durban is really lovely. If you choose your time.' Her companion, a fat woman with rolls of grey hair said, 'I shall bide by that decision.' They both got up and went to the paper stall.

At London Airport, K.H. came over rather stuffy, looking at the main entrance hall, crowded with people, he said, 'What extraordinary people to be at London Airport at this time in the morning.' When we went into the departure lounge he said, with relief, 'I see we've a better lot of people in here. Those out there were only visitors. They really shouldn't allow that kind of riff-raff in the airport at all.' When I pointed out that his remarks were pretty amazing considering the circumstances, he said, 'I don't want a lot of people about in the airport I'm leaving from. It's spoiling everthing.' He then went to the duty-free tobacconist's and bought a hundred Sobranie cigarettes. He sat next to a Pakistani and his wife and opened the cigarette carton. A customs official appeared at his side, 'Excuse me, sir,' he said, 'did you buy those cigarettes here?' Kenneth said he did. 'Then you're not supposed to break the seal, sir. You are infringing the regulations. I must ask you not to smoke them or they'll have to be confiscated.' Kenneth looked furious and embarrassed. 'Dreadful petty officials,' he muttered as the man went away. 'There's absolutely no need for all that kind of thing.' 'I told you to leave them sealed,' I said. 'If you'd allowed me to put them in your satchel like I suggested none of this would've happened,' Kenneth said very crossly. The flight was then called and we boarded the plane.

On the plane we were sitting immediately behind a fat, balding Libyan, his aged friend, his wife (or daughter) and two children. The man had a loud voice and looked like an East End barrow-boy. K.H. and I called him Mohammed el-Common. 'I suppose some oil company struck rich in his cabbage patch,' Kenneth said. Mohammed el-Common kicked up a terrific fuss about where he was to sit, who he was to sit with and where he was to put his hand baggage. Finally the plane took off. Mohammed el-Common ordered whisky and soda and the rest of his party had soft drinks. The plane otherwise was full of middle-class women and horrible children who kept being sick. When I went to piss a curly-headed, long-nosed child was tugging at the stewardess's skirts and saying, 'I'm to be sick, please.' The stewardess said, in an alarmed way, 'Where's your mummy? Are you travelling with mummy?' The child kept repeating 'I'm to be sick, please.'

We had a good flight. The sun shone from a cloudless sky right through France, down Italy and Sicily. We arrived in Tripoli about five-ish. The stewardess had a long argument with Mohammed el-Common, who'd bought two packets of cigarettes and had only given her one pound. 'I need another pound,' she was pleading. He didn't understand. Or pretended not to understand, his little, cunning, piggy eyes flashing to and fro as he waved his great paws about. I didn't hear the end of the incident. A second stewardess suddenly hurried around collecting our passports. 'What does she want them for?' Kenneth Halliwell said, alarmed. 'She shouldn't have our passports.' I was heartily sick of the whole plane-load of people by now and didn't reply. We got down from the plane. Kenneth and I were the first out of the plane and were escorted across the tarmac by the usual moustached, glittering policeman to the customs post. The first thing they wanted was my passport. 'I haven't got a passport,' I said. The Libyan policeman looked stunned. Another policeman at another desk called over, 'Come here!' I went over. 'Where's your passport?' 'The stewardess took it,' I said. Kenneth H. hovered in the distance. 'Go and get it!' the policeman said. 'I went back to the plane. The stewardess was now surrounded by passengers demanding their passports. We got ours and went back to the customs post. By now it was crowded and we had to wait, fill in absurd forms, get them stamped and finally were allowed into the country.

Idris Airport is very beautiful. For an airport. It is set among gardens and pepper trees. The main airport building is big and cool. Kenneth Halliwell says it's an aeroplane hangar left over from the war. He may be right. Outside the main building was a group of stuffy, tight-arsed English and American business-men. 'I've never been here before,' I said to one of them. 'Can you give me the name of a good hotel?' He looked at me in a pondering sort of way. I expected him to turn on his heel and walk away. At last he said, 'Haven't you made a reservation?' 'No,' I said. 'Well, you may find it rather difficult to get into a hotel.' This brought me up sharp. I caught a glimpse of Kenneth's face looking as though he'd been pole-axed. 'It is difficult then?' I said. 'Yes,' the man said. 'Try the Libya Palace. And if you can't get in there I'd go to the Delmahari.' He shuffled away, uneasy; as though not wishing to be associated with such people. I called a taxi and told them to take us to the Libya Palace. The fare was £4.

The Libya Palace hotel is modern. It has a dim interior. A desk clerk came forward, though it took him seven or eight minutes to decide whether to do so. 'I'd like two single rooms,' I said. 'Have you made a reservation?' he said, looking me up and down. 'No,' I said. 'We have no room.' He didn't say anything else but turned abruptly to a businessman and his dowdy wife who'd just arrived. I went outside and called another taxi. 'The Delmahari Hotel,' I said. 'Ask him how much it's going to cost, for Christ's sake!' Kenneth said. 'What's the use?' I said. 'We've got to get there. There's no other way of doing it.' Kenneth, tight-lipped and angry, said, 'I'm not staying here. You know that, don't you? I can tell already that it's dreadful. It's everything I feared.' The Delmahari Hotel was perhaps one hundred yards away. The taxi cost 10s.

The Delmahari was full. 'Take him to the ship,' the desk clerk said to the taxi driver. We were led away from the hotel and back to the taxi. 'A ship!' Kenneth gave a cry of alarm, 'We'll find ourselves in Saudi Arabia branded as slaves.' 'Ship very good hotel,' the taxi driver said. 'Hot and cold in all rooms.' He drove at a rapid rate onto a quay, stopped with a jerk, flung open the doors of the taxi and welcomed us to the TSS *Carina* billed (on the side of the ship) as 'Libya's only floating hotel'. We paid the taxi driver and climbed the companionway.

The *Carina* was a second- or third-class ex-German cruise ship. It was moored to a wharf. The town was around the ship in a half-circle. Inside the ship we found our way to the reception desk. I asked for two single rooms. 'We have no single rooms,' the manager said. (He was fat, Greek or Levantine, he had dark glasses and kept them on always, even at night.) 'We have only double room.' 'How much?' I said. 'Eight pound ten,' he said. 'For two?' He gave a smile and a shrug, 'I'm sorry, for one.' 'Eight pounds ten a week?' I said. 'A night.' 'I'll take a double room,' I said. The manager called a young boy to attention. The boy was fair-haired and plain in a pretty uniform. 'Take the gentlemen to 112,' he said. The boy, who didn't understand, or even care what the manager said, immediately disappeared down a stairway. We waited for ten minutes until he returned. More businessmen arrived and, upon being told the price of the rooms, swallowed hard and paid up. Our passports were taken away by a pleasant-looking Libyan who was next seen examining them in detail in a glass booth. The pageboy had parked Kenneth and I outside a cabin and left us after discovering that the cabin was already let. It took another half an hour, as the manager, the page and the steward, separately and together, opened the door with a pass-key and stared in at two suitcases on the floor. After a long while they went away and left us alone in a tiny corridor outside a door marked, in fading, scratchy paint 'Herren'. 'Oh, my God!' Kenneth said, rounding upon me savagely. 'Look what a mess you've got us into now! Dumped on a ship in the middle of some wretched fascist state! I'm going to faint!' I found myself saying, 'Pull yourself together! There's no need to behave badly.' 'I warned you what it would be like. No travel agency does Libya. And I'm not surprised,' Kenneth said. 'This is probably a brothel!' Even this would've been interesting but, as though to prove him wrong, a plum-faced matron was seen shepherding three young children down the corridor to the loo. 'This way, sir,' the manager said at my elbow, 'there's been a mistake.' Behind me Kenneth said, 'What's going to happen if they're full here? We shall be sleeping in the open.' 'Don't be ridiculous,' I said, 'I shall go to the British Consul.' 'He's probably an Arab!' Kenneth said. 'That'll land us in a worse mess than ever.'

The fat manager opened the door of Cabin 115 (also outside a door marked 'Herren') and showed us what we were getting for £8 10s. a night. Or rather, as Kenneth who'd been listening to the conversations at the reception desk, said, 'Ten pounds a night each with taxes added.' It was a cabin with two bunks, both already made up for the night; the sheets were spotless, the blanket obviously freshly-laundered. The whole area of the cabin would've been a generous linen cupboard. 'The room also includes a shower,' said the manager rather proudly attempting to fling open the door of the shower and finding that it needed a little effort to do so. The shower was in the lavatory and so, as I later discovered, it wasn't possible to use the lavatory after a shower because the shower saturated the lavatory pan and reduced the toilet paper to a pulp. The manager went away leaving us alone.

'We could stay at the Hilton for this price!' Kenneth screamed with rage. 'I'd rather not discuss it,' I said. 'We must make the best of it.'

When we'd changed, we went onto the upper deck. Around us were several oil tankers floating on the swell. The evening was warm, like an English spring. 'Well, the weather is perfect,' I said. Kenneth, who'd recovered a little, said, 'It should be at this price.' A man and woman loomed towards us in the twilight. 'Are you English?' I said. This seemed to bring them up sharp. 'We're Americans,' the man said. I felt he rather resented my speaking to him. As though, like English ladies at the turn of the century, he expected to be properly introduced. He had pale blue eyes and a wooden manner. 'Are you staying here?' I said. 'I live here,' he said. 'I work here.' His wife, an ex-fluffy blonde, nodded. It was as though someone were pulling a string behind her. She'd obviously never been taught to speak. 'How do we get out of this place?' Kenneth said. The man said, 'I work for one of the oil companies.' 'Do they usually charge these prices?' I said. 'What are you being charged?' the man said. I told him and he said he thought that was usual. 'This is all most weird,' Kenneth said. 'I feel as though this ship is going to sail away and we're going to be sold into slavery.' Both the man and the girl were considerably put out by the turn the conversation had taken. The man shook his head, 'I don't think there's any danger of that,' he said, without even a twinkle in his eye. Somebody pulled the strings behind the girl and she wobbled about agreeing with her husband. 'How do we get out of here?' Kenneth repeated the question, which neither the man or his wife had cared to answer the first time round. 'Well, there's a plane to Malta twice a day,' the American said. 'I believe it's quite easy to get onto that.' We asked him how to go about booking a ticket. He didn't seem inclined to give away that particular secret and we parted. The puppet-wife nodded a lot as she left.

'We must get a plane to Malta tomorrow,' Kenneth said. 'It's bound to be horrible and English, but anything is better than the robot slaves of Esso and Shell.' Another man came on deck and sniffed at the air. 'How much is a taxi from the airport?' Kenneth said, addressing the man abruptly. The man turned and smiled in a thoroughly English way, 'We usually tell our people no more than £4,' he said. 'Though, I believe, they'll ask for as much as six.' 'We were charged four,' Kenneth said. 'You can get them to do it for three,' the man said. 'But four is fair.' 'We've come here for a holiday,' I said. 'A holiday?' The man raised his eyebrows. 'What did you do that for?' 'I thought it'd be like Algiers or Tunis or Tangier,' I said. 'Oh no,' the man said, in a kindly tone, 'it isn't a town like that at all.' 'Isn't it strange to be asked this kind of price for a cabin on a cruise ship?' Kenneth said. 'You're much better off here than at the hotels,' the man said. 'The food is quite edible, you know. Breakfast was excellent this morning. The lunch was a bit greasy, but quite edible.' He said that the hotels in Tripoli were always full. 'And, you know,' he said, in a nice, open way, 'all our people go to Valetta when they want a holiday.' He said he was expecting people to join him on the ship for dinner. And, then he said, 'It's jolly here. They have a band. It was quite noisy until three o'clock yesterday morning.' It was unpleasant to realise that, far from staying in a dump, we were booked in at the local swinging place where the in-crowd went. As though, stumbling upon the Battersea Dogs' Home, one had been informed that it was Crufts. 'I'll leave you now,' the man said. 'I see my party arriving.' He waved to a number of men and women who all greeted him with cries of 'Hi.' 'You made it then?' he called. The crowd, climbing the gang-plank, called back gaily that they had. Assuring ourselves that dinner wasn't included in the £20 or so a night, Kenneth and I went for a walk.

We strolled along an embankment into the city. Cars roared past. An old man driving a horse-driven hansom cab trotted by. A few depressed and aged Libyans were seen at intervals under trees. It was altogether like a balmy night in Hull or Birkenhead. At the end of half an hour's walking, we came to some traffic lights and crossed the road. We explored a side-street which wound in an odd way among a strange collection of buildings, semi-ruins and what looked like overgrown bomb sites. Inexplicably there would be a modern plate-glass-fronted showroom and next to it an old warehouse. We turned back and, in doing so, I noticed a BOAC poster in one of the glass-fronted showrooms. We'd found the place we were looking for: a large travel agency. 'Our walk hasn't been in vain then,' Kenneth said. We walked back to the ship.

On board, the evening was just beginning. Large numbers of English, American and German middle-class men and women (all the women seemed to be the same dyed-blonde hag) were laughing in loud, raucous tones. A few middle-class Libyans were strolling about. 'Wog bourgeoisie is even worse than the home product,' I said, rather wishing that Kenneth was in a better mood to appreciate the remark. 'Shut up!' Kenneth said, pushing crossly past a gaggle of excited young women. 'I'm in no mood to appreciate your remarks.' We went to our cabin. I took a shower, Kenneth took his clothes off and then discovered that the curtains didn't fit properly over the windows. The window gave onto the deck and anyone strolling by could see right into the cabin. Whilst I was having a shower Kenneth discovered that it wasn't possible to open the windows more than an inch and that the ship had central heating. We were being suffocated in our cabin. 'Go and have a shower,' I said; 'it's supposed to be good for the nerves.' 'Fuck the shower!' Kenneth said. He hung a bath towel over the window to hide us from the world. 'I must have a drink of water,' he said. He then filled a glass with water from the washbasin and put an Alka-Seltzer tablet into it, though as I pointed out Alka-Seltzer wasn't sold as a protective against typhoid. 'It makes the water taste better, though,' Kenneth said. We both sat on our bunks sipping Alka-Seltzer and listening to the bumping from the upper deck and the shrieking, laughing people pushing into the lavatories just outside our paper-thin door. 'Sleep will be impossible tonight,' Kenneth said. 'We might snatch an hour or two,' I said. 'What've they all come here for, I wonder?' The answer wasn't long in coming, for a band, in the 'ballroom' just down the corridor, suddenly struck up 'South of the Border' and the dancing began.

Until half-past two the next morning the band played a selection of dance tunes from the early forties. 'Put the blame on Mame, boys', 'Begin the Beguine', 'You'd be so nice to come home to' and 'Maria Illena'. 'It's as though they're still fighting the desert war,' I said. 'I wouldn't be surprised if Rommel suddenly appeared on deck.' I dropped off into a kind of delirium at two o'clock and woke up to hear an American woman saying 'I'm going to the "little girls"', a lot of laughter and a man's voice saying 'Me for the "little boys"', more laughter. More hysterical conversations from drunken gay oilmen and their drunken gay wives. Almost everything they said seemed to be in inverted commas. At the end of a hush which fell upon the ship at three o'clock, a steward knocked on the cabin next door and said 'Your five o'clock call, sir.' Kenneth and I engaged in desultory conversation until seven when we got up and dressed. I couldn't be bothered shaving. We went to breakfast at eight.

Breakfast was, as the Englishman had told us, surprisingly good. Just bacon and eggs, coffee and rolls (the most expensive I've ever eaten), but they were well cooked, the rolls were fresh and the coffee excellent. It could've been worse. The ship now, inexplicably, seemed to be full of a Libyan athletic team. They were eating at tables down the opposite side of the ship. 'There's a kind of dreadful apartheid in this place which is very unpleasant,' Kenneth said. But I thought it might be his imagination. Though certainly, the Europeans and the Libyans weren't mixed. I recalled for a moment a remark the Englishman had made the night before: 'The police are very good here. They're British-trained. The natives are terrified of them.' 'You see,' Kenneth said, feeling much better after a meal, 'instead of the British Raj you've got the Oil Raj. And honestly, Queen Victoria was better than Shell.' We went to the travel agency at nine o'clock.

The travel agency was open. A most courteous Libyan attended to us. Kenneth had had an inspiration earlier, during the long night, spent listening to alien gaieties outside our door. 'The VC10 we came on goes on to Accra,' he said. 'It must turn round and come back today. We can get onto it if there's room.' We enquired if there was a plane to London. There was. It left Accra earlier in the day, arriving at Tripoli about 4.45. With a feeling of relief I booked two seats. The travel agent looked at our tickets. 'You came only yesterday?' he said, in surprise. 'Yes,' Kenneth said. 'The hotels are full.' The man nodded. 'The hotels are always full,' he said.

The rest of the morning was spent waiting. We sat on the top deck in the sunshine (cool, like a fine June day in England). We took about a dozen black and white snapshots (to use up the remaining reel of black and white film in the camera and to have some kind of souvenir), and then we had lunch. Very good. The waiter said 'What is the number of your cabin?' '115,' I said. 'I haven't brought my key with me.' 'That's all right,' the waiter said. 'I'm Greek. I'll trust you. You are English?' 'Yes,' I said. He smiled. 'We are Europeans,' he said, 'we'll trust each other.' I was surprised by this remark and he lowered his voice and pointed to the Libyan athletic team. 'They don't trust each other,' he said, by way of explanation.

At 2.30 we left the ship. At 3.30 we were at Idris Airport. At 4.30 we waited to board the plane. The passengers were the by now familiar oilmen and a sprinkling of oil executives who chattered with a sort of suppressed excitement at going away. 'Done your "stint" then?' one man laughed to another. The other replied in an undertone and the first man said, 'You should pay "the company" for allowing you to work for them.' Everybody laughed and nodded in a knowing sort of way. A perfectly idiot American was taking moving pictures of the various passengers leaving the departure lounge. Not people he knew or had any interest in, just people, strangers, leaving an anonymous doorway. He sat behind me on the plane and, every half-an-hour or so I'd hear a whirring, like an alarm clock. I realised at last that he was taking pictures from the plane window. Inexplicable shots of cloud formations seen through dirty windows. His home movies must be stunning to see on dark winter evenings.

The stewardess was surprised to see us on the plane. The journey home was uneventful. The weather for most of the way perfect. The views, from the window, of the Alps was breathtaking. I noticed that, as we passed from Turin over Mont Blanc to France, the American with the camera was busy chewing gum and drinking scotch. He only got out his camera when we approached the French coast. He took some interesting shots of anonymous landscapes wreathed in the gloom of a winter afternoon. To preserve the memory of his flight home, I suppose.

On the way home, in the airport bus, I sat in front of a black lower-middle-class Noël Coward[1]. He was with his fiancée and kept up a constant stream of dated badinage interspersed with outmoded forms of imperialist thought like, 'I

---

1 Sir Noël Coward (1899–1973). Actor, composer and playwright. Coward became increasingly the spokesman for reactionary positions. In one of his diatribes against the 'kitchen sink' dramas of the early sixties, which he called 'the scratch and mumble school', he wrote: 'Duchesses are quite capable of suffering too.'

fight with my hands'. 'To use a knife is cowardly', 'I never swear in front of women', 'I always wear a tie at functions' and even 'The RAF is the finest body of men in the world'. This mixed with the kind of facetious chatter that would be howled down in the fourth form. 'The depressing thing about a lot of coloured people,' Kenneth said, 'is their pathetic imitation of everything that is bad in the white races.' 'Did you hear his remarks on Communism?' I said, suddenly remembering a stretch of dialogue I'd forgotten. 'He said, "We should shoot the bastards. They are ruining the economic trade of the world."' 'What was he like?' Kenneth said. 'Oh, about thirty-five, bespectacled,' I said. 'I thought he was about seventeen,' Kenneth said. The taxi drew up at the flat and we both stumbled out – home again after a day trip to Tripoli.

Saturday 4 March

Spent this morning ringing up P. Willes, Peggy, Michael White and Oscar. P. Willes, predictably, said 'Oh, you fool! Why didn't you go down the coast?' 'Where to?' I said. 'You could've stayed at an Arab house.' 'Don't be ridiculous,' I said, 'I don't know any Arabs.' 'You should've asked any taxi driver. You should've said "Take me to your house, I wish to stay with you",' Willes said. 'But then he'd think I wanted to sleep with him.' 'Well, why not?' Peter said. He became hysterical with anger that I'd spent £100 on the trip. 'Just for yourself?' he said. 'Yes,' I said. 'Kenneth's was another £100.' 'Oh, good heavens! How scandalous! I'd've flown over myself and put you right for that. I see you've started already. Just like Harold.[1] The problems of the rich.' 'But there was no problem. I hated it and came back. You can do that when you're rich.' 'Well, it's disgraceful. Oh, I shall have to go and have a cup of coffee with my mother. This has been so upsetting! You should've asked to be taken to a brothel. You should've said, "Take me to a brothel"'. 'I wasn't feeling like sex,' I said, feebly. 'Any taxi driver would've taken you to a brothel and you could've said "If any of the gentlemen fancies me I'm only too ready to oblige".' 'That wouldn't've solved the accommodation problem,' I said. 'Any Arab, if you say to him "I wish to sleep with your nephew or your son", will be delighted to arrange it,' Peter shouted down the phone. I was alarmed by the way the conversation had gone off the rails and called, in a voice loud enough to be heard without the telephone, 'Sex was of secondary importance!' 'Well, it's all too terrible. Too terrible,' Peter said, 'and I'm in the middle of Easter eggs. I've got a party of children coming tomorrow. This has really upset me. Such a fool you are!'

Peggy said, 'How splendid. To come back like that. Rather magnificent. The papers have been onto us ever since the announcement of the film rights. Come

---

1 Harold Pinter. 'Joe was quite proud of his friendship with Pinter,' said Kenneth Cranham. 'He liked Pinter's work, but he scoffed at the way he lived.'

down on Monday and I'll give you the people you're to call. I expect this little incident will be quite good publicity. And, don't forget, you can put the trip down to "collecting local colour for a play" and get it off tax. Kenneth's too. You simply claim that he's your "personal assistant".[1]

Michael White said, 'But I thought you knew that it was awful.' 'No,' I said. 'Oh, yes,' he said, 'a psychiatrist friend of mine and his wife went and they said just the same. A town run by the oil companies.'

Oscar said his chauffeur had wondered why Joe Orton was going to Libya. 'No one does that,' he'd said, 'unless they were there in the war.'

I went to the Criterion to tell the cast of the adventure. Sheila B. said 'How fortunate you went. I was determined to go there myself. I shan't now.' Simon said someone he knew had told them about Tripoli and they'd had a wonderful time. 'But, he stayed with some people,' he said. 'Well, of course,' I said, 'if I'd been staying in a private villa it would've been much better. I would then have had a base of operations.'

The publicity has been good for the play. Mark tells me that the matinee was up and the evening performance was sold out except for a few seats. When I left, I took the Piccadilly line to Holloway Road and popped into a little pissoir – just four pissers. It was dark because somebody had taken the bulb away. There were three figures pissing. I had a piss and, as my eyes became used to the gloom, I saw that only one of the figures was worth having – a labouring type, big, with cropped hair and, as far as I could see, wearing jeans and a dark short coat. Another man entered and the man next to the labourer moved away, not out of the place altogether, but back against the wall. The new man had a pee and left the place and, before the man against the wall could return to his place, I nipped in there sharpish and stood next to the labourer. I put my hand down and felt his cock, he immediately started to play with mine. The youngish man with fair hair, standing back against the wall, went into the vacant place. I unbuttoned the top of my jeans and unloosened my belt in order to allow the labourer free rein with my balls. The man next to me began to feel my bum. At this point a fifth man entered. Nobody moved. It was dark. Just a little light spilled into the place from the street, not enough to see immediately. The man next to me moved back to allow the fifth man to piss. But the fifth man very quickly flashed his cock and the man next to me returned to my side, lifting up my coat and shoving his hand down the back of my trousers. The fifth man kept puffing on a cigarette and, by the glowing end, watching. A sixth man came into the pissoir. As it was so dark nobody bothered to move. After an interval (during which the fifth man watched me feel the labourer, the labourer stroked my cock, and the man beside me

---

1 Orton did just that. Halliwell received a salary for his 'editorial services'. The irony was not lost on Halliwell who signed a letter to Peggy Ramsay, 3 May 1967: 'Secretary to Joe Orton'.

pulled my jeans down even further) I noticed that the sixth man was kneeling down beside the youngish man with fair hair and sucking his cock. A seventh man came in, but by now nobody cared. The number of people in the place was so large that detection was quite impossible. And anyway, as soon became apparent when the seventh man stuck his head down on a level with my fly, he wanted a cock in his mouth too. For some moments nothing happened. Then an eighth man, bearded and stocky, came in. He pushed the sixth man roughly away from the fair-haired man and quickly sucked the fair-haired man off. The man beside me had pulled my jeans down over my buttocks and was trying to push his prick between my legs. The fair-haired man, having been sucked off, hastily left the place. The bearded man came over and nudged away the seventh man from me and, opening wide my fly, began sucking me like a maniac. The labourer, getting very excited by my feeling his cock with both hands, suddenly glued his mouth to mine. The little pissoir under the bridge had become the scene of a frenzied homosexual saturnalia. No more than two feet away the citizens of Holloway moved about their ordinary business. I came, squirting come into the bearded man's mouth, and quickly pulled up my jeans. As I was about to leave, I heard the bearded man hissing quietly, 'I suck people off! Who wants his cock sucked?' When I left, the labourer was just shoving his cock into the man's mouth to keep him quiet. I caught the bus home.

I told Kenneth who said, 'It sounds as though eightpence and a bus down the Holloway Road was more interesting than £200 and a plane to Tripoli.'

Monday 6 March

Kenneth Williams rang first thing. I'd written a note to Kenneth saying Tripoli was disaster – 'Not a sign of a cock – except my own and that only glimpsed briefly in a cracked mirror' – he was very interested to hear the news. He said he'd had a similar experience in Beirut. 'I was charged 12 guineas a night for a room,' he said. He did have the consolation, though, of staying in the poshest hotel. Not like me – a dump. He said he was recording his radio programme today and his television programme tomorrow but he'd ring on Wednesday and come round.

Had my hair cut at a new hairdresser's in Knightsbridge. Cost a guinea for a style. But it looks pretty good. It appears to be quite natural whilst in actual fact being incredibly artificial. Which is a philosophy I approve of.

Went to Peggy's office. We decided to send Shenson *Up Against It*. No point in hanging on to it. Tried to get in touch with him with no success. I said I'd try later on in the morning. Came home. Went to Shenson's office at 2.30 and delivered the script. He was very surprised to get it so soon. He's off to California in the morning. Epstein is in New York but will be back next week. Shenson said he'd ring me tomorrow morning about ten-ish. He's going to read the script tonight. Peggy said she feels it will be too much for him.

I'm reading the Savoy Operas[1]. Very good. I very much like the following (about England) from *Utopia Limited*:[2]

> She terrifies all foreign-born rapscallions;
> And holds the peace of Europe in her hand
> With half a score invincible battalions!
> Such, at least, is the tale
> Which is borne on the gale,
> From the island which dwells in the sea.
> Let us hope, for her sake,
> That she makes no mistake –
> That she's all she professes to be!

Tuesday 7 March

Kenneth suggests that, with the money coming in so fast, I buy a house in Brighton and keep on this flat as a pied-à-terre. Sounds a good idea. Brighton is only an hour away by electric train. Kenneth has already started looking in *Dalton's Weekly* for suitable properties. Peggy invited us down to stay at her place in Brighton. We are going down there on Sunday.

Shenson rang this morning. He'd read only half the script (to the prison sequence) and confessed to finding it 'fascinating'. I gather, though, that he's jittery. He also thinks that either it should be made much clearer that the four boys are merely aspects of one person or, as I suggested, that there are four boys. He's worried by the fact that, as the script goes at the present time, it would be impossible for there to be only one boy. He's obsessed by the fact that 'as you know, Joe, we're all of us different people. And we have to learn to live with those aspects. I understood that the original idea was to show how a man came to live with himself.' Which I think is pretentious shit. I can't write that or, what is more important, alter my script to fit in with that idea. I'd much rather have it about four boys anyway. Shenson is going to speak to Epstein from Los Angeles tonight. He has suggested Antonioni[3] to direct. Rubbish!

Wednesday 8 March

Surprised to see the Cordens' car outside the flat. When I went down, Mrs Corden said, 'We had to return. We'd left a lot of crockery in the drawer of the

---

1 Written by Sir. W. S. Gilbert (1836–1911) and Sir Arthur Sullivan (1842–1900), between 1881–1896. So named for the Savoy Theatre built by Richard D'Oyly Carte and opened in 1881 with *Patience*. Artists associated with the productions were called 'Savoyards'.
2 *Utopia Limited*, 1893.
3 Michelangelo Antonioni (1912–   ). Director. His films include *The Red Desert*, *Blow-up*, *L'Avventurra*.

cooker.' Mr Corden beamed and said, 'We couldn't imagine where the various articles we sought had disappeared to.' Mrs Corden, after telling me how well Miss Boynes was 'down at Holland', suddenly began a tirade on the fact that 'it's quite impossible to obtain homogenised milk down there.' She'd bought seven pints in London to take back. 'I spoke to an inspector. I told him of the difficulties I was having. And he said "Perfectly ridiculous. We supply homogenised milk all over the country." And so he promised to get in touch with my dealer.' 'What do you want homogenised for?' I asked. 'Well,' Mrs Corden said, 'it's very good for stomachs.'

We went to see *The Night of the Generals*[1]. Not a good film. Rather a mess. But (apart from some boring sex scenes between Tom Courtenay[2] and a dreary girl) quite worth watching. I don't know why there keep being scenes on beds in films, where the two people concerned are supposed to be in the throes of sexual passion and yet insist upon keeping their clothes on.

I was in bed at ten. The phone rang. It was Budgen. He's having difficulties in getting a hotel in Cyprus in June. This made me depressed. Obviously Cyprus has become 'a tourist paradise'. Budgen also said that Agadir was 'nice' but trade difficult because the hotels don't allow dragging back. He said Marrakesh was good. 'I've already decided to go to Tangier in May and June,' I said. 'If I can get a flat.' He persuaded me to write immediately to Reginald Allen[3]. Not to delay another day. He himself is off to Morocco on Friday.

Thursday 9 March

Kenneth suddenly showed me a lot of spots on his leg and thigh. 'I've never completely got rid of those scabies,' he said. Find this difficult to believe as, with one application of benzyl benzoate supplied by the skin hospital mine cleared up completely. Kenneth has had a second application since then. I went with him to the doctor's this evening. Pouring rain and a high wind. The doctor assured Kenneth that benzyl benzoate isn't dangerous and anyway, as it is only applied on the outside of the body, couldn't (as Kenneth says it does) make his heart beat in an alarming fashion. Would have thought this myself, but don't particularly trust the doctor to know. He seemed embarrassed by the fact that he'd diagnosed 'an allergy' when I'd caught the scabies. I asked about injections for typhoid as I'm going abroad. He said he'd arrange that. 'And what about polio,' I said. 'I've never had an injection for that.' 'If you'll forgive me for saying so,' he said, snuffling, 'I think you're too old to catch that.' Which, if I believed him, would be a relief.

1 *The Night of the Generals* (1967). With Omar Sharif, Donald Pleasence. Directed by Anatole Litvak.
2 Tom Courtenay (1937–   ). Actor.
3 Hon. Reginald Allen (1915–1985). Estate agent.

Kenneth put some benzyl benzoate on his spots and, at about two in the morning, I was woken up by hearing a fizzing. He was sitting up in bed drinking Alka-Seltzer. 'I've had those unpleasant side-effects again,' he said. 'There's a pain in my chest caused, I'm sure, by the benzyl benzoate.' I suggested that he should go to a doctor about the pain in his chest, but that I didn't see how the small amount of benzyl benzoate put on the spots could cause palpitations of the heart and a pain in his chest. Long, neurotic argument. Kenneth said, 'You're turning into a real bully, do you know that? You'd better be careful. You'll get your deserts!' Went to sleep.

March 10 Friday.

Bright sunny morning, though the wind howled around the streets. Kenneth v. depressed. I was feeling merry. I'd finished cutting *Entertaining Mr Sloane* for Rediffusion and now have no work to do. I'm quite free. The BBC wrote asking me to do a play for their Wednesday Play series. I shan't, though. I don't want to do anything this year except perhaps the second draft of *Up Against It* and the final recension of *What the Butler Saw*. If I've time on my hands at the end of the year I'd like to amuse myself by writing a bit of rubbish under an assumed name: in the nature of a joke play.

Kenneth and I went to see the film of Olivier's *Othello* at the Academy Cinema this afternoon. I went in a sceptical spirit. I was prepared to hate it. The opening scene between Iago (Frank Finlay)[1] and Roderigo (Robert Lang)[2] I found very good. Then, when Olivier came on, I was staggered. He was certainly giving a remarkable performance of a negro. He looked perfect. The slight negro accent didn't bother me much. At least not for the first scene. Came the senate scene and the 'Most potent, grave and reverend signors . . .' and I realised that although he looked Othello (so that Brabantio's lines about Desdemona being frightened to look upon him were, for the first time, credible) he couldn't play Othello. He mangled the verse. He should be called 'Butcher' Olivier. When Maggie Smith entered as Desdemona, one felt cheated. After all that build-up about her youth and beauty to find a thirty-seven year old spinster entering! The feeling that they were playing some other play of their own invention grew and grew. Olivier entered on Cyprus dressed in the full gear of Islam looking like a Turk. Yet it's quite clear that he's a Christian and a general of a Christian power. Olivier had a scimitar. Why? Nobody else in the play did. And Olivier's costumes were just fashionable beachwear and lounging clothes. A selection of 'shortie' nighties and dressing-gowns. I found myself cursing Shakespeare for his stupid plot. And then, with a feeling of guilt, realising that the production and acting were at fault

1 Frank Finlay (1926–). Actor.
2 Robert Lang (1934–). Actor and director.

and I was blaming the play. Like people had blamed my own plays. The impression grew, as the film wound to its weary conclusion, that this was an opera without music. Like watching the libretto only. The last scene was made nonsense of by Olivier committing suicide not with the sword of 'the ice-brook's temper' but by doing some inexplicable action with an invisible instrument at the back of his neck. And the last shot of the bed seemed to stretch out to eternity.

Olivier is a great impersonator, not a great tragedian. I've started to re-read *Othello* just to assure myself that it is a work of genius. It is.

Saturday 11 March

Rain and high wind this morning. Kenneth W. rang. Invited him round for a meal. He's coming at two-ish. Went out and bought a couple of pounds of smoked haddock. Reading *Othello* I found a quotation for *The Erpingham Camp*: 'We cannot all be masters, nor all masters/Cannot truly be follow'd.' As far as I recall this was cut in the film. As was the line, 'A fellow almost damn'd in a fair wife'. Kenneth Halliwell suggests that, for *What the Butler Saw*, the quotation from Juvenal '*Quis custodiet, ipso custodes*'[1] would be apt.

Kenneth Williams came round at two. He was wearing a most peculiar dust-coloured mac. His clothes are really most odd. Not fashionably odd, but sort of middle-range bank clerk odd. He took off his mac and revealed a nondescript suit and tie that wasn't exactly quiet, more mumbling. We talked of the Libya trip. He said 'Exactly the same thing happened to me! Same thing to a tee. I went with this great queen to Spain. "No need to book," she said, "it's February. We're bound to get in at some lovely ritzy hotel. And there's your marble shower and your cool linen sheets. And whatever you fancies in the way of extras." Well, we drove from Gib. We went to Malaga. Not a hotel room to be had. All these old norms, darling. All norming about. "Come along, Millicent, we'll sit over here. Where we can catch the warmth." Well, I was furious, but what could we do? We went to some horrible motel place called "RAF Log-cabin Lounge". We went in. There were your communal tables and dreadful English kiddies: "We've been on the beach all day! We're writing to Mummy!" They'd been brought there by their English school-teachers. Some great bitch came up and said, "You're an actor, aren't you?" I said, "Yers," and she looked straight in my face and said, "Well, all actors are hypocrites". I was astounded. So this great queen I was with said, "Let's go into the bar." We went into this quite nice bar. Log-fires, Spanish ironwork. We'd just ordered a drink when these school-teachers came in. "There's the hypocrite," one of them said. Oh, the rudeness of people is simply unbelievable. "I'm going out," I said. Well we went out and came to some transport café and this great queen I was with said, "I bet that's interesting."

1 Juvenal: Quis custodiet ipso custodes (Who guards the guards themselves?).

"It's a transport café," I said. She winked, "I bet it's interesting, though," she said. Well, we went in and there was a bunch of poor queens at the bar. The air was hot with sibilants. We had a drink and I saw this Spanish dish wink at me from the other side of the room, "'Allo, English." So I said to these queens, "I'm going to see what happens with that one." Well, the ugliest of these poor queens said, "No! I wouldn't. He's rent, you know!" "Oh, piss off," I said. I was feeling so rude by this time.' After this there was a sort of gap in the story because, as is usual with Kenneth W's sexual adventures, I gathered it ended rather lamely. He said the boy had demanded money and threatened him. Though I never understood what, if anything, had happened. Kenneth W. began another story about Henry Budgen, who'd been taken back to a flat after a party. 'He got into bed, lovely body he had, French-style body. He undressed and got into bed and then he watched Budgen undress. And, as you know, Henrietta has those rather unfashionable underwear, not these briefettes like all the queers wear, and he has bum trouble and his pants were stained and this great queen he'd gone home with looked at him and said: "Well, they're passion-killers, aren't they?" Budgen got into bed and put his hand on the cock. There wasn't a murmur. "It must be the drink," the queen said. Henry knew it wasn't. He got dressed. Awful, it was. Oh, the failure, the humiliating failure.' This sudden flash of truth put a damper on the conversation. He turned to more gloomy subjects, telling how he'd been insulted at a restaurant the other night.

'I was in Biagi's with this fat queeny friend of mine and suddenly I heard this old couple at the table talking about me. The woman said, "He's imitating the waiter and he's not succeeding very successfully." I couldn't believe my ears. I thought, "Not in England, not in this day and age." And then the old man said, "Where are they?" "Behind you", the old woman said. And he turned round, turned his chair round and stared at me! Then the waiter came and the woman said, "I'm not going to give you a tip." The waiter looked flabbergasted. "No tip?" "No," the woman said, "we're from East Africa and we're staying in London for a while. We shall be dining here often. And we'll give you a tip at the end of the time." Awful, awful people,' Kenneth W. said. Though, as I remarked to K.H. later, he probably had been imitating somebody in a loud voice. And although these refugees from the colonies are loathsome, they have a perfect right to insult one if one insults them. It's no good making a show of affronting the middle classes and then being surprised if your enemies retaliate in their own nasty way. That's what enemies usually do.

Kenneth W. told a lot of stories during the evening, so many that I can't possibly remember them in sequence. He said Maggie Smith had told him an interesting story about Olivier. When, during the rehearsals for *Othello*, he'd taken up a rigid routine of physical training, he broke his Achilles tendon on the Brighton seafront and lay in agony by the side of the road, not able to move.

Nobody came to his assistance and finally he had to call, 'I am Sir Laurence Olivier! I need help!'

He said that somebody he knew had been robbed in Sicily, and that in Naples all the boys in the Gallery Umberto were only interested in robbing and beating up people. 'The same with the Spanish Steps in Rome,' he said. 'I knew somebody who went back with this marvellous bandit-type youth,' he gave a haughty look down his nose; 'he threatened to bash her.' 'But, Kenneth,' I said, 'all those male whores can't be beating people up all the time, otherwise it would get to be well-known that that's what happened and they would find customers hard to come by, surely?' He failed to see the logic of this. Sexually he really is a horrible mess. He mentions "guilt" a lot in conversation. 'Well, of course, there's always a certain amount of guilt attached to homosexuality.' For him, perhaps, too much. 'I never feel guilty whatever I do,' I said. 'Why should you?' There's no answer to this and it would be futile to attempt to find one. Kenneth W. isn't able to have sex properly with man or woman. His only outlet is exhibiting his extremely funny personality in front of an audience and when he isn't doing this he's a very sad man indeed.

He talked of the tour of *Loot*. 'Remember that party in the Royal Crescent?' he said. 'No,' I said. 'There was this party who'd been to see *Loot*, and the woman said, "Well, I mean, it's all about pregnant women and Jesus Christ and we all know about them!"' He then told a story of how a woman had come up to him and said, 'You're on in that play at the Theatre Royal, aren't you?' And when he'd replied that he was, she said: 'Disgusting play. I walked out half-way through. What happened at the finish?' Kenneth said that Gordon Jackson who was with him said:'By walking out madam, you forfeited your right to know.' 'Marvellous reply, wasn't it?' Kenneth said, his eyes shining.

He talks a lot about a friend of his who committed suicide. 'Found in a cottage she was,' he said. 'They gave her the choice of gaol or a mental home. She chose the mental home. "Well," she said, "there's all the lovely mental cock. I'll be sucking all the nurses off. I'm sure it'll be very gay."' Kenneth said this man went into the mental home and was given some kind of treatment 'to stop her thinking like a queen.' The man apparently was very depressed after this and committed suicide. Kenneth then spoke of all the people he'd known who'd killed themselves. Someone threw himself from a high window and died in the ambulance in agony. His father, I believe, swallowed disinfectant. He told all the stories in a way which made them funny, but it was clear that he thinks about death constantly. He is afraid also of being alone. When I mentioned that I didn't mind being on my own, in fact I liked wandering about by myself, he shuddered and said, 'Can't stand it. Can't abide being alone.' He stayed till ten o'clock and I took him to the bus-stop. 'I wish you'd come to Tangier for Easter,' he said. 'I can't, Kenny,' I said. 'I'm going for May and June.' 'I'll give you a ring before I go,' he said, and climbed aboard the bus.

Monday 13 March

Went to Regent's Park. Weather, early on, was perfect: clear skies, sun shining. At midday it clouded over. I decided to go to Peggy's office. She'd promised to bring a map of Brighton and details of the properties she'd seen for sale. We walked down the Tottenham Court Road. I left Kenneth at St Giles Circus. Went down past Foyles. Noticed somebody had got a large and impressive book called *The English Organ*. It'd be nice to have the cover. I'm not interested in music. A cinema had a horror film on. It was advertised as 'the awful girl-stalking vegetable!' Saw Peggy, collected the map etc. Signed a contract: (the BBC are paying me £50 for a short sketch (*An Unsavoury Interlude*). They did it very badly on *The Late Show* a week or so ago. Came home. Very tired. Went to sleep. Thunder and rain this afternoon. Rang several estate agents in Brighton. Made appointments for viewing on Thursday morning. One agent's advertisement said 'unusual property'. I rang and said, 'What is unusual about this property?' And a rather dim-sounding girl said, 'Well, its very central. On a corner. And it's quite modern throughout.' 'I thought "unusual" meant architecturally,' I said. 'Yes,' she said, 'it's longer from back to front than it is from side to side.' Made an order to view with some interest.

Tuesday 14 March

Kenneth got up this morning and felt sick. He looked a ghastly yellow colour. So he went back to bed. Some bug, he says, he's picked up. I felt OK. Though I remembered I'd felt sickish in the night. Sunny day, just a few clouds.

Went to Rediffusion to order six prints of photographs taken during the filming of *The Good and Faithful Servant*. Rather dull pictures, I thought. Bought half-a-dozen at 5s. each. Took the cut version of *Sloane* to P. Willes who'd just had the playback of the first of the *Deadly Virtues* series[1]. A play by Bill Naughton[2]. I'd met B. Naughton before. And, as I went into Willes's office to deliver the script, Naughton was there. He said how much he admired *Loot*. And the way I wrote. He said my work was absolutely original. It never fails to amaze me how kind and generous people like Bill Naughton and Lord Willis are to me. I wouldn't've supposed, judging from the things they write, that I'd appeal to them. Yet they seem perfectly sincere in their admiration. I can't be generous. I've never liked

1 Orton's *Funeral Games* was commissioned for this series to dramatise Faith and Justice. The title *Funeral Games* was the original title for *Loot*. Orton was also considering 'The Comedy of Horrors', because as he wrote Michael Codron on 15 October 1964, 'It has a nice play on Chamber of Horrors and *Comedy of Errors*. Or is that too high for the public?'
2 Bill Naughton (1910–). Playwright. His plays include *Alfie, Spring and Port Wine*.

anything either of them has written. It's like Rattigan's[1] eulogies: I can't return them with any degree of conviction. I'd like to think I'd be as nice to somebody if I admired their writing. But who could it be? 'God,' Kenneth Halliwell says.

I've received an invitation to a banquet given by the Lord Mayor of London – just like Mr Pooter[2], Kenneth says. I shan't be able to go because, I hope, I'll be in Morocco for May and June. The banquet is on 8 June. It's really a little absurd, though. The letter says that the banquet is being held 'in honour of those eminent in the arts, sciences and learning'. 'It's just because of the £100,000,' I said to P. Willes. 'They've realised that I'm as rich as they are and now they invite me to their rubbishy dinner.' P. Willes looked shocked. 'I really don't think you should talk about the Lord Mayor's banquet like that,' he said. 'I believe they have excellent turtle soup. You should go. You might like it.' 'I'll be away,' I said. 'It'd be excellent copy.' 'I would go,' I said, 'but I'll be away.'

I walked with Bill Naughton down to Peggy's. He told me that *Spring and Port Wine*[3] has been transfered to an American setting. 'I've never seen such disaster,' he said. 'Absolute disaster.' 'Why did you allow it?' I said. 'Well, I supposed it would make it better for them. I mean, Joe, I'm not interested in impressing the Americans artistically. God knows all I want is their money. They wouldn't be interested in art.' I agreed, having had an experience on Broadway. 'They're a very ingenuous people,' I said, apropos of nothing really, but it's the thing that one says when America crops up. 'Oh, pure simpering shit,' Naughton said. 'I've no use for them.' He seems an intelligent man. 'You'll have to have a stoup of holy water in the foyer of the theatre where *Loot* is playing,' he said.

Saw a poster for a film called *Libido Means Lust*. It said, 'What happens when a sadistic sex maniac falls in love!' On the way home I noticed a crit of *The Diary of a Madman*[4] which is being presented, for four weeks, at the Duchess with Nicol Williamson[5]. I thought how fashionable madness is at the moment. The film of the *Marat/Sade*[6] is just out. Of course it's the perennial fascination of most

1 Sir Terence Rattigan (1911–79). Playwright. He championed *Entertaining Mr Sloane* and invested £3,000 to insure a West End transfer. 'I don't think you've written a masterpiece,' Rattigan wrote Orton, 16 May 1964. 'But I think you have written the most exciting and stimulating first play (is it?) that I've seen in thirty odd years of play-going.' About *Loot*, Rattigan wired Orton: 'IT IS THE BEST SECOND PLAY I HAVE READ IN FIFTY YEARS AND DON'T TELL ANYONE I WAS READING ARISTOPHANES AT THREE STOP IT IS SO GOOD THAT I HATE YOU ALMOST AS MUCH AS I LOVE YOU . . .'
2 The prim, social climbing fictional diarist in George (1847–1912) and Weedon (1852–1919) Grossmith's *Diary of a Nobody*, 1892.
3 By Bill Naughton, 1964.
4 *Diary of a Madman* (1962). Adapted from a Maupassant story.
5 Nicol Williamson (1940–). Actor.
6 *Marat/Sade* (1966). Written by Adrian Mitchell from the play by Peter Weiss. Directed by Peter Brook. Music by Richard Peaslee.

people with watching lunatics. Four hundred years ago they'd've gone to Bedlam for the afternoon. Now a director and actors recreate a madhouse in a theatre. Let's look at mad people. At queer people. They have only to look in their mirrors. Kenneth H. said, 'In *What the Butler Saw* you're writing of madness.' 'Yes,' I said, 'but there isn't a lunatic in sight – just the doctors and nurses.'

Wednesday 15 March

Went to see my accountants today. They suggested I buy the house on a mortgage. Makes tax easier. Also that I buy tax redemption certificates. Solves a lot of problems. They said, 'Are you married?' 'No,' I said. 'Any prospects of you getting married in the near future?' 'No,' I said. They almost advised me to find a wife and children. Makes tax easier. Solves a lot of problems.

Plays and Players have printed the letters from Donald H. Harley[1] and Edna Welthorpe[2] condemning and praising *Loot*. I shall write more jokey letters this month. I'm feeling idle and full of fun.

I heard a woman with stringy hair saying, on passing the Shaftesbury Theatre where *Big Bad Mouse* is playing, 'I wouldn't see that. Not for the world!' And the man with her said, inexplicably, '*South Pacific* was a lovely show.' The woman looked at him narrowly, 'Who did you see that with?' she said. 'Who did I see it with?' the man said, put out by the question. 'I don't know. I really can't recall. It must've been five year ago.' There was a long sullen silence and the woman suddenly broke it with: 'Oh, you can remember *some* things.'

Thursday 16 March

Kenneth H. and I caught the nine o'clock train to Brighton. We had a list of houses which we intended viewing. Sunny morning. Very pleasant. We arrived in Brighton promptly at ten o'clock. Looked at one or two houses in Guildford Street. Number 42, with a spiral staircase, appealed to me. Didn't go in. Our appointments were for later. Looked at the outside of another property at Ditchling Road. This was the house advertised as 'unusual'. It looked the kind of property one could make interesting. I wondered, at the time, though, whether the noise of traffic wasn't going to be against us there.

Strolled around for a while. Most of the houses, vaguely termed 'regency', aren't. The ones around the station appear to be 1860-ish.[3]

Got the key of number 42 Guildford Street from the agent. The price (originally £4,995) has dropped to £4,100. Another house in Guildford Street,

1 See page 284.
2 See page 287.
3 Kenneth Williams: 'When Joe said to me, "I'll never leave Kenneth", he meant, "I'll never forsake him." He said, "I'd have the flat to do what I like. I'd go down to Brighton on weekends." They'd still be together, but in London he'd be free. You see he had no place to bring these pick-ups.'

number 29, was for sale. 'A gentleman will be on the premises to let you in, sir,' the agent said. We went to 42 first. Very nice house. The front two rooms had been knocked into one room. A gas fire – one or two of the elements were broken. Two bedrooms. One with a new floor. It seemed excellent. The large basement had been turned into a kitchen. The bathroom and lavatory were off the kitchen. Kenneth noticed first that the walls were damp, in fact the plaster was crumbling in several places in the kitchen, and that the bathroom had no ventilator for the steam to disperse. There was a window, but it didn't open. It appeared almost impossible to get the dustbin up the spiral staircase to the front door. These details, but mainly the damp condition of the walls in the kitchen, decided Kenneth against it.

We couldn't get into the house which we (mistakenly as it happened) thought was 29. It was empty. We knocked and decided to come back later. From another agent we got the key of number 6 Guildford Street. On the opposite side of the road to 42. This had no basement. The two rooms on the ground floor had been turned into one. But the room had two doors leading into it: one of the doors not having been blocked up. Also part of the room was panelled in wood. Just two walls. Upstairs the bathroom had a hideous new pink suit. Although Kenneth was not against it as I was, we decided not to bother with that one either.

We made another trip to Ditchling Road. Looked at the place. Rather a rum sort of house. The 'walled garden' turned out to be a shared garden. We went to the agents and he came over with the key. The house was ideal in many ways. It even had a telephone. But the noise of traffic was too much. We said 'no' to that one. We had a meal at a café. Attempted, after the meal, to get into 29 Guildford street by knocking. Realised that we were knocking on the wrong door. Found 29 and even from the outside thought it too hideous and came away. Went to a number of houses. One in Queen's Gardens (the owner was out). Looked down Frederick Gardens (too sordid) and decided that most of the property we'd been looking at wasn't worth buying. Victorian slum with a coat of whitewash. We returned the key of 42 and I had a chat with the agent who said, 'Well, there is this property at Kemp Street, sir. It's been completely modernised throughout and redecorated at a fantastic cost. The owner wanted it for a weekend cottage but is now unable to visit Brighton as often as he'd like. Consequently, he's put it on the market.' We said we'd have a look at that one.

The agent drove us to Kemp Street. We looked over a tiny house. It was obvious from the moment that we got inside the door that an outrageous queen had been at work: all carpets in delicate pastel shades, the furniture, gilded antiques, the fixtures included a 'display cabinet' with bits of regency rubbish illuminated from behind, in each bedroom and in the bathroom were things called, in the agent's catalogue, 'vanitaries' – built-in dressing-tables with mirrors – the kind of thing actresses are often shown at whilst engaged in emotional scenes with their lovers. The light fittings appeared to be made of gobs of gold and crystal. The staircase had wrought iron bannisters. The iron was twisted like leaves in a particularly offensive manner. The bathroom was excellent except that above the bath was a mosaic of bits of coloured glass. The curtains (which had to be bought with the house) were in a floral pattern and too nauseating. 'I suppose the man's wife has been responsible for the decorations?' I said to the agent. He made a non-committal reply. I said I'd think about the idea and we left. We caught the train home.

'If we bought Kemp Villas,' I said to Kenneth, 'we'd have to rip down the curtains, change the light fittings, tear down the display cabinets and vanitaries and repaper or whitewash the walls.' 'You're paying for those things,' Kenneth said. Number 42 was the only possible house. And that was damp.

Friday 17 March

Kenneth suffering from a tightness in his chest. Rather a row this morning. I went down to collect photographs of *The Good and Faithful Servant*. Called in at Peggy's. Signed a contract or two. Went on to the Criterion to book seats for next Saturday. Leonie and George are supposed to be coming up to London. The woman at the box office said, 'A Swedish producer has been to see *Loot* three times. And now he's bought the book.' 'Is he doing it in Sweden?' I asked. 'He says he's having to think hard,' she said. 'He says that you can't shock the Swedes on certain subjects, but this would shock them very much.' 'How typical!' I said to Kenneth H. when I got home. 'Like saying the nineteenth century wasn't shocked about certain subjects – like polished floors and bonnets.'

The Swedes, like the French, have a strange reputation for broadmindedness and unshockability. On the strength, I suppose, of a few films in which 'free love', 'lesbianism' and 'nude bathing' are indulged in.

And Paris has been living on a reputation for 'naughtiness' for a century or more by the expedient of pretending that 'adultery' and 'little women down the road' are the height of rudery and licence.

America the same. All of them like fifty-year-old virgins talking about the pleasures of sexual intercourse and knowing nothing about the subject – except in theory.

Saturday 18 March

Exhausting wrangles over trivia. Kenneth, lying in bed, suddenly shouted, 'I hope I die of heart disease! I'd like to see you manage then.' He talks a lot of *The Dance of Death*. 'We're living it,' he suddenly said. 'This is Strindberg¹!' Soothed

---

1 August Strindberg (1849–1912). Swedish playwright and author. *The Dance of Death* (1901) was about the brutalising battle for psychic survival in marriage.

down the situation only to have it break out later. 'You're a quite different person, you know, since you had your success.'

In the evening we went to the doctor's. Kenneth wanted to ask about the tightness in his chest. We both had typhoid vaccine and wished for an injection. When we arrived, the surgery was full of Indian women with their children, all of whom had whooping cough and measles. Read disconsolately a copy of *Country Life* and several editions of the *Times* colour supplement. Kenneth went into the surgery first, was away for ten minutes or so and came back to call me in. The doctor had given him his typhoid injection. He gave me mine and after a few pleasantries on the subject of vaccination we left. 'What did he say about your heart?' I said. 'He's prescribed some tablets. I have to take three a day,' Kenneth said. We went home. I've finished the *Savoy Operas* which I've been reading and have now begun the collected works of Tennyson[1]. 'Maud' a really rather remarkable poem. 'The Princess', apart from the lyrics, as ludicrous as the day on which it was written. Went down to the Criterion.

The cast were in diminished spirits, having read in several papers that Malcolm Muggeridge[2] was likely to move into the Criterion in May with *An Evening with Malcolm Muggeridge*. These evil old atheists are everywhere lately.

Kenneth Cranham's hair shone like burnished copper. 'What a wonderful sheen your hair has,' I said. 'I've had a rinse,' he confessed, a little sheepish. 'It looks very nice,' Sheila Ballantine said. 'Lovely under the lights.' 'It does look better,' I said, 'and entirely natural.' Michael Bates depressed us all by announcing that 'all the old ladies will simply flock to see that old fucker Muggeridge.' Came home feeling weak and weary. We've done over 200 performances. The board will be up on Monday, so Mark says.

Sunday 19 March

Kenneth is quite different since he has started taking tablets. So tranquil. I'm shagged out. Like a limp rag. The Sundays have given Muggeridge horrible notices. But if D.A.[3] is determined to bring it in that won't stop him. Walked through the city, past the Barbican development area. How nice it was ruined.

Monday 20 March

I've had a pain in my arm since the doctor's typhus injection. It's subsiding now. Long walk through Regent's Park. Sunshine and the first ghastliness of Spring. Found that the café in the park was partially open. Bought an orangeade and a Coca-Cola. Sat in the blazing light and noticed how hideous the bright sunshine

---

1 Alfred Tennyson (first Baron Tennyson) (1809–92). Poet. 'Maud' (1855), 'The Princess' (1847).
2 Malcolm Muggeridge (1903–). Journalist, author, TV personality.
3 Sir Donald Albery (1914–). Theatre manager and producer.

made everyone (including myself) appear. Like blanched and unsavoury apes. Felt scratchy and soiled. We walked from the park to Oxford Street where we had a cup of tea and a cake at Woolworth's. And then we went to see a Japanese film called *An Actor's Revenge*. Breathtaking direction and photography. Wasn't too keen on the acting. And the storyline wobbled a bit. But I liked it. Not an afternoon wasted.

Peter Willes rang up. 'What do you mean by sending me such an atrocious script?' he said. 'What?' I said. 'All the "O's" are out of line. I can't read a script like that. Haven't you another copy?' 'No,' I said. 'I'll have to get it retyped,' he said. 'I can't let actors see a script in that state.' 'Did you read the script?' I said. 'A little.' 'What did you think of it?' 'I thought it rather dated,' he said, 'though that may have been the effect of the "O's".'

He's going to have lunch with Robert Stephens, who we want to play Eddie, on Wednesday. 'Would you like to come?' he said. 'All right,' I said. 'And for goodness sake buy a new typewriter,' he said, as he rang off.

Tuesday 21 March

Another bright spring day. Feel so weary that, although I haven't been out much, I can hardly move the keys of the typewriter to write this. By the first post came a stupid letter from H. Budgen in Tangier. 'I've fixed a flat for you – in the Socco Chico'. I could've wept with rage. The Socco Chico is the last place I'd want a flat. I'd like to shove something hard and non-human up Budgen's arsehole. He behaves like an escapee from some upper-class hideaway for loonies. Wrote an immediate letter back. Posted it to Kenneth Williams[1], who is going out on Friday.

Willes rang, 'I don't think I'd better take you to lunch tomorrow. It wouldn't be wise.' He said that *The Good and Faithful Servant* is getting the cover of the *TV Times*. A great yawn day. Went to the West End. A hot sun and I wore a great fur coat. Stifling with heat. On the way home I sat behind a young guardsman who was with his mother. He was blonde and as thick as shit. But an interesting type. Dragged myself back home. Have scarcely been able to move with lethargy ever since. Yet feel vaguely restless.

Wednesday 22 March

Kenneth has a pain in his chest when he doesn't take his tablets. He told me this morning. 'They don't last eight hours,' he said. 'When the effect wears off the pain returns.' I hope there's nothing seriously wrong. 'You must go to a specialist if it doesn't get better,' I said.

1 Orton to Kenneth Williams, 16 March 1967: 'Please find a letter enclosed to Henry. Oh, the insanity of the man. He writes to tell me that Reg Allen has got me a flat on the "Socco Chico". He says, "It's very discreet" – only on top of the fucking police station!'

Went to a press conference at twelve. A fat, queeny man welcomed me into the room. He had a brown suit and a jolly queeny face. 'I *do* admire your work,' he said. 'How *do* you think of all those witty remarks?' He gave me some coffee and I had a sandwich. 'Prepared with my own fair hands,' the queeny, red-faced man said in a gay, camp voice. Everybody laughed. A lot of other people came in, all laughing and looking around eagerly to see if any celebrities were about. The only one in sight was Hermione Baddeley.

Peter Willes came up to me with a wonderfully-typed copy of *Entertaining Mr Sloane*. 'There,' he said, 'I've had three copies and they've cost me £20.' I examined the script. 'Very good,' I said. 'It's not for you,' he snatched it away. 'I'm going to give it to Robert Stephens at lunch.' He hurried away.

I was pleased to see that the photographs of *The Good and Faithful Servant* were prominently displayed. More prominently than any of the other plays. This made me glow with pride and a secret glee. I felt rather nasty as I looked around the room. Hermione Baddeley invited me out to lunch. We went to the Wig and Pen Club near the Law Courts. 'Everyone who has a divorce always comes out of the Law Courts and has lunch over here,' Hermione's agent said. He had an enormous meal of gammon and chicken. I had steak and kidney pie and leeks. I love plain food. It tastes better. 'Something simply frightful has happened to my agent,' Hermione said. She meant the senior partner, not the one we were lunching with. 'Dreadful things have taken place,' she looked about her, all pink and powdery like a glamorous marshmallow. 'He's absconded with a lot of money from his clients.' The partner we were lunching with said, 'He appeared in the office and said "I've booked a plane for Durban. If you try to stop me I shall kill myself," and he left.' 'Oh, it's simply frightful,' Hermione said. She was tucking into her food and shaking her head. 'He's an alcoholic,' she said by way of explanation.

When I got back home I found that I'd left my key in the pocket of my jeans. Kenneth was at the dentist's because one of the crowns on his teeth has broken. So I had to sit on the step and wait for nearly an hour till he came back and I could get in.

Thursday 23 March

Post brought a reply from Kenneth Williams to my letter complaining about Budgen's ridiculous behaviour. V. amusing letter. Though I think the spirit of Edna Welthorpe is taking over his personality. He is head over heels in love with her. 'Budgen's a perfect *fool*!' he said. 'You can't entrust her with a thing!' I said I thought class entered into it somewhere. 'The Hon. "Reg" Allen had no difficulty in letting flats to his own kind.' 'You're right there,' Kenneth said. 'She sent me a letter – "it's a good flat – so mind how you go." "Mind how you go." Me! She thinks I'm going to spill wine over everything and set fire to the place.' We talked about *An Actor's Revenge*, which he had seen. 'Everything was integrated into the director's original conception,' he said. 'Not like over here – bits and pieces stuck on – directorial tricks.' He said he had to rush and promised to send me a card from Tangier. 'And don't worry, my darling. I'll fix you up with something nice. Trust your auntie.'

Kenneth H. and I went for a long trot and argued most of the way – traffic and heat aggravating the argument to fever pitch. The argument was about Ivan the Terrible. I forget how it began or ended. At one point Kenneth said, 'You know I'm taking these tablets. They calm me down. And you're working overtime to override the effect of the tablets, aren't you?' When we got home we had a cup of tea and it was smiles until bedtime. These hot, dusty London pavements are no pleasure.

P. Willes rang. 'Robert Stephens was very excited,' he said. 'He's going to let us know on Tuesday.' 'He didn't look as though he'd be shocked,' I said. 'Oh, good gracious me, no!' Willes laughed and I heard something rattling down the wires. 'He thought Patricia Routledge's reactions most amusing.' 'He sounds a nice man,' I said. 'Oh, he's a frightfully nice man,' Willes said, and rang off after a lot of talk about a play by David Rudkin[1], 'which he's written entirely in Japanese. Well, it might just as well be. Japanese and pictures. I simply can't understand it.'

Friday 24 March

Day began sunny. Went for a walk. Caught a bus back at Euston. Kenneth is off to hang his collage-pictures at Freddie Bartman's antique shop, Anno Domini, this afternoon. At two Freddie rang and said he hadn't any nails. Kenneth found that we had some in a tin. He went down to Chelsea by tube at half-past two. The pictures, about twenty in all, we framed a while ago.

After Kenneth had gone I cleaned the bathroom. Then I had a glass of milk and went down the Holloway Road in search of a bit of sex. It was a grey day. The wind blew dust in everybody's eyes. I went round a back street near the tube station and into a lavatory. Only a fattish man in a blue woolly. I wasn't particularly interested. Several more men drifted in: all ugly. In the end the place was full and I decided to leave. I passed through the place, looking to see if any were worth having and suddenly noticed that one – a youngish man – wasn't bad. He followed me out and we walked under the bridge. He was Irish. He had a pale face, hollow cheeks, but pleasant. I said, 'Have you got anywhere to go?' 'I share a room with a mate,' he said. I thought this meant that he had nowhere to go. So I said, 'I don't know anywhere round here.' 'D'you like threesomes?' the

---

1 David Rudkin (1936–). Playwright. Author of *Afore Night Come, Ashes*; and co-author with Francois Truffaut of the film *Farenheit 451*.

young man said. I shrugged. 'It depends who the other fellow is,' I said, thinking at the time that this was a very sensible remark because his mate might be hideous. 'You can come back with me,' he said, 'if you like.' 'Won't your mate mind?' I said. 'I wouldn't be taking you back if he did, would I?' he said, which was another sensible remark to put with mine.

His name was Allan Tills. He was a security guard. I thought he meant police at first, but this wasn't the case. His mate worked in a bar. They had a flat in Highbury. The flat was in a big Victorian house painted blue, and in good condition. His mate was in when we got to the door. I went for a piss and when I came back his mate was introduced to me as Dave. I realised at once that luck was with me: he was well-worth the effort. He had pale blue eyes and had a day's growth of beard. He wore jeans and a check shirt, under the shirt a white vest. He was about twenty-five years old and came from Burnley in Lancashire. He had a softness about his body which wasn't the softness of a woman. I hoped he would let me fuck him. I didn't anticipate having to persuade him. 'D'you want anything to eat?' he said. I said I didn't. 'We're going to have a meal,' A. Tills said, 'I'm famished.' We went into a kitchen. They got fish and chips for themselves and I had a cup of tea. 'Where d'you work?' blue-eyed Dave said. 'At the British Drug Houses,' I said, thinking that it would be ridiculous in a situation like this to tell the truth. 'Where d'you come from?' he said, a bit later. 'Leicester,' I said. 'I've got a mate who plays for Leicester City,' he said. 'I slept with him on the night before his wedding.' 'You must've ruined his wedding night,' I said, more for want of something to say, since the remark hardly made sense. 'Yer,' Dave said.

We went into the bedroom after this. It was a large room with a print of ships in a harbour on the wall. There were two beds – a double one and a single one. On the single bed was a lot of clothes. 'For the laundry,' A. Tills said. He came round and kissed me. 'D'you mind threesomes?' he said, in a rather prurient way I thought. 'No,' I said. He got undressed. He had a thin body, a fuzz of black hair on his chest, a large cock. I didn't take my pants off immediately. Neither did Dave. I remembered that in Tangier Marzuk wouldn't either. In the bed everything went remarkably well. I necked with A. Tills more to show willing than anything else since I'd much rather have begun on Dave. It was like having to eat bread before touching the jelly at school parties. After a decent interval I turned and necked the blue-eyed Dave who had a very sexual body. A. Tills sucked my cock. After a while I turned Dave over and shoved my cock up his arse. He gave a yelp and I took it down. A. Tills produced vaseline and I put it on my cock. A. Tills put some up the blue-eyed Dave's bum and I began again. It went up like a treat. 'Flat! Lie flat!' I said. He did so. Whilst I fucked his arse, A. Tills pulled himself off. Also, and I remember thinking, 'Kinky Irish Catholic get', he kept smacking my buttocks. Actually it was quite exciting. After I'd come and withdrawn, I noticed A. Tills had come. Dave rolled on top of me and rubbed himself off on my belly. We lay in bed for a while, half-asleep. The ceiling was v. clean. Moulding of leaves. An alarm clock beside the bed said 4.00. 'I must go at five,' I said, thinking that Kenneth would be back by then.

A. Tills became amorous again in about fifteen minutes. I got the horn. But didn't really want to be bothered doing much. I got on top of him and began necking him. He moaned a lot. Then, rather to my surprise, the blue-eyed Dave, also with his second wind, began to push his prick up my arse. It seemed rude to refuse to let him do to me what I'd already done to him. And so I let him fuck me. Whether he came or not I don't know. A. Tills said afterwards he felt crushed flat. 'Come again sometime,' Dave said, switching on the television set which burst into life with *Winnie-the-Pooh* by A.A. Milne[1]. 'We'd love to have you.' I did take the address. Whether I'll call again is another matter. 'The best night for us is Monday or Wednesday,' A. Tills said, as he let me out of the front door. I thought they were both very nice fellows.

Saturday 25 March

Fine day. Sunlight. A little wind. Kenneth told me that Freddie Bartman had refused to hang two of the collage-pictures on the grounds that 'some of my friends have warned me that I could be liable to prosecution.' The two pictures are a nude Venus and a picture called *Cosy Couples* – several sections of young men cut from physical culture magazines juxtaposed with large flowers and distant views of houses. Freddie B. is a nervous twit. Like all the middle classes. Too nervous to live. He was even timid of using Kenneth's poster which makes use of Steinberg[2] drawings. 'As though,' Kenneth said, with some truth, 'anybody will go and see the pictures stuck away at the wrong end of the King's Road.' Today I received a fatuous letter from Reginald Allen, an estate agent in Tangier and a friend of H. Budgen's, informing me that he had a flat for me 'in the Grand Zocco'. It was 'sparsely furnished' at the moment, but he hoped the owner 'would spend a little money on it.' Wrote an angry letter suggesting, in a perfectly polite way, using the language of diplomacy, that he ram up his arsehole the flat and what little contents it possessed. I want a decent flat where I can hide from the lousy Tangier wind. Not a hellish dump within a stone's throw of the casbah, the lure of which has long since departed from me. Dropped a note to K. Williams complaining bitterly of the thick-witted friendship of Budgen and a few lines to Budgen letting him know that he is a fool and consequently can stop

---

1 A.A. Milne (1882–1956). Prolific author of plays, novels, biography and essays, all over-shadowed by his children's books. *Winnie-the-Pooh* (1926).
2 Saul Steinberg (1914–). Rumanian-born American cartoonist.

studying to pass the entrance exam into the duffer's club.[1] 'The trouble with all these middle- and upper-class idiots,' Kenneth H. said, 'is that all their paltry lives they've been insulated against the opinions of other people by the thick wads of money surrounding them. Nobody ever says to them "You're a fool." Boring, nutty, fatuous ex-public school layabouts.' They also imagine that anyone from the working classes is automatically going to accept their old buck on any subject. I hope they're sadly disillusioned in my case. 'It's not the working classes who're likely to misbehave in a flat,' I spat angrily at K.H. wishing he were Budgen. 'It's their lousy gin-drinking class: spilling cigarette ends and vermouth over the carpets. Some of the dirtiest eaters I've seen have graduated from stately homes. And are proud of it.'

I've read *Black Mischief*[2] (patchy – Waugh isn't up to Firbank[3], the source); *Iolanthe*[4] – (good on the printed page, mangled by Sadler's Wells); *Caprice*[5] – (Firbank is the only impressionist in the English novel). And *Our Theatre in the Nineties*[6] (it might've been written last Sunday – very depressing). Went for a walk tonight. They seem to be pulling down the Imperial Hotel. How many more interesting buildings will go west? As we walked along the Euston Road, St Pancras Station came into view. It won't be much longer before the vandals attack that.

Leonie (seven months pregnant) and George came to London. I met them outside Lyons in Coventry Street. Brought them back home rather than wander around for several hours until the curtain goes up on *Loot*. Talked. Leonie keeps looking up articles on childbirth in dictionaries and women's magazines. We went to see *Loot*. I had a word with Sheila and the boys before curtain-up. Michael Bates over-acting, so I was told. Saw the performance which was excellent. Audience reaction v. good. Shocked and delighted in the right quantities. I heard a woman saying, on leaving the theatre, 'I thoroughly enjoyed that,' and her husband asking, 'I was right then to get the tickets?' One of the first overheard remarks that've been favourable. Simon Ward said, 'It was very good tonight,

---

1 Orton to Kenneth Williams, 25 March 1968: 'This morning (Saturday) I received an absolutely fatuous letter from R. Allen. He offered some crumby flat in the Grand Socco. (Not Socco Chico as Beau-jean informed me – I have the letter before me in H.'s own handwriting. Needless to say I don't want the Grand Socco – all those wretched native fiestas. In any case Eliot makes the flat sound like a Joan Littlewood set. "At the moment it is sparsely furnished; but one of the owners will be here next week and I hope he will spend a little money on it." Thank you very much. I hope you'll explain that unless Eliot can offer something civilised, he can go and get fucked!'
2 By Evelyn Waugh (1903–1966), 1932.
3 Ronald Firbank (1886–1926). Novelist. For his influence on Orton see *Prick Up Your Ears*, pp. 125–8.
4 By W.S. Gilbert and Arthur Sullivan, 1882.
5 By Ronald Firbank, 1917.
6 *Our Theatre in the Nineties* (3 vols.). By George Bernard Shaw, 1932.

didn't you think so?' 'Yes,' I said. 'That's because you were here,' he said. 'It was a different performance.' Promised to see the show at least once a fortnight. Introduced Leonie and George all round. Took them to St Pancras where they were catching the train to Canning Town to spend the night with George's auntie. 'Don't suppose we shall be able to stay in London again until the baby is walking,' Leonie said. On the tube, Sheila and I got into conversation with a drunk South African who'd been celebrating the boat race. When we got up at Kings Cross, he followed us. 'Is he coming with us?' I said to Sheila. 'I hope not,' she said. George stopped to look at a poster and we waited. The pissed South African disappeared. We left Leonie and George. 'I'll take you home if he looks like following,' I said, not relishing the thought of travelling to Belsize Park and then having to make my way back. When we got to Sheila's platform there was no sign of the drunk. I kissed her. 'You shouldn't talk to these strange men,' I said. 'It's the story of my life,' she said, getting on the train. I went home and Kenneth was in bed. 'They liked it,' I said. 'They thought it a better play than *Sloane.*'

Sunday 26 March

Easter Day. Nothing on television but uplifting programmes. BBC crooning to itself as usual. Spent the day reading. Didn't shave. Went for a longish walk. Kenneth, who read *The Observer*, tells me of the latest way-out group in America – complete sexual licence.[1] 'It's the only way to smash the wretched civilisation,' I said, making a mental note to hot-up *What the Butler Saw* when I came to rewrite. 'It's like the Albigensian heresy[2] in the eleventh century,' Kenneth said. Looked up the article in the *Encyclopaedia Britannica*. Most interesting. Yes. Sex is the only way to infuriate them. Much more fucking and they'll be screaming hysterics in next to no time. 'Innocent III', Kenneth said, 'did for them.' 'It isn't going to be so easy to mount a crusade this time,' I said. We watched an unbelievably awful film with Gregory Prick[3], *Twelve O'Clock High*. Some kind of tract on 'team-spirit'. 'It's all like a particularly intense girls' gym team,' Kenneth said. Film ended with Gregory Prick having a kind of brainstorm. Only a plentiful supply of peanuts at my elbow prevented my own brain from whirling into a hurricane.

Wednesday 29 March

Easter celebrations over. Feel in a better mood. Rang Peggy about the Beatles' film script. She promised to write a letter to Shenson. The real trouble, she feels,

1 The Living Theatre, founded by Julian Beck (1925–1985) and Judith Malina (1926–   ).
2 The Albigensian movement, which gained popularity in the eleventh century, believed in the coexistence of God and the Evil One. They saw a conflict between soul which was from God and creation which came from the devil. Man was a fallen spirit imprisoned in an evil body and circumscribed by an evil world. They renounced the material order, promoting extreme asceticism, absolute chastity, abstaining from meat in all its forms, including milk and cheese. In 1208, the Pope proclaimed an Albigensian Crusade. They were stamped out with considerable cruelty.
3 Gregory Peck (1916–   ). Actor and producer.

is Epstein. An amateur and a fool. He isn't equipped to judge the quality of a script. Probably he will never say 'yes', equally hasn't the courage to say 'no'. A thoroughly weak, flaccid type. Oscar is keen to do the script of *Up Against It*. He probably would do it better anyway. Extraordinary the way someone like Epstein has absolutely no idea how valuable a property the Beatles are. Having commissioned a script he can waste time until it is taken from him. He'll then be back at square one with the original script (which was dull and of no interest), or faced with the job of commissioning another script from another author.

Letter from Kenneth Williams in Tangier. He says he's enjoying himself immensely (though considering that the letter was posted on the 25th and he only arrived on that day how he can be enjoying himself yet is a mystery). He complains that the letter I sent H. Budgen is unpleasant. Imagined at first that he had received already the letter I posted on Saturday. Rather put out to realise that K.W. was talking of the letter I gave him to pass on to H.B. As the first letter was reasonableness itself (with a sharp word or two for sauce), I'm apprehensive of the letter posted on Saturday. I imagine Budgen bursting into tears on receiving it.

I'm reading Swift[1]. *Gulliver's Travels*[2] – Lilliput and Brobdingnag amount merely to trick photography – Laputa a bit strained, though the section on the scientists was pungent enough. The most superior part of the book is the last part among the Yahoos. On the whole I rather agree with Dr Johnson[3] – Swift is an overrated writer. Have now read *The Tale of a Tub*[4]. Far superior to *Gulliver's Travels*, though the digressions are over-played, also the trick of pretending a gap in the text. The whole scheme clever, but not sufficiently worked out. The ending a disappointment. *The Battle of the Books* really isn't up to standard. *The Bickerstaff Papers*[5] quite a good practical joke, nothing more. I'm inclined to think that the main fascination of Swift (as with Dylan Thomas[6], Brendan Behan[7] and many other writers and artists) is with his life. His art certainly doesn't warrant the merit attached to him.

1 Jonathan Swift (1667–1745). Irish satirist.
2 By Jonathan Swift, 1726. Nearly all Swift's writing was originally published anonymously; and this satiric novel was the only one for which he was paid (£200).
3 Dr Samuel Johnson (1709–84). Critic and poet.
4 By Jonathan Swift. A satire on the 'corruptions in religion and learning'. Published together with *The Battle of the Books*, 1704.
5 *Bickerstaff Papers*. Isaac Bickerstaff was a fictional character invented by Swift much as Orton had invented Edna Welthorpe. In 1708, Swift published a parody 'Predictions for the Ensuing Year by Isaac Bickerstaff'. One of his predictions was the death of John Partridge, a cobbler who claimed to be an astrologer and published his prophecies in an almanac. Swift then published a letter claiming Partridge had died. Partridge countered with an irate letter claiming he was alive. Swift had the final laugh in 'Vindication' which 'proved' that Partridge was dead.
6 Dylan Thomas (1914–53). Poet.
7 Brendan Behan (1923–64). Irish playwright.

Thursday 30 March

Kenneth and I went to see Hermione Baddeley in *The Killing of Sister George*. Really, I suppose, it would've been better to see her at an evening performance, but the idea of traipsing all the way to Wimbledon to witness a performance of a play which I don't particularly fancy, and have seen once anyway, at eight o'clock at night and getting back about twelve didn't appeal to me. Yet I'd promised Hermione that I'd come. So the matinee it was. Actually it was fun. The place was full of Wimbledon matrons of the nastier sort and old people in various stages of mental and physical decay. The theatre was crumbling, the paintwork dirty, the carpets threadbare: the house had seen better days. Two or three usherettes in rusty, black dresses bustled about, taking orders for tea during the intervals.

Kenneth and I found our seats, on the aisle, row N. There was an elderly woman sitting in one of them. We showed her our tickets. 'The lady said I could sit anywhere,' she said. 'I've only got one eye.' This gave us pause for thought. 'Well, you can have the seat if you like,' I said. 'No, no! I'll go somewhere else. Only with my eye I have to be so careful or I can't see.' I felt very guilty as she hurried away to another seat. The pianist began playing a selection of popular songs of the past fifty years. The audience brightened considerably. There was a buzz of anticipation in the air. A lot more women came in. 'I don't suppose they'll understand what the play is about,' I said to Kenneth. 'Don't you believe it,' he said. 'They'll know very well what it's about.' He was right. It became clear, from the opening scenes, that they understood and weren't amused. Hermione bounced around giving an absolutely outrageous performance. Everyone else in the play was repertory standard. There were hardly any laughs. The lesbianism seemed to stun them. Though I'd thought it was a second-rate play in the West End, light and offenceless, Wimbledon wasn't up to it. Glumly they sat. At the end of the first act the tea-trays were passed around and the piano began to play; this was the part the audience enjoyed. The second act began. There are two scenes in this act. When the curtain came down on the first scene half the audience thought it was the end of the act and the aisles of the theatre were suddenly crowded with old men and women hobbling out into the foyer. Suddenly the curtain shot up on the second scene and, to murmurs of irritation and surprise, the audience slunk back to its seat. During the third act, alarm grew at the (to them) uncontrolled sexual perversion and (to me) flat unimaginative dialogue. At the moment where Sister George orders her companion to drink the bathwater, a couple of old ladies rose and stumbled out. Kenneth and I went back to see Hermione, who looked very rouged and roguish. 'Oh, you naughty thing,' she said, 'you shouldn't've come at a matinee!' 'Why not?' I said, 'the audience gave an excellent performance.'

Friday 31 March

Unpleasant day. Constant rowing over small things. Kenneth suggested we go for a walk to Hampstead Heath. We got the tube to Hampstead and walked up Hampstead High Street. We passed a café called 'Ah, Bistro!' 'Why do these people have to be so facetious?' Kenneth said. We got to the heath without the expenditure of much nervous energy, except that I glumly refused to look in an estate agent's window. We walked across the heath to Golders Green. On the way, minor tiffs occurred – when Kenneth refused to talk about Brian Epstein's extraordinary behaviour in ignoring my film script, and when I refused to go and look at some deer. 'Horrible rat-like creatures,' I snapped, imagining he'd meant the wallabies in the park. 'It's obvious you haven't looked where I'm pointing,' Kenneth said. 'I can't understand you,' Kenneth said, 'you have no liking for the country, have you? You'd be content to walk up and down the Pentonville Road till your balls dropped off.' We took the tube back from Golders Green. Sitting on the platform Kenneth said, 'I get so fed-up with your constant moaning. You're the difficult one to live with. Everybody says so.' 'Who?' I said. 'Oh, everybody. Peter Willes, Peggy. They all know that I'm the easy-going one.' 'Peter Willes thinks *you're* a moan,' I said, stuffily, and got onto the tube.

When we were back at home I settled down to read the *Encyclopaedia Britannica*. I looked up William III, then William II. And then I turned to Queen Anne. I wonder if Lewis Carroll[1] had been reading about Anne's reign when he wrote *Alice in Wonderland?* The Queen and the Duchess seem reminiscent of Anne and the Duchess of Marlborough. Kenneth reading Volume Two of *Our Theatre in the Nineties*. He suddenly looked up and said, 'Sardou's[2] *Divorçons* was playing in London in 1896.' It's been on as *Let's Get a Divorce*[3] for the past six months. 'We ought to see that,' I said. Kenneth agreed and, feeling suddenly merry, I rang the Comedy Theatre to find out the times. We went down and booked a couple of seats at 30*s*.

Before seeing *Let's Get a Divorce*, we went round to the Criterion and talked to the cast of *Loot*. They were feeling happier because the audiences had brightened up. Michael Bates arrived at the last moment having been on a train that was half-an-hour late. We left as the curtain went up.

The Sardou play was grim. Lots of running about, but not a single funny line. A third act that was a joke (unintentional); there wasn't a single situation of any

1 Lewis Carroll. The pen-name of Charles Lutwidge Dodgson (1832–1898). Lecturer in mathematics at Oxford and author of, among others, *Alice's Adventures in Wonderland*. Orton: 'I'm a great admirer of the absolute logic of *Alice in Wonderland* ... It's the kind of logic I put into my own plays.'

2 Victorien Sardou (1831–1908). French playwright. One of the most commercially successful dramatists of his day. Henry James called him a 'supremely clever contriver'.

3 By Victorien Sardou, 1880.

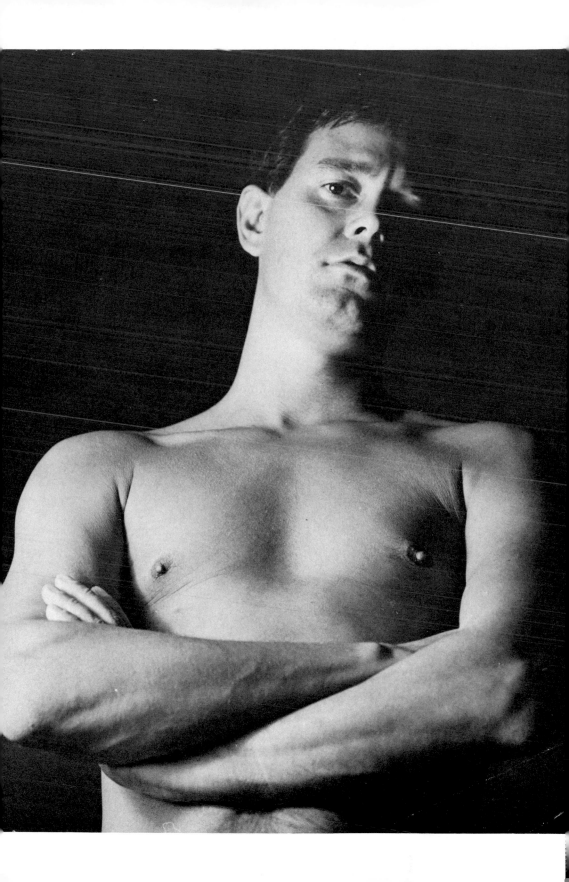

Previous page:
Orton, 1965

Left:
Orton at desk, 1966

Right:
Donald Pleasence and
Hermione Baddeley in *The
Good and Faithful Servant*

Below left:
Peter Gill discusses the set of
Crimes of Passion with cast.
Orton in cap, 1967

Below right:
Orton outside 25 Noel Road

Above: Orton, drawn by Patrick Procktor, 1967
Below: Orton, 1964
Opposite: Orton: 'I shall be the most perfectly developed of modern playwrights if nothing else.'

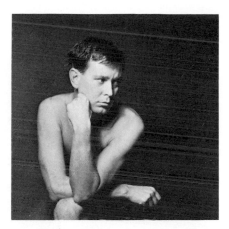
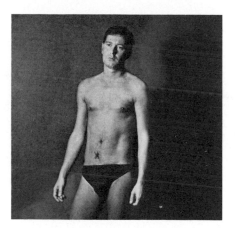

Orton, 1967

Overleaf:
The successful playwright,
1966

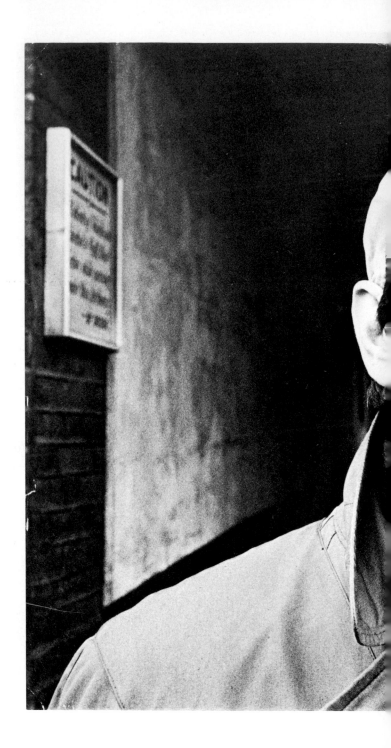

interest. Sardou should be left where he belongs, gathering dust on the shelf in some museum of the commercial theatre.[1]

Saturday 1 April

Post brought a letter from Reginald Allen. He says H. Budgen had misled him. He offered the flat with the terrace garden which Budgen had last year. I posted a cheque off at once reserving the flat for May and June. Both Kenneth and myself feel happier now. Though I'll not be entirely happy until I receive a letter confirming the booking.

Leonie wrote to say that Marilyn had behaved disgracefully last Sunday. She'd promised to have my father for the day and at 7.30 on Sunday morning she turned up to say she was going to the seaside for the day. Would he mind getting his own dinner? He had nothing in the house. He had to go next door. I wrote to Marilyn. Why, I'm not sure. I can't do any good.[2]

Sunday 2 April

Did nothing all day. Rained continually. Couldn't go out. Read *Cards of Identity* by Nigel Dennis.[3] After I finished this I started to read the hymns in *The Book of Common Prayer*. Watched *My Favourite Brunette* on television. This was the film during which, on its first release, I was interfered with. I don't remember much about the film. It wasn't bad. Superficial, though. The gags were mechanical. Only one in ten really funny. Peter Willes rang to say, 'There's a big picture of Hermione in your play in *The Sunday Times*.' I went out and bought *The Sunday Times* and found that it was a small picture. The papers seem to be in one of their simpering moods. A caption of the revival of Coward's *Fallen Angels*[4] reads 'roses all the way' and goes on to say that 'roses, the drinks table and the white telephone is back'. Kenneth has decided that what is wrong with him isn't his heart but his liver. He isn't eating. Just sipping milk every few hours. Most tiresome. I got my own lunch. There was nothing in the cupboard but spaghetti. I had spaghetti and cheese and tomatoes. As Kenneth has decided to go on hunger

---

1 Orton's verdict was shared by G.B. Shaw who coined the phrase "Sardoodledum" for the boulevard entertainments.
2 Marilyn Lock to Joe Orton, 7 April 1967: '. . . I must say how upset I was to receive your letter over such a small matter. I'm not a selfish bitch . . . So you think I want to wash my hands of Dad, do you? Well, if you came home a bit more you would know. I know you are busy but you have time to go on holiday and because Pete and I went away for one day, the whole family goes wild. I do my bit, but at the same time, I have a baby of 18 months old and also a husband and I go out to work full-time. I think I've got my hands full, don't you?'
3 By Nigel Dennis (1912–   ), 1955.
4 By Noël Coward, 1925.

strike I shall now get all my own meals. This doesn't worry me particularly, except that it means we're starting to live quite separate lives.

Monday 3 April

Willes rang to say that Robert Stephens loved *Entertaining Mr Sloane* and would like to do it if his dates fit in. Long argument with Kenneth, the gist of which was 'Tell me what you want for lunch and I'll get it.' 'I'll have eggs and bacon.' 'You can't because the shops are shut.' He then began to argue over suitcases. 'I don't think we should buy new ones.' Since, as I pointed out to him, he was the one who suggested we bought new ones in the first place, this rather surprised me. 'Are you going to wear your blue suit for the summer?' he said. 'No,' I said. 'Then why did you have the trousers altered?' he said. 'If you hadn't had them altered I could've worn them.' 'But if you could wear them,' I said, 'they wouldn't've fitted me. That's why I had them altered.' 'And now they don't fit me,' he said. 'No,' I said. 'But if they'd've fitted you they wouldn't've fitted me. And as they didn't fit me I had them altered. And now I've had them altered they don't fit you.'

Tuesday 4 April

Kenneth, who hasn't eaten anything but milk and grapefruit since Saturday, complains now that he hasn't shit for two days. He took an opening medicine. Arguments continue spasmodically. Breaking out like sudden flames on a dying fire. We went into the West End this morning. I bought a new typewriter. It cost eighty-odd pounds. Then Kenneth bought a tie made of silk which is faked to look like sacking. I bought a pair of corduroy jeans – a sort of parchment colour. Argument over the fact that I bought two typewriter ribbons for 15s. and normally only pay 7s. 6d. for them. Then over socks. I bought a pair for 19s. 6d. and Kenneth claims they're not as good as ones I could've got for half the price. Tiring day.

  Rang Peggy to ask about *Up Against It*. She says that Shenson's secretary rang to tell her that the script would be sent back. No explanation of why. No criticism of the script. And, apparently, Brian Epstein has no comment to make either. Fuck them.[1]

---

1 Joe Orton, *Evening Standard*, 10 April 1967: 'Why, after all, did they come to me? They must have seen *Loot* and know what kind of a writer I am. I gather that the script wasn't conventional enough. But compared to *Loot*, I wrote it with corsets on. I must admit I always thought that the combination of the Beatles, whom I admire very much, and myself, was too good to be true . . .'

Tuesday 6 April

Went to P. Willes's for dinner this evening.[1] 'I've got Lord Swinton[2] coming,' he said. 'Who's he?' I said, imagining he'd dreamed up some chinless wonder from somewhere. 'Oh, good heavens, how ignorant you are,' he said, practically ripping my coat from me in a rage. 'He was the air minister in the war. A great intellectual in his day. Of course he's eighty-four now. I do hope you won't be bored.' 'I won't be bored,' I said. 'But isn't it a bit tactless to invite an old man to see *The Good and Faithful Servant?*' P. Willes thought not. We talked until Kenneth noticed a pair of nutcrackers on the table. They were rather unusual. The end part, where the nut is placed, was shaped like a human head. The nut goes into the mouth and the jaws crack it. 'Do you know who that is?' Willes said, referring to the head. 'It's a portrait then?' I said. 'Yes. He was a very famous man in his day.' 'He must've been,' I said, 'to have been immortalised in a pair of nutcrackers.' We tried to guess who the face was. Kenneth thought it was Owen Nares[3]. I suggested Dr Goebbels[4]. 'It's Austen Chamberlain[5],' Willes said, when we gave up. 'He was Foreign Secretary. I'm going to send them to his daughter. As a joke. She will be crawss.' We all laughed at the idea until the doorbell rang. Willes went to answer it. 'He's dotty,' Kenneth whispered.

Willes came back with an old man. He was slight, with a little fuzz of grey hair over an almost bald head. He stood in the doorway peering about then he changed his spectacles and focused on me. 'This is Joe,' Willes said, 'and this is his friend Kenneth Halliwell.' We all shook hands and Lord Swinton, who wore rather dowdy clothes, stumbled breathlessly to a seat. He looked exactly like an old age pensioner in a back street in Leicester. Willes said, 'What will you have to drink?' 'Eh?' said Lord Swinton, looking up sharply. 'Do you want sherry?' Willes said. 'Is it dry?' Lord Swinton said. 'No,' I said, 'it's very sweet.' 'Will you have a sherry?' Willes repeated. 'Yes,' Lord Swinton said. Willes gave him a sherry and sat down. We began to talk about peeing. 'Joe goes all the time,' Peter Willes said, 'I can't understand him. He's like you.' 'I hardly ever go,' Kenneth said.

1 Peter Willes: 'I was the only gent Joe ever met. I introduced him to a different kind of life and attitude. Like I did Pinter. Joe had refinement by nature. He had charming manners. When I took Dorothy Dickson to *Loot*, he said: "Miss Dickson, I've just been playing one of your records" ... That was a pretty charming thing to say to someone then in her seventies. He was there to meet her in the foyer. A unique thing for a young writer to do.'

2 Lord Swinton (1884–1972). Secretary of State for Air, 1935–8; Minister for Civil Aviation, 1944–5; Deputy Leader of the House of Lords, 1952–5. Responsible for development of the Spitfire. George VI said, 'If there hadn't been a Swinton, there wouldn't have been an England.'

3 Owen Nares. (1888–1943). English matinee idol.

4 Joseph Paul Goebbels (1897–1945). Nazi Minister of Enlightenment and Propaganda. The most educated of the senior Nazi leaders with a D. Phil. from Heidelberg University.

5 Sir Austen Chamberlain (1863–1937). Distinguished politician. Foreign Secretary 1924–9. Received the Nobel Peace Prize for negotiating the Locarno Pact.

Lord Swinton coughed a little over the sherry. 'I really didn't come here to discuss your water-works,' he said. 'Is that sherry too sweet?' Willes raised his voice as though talking to someone in the next room. 'He's deaf!' he whispered to me. 'I wish you'd shut up, Peter,' Lord Swinton cackled, 'I'm perfectly all right.' 'We've been looking at Austin Chamberlain's head,' I said. 'On my nutcrackers,' Willes said, quickly. 'I knew him,' Lord Swinton said. 'Yes, we know that,' Willes said. 'Have you sent them to his daughter yet?' Lord Swinton said. 'No.' 'She'll be very crawss with you, Peter.' Lord Swinton laughed to himself. 'We thought it was Dr Goebbels,' I said. 'Odious man!' Lord Swinton said. On the table was a silver box. It had June 1938 and a coat of arms on it. 'Was it an anniversary?' I said. 'He gave it to me,' P. Willes said. 'He was presented with all sorts of rubbish when he was air minister,' he picked up the box and examined it. 'Does it say who gave it me?' Lord Swinton said. 'No. It just says "June 1938",' I said. 'Is there a coat of arms?' Lord Swinton said. 'Yes.' He took the box and looked at it. Shook his head. 'I can't remember who gave it to me,' he said, and looked sadly about him. 'He forgets, you know,' Willes said. 'I wanted a box and he just picked this up and gave it to me.' Later Lord Swinton was talking about somebody and said, 'D'you remember my remark? I said he was every other inch a gentleman. That's rather good, isn't it. Is it original? Did I invent that?' 'It is good,' I said. 'I shall steal it.' 'I make you a present of it,' said Lord Swinton.

We went out to a restaurant to have dinner. I was talking about realism in writing. 'You must be my literary executor,' Lord Swinton said. 'I thought I was your executor,' Willes said. 'You're an executor,' said Lord Swinton. 'Well, I don't know why I ever consented to it,' Willes said. 'It'll mean a lot of hard work.' 'I'm leaving you £1,000,' Lord Swinton said. Willes looked quite put out. 'Only a thousand? Oh, how mean of you. You can afford much more than that. You ought to leave me £5,000 at least.' He then said that nobody would care if he lived to be a hundred. 'You'd get a telegram from the Queen,' I said. 'I get telegrams from her all the time, God bless her,' Lord Swinton said. 'What's she like?' I said, unable to pretend that I wasn't interested and sinking to the level of a reader of *The Daily Express*. 'Well, you know, she enjoys it,' Lord Swinton said, surprisingly. 'And it must be fun. Anything must be fun. I said to Harold Macmillan[1] the other night – and really he's getting more like Winston every day – I said, "Was it fun being PM?" and he said, "D'you know, it was really." Things should be fun. No point in them otherwise.' He went on to say he'd asked George VI[2] if it was 'fun' being a king. George VI had replied, after a long pause, 'Oh, no. It's not fun.' 'But, surely, sire, I can come and go, but you're here for

1 Sir Harold Macmillan (Earl of Stockton) (1894–   ). British prime minister (1957–63).
2 George VI (1895–1952). On the abdication of his elder brother, Edward VIII, (whom the family called 'David'), he ascended the throne in 1936.

keeps.' 'David wasn't,' the King had replied. And then repeated, 'No, it's not fun.' But, Lord Swinton said, 'I asked the Queen the same question, "Is it fun, ma'am?" And she delighted me by saying, "Yes. It is fun."' 'He's a wonderful old man,' Peter Willes said, nodding over his ice-cream. 'But I do think, Philip, that you should leave me more money in your will. It's disgraceful! Really it is!'

We went back to Willes's flat and watched *The Good and Faithful Servant* on television. It wasn't perfect, but it was v. good. Lord Swinton, rather shattered at first, I thought, but then went overboard. 'Wonderful, wonderful,' he kept saying, 'this boy has real talent.' We talked some more until his car came and he was taken home. Then Peter Willes made some more coffee and we chatted until nearly midnight.

Friday 7 April

Peter Willes rang me at about nine o'clock. 'I simply couldn't wait any longer,' he said. 'I went round at five o'clock and got the papers.' 'What are they like?' I asked. 'Marvellous notices in *The Daily Mail* and *The Sun*. The rest haven't bothered. They've reviewed the posh documentary on witch doctors on the BBC.' Very typical of the puritan mentality; finding that the theatre won't be naturalistic enough for them they invent the documentary and stick to it. P. Willes read the notices out. They were good. I felt v. pleased. Later in the morning Peter Gill[1], who directed *The Ruffian on the Stair* at the Royal Court for a Sunday night performance last year, rang and said that the Court wished to put the *Ruffian* on with another one-act. They've already seen *The Erpingham Camp*. I suggested he read *The Good and Faithful Servant*. It isn't suitable. I haven't yet rewritten it for the stage, but they may as well see what it's like. In the afternoon I took the script down to the Court[2] and had tea with Peter Gill. Peggy v. excited that *Crimes of Passion* (as the double-bill is called) will be going on at the Court.

Sunday 9 April

Once again I was rung up by P. Willes at before nine o'clock. 'A marvellous notice in *The Sunday Times*,' he said, 'nothing in the others.' He then read the notice which was excellent. 'I've had the most startling reactions from Television House,' he said. 'Terrifying ones from some people. They hated and loathed it. One director said you just couldn't write. You were a hopeless writer and that it was ridiculous for the critics to heap such praise upon your head. But other people have been coming up to me and singing your praises. Extraordinary reactions. I've never had a play like it before.'

1 Peter Gill. (1939–). Director and playwright. Plays include *Kick for Touch*, *Small Change*.
2 Orton to Glenn Loney, 12 March 1966: 'The Royal Court are now doing Repertory. And doing it very badly. The rocks are looming for the R.C. (Not the Church, though that isn't looking so good lately either.) The Mermaid is awful. The National is middle-class. Stratford dithers . . .'

Kenneth and I went to see the dress rehearsal of *Rosencrantz and Guildenstern are Dead*[1], a new play at the National. V. interesting. A wonderful idea. I'd give anything to have such an original idea. Unfortunately the only drama in the play is by Shakespeare. There kept being the usual dialogue between two bored people waiting for something to happen and playing games to while away the time. This derived from *Look Back in Anger*[2] and *Waiting for Godot*[3] in equal parts. It's been done many, many times in the last ten years: *Green Julia*[4], *Little Malcolm*, *Won't Somebody Please Say Something*. The interest in this play was that the two who have the duologues are Rosencrantz and Guildenstern. They arrive at Elsinore and we go into the play by Shakespeare for a brief few moments. Then the two students, left alone, comment on what is happening. Knowing nothing of the plot of *Hamlet*, they have to discover the situation for themselves. This is fascinating and terribly funny until the end of the second act. This act ends with Hamlet (upstage) talking to himself – we know he is saying the 'How all occasions do inform against me' soliloquy. When he tells Rosencrantz and Guildenstern to 'go before me' we know that W. Shakespeare (the dramatist in the play) has left us. The third act is the modern author's invention (apart from the pirate episode) and it isn't good enough. In fact it isn't there. What a wonderful idea, though. How I wish I'd stumbled onto it. It should've been about the futility of students – always talking, talking, talking and never doing anything. Great events, murders, adulteries, dreadful revenge happening all around them and they just talk.[5] This is what the play should've been about and wasn't.

Monday 10 April

Spent the day finishing the typescript of *Up Against It* for Oscar Lewenstein. I've turned the four Beatles into three young men. It's a much better script without the weight of stars hanging on it. Kenneth and I went to see *The Deadly Affair*[6] at the local Odeon. V. good film.

Tuesday 11 April

Went to see Peter Gill at his flat. We talked over casting. He made a curious lunch out of a tin. Met Donald Howarth[7] who lives upstairs. V. interesting

---

1 By Tom Stoppard (1937–   ), 1966.
2 By John Osborne (1929–   ), 1956.
3 By Samuel Beckett (1906–   ), 1953.
4 By Paul Abelman (1927–   ), 1966.
5 Orton's *What the Butler Saw* takes this comic tack. Torture, nymphomania, transvestism, incest, blackmail, bribery are what's happening, while the psychiatrists twist the experience into a meaning all their own.
6 *The Deadly Affair* (1966). With James Mason, Simone Signoret. Directed by Sidney Lumet.
7 Donald Howarth (1931–   ). Playwright and director. Literary manager of the Royal Court, 1975–6.

setting. I'm now engaged in rewriting the middle section of *The Erpingham Camp*, which is to be performed with *The Ruffian*.

Wednesday 12 April

Still busy on *The Erpingham Camp*. Oscar rang. He's going to offer me £10,000 and ten per cent of the producer's profits for *Up Against It*. In actual fact I shall be making more money than if the Beatles had made the film.

Thursday 13 April

Oscar rang and asked to see the original Beatles version of *Up Against It*. I'm seeing him for lunch on Friday. Ian Horobin[1] rang and asked me to go to lunch with him on Tuesday. I said I'd be in Tangier from 7 May, all being well. I told him that I was taking a flat behind the Djenina Hotel. 'There've been two murders in that alleyway during the last few weeks,' he said. I've also been asked to go on the Eamonn Andrews[2] programme on the twenty-third of this month. Kenneth Williams came round tonight. He was full of stories of Easter spent in Tangier. 'It was beautiful,' he said. 'I found wild thyme growing on the hillside.' He then said that he and an actor called John Hussey had entered a café run by Lilly, an American woman. She waddled towards them and said, 'Now, how about trying my fish mousse?' 'I'd rather look at your meat loaf,' John Hussey said. Without a tremor the woman replied, sharply, 'With the red cabbage?' 'Yes,' they said. 'And to follow, the prune fool, with hot chocolate sauce?' 'Yes,' they said. At the end of the meal Kenneth said, 'Well, Lilly, we can pay your food no greater compliment than to say we came in without any appetite and we've eaten everything you put before us.' Without pausing Lilly replied, 'Yeah. Well, it's 45 dirhams.' Which is daylight robbery (about £3 10s.).

I told him of my conversation with Ian Horobin. 'Take no notice of her,' Kenneth W. said. 'Those two murders – one was a queen who'd been bashed because she'd promised this kid money and then said, "Oh, I'll give it you tomorrow." She was in Maxim's bar the next night with three stitches in her head. She wasn't dead. Or if she was,' he said, suddenly laughing, 'or if she was she was as big a queen dead as alive. And the other "murder" was some Moroccan thumping a kid because he wouldn't give him some money. He was around the next day as well.' He told us of a drag-queen who'd written to the owner of one of the bars asking for a job. Kenneth W. then gave a long portrait of a dismal drag queen writing a witty letter begging employment. He did it with

1 Sir Ian Horobin (1899–1976). Parliamentary Secretary of Power, 1958–9; Warden, Harfield House University Settlement, 1923–61. MP Southwark Central Div. 1931–5; Oldham East, 1951–9. Author of *Pleasures of Planning Poems*.
2 Eamonn Andrews (1922–   ). TV compere and interviewer.

roguish looks, winks, nods and flips of the hand, sudden climbs in the pitch of his voice which now and then trembled on the edge of hysteria. 'I play to the house. I'll be in the neighbourhood of the Petit Socco in the summer and wonder if you'd like to offer me a job at your delightful bar-bistro. I shan't see much of the ceiling, I expect. Tangier is certainly the place for the homos. Well, cheerio, and keep your cheques and your legs crossed.' He paused suddenly, 'She was dreadful. I mean, "keep your cheques and your legs crossed," did you ever hear anything like it?' He then said that Budgen was shattered by my letter to him. Under Kenneth's influence I typed a letter to him on my new typewriter. ('German,' Kenneth said. 'Six million Jews gassed and you buy their typewriters!') 'She'll put *her* head in the gas oven when she reads that. Poor Henrietta Beaujean.'

Friday 14 April

Spent the morning writing *The Erpingham Camp*. I've now mapped a complete new middle to the play. It seems to be coming rather well. I had an inspiration on the end. In the original television play Erpingham falls from the high-diving board. I'd rather clumsily made this possible for the stage by making him fall out of the window. This isn't good. I'd been trying to think of some way to kill him, swiftly, dramatically, not involving too many production difficulties and possible on the stage, also ludicrous. I had a vision of him shooting up into the air. This wasn't practical – how could someone do that? And then I got it – he must fall through the floor! As long as the Royal Court have a trap it will work.

Oscar wanted to discuss *Up Against It*. He thinks we may have to build up one of the young men's parts in order to tempt a star to play it. He's going to give the script to a director as soon as he's had an opportunity of rereading it.

Kenneth Halliwell has been to a new doctor. The doctor examined him and said he hadn't got an appendicitis. He said it was nervous and has given him some tranquillisers. 'It's because your mother died when you were eleven and it was a traumatic experience.[1] You are imagining this appendicitis out of guilt,' he said. 'Whatever are you guilty about?' I said. 'I don't know,' Kenneth said.

Finished *The Erpingham Camp* this evening and read it through. I'm very pleased with it. It's by far the best thing I've written for the stage so far. I only hope Peter Gill thinks the same.

Saturday 15 April

Letter from Oscar enclosing a copy of a letter written to him by some irate man (or woman) who'd been to see *Loot*. The letter said we should advertise the play

---

1 In September 1937, Daisy Halliwell died from a wasp sting on her finger.

as 'immoral'. Intend to write an Edna Welthorpe letter to them expressing my complete agreement with their disgust.

Went down to the Royal Court. Bought two tickets for their production of *The Three Sisters*[1] on Tuesday. Gave *The Erpingham Camp* to the box-office woman. 'I just had a black-out,' she said, sipping a double brandy. 'Just now. I passed out.'

On our way home we were waiting for the bus when a very fat, pompous-looking woman reeled out of a pub shouting, 'Melancholia? Ad nauseam.' And then she called through the door, 'Hallucination!' And, 'Don't use your fucking foul language on me!' She reeled away and caught a bus.

Peter Gill rang later. He is very impressed by the rewritten *Erpingham Camp*. 'A wonderful job,' he said. 'The speech of the Padre after Erpingham has fallen through the floor is magnificent. Absolutely first-rate.' Went back to my reading of the *Penguin Dictionary of Quotations* feeling relieved and glowing. Watched *Dr Who* on television. Rubbish, but there's a young boy in it who is worth looking at; like an Edwardian masher at a Gaiety show, I mentally undress him. I'm sure the BBC would be horrified if they realised that even a science fiction series can be used erotically. Wrote a letter to the irate man (or woman) who so disapproved of *Loot*. Calling myself Edna Welthorpe I invited them to attend, with me, a meeting at St James's Palace with the Lord Chamberlain 'to protest about plays in general and *Loot* in particular.'[2] 'What will happen if they say "Yes"?' Kenneth Halliwell asked. 'I shall then write another letter making some ludicrous excuse for not going,' I said.

Sunday 16 April

Nothing much happened. Weather bright, sunny, warm. Kenneth read the papers. Reviews of *Rosencrantz and Guildenstern are Dead* hail the play as a major theatrical debut. 'They didn't hail *Sloane* as a major theatrical debut,' Kenneth said. 'Well, it's the second play that's the test,' I said. 'We'll see what happens to Tom Stoppard over the next few years.'

Monday 17 April

Went for a walk. Weather sunny. Bought a copy of *The Transatlantic Review*: a patchy interview with me is printed, tape-recorded and by no means well thought out on my part.[3] A copy of Osborne's *A Patriot for Me*. I'm not likely to see the play and I'd like to know what it's like. And a copy of *Macbird*[4], an American parody on *Macbeth*. Juvenile, undergraduate and firmly rooted in the college

1 By Anton Chekhov (1860–1904), 1901.
2 See page 289.
3 *Transatlantic Review*, 24. Interviewed by Giles Gordon.
4 By Barbara Garson. (1941–).

campus. I suppose the English equivalent is *Rosencrantz and Guildenstern are Dead*. How well the English play stands up to the American. *R & G are Dead* is, admittedly, undergraduate and juvenile, but it has powerful and brilliant writing in it – particularly the scenes with the Player. *Macbird* is the kind of thing anyone can, and a lot of people have, mocked-up to amuse themselves. I remember Kenneth Halliwell and I writing a full-length parody of Dante called *Purgatorio LA*, in which somebody did a tour of Los Angeles (why we had to set it in America remains a mystery to me now). And to be told by Robert Lowell[1] that the writing (of *Macbird*) was 'a kind of genius' makes one's eyebrows flicker in one's hairline like lightning on a summer night.

After *Macbird* I read *Hamlet*. And then I watched *Tarzan* on television. An episode in which they used the Lohengrin–Elsa (who will be my champion?) cliché.

Whilst we were out today I noticed a firm which sold 'paper tubes' and a factory which said over the door 'precision work in plastics', and a woman was overheard to say something about 'a disturbance outside the Nuffield Centre for speech and hearing'.

I rang Peter Willes to say that I wouldn't be going to his place on Thursday for dinner. I said I'd be busy on Thursday afternoon and I'd be too tired. He was most angry. I asked him to come to us for dinner. He rang off in a great huff. Since he is coming the following Wednesday with Dorothy Dickson I'm not sure what his rage is about.

Tuesday 18 April

Curt note from P. Willes saying, 'I shan't be coming to dinner next Wednesday. I'll arrange for a car to collect Dorothy.' How piqued he must be with me not wanting to go to dinner with him on Thursday. 'I thought I was most polite and apologetic,' I said to Kenneth. Kenneth was busy cutting pictures from *The Sunday Times*. He arranged a sort of card which showed a man bending over and underneath, in headlines, a rather cryptic sentence: 'You can fuck five Christians.' 'I'll send that to Willes,' I said. 'As a reply to his cold and formal middle-class note.'

I shaved and went down to Holborn at 12.30. I was to meet Ian Horobin at one o'clock at Simpson's in the Strand. I decided not to post Willes's letter but to drop it in at Television House. As I got to TV House I met Willes's assistant who is a pleasant young man. He laughed when I approached and said, 'You're the last person I'd've expected round here this morning.' 'Why?' I said. He then told me that P. Willes appeared to be having some kind of fit yesterday afternoon, screaming and shouting, 'Joe Orton is the most ungrateful person I've ever met.

---

1 Robert Lowell (1917–77). American poet.

After what I've done for him! To treat me in this disgraceful way!' I laughed a bit about this and then told him that I was going to send him a comic card which said 'You can fuck five Christians.' Willes's assistant turned white with apprehension. 'Oh, don't do that,' he said. 'It really will send him off his rocker.' He spent about fifteen minutes persuading me that P. Willes really might fall into a fit and never put on another play of mine again. So, reluctantly, I decided not to post the letter. I went off to lunch thinking what a nutcase P. Willes was.

Ian Horobin was in the foyer of Simpson's when I arrived. He shook hands and said, rather snobbishly, 'Look here, I didn't book a table till this morning and they're rather full. However, I tried what a title will do and they're seeing if they can fix us up.' After a minute or two the head waiter ambled into view and said they could let us have a table. We sat down, not until Horobin had, in a rather loud and idiotic manner informed the head waiter that I'd just sold a play for £100,000. The waiter stared in blank amazement. Extraordinary how rude these upper classes can be. Fancy crying out in a rather grand restaurant, 'This young man has got £100,000's worth of loot! Tee-hee-hee!'

He was a little more civilised at lunch. We both had saddle of mutton which was delicious. He told his boring joke about how 'Simpson's saddle of mutton had made many Americans curse the loss of union with England.' Then he told me how he'd found a astonishing village down south in Morocco called – I think – Tianiz, 'which is absolutely unspoiled. We stayed at a little place and there were boys galore and so nice. Not spoiled like Tangier.' He then said he'd been to Lisbon, 'which also,' he said, lowering his voice, 'is very good. But you must have a flat, of course. These wretched hotels simply won't allow you to take anyone back.' We talked a lot more bum and then I left.

Friday 21 April

A woman rang from the *Eamonn Andrews Show* asking me to be on it this Sunday. I accepted. They're paying me £100. 'We're going to discuss marriage,' she said, which put me off for a start. They're sending a car to fetch me at seven on Sunday evening. 'We'll be over by 10.15,' the woman said. I shall be back in time to watch the wretched programme which is transmitted at 11.15. I went to see the cast this evening. Told them the news of the *Eamonn Andrews Show*. Kenneth Cranham wanted to know whether *Loot* was coming off. Both he and Sheila would like to be able to do *Crimes of Passion*. On the way back on the bus I heard a mad-looking Irish woman talking. 'I blame the parents,' she said, 'it's the parents. They want for nothing these days, do they?' A pause and she said. 'Bikes ... television ... everything is provided for them.' Kenneth Halliwell grumbles about the weather. 'It's the most terrible spring I've known,' he said. 'It's always dreadful weather in England,' I said. 'Not as bad as this,' he said. 'When have we had winds and rain as cold and as bad as this?'

Saturday 22 April

I went to my hairdresser's today to get my hair cut for the television tomorrow. It's a hairdresser that does women's hair as well as men's. I heard a very well-to-do voice saying to the shampoo girl, 'I've brought my own egg. You never have them in.' I bought a white tee-shirt with red stripes on the way back. Weather cold, bleak. 'I hate this time of the year,' Kenneth says. He's been looking through a property paper and has found a 'marvellous' house in East Croydon. He's sulking at the moment because I've said quite firmly that I won't go and live in East Croydon. 'You're so unadventurous,' he said. We went for a walk. A long walk which took us past the now almost demolished hulk of the old Imperial Hotel. Nearby the almost as splendid Russell Hotel is still standing, but not for long. Kenneth began to carp about the weather and led, by degrees, into a tirade against London and a eulogy of life in the country. I remained unimpressed because although I don't mind moving out of London, I'm not going to be buried in some God-forsaken hole out in the wilds. Kenneth sulked a lot more. In the end I said, 'You're getting to be a fucking *mater dolorosa*, aren't you?' which put an end to the conversation for a time. Saw a headline advertising an article in some magazine: 'MARRIED LOVE – HOW MUCH SHOULD THE CHILDREN SEE?' The King of Greece has organised a coup – Athens is under a cloud from our liberal press. On the television some fool bemoaned the fact that 'Greece, who in fact, invented democracy, has now, we hope not permanently, abandoned it.' 'He can't know much about ancient history,' Kenneth said, 'or he'd know that Athens abandoned democracy pretty soon after inventing it.' I've been reading Sheridan[1]. What perfect plays *The Rivals*[2] and *The School for Scandal*[3] are. Worth any number of Restoration rubbish. I tried to read Dostoyevsky's *The Idiot*[4] and gave up. What a weight of words. Then I had a dip into Virginia Woolf's *To The Lighthouse*[5]. After reading a dozen or so pages I put the book down, wearied by so much thought; beautiful prose stretching into infinity – like viewing the sea from the deck of a liner, at a first glance fascinating, but on the second or third day out one longs for islands, a coastline, even perhaps another ship – anything to break the monotony. What a long-winded art form the novel has turned out to be. At least a play must obey the rules of a 'two hour traffic'. It can go on a bit longer, but it can't turn into a 'two day traffic' as the novel so easily can.

---

1 Richard Brinsley Sheridan (1751–1816). Playwright. His masterful comedies displayed the wit but not the lewdness of Restoration comedy from which they derive.
2 By Richard Brinsley Sheridan, 1774.
3 By Richard Brinsley Sheridan, 1777.
4 Fyodor Dostoevsky (1821–81). 1868.
5 By Virginia Woolf (1882–1941). 1927.

Sunday 23 April

Dreary day. Kenneth in an ugly mood. Moaning. I said, 'You look like a zombie.'[1] He replied, heavily, 'So I should. I lead the life of a zombie.' Read *Love for Love*[2]. Not so theatrical as Sheridan, but a style to be envied. At seven o'clock a large car drew up outside the house and I was taken to the ABC studios at Teddington. The sky was bright. It had brightened up just before sunset. A very Sundayish atmosphere. I got to the studios at a quarter to eight. I wandered around, lost, for a time, as usual. Then I found a commissionaire who directed me to a studio lounge. I found the personnel woman and several executives of the programme there. Eva Gabor[3] was already nosing through her second gin. She'd been to see the play and, fortunately, loved it. She was making a great fuss about her make-up. 'I must do my own,' she said. She was whisked away to a make-up room and reappeared later not only painted a hectic beige, but dolled-up in about fifty yards of satin. The show seemed to go OK. Afterwards I talked a bit and then, at half-past ten, I went home. Kenneth was in bed when I got in at eleven. I made a cup of tea and we watched the programme. I looked very good and came over well. I didn't say very much. Kenneth's tranquillisers worked against too much yapping. I had a dreamy look about me – barbiturates. They photographed everyone to look as pretty as possible and, having no competition, I won.

Monday 24 April

I thought I'd better hold out a flag of truce to P. Willes today. 'Otherwise,' Kenneth said, 'we'll never know whether or not to expect him on Wednesday.' I rang him at ten o'clock. I began by saying, 'Hello, have you stopped sulking?' Kenneth said afterwards that it wasn't perhaps the most tactful beginning to a conversation with the recently estranged. Willes began in a slightly aggrieved tone and went on to say, 'You were horrible on television last night. Terrible, terrible. Everybody here says you came over as smug, complacent, big-headed and a bastard.' 'I'm sorry to hear that,' I said. 'I thought I was too self-effacing.' 'No,' he said, 'everyone said it was a big mistake. You mustn't go on television again.' He is coming on Wednesday. 'I shall arrive with Dorothy at sevenish and I've ordered the car for nine. I don't want to stay up all night and, after all, you may have been for a walk in the afternoon, you'll wish to rest, won't you?' 'Piss off!' was all I could've said. I said nothing. Later Mark rang, and Henry Budgen. Both

1 Eleanor Salvoni: 'I felt Ken changed in the last few months. He wore his dark glasses a lot, which he wore often in any case, even in winter. My son said to me, "Mom, what's the matter with Ken. He doesn't say hello. Joe does, but Ken doesn't." All of a sudden he wasn't talkative any more. Joe was merry-looking; and Ken looked drawn all the time.'
2 By William Congreve (1670–1729), 1695. Orton felt Congreve's style was 'real – a slice of life. It's just very brilliantly written, perfectly believable. Nothing at all incredible.'
3 Eva Gabor (1921–   ). Much married Hungarian-born actress and Hollywood celebrity.

saying how well they thought the programme had gone. Mark said that the box office was fluttery this morning. Libraries and enquiries. Later in the day it was grey and dreary. Kenneth quel moan. I took the opportunity of going to the Royal Court where they're holding a casting session. The only people possible for *Erpingham* are not available, or dead. Saw Gaskill. Fattish and lethargic. Never know how he regards me. With hostility I think. Met Desmond O'Donovan[1]. Overdressed and too thin.

Tuesday 25 April

I took a copy of *Crimes of Passion* to Methuen. I hope they publish. I also dropped a copy of *The Ruffian on the Stair* in at the Court. I've made several additions and cuts. I compared the final recension with the original broadcast play printed by the BBC. It bears only a slight resemblance now. The story is the same, but Wilson's relationship with his brother has developed from a rather vague, repressed, hinted-at feeling, into a full-blown physical passion. The other two characters haven't undergone the same degree of change. Kenneth H. has been sitting in a moth all day. Like a broody hen, I told him. He merely shrugged and looked sulky. He brightened up later when we went down to Kenneth Williams's flat. We were early – twenty to six. But at ten to six another ring came at the door. Kenneth W. let in a young man called Clive. Very ordinary youth. Working-class. Attractive and having an open honest face. 'He's come to mend the telephone,' Kenneth W. said. 'You know where it is, don't you, Clive?' 'Yer,' Clive grinned and went away. 'He's a little sod, you know,' Kenneth W. said in a bridling manner. 'He works on the telephones – he's a telephone engineer.' He went to get a cup of tea and when he came back he carefully closed the door so that Clive wouldn't hear. 'He's a dish, isn't he?' Kenneth W. said. 'He comes from Oxford.' After a bit Clive came in. 'Wal, I've fixed it up like, Ken.' 'A cup of tea?' Kenneth said, brightly. 'I won't say no.' When he came back with the tea he said, 'Go on then, tell Joe and Kenneth about the other day.' 'What?' Clive said. Kenneth W. turned to me and said, 'He was in this block of flats that the GPO were wiring. Empty flats. New ones.' He turned, impatiently to Clive, 'Go on, go on!' 'There's not much to say, really,' Clive said. 'This kid kept messing about – touching me up when I was bending over – and saying, "What a lovely bum, like". I told him to fuck off. And he kept coming back. So I said, "Look

---

1 Desmond O'Donovan (1933–). Director, then assistant artistic director of the Royal Court. Orton to Peggy Ramsay, June 1966: '. . . As for O'Donovan is he "keen on" the rubbish that the Court have been putting on this season? It's been neither an artistic nor a popular success. *Their Very Own and Golden Pisspot, Cresta Run, Performing Giant*. If he's saying *Loot* is inferior to those, I'd better get out of the theatre. If he's saying *Loot* doesn't fit in with the Court policy he's being as doctrinaire as Moscow (or Berlin under Hitler). But scratch a liberal and you'll always find a fascist bleeding . . .'

if you don't stop it you'll get more than you bargained for."' 'And he did!' Kenneth said, delighted. 'Clive had him – with the other GPO men in the next room. Working in the next room they were. Isn't it a disgrace!' 'Codron was shocked by the boys,' Kenneth said later. 'I invited them to have dinner with Codron and me, you know. And over the dinner-table Clive began talking about sex. Afterwards Codron said, "Don't ever bring those boys to my house again. I thought they were nice, innocent lads, and they talked of nothing but fucking and wanking and all that."'

Later on the man Clive lives with arrived. He was about thirty. Nice, but middle-class. He was called Tom. We had a very interesting evening. I told a lot of stories about sex. 'As long as they won't be shocked like the time I told Gordon Jackson how I'd fucked that kid of thirteen,' I said. 'No, no!' Kenneth W. said, 'They love all that filth. Clive's as filthy as you are. And Tom loves it all.' Tom told a joke which I thought was funny. A little boy arrived at school with a new watch. His friend said, 'Where did you get that?' 'It was a present,' the boy said. 'Is it your birthday?' his friend said. 'No,' the boy said. 'Well, why were you given it then?' the friend said. Eventually the friend persuaded the boy to tell him. 'I woke up the other night and wanted a drink of water,' the boy said, 'so I went into Mummy's room. When I got there I saw Dad on top of Mum jigging up and down. They told me to go back to bed. And in a bit Dad came into my room and said I mustn't tell anybody what I'd seen. He said if I promised not to say anything he'd buy me a wristwatch.' The other boy thought about this and he decided that he wanted a present as well. So the next night he waited until his Mum and Dad had gone to bed and after a bit he went into their room. His Dad was on top of his Mum and jigging up and down. When she saw the boy his Dad said, 'What do you want?' 'I want a watch!' the boy said. 'Well, close the fucking door then and sit down,' the boy's Dad said.

Later on Kenneth W. said, 'George Johnson[1], you know, who used to play the violin in the Palm Court, was staying in Bristol in terrible digs. He'd been having the trade back and finally his landlady said, "You've been bringing people back, haven't you?" She looked disapproving and went on, "It's got to stop. You're not to bring any more men back here." So George Johnson didn't. On his last night in Bristol he met a sailor. Very good-looking. And he thought, "Well, fuck it, I'm having this." So he took the sailor back to his room but, so that the landlady would only hear one set of feet he gave the sailor a piggy-back up the stairs. As he passed the landlady's room, carrying the sailor, the landlady opened her door and looked out. She pursed her lips when she saw what was going on and said to George Johnson, "Bringing back cripples now, are you?"' Kenneth said that they

---

1 George Johnson (1920–1975). Violinist.

just went on into George Johnson's room. 'Sex was very difficult because they kept laughing,' Kenneth said.

When we left Kenneth I gave Clive and Tom my telephone number. 'You should've asked for theirs,' Kenneth H. said. Later on he said, 'Which one did you like?' 'Clive, of course,' I said and was both surprised and delighted to realise that Kenneth H. had infinitely preferred, for company and sex, Tom.

Wednesday 26 April

I wrote a letter to Kenneth Williams asking for Clive's telephone number.[1] At three o'clock this afternoon he rang and gave it me. The GPO must have shot it round very quickly. After my appearance on the *Eamonn Andrews Show* the box office has gone up with a leap. Willes arrived tonight with Dorothy Dickson. They came at seven and were gone by nine. Not a particularly exhilarating evening. Whether Willes has forgiven the imagined insult or not is open to conjecture.

Thursday 27 April

Did nothing today. Weather fine and sunny. I went to Foyles bookshop in the Charing Cross Road. I wanted to buy the collected plays of Wycherley[2] and Farquhar[3]. I couldn't find them in print. I bought a copy of Middleton's *The Changeling*[4]. Peter Gill said I should use the subplot in a play of my own someday. Went to the Royal Court at five to see a man called Roger Booth audition for *Erpingham*. I rang Clive first. Tom will be away most of next week and so I suggested Clive come to the theatre to see *Loot*. 'I don't know what you want to do that for,' Kenneth H. said. 'It means having sex at midnight.' I invited Tom and Clive to come over for a meal on Monday.

Roger Booth gave a good reading of the part of Erpingham. He then read the Padre. I preferred him as the Padre. He could, though, at a pinch, play Erpingham. Later on in the evening Tom rang. Kenneth spoke to him. Then I did. He said Clive was sitting looking rather shattered. 'Why?' I said. 'Oh, he's

---

1 Orton to Kenneth Williams, 26 April 1967: 'I can't tell you how I enjoyed yesterday evening . . . And the filth, far from reacting upon me as upon a famous London impresario, added fuel to the fire of enjoyment. I gave Tom and Clive my telephone number when we left, but K. Halliwell said this morning, 'You did your usual choking off bit, didn't you?' 'I was most friendly,' I said, 'only I didn't want to seem as if I had a hard on.' (Which I had and the off-hand manner must've been the effect of a strangulated horn.) Anyway, I'd like to invite you both over to taste my haddock! . . .'

2 William Wycherley (1640–1716). Restoration dramatist whose satires were as savage as they were lewd.

3 George Farquhar (1678–1707). Restoration dramatist whose gift for plot and emotion put him above the licentious comedy of manners of the period.

4 By Thomas Middleton (1580–1627), 1622.

been using the sun-lamp. He gets spots sometimes and he uses the ultra-violet lamp to clear them up. It's adolescence.' He paused and said, 'I suppose he's lucky to still be getting them.' We talked for a bit and rang off. 'I don't know why you invited Clive to go to the theatre,' Kenneth Halliwell said, again. 'Tom will be away next week. You could've gone up there and had sex at any time of the evening.' 'But I can't just ring up and suggest coming over for sex,' I said. 'I mean – even for me that's a bit crude. I've got to wrap it up a bit. I've got to at least meet him on his own for a couple of hours and *Loot* is as good a way as any.'

Friday 28 April

The box office at the Criterion played to nearly £400 on Wednesday. And to nearly £300 last night. My appearance must've helped. Last night the doorman at the Cri – Harry – rang and said, 'There's two gentlemen here say you've got an appointment with them.' I'd never heard of this. He put them on the phone. 'My name is Mr Jacobs,' the voice said. 'I believe my secretary rang making an appointment.' I denied all knowledge of this. 'I'm here with the Rev. Dr Peake,' the man said. 'We've a scheme I think you'll be interested in.' I gave them Peggy's number and told them to ring tomorrow (today that is). I then rang Peggy at home and told her not to encourage them because they were probably maniacs. I've heard nothing from her today and so I suppose they haven't rung. A letter in the *TV Times* about *The Good and Faithful Servant*. Liking it.

Saturday 29 April

Kenneth has been to the doctor who changed his tablets from valium to librium. We went for a walk. Grey, dull day. A line in the *TV Times* caught my eye. It was a religious programme, the speaker had taken as his text 'Sin – Is It Our Fault?' Next week the talk will be on 'The Resurrection – Did The Body Rise?' Kenneth H. in a particularly good humour. Oscar has had *Up Against It* printed. He sent me two copies.

Sunday 30 April

Rang Kenneth Williams this morning at 9.30. I arranged that Kenneth H. and I should go down and pick him up at his flat at 10.30. We thought it might be nice, as it was a fine, sunny morning, to go for a stroll in Regent's Park. When we arrived Kenneth greeted us with a beaming smile. 'Here, I went to an amateur revue yesterday,' he said. 'And some of it really wasn't bad. There was this one blackout sketch of two women talking, with glasses in their hands, and one of them said "Isn't this a *terrible* cocktail party?" And the other woman said "Yes. I'm going as soon as I can find my knickers."' We walked into the park. 'Which way shall we walk?' I said. Kenneth tossed his nose into the air. 'Well, I'm not one for your walking,' he said. 'Let's get a deckchair and have a sit down. Watch all the queens passing. That's what I like.' We found three deckchairs and had to wipe the birdshit from them before they were fit to sit on. 'All this excrement is a disgrace!' Kenneth said. We sat for a while in the sun and talked. Kenneth is going to play 'some great German queen' in a film called *Follow That Camel*. 'It's set in the desert. In the French Foreign Legion,' he said. 'We're filming it down at Rye. That'll give you some idea of the care they take with the locale, you see.' He told us how his mother had gone to Athens and a guide had offered to take her round the Parthenon. '"I don't want to see these graveyards," she said. "They keep saying, 'This was your temple entrance, you see. And over there's your sacred enclosure.' 'Is it?' I say, 'I can't imagine it. It looks like a few broken bits and pieces to me'."'

At 12.30 Kenneth suggested lunch. We went to an Italian restaurant called Biagi's. I sometimes go there with Peter Willes. We had lunch. At the end of it P. Willes walked in with a man and woman and a child. When he saw me, Willes smiled and said, 'You aren't allowed in here on your own.' And went to his table. 'Who's that?' Kenneth said, surprised. 'That's Peter Willes,' I said. 'You shouldn't allow him to talk to you like that,' Kenneth said. 'You want to go over to him and say, "Don't talk to me when you're drunk!"'

We went for a walk in Hyde Park after lunch. We listened to the black men and the Irishmen at Speaker's Corner running down the white races and the English in particular. 'All these people are homosexuals,' Kenneth said. 'When you're in the crowd people feel your bum and try all manner of filthy things.' We walked around and Kenneth H. and I got rather bored. It looked like rain. I said, 'It looks like rain, Ken. Shall we be moving on?' to K.W. He nodded in a secretive way and said, 'I'll be getting in contact with you.' He looked absorbed. 'You'll ring me then?' I said, puzzled. He nodded and made a face. So Kenneth H. and I came home on the 73 bus. 'I suppose he was picking somebody up,' I said. 'It'll only end in disaster as usual,' Kenneth H. said.

When we got home we talked about ourselves and our relationship. I think it's bad that we live in each other's pockets twenty-four hours a day, three hundred and sixty five days of the year. When I'm away Kenneth does nothing, meets nobody. What's to be done? He's now taking tranquillisers to calm his nerves. 'I need an affair with someone,' he says. He says I'm no good. I'm only interested in physical sex, not love. 'Your attitude to sensitive people is Victorian,' he said, 'basically it's Dr Arnold[1] "Get out on the playing fields. You won't be sensitive then."' 'All you need,' I said, 'is some field of interest outside of me. Where you can meet people away from me.'

Earlier on Kenneth Williams said, 'Get Clive and Tom to introduce you to the

---

1 Dr Thomas Arnold (1795–1842). Headmaster of Rugby and father of the poet and critic Matthew Arnold (1822–88).

Holloway set. There's this doctor – a queen, but good-natured – and she's bought this house and stocked it with boys. They're all working lads. All from borstal. And she's allotted them their various tasks. One is responsible for the plumbing, another for the electricity. And so it goes on. I said to one of the boys, called Chris, "You do the plumbing – all copper – for cost price?" "Well," Chris said, "he's been good to us. Very good. See I was in borstal and nobody cared about me. And he took me in. Give me a roof over my head. He's been very good to us." There's even a boy responsible for the goldfish,' Kenneth said, more as an afterthought. 'And if any of them neglect their tasks she calls him into her surgery, wags her finger and says, "Now then, Dennis, you've neglected to feed the goldfish. What is your excuse?" And the lad might say, "Well, you see, I had the trade in and I forgot." "Forgot!" this queen will say, "Had the trade in and forgot? You've no right to have the trade until you've fed the fish!"'

Monday 1 May

Kenneth H. had long talk about our relationship. He threatens, or keeps saying, he will commit suicide.[1] He says, 'You'll learn then, won't you?' and 'What will you be like without me?' We talked and talked until I was exhausted. Going round in circles. Later I went out and bought some haddock for the dinner tonight. Kenneth was looking forward to meeting Clive and Tom again. They arrived at half-past seven. We talked for a little and gave them a drink. We had dinner at eightish. They seemed duller than the previous night we'd met them. I realised at one point that Kenneth was saying nothing. They left at nearly twelve o'clock. I thought it something of a let down, but Kenneth, when I arrived back upstairs from the front door, greeted me with a long face. He seemed all right, though, and we made a cup of tea and went to bed.

Tuesday 2 May

At 7.30 this morning Kenneth got up and made a cup of tea. I was hardly awake. I sat drinking my tea and began talking. Suddenly I realised that Kenneth was looking tight-lipped and white-faced. We were in the middle of talks of suicide and 'You'll have to face up to the world one day.' And 'I'm disgusted by all this immorality.'[2] He began to rail savagely at Tom and Clive and, after a particularly

---

1 Miss Boynes: 'Kenneth hinted at the fact that he'd been in a mental hospital. "I've had a breakdown," he said. He said if things got on top of him, he was liable to explode. "I get very tense," he said.'

2 Penelope Gilliatt. Novelist, columnist and critic. Drama critic of *The Observer* in 1965: 'Joe felt corsetted, in desperation like a husband wondering what would happen to his wife if he confronted her with the truth. The truth was he wanted more freedom and a promiscuous life. He just couldn't cope with saying that to Halliwell. He asked me whether he should pretend, deceive, give it up. Then he said furiously, "I can't give up promiscuity and I won't give it up!" He even at one stage asked me to try and talk to Halliwell for him. I said I didn't think Halliwell would welcome it,

sharp outburst, alarmed me by saying, 'Homosexuals disgust me!' I didn't attempt to fathom this one out. He said he wasn't going to come away to Morocco. He was going to kill himself. 'I've led a dreadful, unhappy life. I'm pathetic. I can't go on suffering like this.' After talking until about eight he suddenly shouted out and hammered on the wall, 'They treated me like shit! I won't be treated like this.' I agreed that they both had chosen to agree with me on all things whether sensible or not. 'You had tea, they had tea, you had jam tarts, they had jam tarts. And those photographs of Mustapha – he was so unattractive, and because you'd had him they said "what a dish".' I'd noticed all this the previous evening. I'd also noticed that they'd been over-enthusiastic in praise of anything connected with me. 'Surely you expected this?' I said. 'I expected to be treated with a little respect!' He began to cry. I suspected that the root of the trouble was that Kenneth had built up a totally false picture of Tom. It wasn't possible to have the kind of relationship which Kenneth wants. Tom revealed himself during the course of the evening as a typical and not particularly original queer young man. Nothing wrong with this, I suppose. But Kenneth had imagined that Tom was an intelligent man with whom he could have an intelligent friendship. 'All that typically queer talk,' Kenneth raged, 'I've heard it all before.' After a while he said, 'And he's just a go-getting queen. He's interested in you purely because of your plays.' I said, 'Why are you surprised by this? He met Kenneth Williams by writing a fan letter to the theatre at Oxford where Kenneth was playing. He's a tuft-hunter. I wasn't interested in him. It was you who persuaded me to invite both Tom and Clive over. All I wanted was a bit of a knock with Clive. I'm not interested in futile relationships. You have to have that kind of relationship with your equals. You can't expect to pick up a young Post Office engineer and his middle-class keeper and burst into tears because the keeper is a queer. It's you that are at fault. Their simpering over me was all you can expect from people like that. I saw through it. You saw through it. If I'd been taken in by it then there would be cause for rage. As it is, it looks like Hell Hath No Fury.' The argument, or debate, went on for the best part of the morning with forays into other fields of activity. Snarling rages against me. 'I sometimes think I'm against all you stand for,' Kenneth said. And 'When I'm not here you won't be able to write in this flip way.' The inference that I don't know how cruel, despicable and senseless life is hurt me. 'I won't have you monopolising the agony market,' I shouted at last in a fury. For the best part of the day the to-ing and fro-ing went on. At last the

---

that it had to come from Joe himself . . . Joe sought chaos in promiscuity. I was trying to talk to him about finding chaos in other things, upsetting other orders . . . When I watched them together, Halliwell was very much playing the amusing slattern's role. They would joke together about that. None of it was bitchy. Halliwell was the wife who doesn't notice that her husband is coming up in the world and is changing. Halliwell didn't change and had no capacity for change and no vision of it at all.'

threats of suicide abated until the last one was 'If you have both of them, you can say goodbye to me!' And with that we began to pick up the pieces.

Wednesday 3 May

Kenneth in a better mood. I went to Highgate Station to meet Clive at five o'clock. I waited at the wrong entrance. At five past five I saw him appear looking around him from another direction. He'd been waiting at the other side of the station. He wore blue faded jeans and a grey woolly. Very sexy he looked. He had Tom's car with him. We drove to their flat. It was a nice flat. Two rooms, a bedroom, a separate kitchen and a bathroom and a hallway. Much bigger than ours. We talked for a little. Clive made a mug of tea for each of us. We sat on the settee and talked. He said how someone had sent an anonymous letter to Tom's parents telling them that he was homosexual. There'd been a terrific row. Clive, who was under twenty-one, had to move out of the flat for a week or so until he was twenty-one. And then, he said, he decided to tell his parents that he was homo as well. This seemed a bit pointless to me. However he did and they accepted it as best they could. I'd finished my cup of tea by this time. 'My mum said it was OK as long I just stuck to Tom,' Clive said, 'only she said I mustn't – you know – play around with a lot of men.' He grinned and I judged it about time to begin the main assault. I took the back of his neck in my hand, stuck my tongue down his throat and shoved a hand up his fisherman's jumper. After about a minute I said, 'Can anyone see through that window?' 'Yer,' he said. 'Shouldn't we either close it or go into another room?' 'Well, I've got to shave and have a bath,' he said. 'I've only just come in from work.' We went into the bathroom. He shaved. We talked a lot more. Then he got undressed and got into the bath. He has a nice body. Not over-developed. Heavy shoulders, narrow hips. A beautiful little arse. Not hairy. His shoulders are slightly pock-marked with the remains of adolescent spots. As he finished bathing and I thought to myself, 'I'm going to fuck this before we go to the theatre,' the phone rang. I went to answer it. Someone said, 'Is that Clive?' 'No,' I said. 'Can you get him? It's his mother.' This seemed like a Victorian melodrama to me. I went and got Clive. He came into the bedroom, wet and dripping from the bath and drying himself with a towel. He had a six minute conversation with his mother. About halfway through I took the towel and finished drying him. Then I got behind him, felt him and, when he put the phone down, necked him and shoved him back onto the bed. By this time, as I looked at my watch, I saw it was twenty-past six. 'We've left it a bit late,' I said. He lay naked and didn't even open his eyes to answer, 'We've got to be away by half-past, Joe.' I unzipped my fly, pulled down my underpants and, because there wasn't time for anything else, came on Clive's belly. It was now twenty-five past six. Clive took up the towel, wiped up the come and began frantically to dress. He later told me he'd had it off with a photographer the previous night and so wasn't much concerned with having it away himself. We managed to reach the Criterion by seven.

It was an entertaining evening. Clive seemed more relaxed than the other night. The performance was good. Michael Bates told me that several customers walked out on Monday. Stupid middle-class fuckers. We talked to Clive afterwards. I arranged to ring him when I got back from Morocco. 'I'll let you see my tan,' I said. 'You'll be having a threesome with him and Tom, I know you will,' Kenneth Halliwell said, later when we were home. He gave me two valium tablets and a cup of tea and got into bed with me. I had a hard on. And we had a furious sex session. He stuck his finger up my arse and wanked me. And he said I could fuck him if I wanted to. 'I can't overcome that particular psychological inhibition with you,' I said. He sucked my cock. And then I tossed him off after a very long love-making session. I came, but I don't know how much because he'd wiped it up before switching on the light.

Friday 5 May

I spent all day at the Court. I arrived at eleven o'clock. I'd taken two of Kenneth's librium tablets and was feeling jolly. We had a meeting with the designer. I'm worried by the amount of scenery P. Gill has decided to have for *The Erpingham Camp*. I only call for one set – Erpingham's office. The rest I intend to be played on a bare stage. Peter has got the designer to do a series of very interesting sets – not full sets – screens and drops. But they'll all take time to set up. *The Ruffian* is going to be played in no set, just furniture and a backdrop. After the meeting with the designer I saw Douglas Jeffery[1] who'd been asked by the Court to photograph me. We went to Cheyne Walk and he took a series of photographs against gates and trees. At 12.15 we went into the Kardomah for a coffee. I left him then and ambled back to the theatre. We began the auditions at 12.30 with Bernard Gallagher[2]. He's going to play Mike in *The Ruffian*. He isn't at all right for Erpingham. He has no madness. He's prose. But he's a good, efficient actor. There's nobody else. We'll have to have him. And hope to surround him with brilliant actors in the other parts. We next auditioned Roddy Maude-Roxby[3], an inspired amateur. He gave a brilliant reading of the part of Riley. We're having him. We saw a series of boys for Kenny. Only one was really good. He wasn't right for Kenny, though. Too sincere. I suggested to Peter that we read him as Wilson in *The Ruffian*. He's coming back tomorrow. It was now two o'clock. Peter said, 'We'll have a break now.' 'I'm going to have lunch,' I said, 'I'm not like you neurotics. I must have a good meal inside me.' He was just eating a sandwich. I

1 Douglas Jeffery (1927–). Theatrical photographer.
2 Bernard Gallagher (1929–). Actor.
3 Roddy Maude-Roxby (1930–). Actor.

went to Lyon's Corner House and had steak pudding, chips and cabbage, a cup of tea, a roll and a cake. Then I went into a record shop to see if there was an LP of *Privilege*. There was. But the only numbers I wanted – the pop versions of 'Onward Christian Soldiers' and 'Jerusalem' weren't on it. So they can stuff it up their fundamental gap. At 2.30 the auditions began again. We found a Kenny. At 4.30 I had to go to Patrick Procktor's[1] studio in Manchester Street. 'To be drawn,' Peter Gill said. 'Have you been to his exhibition?' 'No,' I said. 'Oh, it's marvellous. There are terrific drawings of the Rolling Stones in drag. And paintings of Chinamen. And wonderful ones of young boys in their pants.' 'Perhaps you'd like a picture of me without my clothes,' I said. Peter's eyes lit up. 'Would you mind?' he said. 'No,' I said, 'but would you be able to put it in the programme?' 'We'll be delighted,' Peter said. 'Ask Patrick – he's very grand, you know, it's a great honour that he should consent to draw you.' I didn't say anything. I thought P. Procktor was just any old drawer and I was flattered to find that he was quite famous and talented. 'Tell him you don't mind being taken nude,' Peter said. I caught a taxi. It was about a quarter to five when I arrived at Manchester Street. I rang the bell. Patrick Procktor was tall, thin, pallid. Rather queerish. Willowy. I was wearing a green combat jacket, a forage cap and a navy blue woolly. I sat down. He said, 'Do you want anything to drink?' 'I'd like a cup of tea,' I said. 'I make tea all day long.' We talked a lot. I made myself as charming as possible because Peter had said, 'You've got to interest him and then he'll do a good drawing.' 'Did Peter say what kind of drawing?' P. Procktor said. 'Well, it's no use just doing a conventional portrait,' I said, 'because there'll be photographs in the programme and you don't want to compete with them. Peter said to tell him that you can do anything you like. He even suggested I take my clothes off.' 'Would you mind that?' he said. 'No, not at all,' I said. 'Well, we'll do one or two with your clothes on. And then you can take your clothes off.' He paused and said, 'What music do you like?' 'Do you want to listen to pop or classical? Do you like Bob Dylan?' 'Not much,' I said. 'What about the Beatles or the Stones?' 'Yes, I like them.' So he put a record of the Beatles on the record player. He drew several pictures of me in my woolly and cap. Then he told me to take the cap off. After a while he said, 'I'll make some more tea. And then we'll do the nude ones.' So I had a cup of tea. I wanted to piss very badly, but I didn't go because wanting to piss makes my prick swell up and if I went to piss I might be so nervous of taking my clothes off that it might shrink and that would expose me to the disgrace of not looking as though I had a decent-sized cock. After I'd drunk my tea I took my clothes off, and my cock was rather large. So I felt pleased. I remembered the librium I'd taken and thought it might be that too. I sat on the bed and he drew me. Then we talked a little more. And he drew me

1 Patrick Procktor (1936–   ). Painter.

lying on the bed. I kept my socks on, nothing else. I kept my socks on because I think they're sexy. 'I've drawn you looking like a beautiful teenager,' P. Procktor said. 'You'll get a lot of kinky letters after this, I'm sure.' We chatted a bit more and I put my clothes on and went back to the Court. Peter was just reading Margie Lawrence in the part of Joyce in *The Ruffian*. I didn't have much time to say anything except that I'd had nude studies done. He jumped up and down in glee. I hope that they do put them in the programme.

When I got back home, Kenneth H. was in such a rage. He'd written in large letters on the wall, 'JOE ORTON IS A SPINELESS TWAT'. He sulked for a while and then came round. He'd been to the doctor's and got 400 valium tablets. Later we took two each and had an amazing sexual session. I'd decided that I'd fuck him. But it didn't work out. 'I'm not sure what the block is,' I said, 'I can fuck other people perfectly well. But, up to now, I can't fuck you.' This is something quite strange. I had a big hard on. Yet, when I tried to put it up him, it just went off. Anyway we made love and came. He sucked my cock. I've got a mark on it now where he did it too hard.

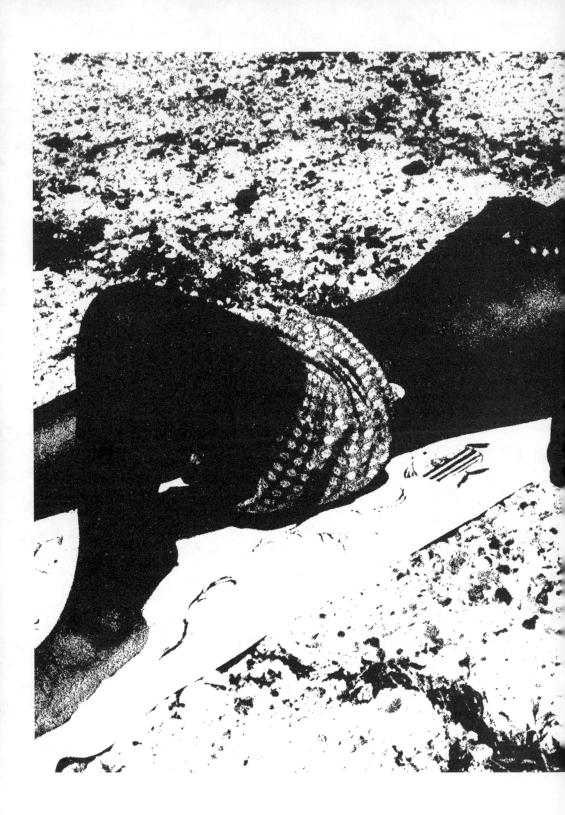

Tangier
May–June 1967

Sunday 7 May

We got up early; a grey morning, drizzle. We'd done most of the packing last night. We had only to pack shaving materials and clothes-brushes. We had one medium-sized suitcase each, and I carried a canvas bag, originally intended for fishermen. At London Airport terminal I bought a Mickey Spillane[1] detective novel from the Smith's bookstand, Kenneth bought the paperback edition of *A Case of Human Bondage* by Beverley Nichols[2]. We neither of us read them on the plane.

We had an uneventful journey. We saw Bill Fox, an acquaintance from last year, on the plane and chatted to him. He had a woman with him. 'She's some silly whore I picked up at the customs,' he said. 'You didn't think I was a convert, did you?' 'I wondered,' I said. 'Good God no!' he said, 'I shall be taking it up the arse as usual during the next fortnight.' We talked a little more and he went back to his seat. We waved goodbye at the airport at Tangier.

We were driven into town to the flat which is actually half a villa in an alley way called the Rue Pizzarro[3]. The actual owner – a gentle French homme-femme – showed us around the place. It is furnished in a most 'luxurious' manner – antique furniture and mirrors, gilded chandeliers – awful shit, but comfortable. The kind of taste I abhor, but as I am staying in Tangier for two months I want privacy, comfort and quiet. If I have to have a flat decorated by a gentle French queer it's a small price to have to pay. The main advantage the flat has is a terrace overlooking an enclosed garden and so when the hellish Tangier wind blows – as it is sure to do – we have a sheltered spot out of the way. We have to

---

1 Mickey Spillane, the pen-name of Frank Morrison (1919–   ), author of hard-bitten detective thrillers.

2 Beverley Nichols (1898–1983). English journalist and novelist.

3 The flat – No. 2 Rue Pizzaro – is where Tennessee Williams wrote *Suddenly Last Summer* which dealt, in part, with cannibalism and the barbarity of sexual promiscuity, of which Orton got a glimmering on this Tangier visit. One of Williams's last plays, *The Blonde Europeans*, is dedicated to Orton. 'Tennessee Williams has been to see it twice,' Orton wrote to Halliwell in October 1965, about the Broadway previews of *Entertaining Mr Sloane*. 'And, so I'm told, is wild over it. Says it's the funniest play he's ever seen.'

lock the place securely when we go out, including pulling shutters over the windows because 'the Moroccans get in'.

After changing we went down to The Windmill, a beach place run by an Englishman (Bill Dent) and an Irishman (Mike). The Windmill is right along the beach and so it is very quiet. Bill D. gave us a long talk about his health – he has shaking fits, he looks thinner than last year. Kenneth Halliwell says, with some truth, that what most of the Tangier regulars suffer from is drink. 'He's got cirrhosis of the liver, I bet,' K.H. said darkly. Mochtzar – who I had briefly last year – is now a sort of waiter at The Windmill. 'He's going into the army in June,' Bill Dent said. 'I'll have to have him quick then,' I said. We had tea and went out on the terrace, which is by the railway line. As I was sitting half-asleep, a small voice said 'Hallo'. It was a little boy. I had a little conversation. He asked my name. 'Joe,' I said. He nodded. 'Joo,' he said, 'yes.' 'Are you going home now,' he said. 'No,' I said, lying, 'I'm staying with friends.' He spoke then of how he was at school and was learning English. After more conversation, during a lull, he said, wistfully, 'Do you like boys?' 'Sometimes,' I said. He nodded. 'You fuck him?' he said, nodding at Kenneth. I shook my head and he said, conspiratorially, 'He is asleep.' And then, 'You will be here many days?' 'Yes,' I said. 'Goodbye,' he said, with a smile and stopped. 'I am Hassan,' he said. After he had gone, K. said, 'You can't have him – he is about ten.' 'It'll have to be a cabin job,' I said. 'They won't allow him in the cabins,' he said. 'Along the beach then,' I said.

We came home and Kenneth said, 'You go for some tea, bread, sugar, etc. They think you are poor and are nicer to you.' So I went to the corner shop and a fat, very friendly boy served me with provisions. When I got back, I had a cup of tea and two of Kenneth's librium tablets. They are excellent and make me feel wonderfully relaxed and confident. We had dinner at a small French restaurant. We had a pleasant stroll along the boulevard and down to the Petit Socco. We bought two coffees and spoke to a youth. He seemed a nice bit of rough – though he had clearly been on the Kif. 'I'm much too tired for anything tonight,' I said to Kenneth. We said goodbye, drank our coffee and strolled past the Hotel Mamora which, from being a semi-brothel two years ago, is now a 'tours' hotel with fat women and children sitting eating and drinking under pink lighting. When we were at the steps leading from the casbah, three very beautiful boys approached. 'You English?' 'Yes.' 'You like to come for a ride in a taxi?' the prettiest one said. We were too wise to be caught in that trap and we said 'no'. 'I'll take a single one back sometime,' I said to Ken. 'But not three and not in a taxi.' 'The taxi driver is probably in the act,' Ken said. We walked on and met a couple of Moroccans we knew from previous years. The effect of the librium was wonderful, so calming. We were able to carry on perfectly warm, friendly conversation in a most un-English way. 'The funny thing is,' Kenneth said, 'they're so surprised by the complete lack of nervousness on our parts that they don't try to pester us at all.'

When one of them suggested that we come and smoke Kif I was able to say 'no' in a firm, yet friendly way. I was really tired, and went to sleep having no sex, no inclination for any.

Monday 8 May

Kenneth worried about changing money. The £50 allowance simply won't take us to the end of June. We must find someone who will cash sterling and travellers' cheques of which we have £400 worth. We went to Kents (the Moroccan Woolworth) and bought shaving cream. The morning was cloudy. No sign of the sun, but it was pleasant and relaxing to stroll in the warm air. We saw Bill Fox sitting and drinking coffee at a café. He said, as we sat down, that he's had a little chicken who'd sucked his cock. 'He said he loved it,' he laughed. 'I thought of you immediately Joe, though he's too small to fuck, I'm sure.' I asked him his name. 'Hassan,' he said. 'That's the one I spoke to at the Windmill,' I said. 'I must have him, only I can't take him back to our place. Not after last year, and we are staying the summer.' 'You can have him at my flat,' Bill said. 'I'll fix it up for you.' He then took us to a woman who changed all Kenneth's cheques on the black market, and so that problem was settled. We all went to The Windmill for lunch. Met a nice ex-Merchant Navy man called Alan. Seems a good, decent type. 'I like doing anything,' he said. 'I've tried women and I have come to the conclusion that two men in bed together can enjoy themselves ten times more than with a bird.' We're meeting him tonight for a meal. We've locked the main salon of the flat, which is enormous and gives an impression of millionaire elegance. We'll just pretend that the flat consists of the kitchen bathroom and two bedrooms. Kenneth worried. 'It's so dangerous,' he says. 'Look,' I've said perhaps rashly, 'if there's a real nastiness we can just sling him out. We're never having more than one in at a time, our money is locked away, and, up to date, I've *never* had any trouble with a boy.' 'There's always a first time,' Ken said darkly, with which I can't argue.

We had dinner at a restaurant called Nino's. A notorious Italian runs it. When we asked what had become of Abdul-Kador, the waiter he employed last year, he pursed his lips in disapproval and said simply, 'A prostitute.' Kenneth gave me four librium tablets and then gave Bill Fox two, and the ex-navy man called Alan two also. They seemed to have an alarming effect on Bill, who was drinking wine with his meal. 'I simply *must* take it up the arse tonight,' he said, 'or there will be no doing anything with me tomorrow.' He said he had been a miner when he was fourteen. 'I was first fucked down a mine,' he announced to Nino. 'Yes?' Nino said, not understanding. 'Among the coal,' Bill said, trying to explain. 'A miner did me.' Nino shook his head. 'Another prostitute, yes?' 'She thinks I did it for a bucket of coal,' Bill said.

Tuesday 9 May

We went down to the beach early today. It had cleared up. Clouds passing over the sun, but enough heat to be pleasant. We were hailed with 'Hallo' from a very beautiful sixteen-year-old boy whom I knew (but had never had) from last year. Kenneth wanted him. We talked for about five minues and finally I said, 'Come to our apartment for tea this afternoon.' He was very eager. We arranged that he should meet us at The Windmill beach place. As we left the boy, Kenneth said, 'Wasn't I good at arranging the thing?' This astounded me. 'I arranged it,' I said. 'You would have been standing there talking about the weather for ever.' K. didn't reply.[1]

I borrowed the keys of Bill Fox's flat – (because I thought I must test the boy out in less grand surroundings than the flat we've taken) and went over to the boy. He was standing under a tree in the rain. He smiled, I nodded in the direction of the waste ground opposite the beach. He took my hand and we ran across the wasteland in the rain. We reached the flat and I had difficulty in finding how to open it. Fortunately nobody came up. I was dressed poorly myself in a pair of ordinary trousers and a polo-necked jumper – now wet with rain. I got the door open and we went inside – I pissed. The boy stood in the centre of the room. I tried to explain that this apartment belonged to a friend. He seemed to understand neither French, English or Spanish. I took him to the bed. Kissed him. He was shy and didn't open his mouth. He got very excited when I undressed him. I undressed myself and we lay caressing each other for about ten minutes. He had a heavy loutish body, large cock, but not so large as to make me envious or shy. I turned him over. He wouldn't let me get in so I fucked along the line of his buttocks which was very exciting. He'd wiped his spit on his bum. When I'd come a great patch on Bill Fox's coverlet, I went and fetched a towel – then we kissed some more, neck, cheeks, eyes – he still wouldn't open his mouth – strange for an Arab boy – he must be about fifteen, surely he'd have learned (I later was told that he had only recently come up from the country). He then turned me over and came along the line of my buttocks in the same way. Suddenly he stopped and said, 'How much you give me?' 'Five dirham,' I said. 'No, please, fifteen.' 'No,' I said, 'five.' He grinned. 'OK,' he said and went on. He took a very long time to come. We lay together for an hour afterwards while the rain poured down outside and the thunder roared. His name is Mohammed.

1 Sir Terence Rattigan: 'It was perfectly plain to me – and this isn't being clever after the event – that Halliwell was wildly jealous of Joe's sexual escapades, and it was perfectly clear that Joe didn't give a fuck. Halliwell lied about his age. For every erotic triumph that Joe described, Halliwell described five of his own. That was obviously phoney. I think I got as far as asking Halliwell: "Don't you mind when Joe goes and does these things?" He may well, but he wouldn't be doing it with any success. He resented Joe's success in that sphere as well as the other. That was one part of Joe's life he couldn't collaborate in.'

We then took a shower together. I then gave him five dirhams, slipped it into his pocket. He said, 'Please, one more.' Because he was sweet, and even on a matter of one dirham, they like to gain a victory, I gave him an extra. He kissed my cheek, I hugged him and said I'd see him again. He left the flat first. I wiped up the floor in the bathroom, which was swimming, and left. Alan, who had had a most unsatisfactory experience with a drunken English sailor the night before, said, 'Well I don't really mind,' and laughed. He went off with a very attractive but very young boy later, after inviting Bill Fox, Kenneth and I up to his flat for a glass of wine before dinner. Bill Fox told me that the Baron Favier (from whom we rent our flat) likes to dress young men up in military uniform. 'One night,' Bill said, 'he picked up a sailor in uniform, he took him back, made him take off his naval uniform and put on a military uniform before he could have him.' Bill went off with a waiter, a nice Moroccan in his twenties. Not pretty but a good, friendly man. 'Lovely sex, dear,' Bill said. 'He's promised to make me some hashish cakes.' These are cakes made with hash – they look the same as ordinary confectionery but are greatly superior to anything sold at Fullers . . .

Wednesday 10 May

Weather very bad. Cloudy. Pleasant to walk around. We met Bill sitting on the boulevard. He looked very happy, having had another sailor. Kenneth and I went down to The Windmill and I was going to have Mohammed again only Kenneth said, 'Larbi is coming at four for tea – I shall not want him, so you can have him.' So, I gave Mohammed a couple of dirhams, though I would much have preferred to have had him. Then we met the two thirteen-year-olds from last year, Mustapha and Absolem. But it really is too dangerous to go with the little ones so I said 'no'. We went back to the flat. We had tea and Ken and Larbi went into the bedroom. I'd had a couple of librium tablets and switched all the lights out in the salon and lay on the leopard-skin couch and dozed off. When Ken came back, they had had sex. 'I've arranged for you to have him tomorrow,' Kenneth said in a confidential tone when the boy was out of the room. 'But I've already arranged to have Mohammed tomorrow,' I said. 'I really wish you wouldn't play the procuress quite so much. I'm quite capable of managing my own sex!' Kenneth then went into the bedroom to put his tie on and I sat next to Larbi and kissed him. We then lay on the couch. I put my hand between his legs and felt his arse, to which he had no objection. 'We make *l'amour* tomorrow?' he said. I nodded, excited by the prospect, yet wondering how to put the other one off.

Thursday 11 May

Weather a little better, the sun came out and was very hot. Got slightly burnt across the shoulders. I arranged to go with Mohammed tomorrow, and in the early afternoon Ken and I went home to the flat. I took three valium tablets which had the most odd effect of making me take hours to come. I fucked Larbi a bit up the bum, with him making grunts and then, the valium, I suppose, I lost the hard. I went to the loo and had a piss, came back, tried to turn him over again. He shook his head and said, 'No, please.' 'You don't want me to fuck you?' I said. 'No,' he said. We made love a lot longer and I came on his belly. Then he made me toss him off with my come. We lay for about half an hour after this, stroking each other, and then took a shower. Later Ken and I went out to dinner. We've seen no sign of Bill Fox all day.

Friday 12 May

Weather still cloudy. We went to The Windmill. I wanted to see Bill Fox. There was no sign of him. I couldn't explain to Mohammed about the flat and Kenneth says I am not to bring him back until I know him better. In the end Mohammed had an idea. He gave a loud whistle and a younger boy came running. He could speak a little English, so I explained how it wasn't possible for me to take him to my friend's flat. He looked puzzled and said, 'Malabota? Yes,' and pointed into the country. I agreed to go into the country with him at three. It turned cold at about eleven, so I went into The Windmill and said to Kenneth that I was going back to the flat for my woolly. I walked along the rue d'Espagne and met Abdullah, who I always called Paddington, because he said he had once worked in Paddington. He had a friend with him and they said they'd like to buy me a mint tea. So we went into a café, drank mint tea, and I was given two pipes of Kif to smoke. They said would I like hashish. I said, 'Yes.' They tried to sell me a piece for 50 dirham which is ridiculous. Then they said, 'How much you give for this?' 'Ten,' I said, and immediately realised that even ten was ridiculously expensive. Anyway I bought it. 'Crumble it up in a little soup,' Paddington said.

I went back and faced Kenneth in such a rage at The Windmill. 'Where've you been? You have been gone an hour and a half. I was nearly out of my mind with worry.' With that, on the terrace of The Windmill, he burst into tears, to my own embarrassment. 'My nerves can't stand you going off without my knowing where you are.'

After a great scene, he said that Mohammed el Khomsi with the gold tooth, a boy of about eighteen, had been looking for me. 'I've arranged for him to come to the flat tomorrow,' he said. I was rather choked by this as it ties me down. 'Well you said you wanted to fuck him,' Kenneth said peevishly, 'and he's going to Gibraltar in a fortnight to work as a page-boy in a hotel.' He then began complaining about my liking Mohammed (the first one) and how he was a nasty bit of work. 'And you're mad to go along the beach with him. Absolutely mad.' He then began saying I would get into trouble. 'That boy of yours looks a nutter to me.' In the end, fed up to the back teeth with nagging, I said, 'Every boy in town is no good except the marvellous one you attach yourself to.' K. calmed down later. I had lunch. Chicken soup and I crumbled some hash into it. Then I went with Mohammed into the country, walking down dirt-tracks among the donkey shit. We walked for a mile or more and then he stopped at a village shop, very tumbled-down, and went inside. He came out again with a half loaf and two oranges. The half loaf had fish in it. He ate this himself. He gave me the two oranges to eat. We walked on and lay in the grass. Found it was possible to be seen by the odd person from the road, the railway line, and even from houses and a bridge across a stream. 'No good,' Mohammed said and suggested the German baths. It was much too late by now to go into the casbah to the baths – especially as I had told Kenneth that I would be back by four and I couldn't risk a repeat of this morning. So we walked back. I stopped at The Windmill and asked Mike if I could take the boy into the beach cabin. 'Oh no,' he said. 'I have to be so careful you see.' Stupid cow! What had he to be careful over? I told Mohammed it was too late. Gave him a couple of dirham and came home. By now the hash I had taken earlier had begun to work – I felt very confident, very lovely, had tea. Larbi had also taken hash and so had K. by this time, and so we had a rather hysterical time. Then I lay on the leopard-skin couch and had a siesta.

Saturday 13 May

Felt very good today. Very relaxed after hash. The sun shone out of a clear blue sky all day. Got very sunburnt today. Mohammed Khomsi arrived at The Windmill. He's full of the fact that he's starting life as a page-boy at a hotel in Gibraltar. He's the perfect fantasy page-boy. He's small, happy-looking and nineteen. He has a good body, not over-developed, not under-developed. I don't know, though, it doesn't seem to work with me. He's a sweet boy, though, and so I invited him back to the flat for tea. Larbi came later, bringing three sticks of hashish at 50 francs a piece. He had already eaten two sticks so was in a very giggly mood. I went to bed with Mohammed Khomsi. We had a long love session. 'Please, I must fuck you,' he said, 'I've had no *l'amour* for many weeks.' I let him. He didn't get right in though. He came. We went on with the session. Stroking each others bodies. Kissing necks, tits, running the finger over every part. I found something wrong, I've always been unexcited by Mohammed Khomsi. After a long while he fucked me again. Right in this time. I went for a piss and he tossed me off, shrieking with maniacal laughter as I came over the top of his head. Why can't I fuck him though? He's quite young and pretty. What chemical is missing that makes him, for me, totally unexciting? We lay for a while longer and got up and took a shower. Kenneth later said that Larbi had been half asleep with the hash. When Mohammed had gone, Larbi had a cup of tea and then had to run to the lavatory to be sick. He looked very shattered. 'Too much hashish.' He went. I told Kenneth how Mohammed had wanted to have a threesome with a girl. 'You me and girls,' he said. 'But where?' I said, not going to go in for that kind of thing in the apartment. 'Along the beach,' he said. I said 'perhaps'. We saw Bill with a very dreary American. Bill said he'd be at the Oriental Palace tomorrow afternoon and I could have the key to his flat if I wished, and so I shall take Mohammed (1) to Bill's flat if possible.

Sunday 14 May

Ridiculous day. Mohammed (1) outside beach bar from eleven to two. I'd arranged to meet him at three. Found Bill. Got key to flat. Bill said, 'When you've finished bring the key to me at the restaurant across the road.' I went back to The Windmill. No sign by now of the boy. No sign at 3.15. Decided to scrub the idea. Went in search of Bill to give him the key back. The restaurant was closed, it being Sunday. Couldn't find Bill. Walked up and down the street. Met Kenneth coming home, who said my life was one long round of ridiculous complication. Then we saw Bill and a good looking American called Gerry. I handed Bill back the key. The American came back to the flat with Kenneth and I. I had promised to give him a stick of hashish candy. I gave him half a stick, then Larbi arrived. We all drank tea. The American said that Bill had a youth from Meknès coming at five and why didn't I come over and have a threesome. I said 'OK', Kenneth being occupied with Larbi. We walked along the rue d'Espagne and met Mohammed (1). It was now 4.30. I'd arranged to meet him at three. The American suggested we take him to Bill's. I said, 'But he won't want the flat full of Moroccans,' so we parted from Mohammed (1). We got to the flat. I waited till 6.30. No boy turned up. Several little boys of about ten rang at the doorbell, but I'm not interested in them and Bill turned them away. Finally I came home. Kenneth had arranged for us to go to the Mauretania Cinema tonight where we were supposed to be seeing Moroccan dancing – the original dancing boys, etc. It turned out to be the Senegal National Dance Company.[1] I left at the interval finding it very boring.

Kenneth has now arrived home with the Moroccan boy, Larbi. I don't mind

---

1 Orton to Kenneth Williams, 14 May 1967: '. . . Kenneth and I were persuaded to see an exhibition of "Moroccan dancing" given at the Mauretania Cinema. I, of course, expected dancing boys, etc. When we got there (we went, God knows how, with 4 or 5 rather stuffy people and a couple of Moroccans – middle-class!!) Kenneth had a nice boy with him. I was lumbered with the shit. The dancing turned out to be the Senegal National Shitpot Company who are always performing at the Saville Theatre in London. By the interval, I'd had about enough of these fat, horrible dancers with their lunatic costumes with Carmen Miranda hats squealing and fart-arsing about, and as we stood making small talk in the foyer, I said to one of Moroccans – quoting a famous London wit, "Well, it's coats girls." The Moroccan said 'What is this "coatsgirls"?' I said, 'Oh, when we've had enough of a good thing in England we say, "I think it's coats girls."' The Moroccan beamed all over his face, and said in an extremely loud voice to these stuffy twits, "Well, come along now, it's coatsgirls." He kept repeating it, beaming around the company totally failing to comprehend the frosty smiles he was getting.'

him but when one considers the restriction placed on my own freedom, the nagging, the rows, the constant complaints, I feel like pissing off and spending the night in some Arab doss house. Later Kenneth and Larbi made such a racket, talking and laughing, which could be clearly heard through the communicating doors of the two bedrooms, that I picked up a blanket and pillow and went into the main living-room, locking the door behind me, and spent the night on the couch in quiet.

Monday 15 May

Mohammed (1) turned up at The Windmill at twelve and suggested we go to the baths. So I followed him into the casbah. On the way we met Nasser, the waiter from the Hotel Cleleh, who is going to make me some hashish cake. Kenneth says it won't be as good as valium or librium with a glass of wine. He looked at Mohammed (1) and said, 'This your friend?' 'Yes,' I said. 'Good,' he said in a very appreciative way. 'A good boy.' I arranged to give him five dirham for the ingredients and then he'd take them to Bill Fox's flat. We walked a little way and then Nasser left us. Mohammed (1) pinched a lot of monkey nuts from a cart which was going by loaded with them, and gave me a handful. We went through miles of twisting evil-smelling alleys and finally got to the Spanish Baths. There were small cubicles and a heated room. The Moroccan attendant smiled and said something to the boy, who nodded. We went into the room, undressed and lay on the heated, tiled floor.

I found it less exciting than I had at first imagined. The boy was as beautiful and as willing, though I found the heat unbearable. I tossed him off. He came only a small amount. They're pulling their cocks twenty-four hours a day I suppose ... We went into the other cubicle, where I realised that he'd forgotten to bring in a towel. I opened the door and the attendant appeared. He immediately looked down in the direction of my prick, which, since it was still semi-hard, was impressive enough. 'Towel,' I said. He disappeared and went for a towel. We dried ourselves and went outside. The attendant asked for five dirham each from me and the boy. Daylight robbery, but they know that the bath hadn't been used for bathing. Mohammed (1) said 'Too much money,' when we were away from the baths. 'You English they want too much money.' I gave Mohammed (1) five – he asked for two more. I gave him one more. He smiled, shook hands and we parted.

Later, after sunning myself for the rest of the morning, we talked to a very beautiful German girl called Vipsil. She is one of the most beautiful people I have ever met. Larbi, who fancies himself as a lady-killer, was trying to interest her in him. But, like most Arabs, his technique with women left a lot to be desired. It consists of flashing eyes, the grin and a barrage of more or less direct questions. When she tried to read her book, he suddenly said, 'Hey, you. Why you not speak?' The girl got more and more irritated until I said in a quiet voice, 'They're rather boring when they are trying to impress, aren't they?' She immediately smiled and said, 'They are, yes.' When we left, Larbi said, 'Girl she likes me, yes?' Ken and I laughed. Larbi, whose sense of his own sexual attractiveness borders on the insane said, 'Tomorrow I speak then I fuck her.' I said, 'I'll fuck her before you do. If you get your hand anywhere near her cunt I'll give you 50 d.' '50 dirhams if I fuck her?' he said. 'OK.' We all laughed, especially as I learned later that the girl couldn't stand these boys. We got home, Larbi disappeared into the corner shop and came back with spaghetti. He insisted on making a meal, he said, for himself, Kenneth and I. Also Mohammed Khomsi, who had just arrived. Kenneth and I had had a meal earlier. Larbi said, 'I make eats for Joe, Kenef and you perhaps?' In the end Mohammed and Larbi ate the spaghetti, which, in fact, was extremely well cooked. I had some myself and Larbi is a good cook (judging by his spag). I went into the bedroom with Mohammed later. I wasn't really feeling very much like sex after the baths this morning, but I took two valium tablets which seemed to work. Mohammed did the full love-play bit, kissing all over, lips, eyes, belly, the stroking and the exotic positions. Then he fucked me and afterwards a lot more love, and he slowly tossed me off.

We went back into the salon after a shower and sat talking. 'I like you very much,' he said. 'You very nice.' Then we spoke of his forthcoming job as a lift-boy in a Gibraltar hotel. He told me how he had worked for a time for a bank manager. 'Another boy work also. One day I come back with my patron and find boy fucking Moroccan boy in house. My patron say, "Off out of my house, I no want boys to fuck in this house."' He said how his patron, who was employing him in the Gibraltar Hotel, had interviewed him. 'Does he like boys?' I said. 'No,' Mohammed said. 'He likes big boys, gentlemen with a big cock.' He nodded saying, 'When I grow bigger I fuck him too perhaps.' We talked in this fashion for two hours until Mohammed said of Kenneth and Larbi, 'What they do in the bedroom, eh?' I had been wondering this for a long time and I went to the bathroom door and opened it. Kenneth was standing just inside looking worried. 'You'd better go and get rid of Larbi,' he said. I went into the bedroom and Larbi was lying on the bed naked, playing with his cock which was completely limp. 'He hasn't been able to get a hard on!' Kenneth said in tones of the utmost disapproval. 'A fifteen-year-old boy and he can't get a stand on. It's absolutely shameful.' I felt very excited by Larbi's complete passivity, brought on by the hashish and whiskey. However, I thought it was much too late, seven o'clock and two orgasms too late, to turn him over, so I picked him up and carried him to the shower. When I poured cold water on him he shrieked and giggled hysterically. 'He likes being manhandled,' Kenneth said bitterly. 'Larbi said that when he'd left here early this morning he'd gone into the lavatory of his house and wanked himself off, like any English schoolboy,' Kenneth said, though Mohammed said he'd been with tourists. 'I fuck him,' said Mohammed, 'sure I fuck him.' But Mohammed isn't always to be trusted.

Tuesday 16 May

It was a grey day. A chastened Larbi rang this morning. 'Allo's at Joo?' 'Yes,' I said. 'Ow are you?' 'Very well,' I said. 'Are you still *malade?*' 'No,' he said. 'Tranquil. I see you on *la plage*.' 'Yes,' I said.

We went to The Windmill at about eleven. At half-past it began to rain. Poured and poured for two hours or more. Larbi appeared in a djellabah and, after about three quarters of an hour, disgraced himself by getting over-excited, and had to be sent away. When it became clear that the rain was going to continue, everyone drifted away. Ken and I couldn't find a taxi. We waited and Nasser appeared with bags of nuts, raisins and sunflower seeds which, so he assured me, were going to make the cake. He wanted money now to buy the Kif so I gave him five dirham. He went away. Long disapproving looks from Mike, the part-owner of The Windmill, who is a stuffy Irish queer. Ken and I decided to walk home in the rain, but then caught a taxi about ten yards away. We got home at two o'clock; the doorbell immediately rang. Kenneth said he wouldn't answer it. 'I don't wany anybody to come in,' he said, 'not till about four.' I went to the door. It was Larbi. I said, 'No, no! Later. Four. Mucho trabajo.' He looked cross but went away. Ken and I had a quiet couple of hours. I had time to write up my diary. Ken read a newspaper. We had some tea. Prompt at four, Mohammed Khomsi arrived. Then Larbi. Later I had Larbi. Afterwards it took me ages to toss him off. Finally I gave up, allowing him to wank himself, and only at the last minute did he force his prick into my hand, I pulled him off whilst sticking my tongue half-way down his throat. We took a shower. Mohammed, after swearing life-long friendship to me yesterday, seems quite content to do the same to Kenneth today. Kenneth said they wanked each other. K. having a psychological (or physical) block about taking it up the bum.

George Greeves[1] rang and suggested we go out to dinner this evening, it being rather dreary weather. K. and I arrived at his flat in the rue Goya at a quarter to eight. George was talking business. We went into the next room. We could hear snatches of conversation. 'Yes, she looks like a poisoner, doesn't she?' and 'I want nothing to do with that filthy rotten bitch. I would shit on her stinking face if I could.' Finally the man went and George appeared in a suit and tie. We went out to dinner and met Dai Rees-Davies (M.A. Oxon)[2], reputed to be persona-non-grata in England. He looks like a frog and has only one eye. 'He takes it out, you know,' George said later, 'takes it out and frightens the shit out of these kids. I

1 George Greeves (1900–1984). Reuter's Morocco correspondent.
2 Dai Rees-Davies (1910–1985). Antiquarian.

remember once I was having dinner with him and he took it out and wiped it. It slipped from his hand and fell straight into the pudding. What a fucking carry-on there was. This dirty, shitty, Welsh fucker searching in the ice-cream for this rotten, filthy, glass thing that'd slipped from his poxy head. I had to refuse the pudding after that. The dirty shit though.' His stories are endless. He keeps up a constant stream of foul-mouthed commentary – life and death, nobody is saved. His chief target the rich and pompous. 'I hate the fuckers,' he said. 'I'd like to line them up and shit on their rotten faces.' He told a story of Auden[1] when young; 'I gave a party,' he said, 'all the fucking queers for miles flocked in. I believe we even invited the Bishop of fucking London but he had the piles and couldn't come. Well, Auden who'd been had when he was fourteen (that was a year before this party – ah, this party was, let me see now, 1936) – Auden was receiving the King's gold medal for poetry or some shit so he said he might be late. "Come when you like," I said, "and we'll go round the Hammersmith Bridge afterwards looking for a bit of young trade," I said. Well, in spite of the absence of the fucking Bishop and her piles, we had a hell of a time, and Auden finally turned up. When I opened the door he said, "Ah, I've just come from one George to another!"' George said, 'The whole thing was a bit of a fiasco really. I mean George V[2] at the best of times wasn't fucking all there, and he'd been given this bit of paper by Masefield[3], who's just kicked it, and about fucking time – he's been a disgrace to poetry for ninety bleeding years. However, the King had read this bit of paper and he said, "Now, Mr Auden, I very much admired that poem you wrote in 1826." Auden thought, "Oh Christ, he's really done it now" – "Ah, I mean 1926," the King said. After a bit of a natter the King said, "And how are the boys?" Auden thought he's tumbled, d'you see – he thought he's tumbled the trade he'd had under Hammersmith Bridge. So Auden turned and muttered something about the King. Turns out that on the piece of paper Masefield had presented the King with, it turned out that it said Auden had been a prep school teacher. It really gave W.H. the shits for a minute or two, I can tell you.'

George was drinking mineral water, he isn't allowed to drink much else now. He walks with a limp. He's fat and a big man with an Australian accent. He was off again telling a frankly invented story, but telling it with such a straight face that I was taken in and until quite later on believed it to be true. 'There was this poor queen, d'you see? She had nowhere to go. She was a starving poor old cow. "Oh where shall I lay my weary old head," she said to a queen who had befriended her. "Don't you worry, mother," the young queen had said. "You can come and live with us. We'll give you a bed and food. You'll be OK." Well this

---

1 W. H. Auden (1907–73). English poet.
2 George V (1865–1936). King of England, 1910–36.
3 John Masefield (1878–1967). English poet, who was Poet Laureate from 1930.

poor old queen went and lived with these young queens in a pretty old boarding-house somewhere in London. After a bit she got on her feet and starting coming it. "I can't eat that," she'd say, "and I must have things just so." The young queen got choked off with it and, in the end, said, "Now look here, you're no fucking ornament Auntie, you can have your bed for another month but you'll get no food. Get your smelly arse out of here and get yourself a bit of the ready." "Oh dear," the poor old queen said, knowing full well that she'd gone too far and wringing her hands, "whatever shall I do?" So the queen goes down to Leicester Square. It was a foggy night and she was frozen. She stood outside the Gents and prayed "Oh Holy Mother of God, send me a big prick".'

We all laughed loudly at this and several English tourists looked on in evident disapproval having heard the last remark. 'Anyway, just about when she'd given up hope,. a very properly-dressed man came by. "Goodnight," the queen said. The man looked her up and down and said, "Are you a queen?" "Yes," the queen lisped. "Well I am an opera singer. Would you like to come along with me?" "Yes, I certainly would," the poor queen said. So the man hailed a passing taxi and said "St John's Wood." When they were in the man's house, he said, "Now, I'm a leading tenor and I want to sing at the institution." So he began to sing, "Take down my trousers. Take them off. Suck my cock into your mouth. Suck my balls and suck on my cock. Onward, onward, up your bum and round and round." This went on for hours and hours until about three in the morning. The man came and the poor queen put on her clothes. The man went to a drawer on his desk and the queen thought, "Ah, now he's going to give me the money – now it was all worth it." The man came forward and said with a beaming smile, "I told you I was an opera singer – here are two tickets for Covent Garden." The poor old queen looked at them in amazement. "But I can't use these," she said, "I'm hungry, I want bread." "Bread?" the man said. "Then you should have been fucked by a baker!"'

Wednesday 17 May

Bill Fox behaving most oddly. Have hardly seen him since the beginning of this week. A Moroccan who he was having last year, called Nasser, promised to make me some hashish cake. So today I followed him for miles into some Moroccan district. Full of winding alleys – it wasn't the Medina though, but a district further out. We found his house and I sat outside whilst he went in. He came out with a bag of stuff and asked for three dirham for the hashish. He went back and returned with a packet of what looked like heather. Then we went in search of some special butter. He stopped at one stall in the market and asked to taste some. He gave me a piece to taste. It was very hot. Probably goat or some other incredible animal. He bought a piece. And a piece of a round flat white cheese. I thought this odd for a cake, but he tasted it and gave me a piece as well. We got back to the flat eventually, and he began to make the 'gateau'. He boiled the heather stuff and then strained off the juice. After this it would have been perfectly simple, I would have thought, to have bought a cake mix and use the hashish liquid instead of water. But no – he mixed in nuts and raisins and flour and butter. Then there was a lot of liquid left over and the cake mixture wasn't firm enough. He made a couple of pancake-like things. Then we smoked a pipe or two of Kif and he said, 'You like boys?' I said, 'Yes.' He nodded thoughtfully and said, 'You wouldn't consider tomorrow with I?' He's about twenty-five, by no means good-looking, but he has an honest, solid, very square look about him. I said 'No,' but we went into the bedroom, stripped off and lay in the bed making love. He has a nice body and a very well-shaped prick – smooth and, of course, with reference to the religion of the country, circumcised. He asked that I should be his friend – his amigo. I said 'But, I like boys.' We made love a while longer, and he asked if I'd let him fuck me. I turned over, though with some reluctance and a show of modesty which must have been very provocative. It's the kind of thing which makes me go wild sexually when the circumstances are reversed. He didn't get it right in. 'Next time I fuck you properly,' he said, after he'd played with my cock and tossed me off. I shrugged and we got onto the subject of payment. I gave him six, and a packet of Ken's cigarettes. 'I like boys too,' he said as a parting shot. He promised to come back at 1.30 tomorrow for the rest of the baking and bring a baking tin.

I sat on the terrace and sneezed once or twice. I've caught a cold I suppose. Kenneth returned at four-ish with Larbi. 'Where are they?' he said. 'What?' 'The cakes.' 'Oh he hasn't made them, just done the mixture.' 'You've had some though, haven't you.' 'Well he made a couple of pancakes.' Kenneth said, 'It really isn't fair, I might have known you'd find a private paradise by hook or by crook. You knew the place was heaven and you've gone and found an exclusive little Garden of Eden somewhere – selfish little whore!' He went away and investigated the contents of the bowl of mixture, which he said tasted foul. But he then had a couple of spoonfuls of the green liquid in the other bowl. By the time Mohammed arrived at five, Kenneth and I were feeling very happy.

The next hour or two seemed rather vague. I remember Larbi and Kenneth taking my clothes off and I did a belly dance to rounds of applause. I then put my clothes on and had a wrestling match with Larbi, and knocked over a rubbishy antique piss-pot or something, which was fortunately made of unbreakable teak or something, and didn't smash. Mohammed looked very disapproving.

Larbi, I suspected, was on the hash. Mohammed wasn't – we went into the bedroom. Mohammed did the full 'pleasure of sense and senselessness' bit, kissing me up and down. I kissed him. We got very sweaty – I find him a terrible little bore. I came again. He had it up me. Even when he kisses my arsehole he bores me. I believe he is happy in his work. When Mohammed and I had had our shower, the bell rang. It was Nigel, a very intelligent Englishman we had met, or rather Kenneth had met. Nigel had been a school-teacher. He's very middle-class but it doesn't show too much. Not in the least queer-looking. I looked out of the lavatory window. 'What do you want?' 'I wondered – ' he began and then said, 'I'm not interrupting anything, am I?' 'No,' I said, 'we've just finished, I'll let you in.' So I went to the door and let him in. 'I wondered if you were doing anything tonight.' 'No,' I said. 'We might have dinner together,' he said, which was perfectly acceptable. Until Kenneth appeared we talked. Nigel had practically no sex at all until five years ago – he's now forty-five. 'None?' I said. 'A little at school,' he said. 'I'd pick up a woman occasionally, but I had no homosexual relationship until I came out here. Of course, I'd always wanted them.' 'Wasn't it easy being a school-teacher?' I said. 'Oh, it was,' he said, 'it was terrible. And the boys, you know, are such terrible tarts. Once one of them called me into the music room and we sat down and he kissed me, and I mean, what can one do? I didn't dare respond. So I simply smiled and pushed the boy off, with instruction to continue the five-finger exercise. I'd set him to make a real assault on "Bluebells of Scotland", which was his examination piece.' Kenneth came out of the bedroom – Larbi was still preening himself in front of the mirror. 'He looks at himself and says, "Oh you beautiful boyee. If only I could have you!"' Kenneth said. Nigel spoke to Mohammed who, seeing an important Englishman, went stiff and formal and said, 'In ten days I go to Gibraltar. I work as a page in hotel.' 'How interesting for you,' Nigel said, 'I'm sure you'll do well in your chosen profession.' 'Yes,' Mohammed said pompously. 'I like the work, always I like the work. Beach no good! No good boys on beach.' 'He's doing his Manon Lescaut – Moll Flanders bit now,' I said to Nigel. 'I gave up going to the beach.' 'He who made the Great Renunciation,' Kenneth said, a quote by Dante[1] that nobody got but me. 'What is the name of the hotel,' Nigel asked, 'the Crater Palace?' 'It's the Clitoris Palace,' Kenneth said. 'Yes,' Mohammed said, flashing his teeth. 'The Clitoris Palace.' After we'd got rid of Mohammed and Larbi I said, 'I'm not having Mohammed much longer, he's such a bore.' 'Does he perform well?' Nigel said. 'Oh yes,' I said, 'but even his expertise is a bore.' I came out here determined to fuck him. I'd had the vision of him all winter. I saw his face, his body. If I'd met him in London, I would have fucked him like a slob, but somehow, although one can be bored and passive, one can't be bored and active, and so I've never fucked Mohammed though he's willing, and indeed he's had his arse stuffed by every Moroccan in sight.

We went out to dinner at Florcan. We had to wait for half an hour while both the Florcans – father and son – flounced about in carpet slippers and wouldn't

---

1 Dante Alighieri (1265–1321). Italian poet. According to his first biographer, Boccaccio, 'that singular splendour of the Italian race'.

do anything as mundane as taking orders. Later we had coffee at the boulevard. Met a funny old man who looked like a gnome with a white moustache, called Frank. He was a professor. He was full of the fact that he'd lost his voice. Kenneth in his element and holding forth. I'm glad he's happy for a change.[1]

Thursday 18 May

Went to The Windmill early. The weather after having poured with rain for the last two days cleared up and is perfect. I came back to the house at one to begin slaving over a hot stove with these wretched cakes. Nasser has made enough fucking mixture to drug a regiment. I'd already discovered how to work the oven. He made about two dozen cakes, and asked if I wanted l'amour. I said, 'No,' and then he suggested that he came back later and 'fabrique' more. I said, 'No,' I'd bake the rest. I said I watched how to do it – which was rolling it into balls and sticking them in the oven – and I was perfectly capable of doing that. So I got rid of him. Took his cakes out of the oven and nobbled one or two and put the rest of the mixture in a tin to bake as a whole. I had no idea how long to leave it in the oven. It was as hard as a biscuit. 'You've over-cooked it,' Kenneth said, when he returned from the beach. 'I've had a couple of small cakes.' Mohammed, thank God, isn't coming today. I told Nasser to come on Monday at one o'clock, so I lay on the settee in a beautiful daze just thinking, while Ken had sex with Larbi. Later we met George Greeves at the boulevard. He told me of a woman he'd helped by forging someone's name on a legal document. 'And I thought to myself as I did it, well you've been a sodomite, and every other shitty thing you can think of and now you're committing forgery.' Walked home with him and he suggested that we go with Dai Rees-Davies, the notorious one-eyed Tangier pirate, to Asila.

Friday 19 May

Fine brilliant weather. We had a walk to the Boulevard Pasteur in the morning to find vaseline. I went into a chemist's where, two or three days ago, I had asked for benzyl benzoate. (I'd a couple of spots round my cock and, though I'm sure now it's nothing serious, I thought I'd better be perfectly sure.) I'd explained what I wanted, when he hadn't understood benzyl by scratching my cock. The French bourgeois shopkeeper had given a horrified, 'Non!' and practically shoved me from his shop. When I went in for 'le tube de vaseline,' he looked on in disapproval as I bought two tubes.

Went to The Windmill and, because the beautiful German (or Danish) Vipsil wished to buy some souvenirs, I walked her into the casbah. How slow women

---

1 Orton to Kenneth Williams, undated postcard: '. . . Kenneth's having a marvellous time too, which is a great help all around . . .'

walk. She talked all the way of how in Islam women were 'treated so bad you know'. How she couldn't walk down the street without 'the bad things being said to me, you know'. And I thought, what a beautiful cow, and how right the Arabs were about women. I enjoyed the looks of envy as I walked along with her. In a shop a shopkeeper lifted a silver chain and offered it to her. 'Where does it go?' she said. He was just about to put it round her waist when I took it from him and put it round her waist. He completely accepted the reason for my taking the waistband from him, accepting also that she, whilst in my company, was my possession. And so, in fact, for a morning's walk around the town, I possessed the most beautiful and desirable girl in Tangier. I was curiously excited by this fact.

I showed her the flat. She seemed very impressed. Then I took her back to the beach, having bought nothing. 'It is all so bad,' she said. 'What rubbish,' I said. On a great Moroccan plate was stamped 'Made in Belgium'. Stayed sun-bathing until 2.30 when I went down to The Pergola – the beach place where the uglier queers in Tangier gather to stare at each other across professional beach boys. Larbi's father is the cabin attendant. I was hailed by the proprietor, Peter Pollock. Very blonde, almost certainly dyed, a sort of demi-queen, more queen by desire than nature. He has a shy, winning smile. He asked me to have a drink. 'I don't drink,' I said, 'but I'll have a Coca-Cola.' It was nice to think that before *Loot* and the £100,000, I wouldn't have been such a desirable personage. The Pergola had always slightly frightened me. A large bank balance in a gathering of queers is as popular as a large prick.

I drank my Coke and went for a drink with Larbi and a friend. We swam. I dived from the top board, something I'd done only once before – a day or two ago – to impress Vipsil – why I should want to impress her is impossible to imagine. Ken and I were supposed to be having a Dutchman, resident for fifteen years in Paris, to tea. But he didn't show up at The Windmill by 3.30, so we went home. We found that the Fatima had done all the weekly work and left all the clothes in water and bleaching solution, in the bath. Also that the stove wouldn't work. Larbi arrived and, when we told him that the stove didn't work, he grinned and said, 'I make it work, I fuck it good, yes?' He showed his cock. Laughed. Went into the kitchen and found that the Fatima, for some reason not able to be explained, had turned the gas off at the mains. So I got on to Agipgas and cancelled the order. Kenneth and Larbi went into the bedroom. I said to Mohammed, 'I shall give you a *petit cadeau*.' He immediately looked interested. 'These,' I said, indicating the trousers I was wearing. He looked put out because, as it turned out, he wanted the other, more expensive pair which I'd no intention of giving him. 'No *l'amour* today,' I said. 'Pourquoi?' I suddenly remembered it's always 'Why? Why?' with Mohammed. 'I don't feel well, I have a cold,' I said, and then desperately, 'I have syphilis.' 'Show me your cock,' he said, becoming most professional. I did. He examined the spots and said, 'This isn't syphilis. You can have *l'amour* today.' 'Non,' I said, 'today no *l'amour*.' I gave him the trousers, refused to give him the belt. He went and knocked on the door of Kenneth's room, had a long emotional scene in which he said I was behaving badly and didn't like him. 'For Christ's sake, give him five dirham!' Kenneth shouted. 'That'll make him shut up.'

So I took Mohammed back into the bedroom, explained that though I didn't want *l'amour* I would still give him the money. 'I know that,' he said, indignant. 'You give me money, yes – but me want *l'amour*. Me like you. Me want *l'amour*.' So we had sex, or at least I lay and allowed him to fuck me, and thought as his prick shot in and he kissed my neck, back and shoulders, that it was a most unappetising position for a world-famous artist to be in.

Kenneth and I went to dinner at a restaurant called Grillon. An American woman runs it. She looks as if she's Eve Arden's[1] stand-in's stand-in. She makes witty wise-cracks throughout the meal. She's not a bad type and her food is good. We saw George Greeves again on the boulevard as we strolled along. George was with a rather stuffy man with gingery hair, nearly bald, who he introduced as Somebody St. John. The man chatted – when he finally got up I said, 'Who is he?'

'Oh,' George said, 'she's a silly queen who's lived out here for years. She's doing some typing for me.' 'He looks rather tight-arsed,' I said. 'Don't you believe it, laddie, she's had camels up her ring-piece. I don't mean their pricks,' he said, as an afterthought, 'I mean their heads.' A little later the Dutchman, Stalk, sat with us. He looks like a fucking stork. Very tall and blonde. Looks as if he ought to be singing songs in praise of beer in some dreadful German shitty musical. He behaved like a pest.

Two boys went by, one of whom was Absolem, whom I had had last year, but found him too lethargic, like something off a Rubens canvas. I didn't want the whore sitting next to me, but Stalk spoke to them and, before we knew where we were, the great beauty rose was parked next to me and asked 'Why no *l'amour* for me?' Frank, the little old man of seventy-six with the white moustache who'd lost his voice the previous night, having found it again, sat with us. Absolem said to me, 'Frank very good friend of mine for two years – why he no speak to me now?' 'I don't know,' I said. 'He's probably found someone with a bigger prick than yours.' He was most put out. 'I go and speak with him.' He went and sat next to Frank, who was rather annoyed and tetchy. He's frightened of these boys I think. I heard Kenneth saying, 'Oh Frank, we're too middle-class to deal with them. Joe can deal with them. He comes from the gutter like they do.'

Absolem's friend then said to me, 'Hey, you had six today?' 'Six?' I said. 'No

---

1 Eve Arden (1912–   ). Wisecracking American film actress.

only one.' 'Six,' he said. 'Fuck?' 'Yes,' I said. 'You like to be fucked or fuck?' he said. 'I like to fuck, wherever possible', I said. He leaned across and said in a confidential tone, 'I take it.' 'Do you?' I said. 'Yes,' he said, 'up to the last hair.' 'You speak very good English,' I said. 'Where did you learn?' 'In school,' he said. It crossed my mind to ask who had taught him a sentence like the one he'd just used. 'Where you go tomorrow?' he said. 'Malabata,' I said. 'We could fuck at Malabata if we took enough towels,' he said, 'and the vaseline.' I was quite bowled over by his command of the English, and said again how excellent his command of my native tongue was. 'No doubt the command he had over his own tongue was even greater,' said Nigel, who'd just joined us. 'I have very good English,' said the boy, whose name was inevitably Mohammed, and he produced a battered book, *Colloquial English for the Beginner*. I leafed through it but found hardly a reference to vaseline and none to taking it up to the last hair. 'We must make a date,' the boy said. 'I'll see you sometime,' I said, refusing to make any more dates. My life beginning to run to a timetable no member of the royal family would tolerate.[1]

Saturday 20 May

Day fine; clear, brilliant sun. Met Stalk as arranged and, under Larbi's guidance, stood by the bus-stop. We met Mustapha. He was about fourteen. 'We're going to Malabata,' I said. 'Would you like to come with us?' He made no objection and we waited for the bus. However, there was the prospect of fucking Mustapha in the hills outside the town and I endured all with patience and thought of the tube of KY Jelly in my haversack along with the bottles of lemonade.

At last Nigel drew up in his car. It's a four-seater and he offered to give us a lift. However, he hadn't realised that Mustapha was with us and chickened-out of taking him on the grounds that he couldn't carry six. I wanted to get out with Mustapha and wait for the bus, but Kenneth objected and said, 'No, let Mustapha join us at Malabata.' 'But,' objected Stalk, 'he won't do that.' 'Yes, he will,' said Kenneth.

By now I was in a great rage. 'I'll get out and get the bus with Mustapha,' I said. 'No, no!' Kenneth said and, foreseeing great scenes ahead if I did get out, Nigel drove off, and before we were out of sight we saw the boy speaking to some tourist. I sat sick and glum. 'It's too dangerous to take boys of that age in the car,' Kenneth said. Nigel agreed. I said nothing and went into a world of my own for

---

1 Orton to Kenneth Williams, undated postcard showing 'Typical Morocco' – a woman at her loom: 'I'm sure you'll be interested in this totally unexpected local trade. Anglo-Arab relations here really couldn't be bettered. My memoirs will be bid for with avidity, but they'll go to you for a song (you can choose the song!).'

the rest of the day, shutting the door and refusing to speak to anyone on the ill-fated trek to Malabata. Sulking in the hot sun, refusing even to drink and thinking of the wasted KY Jelly liquefying at the bottom of the bag.

I began to walk back. We strolled along the sand for miles, back to Tangier. I said nothing and the others chatted. I went and had a bath and lay on the bed. I made a cup of tea, drew the blinds and dozed until 5.30. Sat writing this diary until the doorbell rang. It was Nigel with Larbi's jacket, which he'd left in the car. I spoke to him. 'Do you want to come in?' I said. 'I warn you though, I'm still sulking.' 'Oh, good heavens, I wouldn't want to disturb you,' Nigel said and left.

We met him again later, at dinner. He had a curious man with him, the Marquis of something or other. A man who said a pipe of opium was pure heaven, and who I suspected was wearing a toupee, though I couldn't be sure. He took us back to his house and name-dropped. 'I remember the Duke of Windsor[1] saying his mother the Queen Mary[2] never had a new dress in thirty years. And I was there when Madame de Gaulle[3] made her famous gaffe, you know. Somebody asked her, "What are you looking forward to when you retire?" "I am looking forward most to a penis," she replied. After a pause somebody said, "Oh, oui, happiness, madame?"'

The Marquis' house was crammed with junk. It looked like a Chelsea antique shop. Rubbish from the rag-bag of eighteenth-century culture. Mirrors with the original glass – so cracked that to see one's self in them was to have a vision of what one's face might look like on the Day of Judgement, the marks of the grave upon it. 'What shall you have to drink?' the Marquis said, leading me away from a monstrous, over-sized, headless nude statue of a man. 'Coca-Cola,' I said, feeling that the mere pronouncing of the word would dispel the mucky grandeur of the past. The Marquis looked put out. 'You would not prefer . . . ?' and he said the name of some unsavoury and unpronounceable drink to match the furniture. 'No,' I said, 'just a Coke.' We sat drinking and he told us of 'the Princess Marina[4],' and 'What do you think of the Earl of Snowdon[5]? Do you not think he's an unhappy man?' 'The royal family is a noose,' I said. 'You don't have to put your head into it. If a man does so, he must expect to be unhappy.' 'Ah, oui,' said the Marquis, shrugging his shoulders and trying to look like a character in Proust[6]. We were sitting on the most uncomfortable chairs I have ever bummed.

1 Duke of Windsor (1894–1972). As Prince of Wales, he succeeded his father to the throne on 20 January 1936 as Edward VIII; but abdicated on 11 December after the furore over his proposed marriage to the American divorcee, Mrs Wallace Simpson.

2 Queen Mary (1867–1953).

3 Madame de Gaulle. Wife of President de Gaulle of France.

4 Princess Marina, Duchess of Kent (1906–1968)..

5 Earl of Snowdon (Antony Armstrong-Jones) (1930–   ). Photographer, then married to Princess Margaret.

6 Marcel Proust (1871–1922). French novelist.

Near me was a table and most conspicuous on it were three photographs, a coloured one of Paul VI[1] (unsigned), a small block of John XXIII[2] with something written on it in the Holy Father's own fair hand, and a large, obviously forties studio portrait of the wartime Pope which said, across the white robe, 'Yours very sincerely, Pius XII[3].'

Sunday 21 May

George Greeves and Dai Rees-Davies picked us up in the car at 10.30. I told George we'd met the Marquis. 'Oh the phoney marquis,' George said. 'Yes, she's a dirty bit of the South of France trade from way back. Now she's a marquis.' 'Well there you are,' I said. 'He has several portraits of the popes.' I told him about the 'yours very sincerely' signed one. 'Oh, she probably signed that herself,' George said. He took us to The Diplomatic Forest. 'This is where to come if you want to get raped,' he said, and then began singing in a loud bass voice, 'Make way for the buggery bus. Here comes the buggery bus.'

We stopped at the beach. Talked to a boy covered in sand. He wanted to come with us. 'No, we'd better not,' George said. 'He's going to be a nuisance with that sandy arse in Dai's car. Dai likes a sandy arse on his face, but not on his upholstery, you fucking old sodomite, you.' Dai beamed his glass eye, catching the light and giving him a positively devilish air – like a picture mothers show their children captioned 'Do not accept sweets from this man.' 'Well,' said George, '"that's the sand in the vaseline," as an old friend of mine used to say.'

We stopped the car several times on the way to chat to boys and give them cigarettes. Very shy boys. 'I like the ones who blush,' George said. 'I remember I used to fuck the blushes off their faces and when they said, "Madre mio. Oh! Oh! Please don't," that's when I used to shove it up.' He cackled and then looked sad at the memory he'd conjured up. Dai said, 'I had a little girl come up in this lift with me once. She got my cock out and began to suck it, and when the lift stopped she ran away and I found my wallet had gone from my back pocket.' 'Serves you right, you dirty old queen,' George said, 'messing with the unclean ones.' He laughed and then began talking of founding a temple. 'I'd have a tall penis on the high altar,' George said, 'and underneath we'd have a furnace for the prudish. We'd throw them down and the smoke would rise and wreathe the glowing altar penis with glory.'

We reached Asilah, a small village 40 kilometres from Tangier. We passed through the most beautiful countryside, the roads lined with mimosa and

1 Paul VI (Giovanni Battista Montini) (1897–1978). Became Pope in 1963. Travelled more widely than any previous Popes.
2 John XXIII (Angelo Guiseppe Roncalli) (1881–1963). Became Pope in 1958.
3 Pius XII (Eugenio Pacelli) (1876–1958). Elected Pope in 1939.

eucalyptus; blue mountains in the distance. The weather was perfect – not a cloud. The sea calm with an hour-glass like transparency. When we got to Asilah we drew up at the only beach place there is in the village. It's run by a Peter Churchill who, I believe, is a relative in some form, though I haven't bothered to enquire, of the Churchill who distinguished himself in the last war by wearing a plum-coloured siren suit. Pete Churchill is tall and grey. Friendly. I had a Coca-Cola. A very attractive fifteen-year-old boy, wearing nothing but a pair of red bathing-drawers, served us. His name was Abdul-Aziz. He had a jut on his bum. His face unfortunately was marred by an eruption of spots. Dai went away to arrange for his car to be looked after and came back saying that a group of boys who had seen us arrive had asked if I was English and 'does he do things?' which is a very sweet thing to ask.[1] 'Very sensible too,' Dai said. 'They're practical people you know.'

We went into the lounging area and, at a table under a sunshade, sat four middle-aged, middle-class English tourists. All women. 'Those fuckers can go for a start,' said George. 'I don't want that kind of shit round me when I am eating my meal.' I heard one of the tourist ladies asking for tea. 'We asked over half an hour ago,' she said so desperately that I had a twinge of conscience. 'I come,' Abdul-Aziz said. 'He'll fucking come,' George said, 'right up your smelly cunt, if you ask him.'

I went away, having been given the key to cabin No. 10 by Abdul-Aziz. The tag came off the key and I left it in the cabin and gave Abdul-Aziz the nude key, and went for a swim. The water was perfect. I swam for about half a mile to a long line of rocks, climbed out and sunned myself near a group of very young boys – an older boy was with them. They asked if I was French. I reluctantly said, 'No, Anglais.' 'Parlez-vous Français?' said one of the boys. I shook my head. 'Habla Espanol?' said another one of the boys. I smiled and said, 'No.' After a general display of friendliness, I ambled away and, before I was out of earshot, I heard 'une petite derrière' blown towards my ear in the breeze – perhaps three of the dozen words of French I do understand.

I swam back to find George, Dai and Kenneth sitting under a vast striped umbrella, eating. Abdul-Aziz still served in his red drawers. He brushed up against me as he served, giving the passing of a sardine a sensitiveness all of its own. 'Does he rub up against you?' I asked the others. 'No,' Kenneth said. 'Oh,' I said, 'I thought it part of the service.' 'That boy,' said George, 'is the boy of

---

1 Orton to Peter Gill, 22 May 1967: 'The other day I visited a small village about 50 miles from Tangier. I went with a notorious one-eyed paederast. As we got out of the car, we were surrounded by boys. Several of them smiled at me and then spoke to the one-eyed paederast in French. "What did they say?" I asked, when we were away from the boys. "Oh," he said, "they wanted to know if you were English and did you do things!" I think that's my philosophy of life from now on: not to look English and not to look as though I do things.'

Pete Churchill.' 'So you'd better watch out,' Kenneth said. 'Oh you don't have to worry,' said George, stuffing potato salad down him. 'Take him down to the cabin and fuck him.' It was a perfect day. I bathed again later. Saw Ian Horobin. 'He's wearing exactly the same get-up as in Tangier,' Kenneth said. 'Perhaps he's come from the sea.' 'He certainly looks like the fucking beast from 20,000 fathoms,' G. said, casting a malevolent sneer in the direction of Ian. 'Do you want to see the Sultan's Palace?' Dai said, 'But when the boys here ask you if you want to see the Sultan's Palace, they take advantage of you in there.' 'He means they get you inside and get you to fuck them,' George said. 'There was one man, I believe,' Dai said, 'who complained that a boy who had taken him into the palace had come too quickly. "Well have me, then," the custodian said. And I'm told he was most satisfactory.' 'Spunk all over the Sultan's fixtures,' George said. 'The buggery always stops at the Sultan's Palace.'

We drove to the palace through winding lanes. We met Ted Woodham, who owns a restaurant in Asilah – the *only* English restaurant. 'Hallo,' he said to Dai, 'nice to see you here. Why don't you come for a cup of tea?' 'Oh, we're in rather a hurry,' said Dai. 'We're going to show these boys the palace.' 'Good luck then,' said Ted. Before he was out of sight George said, 'Did she mean a cup of tea at her place or the restaurant?' 'Oh the restaurant, I'd say,' Dai said. 'Well, the mean old bitch. Fuck her then. I'm not paying to drink her piss.'

There appeared to be no attractive boys round the palace, only the Australian. 'Do either of you want her,' George said. We said, 'No,' and drove home along sun-baked roads, and a sea flat and enamel-looking. A day so perfect that sex really seemed irrelevant. 'So nice to know it was available if one wanted it,' Kenneth said.

We arrived home at four. At 4.30 Mohammed Khomsi arrived. I was angry because I had told him Tuesday. 'No *l'amour*.' He said, 'I want to see you.' 'No,' I said, 'I told you Tuesday.' He said, 'I no come here again.' 'OK,' I said. 'What time Tuesday?' 'Five,' I said. He went, and in another hour Larbi rang at the door. He went into the salon and spoke to Kenneth, and then he came and said, 'You like my friend?' 'Who?' I said. 'Mon ami.' 'Yes,' I said, 'He very good boy,' Larbi said. 'You like *l'amour* for him?' 'When?' 'Today. I fetch him from The Pergola.' He went away and returned with the boy. He looked like the kind of boy I used to go to school with. He was fifteen or sixteen. His name was Mohammed. I started to call him Mohammed Swinnerton to distinguish him from the rest. We sat drinking tea. K. and L. went off into 'la casa'. I got Mohammed Swinnerton on the couch and we kissed. His tongue hovered over my lips and I got harder. So I took him into the bedroom. He was very shy. I thought of George Greeves and shy boys. We lay on the bed in our underpants. Then I took his off. Later my own. He had a beautiful body and a nice prick. I did the full stint this time. Later we showered and went into the salon, where, with my arm around him, he smoked a cigarette. I began to play with his cock. I got a hard on and then, quite suddenly, he fell asleep. I lay on the couch with him for a long time while waiting for Ken and Larbi. As I'd had a large amount of hashish cake (as had Mohammed Swinnerton) I all but fell asleep myself.

K. and L. appeared at last. Went to dinner about eight. But before then we both had a fit of the giggles and the sudden mounting hysteria that gives away the hashish-swallower as surely as a hole in the back gives away a sword swallower. 'We can't go anywhere too respectable like this,' Kenneth said, after we all had hysterics over some weak joke. We decided on Nino's as being the kind of restaurant where we could disgrace ourselves without too much damage being done. The rest of the evening rather strange. I remember meeting George Greeves again on the Place de France, telling him of my rage at the unopened tube of vaseline on the Malabata trip. Later again I said to Nigel how like a frog Dai Rees-Davies looked. 'Yes,' Nigel agreed, 'he does look rather like a frog.' 'But perhaps he isn't really a frog,' I said, turning to the plate-glass window of the Café de Paris behind us. 'If we threw him through these windows he'd turn into a handsome prince.' Nigel looked doubtful and Kenneth said I'd gone too far in fantasy. Came home. Kenneth wanted me to wank him. I said 'OK,' unwillingly because I knew that in the condition of hash it takes so long. He wanted a French letter putting on his cock. I put it on and pulled at his cock for about an hour while he made pleasurable noises, but showed no signs of an orgasm. Finally I gave up and went into the bathroom to clean my teeth. I saw him masturbating himself, and closed the bathroom door. Evident enjoyment was on his face.

Monday 22 May

Weather misty. Not good in the afternoon. Good in the morning. K. and I went to the beach at 10.15. Vipsil leaving today. Bill Fox very oddly left yesterday without appearing again. Saw Mohammed Swinnerton. Spoke to him bitterly. I'd got Nasser coming at one. So I didn't want to complicate life too much. I bathed. The water was cold. Then I came home at 12.45. At 1.15, no sign of Nasser. I went to the corner shop and bought 50 francs worth of cheese and ate it with a piece of bread for my lunch. No Nasser looked like appearing.

I received a letter from Peter Gill at the Royal Court – there seems no serious cause for alarm at his final casting, though except in one or two cases, no cause either for great expectation.[1] It's very much a Royal Court cast. I hope the plays work under those circumstances. Certainly they have no worse casts, in some

1 Peter Gill to Joe Orton, 18 May 1967: 'There are many problems – I hope not insurmountable ones: Avril to be phlegmatic enough; Michael Standing to be internal and young enough; Bernard as Erpingham; Roddy to be Irish; Yvonne Antrobus to be real; and also the "Lord Chamberlain".'

cases better, than *Sloane* or *Loot*. I don't think there'll be a performance like Michael Bates, and *The Erpingham Camp*, of course, is simply *Hamlet* without the Prince. Bernard Gallagher never could be brilliant as Erpingham. He's totally miscast, though there isn't much else one can do except have Erpingham played by a good serious actor, and surround him with comedy 'cameos' – the staff. It should, of course, be a comic lead of the Truscott kind, surrounded by a staff slightly less ludicrous than the central figure. Wrote to Peter. Also to Peter Willes, because Nasser didn't arrive. This isn't serious as far as sex is concerned, but it is serious in that Nasser is our one *good* contact for hashish. He knows where to buy the pure, first-class stuff to boil down and use in cakes. Ken arrived home at three. Frank told me a story about a soldier who was in a military hospital and one of the nurses came from behind the screen and began laughing. 'What are you laughing at?' her friend said. 'The patient in there has "Son" tattooed on his penis,' the nurse replied. 'Oh, it read Sachatuon when I saw it,' her friend said. Kenneth and I both had a piece of hashish cake. I broke a large piece off the cake I made. Kenneth had a small piece of mine and one of the scone-like things which Nasser made. Larbi arrived at four. Later we had a curious violent wrestling match. Larbi fostered a candlestick between his legs and was running around giggling that it was 'une grande cock.' He dragged me into the bedroom. We fell onto the bed. Larbi began tearing my clothes off. 'No! No!' I struggled to get away from him and suddenly saw that the table lamp was about to topple over. The bed creaked ominously. I realised also that he must have had more of the stuff than me. He rocked to and fro and suddenly the doorbell rang and we got up. Kenneth mustered Nigel, Frank and Stalk into the salon. Larbi, still very giggly, entered buttoning his fly. We talked for a while. Mostly about the flat which Stalk says is really full of valuable period furniture. He looked into my bureau. 'This bureau,' he said, peering at a really dreary chest of drawers, 'is really beautiful. It's Louis Quinze.' 'It has convenient drawers,' I said, opening one. Inside was a used French letter. 'Good gracious,' said Stalk. 'Is that antique as well?' asked Nigel. 'Kenneth will leave them lying around,' I said, 'or else he fills my pockets with the things.'

We drove off to the mountain. The English colony have succeeded in turning a fair-sized hill near Tangier into a replica of a Surrey backwater. Twisty lanes, foxgloves, large pink rambling roses, tennis courts and gardens watered by sprinklers. Only here and there does the presence of a palm show that Africa is waiting. We drove through an olde English garden and were welcomed by a man called Kevin, who is, I was later told, a millionaire. He was of middle height and had a pleasant face, always smiling. He was also a bit fattish. I'd say he was in his early thirties. He had a Moroccan youth with him. Later Frank said the boy had 'classical good looks' and this confirmed my own impression of him as resembling a ginger-coloured Ivor Novello[1]. We were led into a large entrance hall differing from that of the British Museum entrance only in that there was no postcard stand. The vast interior was decorated with urns and hubble-bubbles which were fastened to the floor. On the second floor was one big living-room, several small lavatories and something for preparing drinks. I saw no bedroom. The view from the terrace was beautiful. The town lay spread beneath us, and the bay and the mountain in the distance, a soft almost purple light covered the whole scene. I was aware, by that time, that the hashish was having an effect on me, and because I'd been warned not to do so, I had a double whiskey. Kenneth at the same time had a large gin. The world became even more wonderful, my limbs felt as if they were made of rubber and, catching sight of myself in the mirror, I gazed, without self-consciousness, for perhaps five minutes, or so it seemed, into my own eyes.[2] The conversation was deathly dull as a whole. I believe, without the aid of the drugs, it would have been unbearably tedious. But I felt elated, danced a wild dance around the hall, positively spinning round the urns and hubble-bubbles, like a teetotum. The others came down the stairs talking in mellow English tones, and upon seeing me, Nigel remarked, 'Is this his farewell performance?'

At the end of dinner, which we had at Nino's, Kenneth looked, and said he felt, suddenly sick. We'd paid our bill when Madame Jungles swept in. He is a most extraordinary person. Having no talent for female impersonation at all. He is simply a dowdy, suburban housewife who has chosen to pass herself off as a perverted female impersonator. 'Hello, Joe,' he said. 'By the way, I saw your show in London and I thought it was fabulous.' She turned away. 'When are you going to write a part for me?' She suddenly was serious. 'No, I shouldn't have said that. It was rude of me.' After a few seconds of polite chit-chat I got away. 'What a terribly sad creature that man is,' Nigel said. 'He's a woman really, isn't he?' I felt rather tired and had a headache and felt lost by this time. I was very glad therefore when Nigel decided not to have coffee, but to go straight home. Kenneth and I did the same. 'I'm not taking drink with hash again,' Kenneth said. 'I felt as though I was going to be sick in there.' I was by no means feeling well, but we were considerably heartened by the sight of an ornamental electric arch, erected to span the boulevard and delight the tourists, in ruins having been struck by a passing car and toppled over to the shrieks of alarm and superfluous horror from the ruled women of the East.

1 Ivor Novello (1893–1951). Welsh actor, composer, songwriter and dramatist. His song 'Keep the Home Fires Burning' was one of the most successful in World War I.
2 Kenneth Cranham: 'He thought he was really beautiful, Joe did. His real buzz was himself. When he'd leave a room, he would stand in front of a mirror – very upright – and look at himself like he thought he was very butch, very masculine. He was quite small and rather cuddly, really.'

Tuesday 23 May

Felt 'hangoverish' this morning and, as I've never known hashish leave me with any unpleasant effects, I concluded that the whiskey had been responsible and will never mix the two again. Wine seems to mingle with hashish very well. Spirits apparently do not unite with any harmonious result.

Went to The Windmill to get out of Fatima's way. The weather, dull sky veiled with cloud. Kenneth has several boils on the inside of his thighs which, he says, are extremely painful. By one o'clock we decided that the weather wasn't going to be good enough and came home. At 1.10 the bell rang and it was Nasser who'd mistaken the day. I asked him for a cup of tea. 'I'd have him and tell Mohammed Khomsi to go and fuck himself,' Kenneth said. Nasser had to go at two, so after a directive to appear on Friday at one, we went into the hall and kissed goodbye. We both got very randy and then he had to go because it was two. We had taken the cakes with lemon tea, and just before, I'd had a couple of valium tablets, and the effect was most odd – a perfect contentment. I lay on the bed thinking of the Mohammed Khomsi affair. Even in this state of wake and sleep I was worried by the lack of 'pornographic' element in Mohammed's character. I couldn't, although feeling erotic, feel excited by the prospect of his imminent visit. When he did turn up, I was wandering round the flat in a daze. We talked for a while and then went into the bedroom and I was buggered. He tossed me off afterwards and with his other hand played about my body. He then said he wanted eleven dirham. He owed this to the woman who'd altered his trousers. He produced a letter from somebody in Aden who was proposing sending him twenty dollars within the next week. He painted a truly piteous prospect of the shock it would be for him if he didn't appear, before going to Gibraltar, in new *pantalons*. I finally gave him the eleven when I realised that, as he was going off to his native village on Thursday and when he returned would be off to Gibraltar, this would be the last time I would have to look at his stupid face. Finally he pissed off. Kenneth and I then had hysterics about a letter I had just received from Kenneth Williams in which he describes Baron Favier as a man who 'sometimes effects a lace blouse'. We had got, though, to the giggly stage of the drugs progress and couldn't judge whether the letter was as funny as we thought. Went to dinner at the Alhambra. Kenneth's boils so painful that he could hardly walk. We had coffee and went home.

Wednesday 24 May

Kenneth decided to stop at home today. I went down to The Windmill. Frank, who arrived at 11.30, an hour after me, had a tale to tell of how he was making a papier-mâché mask of Kevin's boy 'because I collect beautiful boys' faces you know.' 'What about their cocks,' I said. 'Well they can't stay hard long enough for the plaster of Paris mould to set,' he said, bitterly. 'I've tried, you know, to discover whether there isn't a quick-drying plaster.' 'You mean some quick-drying emulsion for preserving the pricks of the contemporary male?' I said. 'Something like that,' Frank said.

Went home. Kenneth's boils are a bit better. Larbi arrived at five with no Mohammed Swinnerton. 'Boy crazy, he go off to eat with English tourists.' So no boy. 'I got another boy for you. He's outside. Please look.' So I looked outside, and there was a not bad boy – nothing to give your cock the shrinkings, but nothing to start the balls rolling. I looked back. 'Not today,' I said. Larbi nodded. 'OK. I tell boy,' he said. He leaned round the door and shouted something in Arabic. It sounded like some phrase like, 'You won't be needed tonight.' The boy pissed off. Larbi and Kenneth and I sat talking, and then Larbi and K. went into the bedroom to have sex, and I sat writing this diary. I have just taken two valium tablets to see what effect they have. (Later . . .) The tablets worked to the extent of sending me into a semi-trance for the rest of the evening. Larbi relaxing and perfectly pleasant.

We went to Nino's. It was almost empty except for a party of English women who were busy wondering whether it was *oeuf* or *boeuf* which meant 'beef'. 'Because if it's beef, I've been warned,' one of them said. Later, as we strolled towards the Boulevard Pasteur, a quite nice boy of about seventeen approached me. 'Hallo,' he said. I didn't think I'd ever seen him before but I said, 'Hallo,' and we shook hands. 'You like love with me?' he said. 'No,' I said. 'I do the *soixant-neuf*,' he said and added with a beam, 'I suck you.' This is something I'd never heard a Moroccan offer before. 'Someday,' I said. 'Now,' he said. 'He'll do the 69!' Kenneth said in a loud hiss. 'I'm not keen on that sort of thing,' I said. Kenneth turned to the boy and shrugged at his shoulders. 'He crazy,' he said. The boy laughed too and shook hands. 'Sometime, eh?' I nodded, dazed by the whole episode which I'd only dimly grasped. 'He wasn't trade,' Kenneth said. 'He genuinely fancied you.' 'He was trade,' I said.

We sat at the boulevard and drank Coca-Cola. We were joined by Frank and Kevin (the man everyone calls a millionaire). Very boring conversation, but a succession of very pretty boys to look at passing at intervals. And all available!

Thursday 25 May

Kenneth decided not to go to the beach. His boils slightly better, but still painful. 'Imagine how Job felt,' I said, 'and you'll forget your troubles.' 'Piss off,' he said, 'and get down to The Windmill.' Arrived at beach at about eleven. Weather perfect though a cold wind by the shoreline. On the way to The Windmill I met the boy I'd had at Bill Fox's and at the baths. I had already warned Kenneth that I intended bringing him back if I met him. 'Hallo,' he said. 'Hallo,' I said.

'*L'amour* today?' I said. 'Today,' he nodded slowly. 'What time?' 'Come to The Windmill at two o'clock.' He nodded and went away.

I lay in the sun till twelve. Went for a swim. Talked to Frank. 'My mask of that young Moroccan,' he said, 'came out rather well. I'm engaged on doing the eyes. I colour them the best I can.' 'What colour do you use for the face?' I said. 'Oh I try and get it as exact as I can,' he said, 'though I'm afraid my efforts could hardly compare with the works of the divine Madame Tussaud.'¹ At one o'clock Ken rang. 'Your waiter's just turned up,' he said. 'But I told him Friday at one.' 'He must have lost his appointment diary then,' Ken said. 'I said you were at the *plage*.' A few minutes later Nasser hovered on to the scene. He hadn't understood the day. 'Come tomorrow at one for *l'amour*,' I said, 'to the apartment at one.' He smiled, tossed a few remarks about how 'wapu' I was, and how he liked *l'amour* with me, didn't 'go with tourists'. All of which may or may not be true.

After he'd gone, the boy Larbi brought round last night appeared. I returned his greetings and approached him. He was an English schoolboy too, but the tall blonde type who looks fetching in tennis flannels. I was pretty vague with him. I then saw Mohammed (the one that was coming at two – he wore a yellow jersey and, to distinguish him from the rest of his kind, I'll call him Mohammed Yellow-jersey). So I had a couple of poached eggs and a coffee, and nodded for Mohammed Yellow-jersey to follow.

I went onto the Avenue d'Espagne and Mohammed Yellow-jersey was still following. I let him in and he sat on my bed smiling. Kenneth came out of the bathroom. I went in for a shit. When I came back Kenneth was sitting in a dressing-gown. 'Do you want tea?' I said to Yellow-jersey. 'Yes, please,' he said. I made a pot. He had condensed milk in it and three spoonfuls of sugar. Kenneth and I talked. He had a piece of hash cake. I wasn't going to risk it fucking up the sex. I took a couple of valium though. I usually find a mild muscular relaxant helpful. I took the boy (who is about fifteen) into the room. We took off our clothes and lay together. I stroked him, kissed his nipples. When I'd got a spanking good hard on, I turned the lad over and, using a little grease mixed with my spit, I put my prick up his arse. I found he wouldn't take the cock up the arse. He cried out as it went in. But he allowed me to have the prick between the buttocks which, as I fucked, he agitated in a most alarming way. At this point I, my hand well-greased, put my hand under him and took his medium-to-large tool in my hand. While I fucked him, I pressed his prick between my clenched fist and had a truly satisfactory orgasm.

We dozed for fifteen minutes or so and then he had a *douche*. We smiled a lot and I gave him six dirham and he asked for another, so I gave him seven. We displayed more affection and then he went and drenched himself with a cheap

---

1 Madame Tussaud (Marie Cresholtz) (1760–1850). Swiss-born modeller in wax.

kind of eau-de-cologne which Kenneth had bought for midge bites. I made a pot of tea, had a largish slice of hashish cake and came into the living-room. 'Very good,' I said to Kenneth. 'Just my type.' 'You must let Nasser fuck you occasionally,' Kenneth said, 'or otherwise we shall not be able to get the hashish.'

When Larbi arrived at five, I went to the boulevard to get some tablets for Kenneth. I bought them and sat on the Place de France drinking mint tea. Nearby was a quartet of English tourists and one woman was saying 'Well, the best holiday we ever had was in Plymouth, but we didn't have the weather unfortunately.'[1] As I walked back a Moroccan approached me. 'You English?' 'Yes,' I said. He looked at me. 'You want girls?' he said. 'No,' I said. He paused and coughed a bit and said in a tentative tone, 'You like boys?' 'No,' I said. 'OK. Goodbye,' he said.

I had a very pleasant stroll back, the hash and valium working well. Met Ian Horrible. 'How are you?' I said. 'Alive, I regret to say,' he said. 'Has anything exciting been happening?' he said, and I told him of my Yellow-jersey episode. 'Yes,' he said, 'he's quite a nice kid.' 'A very valuable addition to my collection,' I said. He chortled to himself and gave a spin into a café, leaving me relieved by his departure. I found Ken and Larbi still in the bedroom when I returned. After a while Larbi came out quite naked parading up and down in front of the long mirror in the hall admiring himself. I gave Kenneth the tablets. He took two and said they gave him the most odd feeling on top of the hashish.

We sat talking of how happy we both felt and of how it couldn't, surely, last. We'd have to pay for it. Or we'd be struck down from afar by disaster because we were, perhaps, too happy. To be young, good-looking, healthy, famous, comparatively rich *and* happy is surely going against nature, and when to the above list one adds that daily I have the company of beautiful fifteen-year-old boys who find (for a small fee) fucking with me a delightful sensation, no man can want for more. '*Crimes of Passion* will be a disaster,' Kenneth said. 'That will be the scapegoat. We must sacrifice *Crimes of Passion* in order that we may be spared disaster more intolerable.'

We went to the Alhambra for dinner. I had a glass of wine because it works well with hash. Kenneth already with hash and valium inside him decided *not* to risk vino as well. We went for a stroll. Sat on the boulevard at the Café de Paris and, at ten, rose to go, only to meet Nigel, Frank and Kevin who persuaded us to stay a little longer. In the re-allotment of places, I sat next to a rather stuffy

1 Orton to Peggy Ramsay, 30 May 1967: '. . . Hardly any tourists. Occasionally a cruise ship docks for a night and then we have clumps of the most terrible English middle-classery in flowered frocks sitting at the cafés looking as though rape was imminent. On one of these occasions I overheard a woman, with the sunlight dappling her C and A Modes hat, the exotic palms and the Arabs in their fezzes around her, saying in a loud voice, "The best holiday we ever had was in Plymouth." I felt like pouring my mint tea down her neck.'

American tourist and his disapproving wife. They listened to our conversation and I, realising this, began to exaggerate the content. 'He took me right up the arse,' I said, 'and afterwards he thanked me for giving him such a good fucking. They're most polite people.' The American and his wife hardly moved a muscle. 'We've got a leopard-skin rug in the flat and he wanted me to fuck him on that,' I said in an undertone which was perfectly audible to the next table. 'Only I'm afraid of the spunk you see, it might adversely affect the spots of the leopard.' Nigel said quietly, 'Those tourists can hear what you're saying.' He looked alarmed. 'I mean them to hear,' I said. 'They have no right to be occupying chairs reserved for decent sex perverts.' And then with excitement I said, 'He might bite a hole in the rug. It's the writhing he does, you see, when my prick is up him that might grievously damage the rug, and I can't ask him to control his excitement. It wouldn't be natural when you're six inches up the bum, would it?'

The American couple frigidly paid for their coffee and moved away. 'You shouldn't drive people like that away,' Nigel said. 'The town needs tourists.' 'Not that kind, it doesn't,' I said. 'This is *our* country, *our* town, *our* civilisation. I want nothing to do with the civilisation they made. Fuck them! They'll sit and listen to buggers' talk from me and drink their coffee and piss off.'[1] 'It seems rather a strange joke,' Frank said with an old school-teacher's smile. 'It isn't a joke,' I said, 'there's no such thing as a joke.'

Nigel, who was drinking some strange brandy, got very excited by a girl who passed. She looked like a boy. She was German. We discussed women for a bit and I wrote them off as a mistake. 'Who wants a girl to look like a boy?' I said. 'Or a boy to look like a girl? It's not natural.' 'I really think, Joe,' Nigel said, 'that you shouldn't bring nature into your conversation quite so often, you who have done more than anyone I know to outrage her.' 'I've never outraged nature,' I said. 'I've always listened to her advice and followed it to wherever it went.' We left at eleven. I feel so content.

I slept all night soundly and woke up at seven feeling as though the whole of creation was conspiring to make me happy. I hope no doom strikes.

Friday 26 May

Weather cloudy. I did my exercises, wrote a letter home to Peggy. She has written to say that *Loot* is going on Broadway. Rather stupid as we both agree that it stands no chance whatsoever of success on Broadway.[2] A small theatre off, or

---

1 Orton attributed his arrogance to Tangier. 'This is an arrogant letter,' he wrote Peggy Ramsay, 10 June 1966. 'It must be the effect of living in Morocco for three months. Everybody here behaves in a very "Fuck you" sort of way . . .'

2 Orton to Peggy Ramsay, 26 May 1967: 'Really, though, I think it's a miracle [*Loot* has] run so long. We can't grumble at its falling off. The great middle-brow public *never* took it to their hearts. Which brings me neatly to Broadway. I *curse* Michael White from the bottom of my pitiless soul for getting some sucker to agree to on-Broadway. It will flop in a fortnight. I was looking forward to

semi-off Broadway would have been a better bet. But who cares what the
Americans do – as long as they pay plenty of cash, they can play *Loot* in the
middle of Times Square. Reputations are made in London, only money is made
in New York.

I lay on the terrace from about 11.45 until 12.45. I lay about naked trying to
get my back and buttocks a decent colour. I've burnt my bum a little, but it'll cool
off. I took a cool shower and Nasser arrived at 1.10. He'd been down to The
Windmill, in spite of the fact that I'd told him I'd be at *la casa* today. We had a
long sex session. Finally, wringing with sweat, he rolled off me having not come.
'I love you too much,' he said, by way of explanation. I thought this a piece of real
sexual devotion. I have frequently given my best sexual performance with people
I didn't love, in fact rather despised. I have fucked the arses off aging queens
quite easily, but found a beautiful young boy often too difficult to come, because
I loved him too much. We lay for a long time wrapped in a towel, feeling very
exhausted and *'tranquil'* as he said. He took a shower. I washed my cock in the
approved Moroccan manner. He promised to come on Sunday with some hash to
fabrique un gateau Anglais, or at least I, with the aid of a cake mix, will make an
English cake with a hash filling.

After a lunch of hard-boiled eggs and cold potatoes I lay in the sun for another
hour or so and read *A Case of Human Bondage* by Beverley Nichols. A quite
ridiculous book. A documentary material written in the style of *Aida*[2]. Very
entertaining though. It has the quality of all rubbish and great art of being
readable. Its success is deserved ... Larbi arrived and, after lemon tea and
schoolboy banter, he disappeared into the bedroom with Kenneth, whose thigh
with three enormous boils isn't pretty to behold. Fortunately, as he caught them
off Larbi it doesn't matter, and he says the tablets have worked in that they are
no longer painful except where they press against his clothes. At about five, there
was a ring at the door and Mohammed Khomsi arrived. I looked out of the
lavatory window and he hailed me with 'Hallo Joo, I come to say goodbye.' He
waved his passport to show the truth of the statement. I let him in and after
kissing and smiling and patting each other on the back – all very matey – he is
now sitting watching me smoking a cigarette. 'I am very happy,' he says, 'because
I work now in Gibraltar. I am very happy.' 'And I am happy for you,' I said. I am
quite sober and so my happiness at his happiness is quite genuine, though
probably aided by relief that I shall never see him again. He is looking particularly

---

the Establishment or the Cherry Lane. . . . Still, it's Kismet (Ah, the exotic east is in my blood!). We
can but trust in the will of Allah and insist that we take Michael Bates and Kenneth Cranham to
Broadway. Off-Broadway, I'm told, this isn't possible.
2 *Aida* (1871). Opera with libretto by A. Ghislanzoni and music by Guiseppe Verdi.

nice today. His gold tooth glitters as he smiles. He has just said, 'Hey, Joo, kiss me – I am so happy.' And so I do so feeling very happy for him and for all happiness however small. Because, of course, he'll find in Gibraltar only disillusion. But for the moment, when I kiss him for the last time we are, for different reasons, completely happy.

Saturday 27 May

Posted letter to Peggy. Weather hot, but cloudy, not beach weather. Went to the boulevard in search of ingredients to make an English hashish cake, the Moroccan variety produced by Nasser is as heavy as lead. We bought flour, baking powder, sugar, eggs, blanched almonds, vanilla essence and angelica. Should be OK. But Nasser is bringing the main ingredient. Went to The Windmill and had four poached eggs on toast for lunch. I haven't had hash for two days. I took two librium though before I went out. Saw Mohammed Yellow-jersey. Told him to come to *la casa* at four.

Went to the flat. It was 2.30. At three, a knock at the door. It was Mohammed Yellow-jersey. Of course, as he hasn't a watch he has no way of telling the time. I let him in. The attractive, curly-headed seventeen-year-old also outside and pointed to himself. I shook my head and closed the door. He stayed there for ages waiting. Mohammed very amused. Kenneth not so. 'What is he waiting out there for?' he said. 'It really doesn't matter,' I said. 'He can wait, nobody in this alley sees what's going on.' I took Mohammed Yellow-jersey into the bedroom after he'd smoked one of Kenneth's cigarettes. We had a very exciting sex bout. We were both sweating and exhausted. He almost immediately fell into a deep sleep, snuggling close to me. After a few minutes I also fell asleep and we were awakened an hour and a half later by Kenneth hissing through the door, 'What have you done in there?' 'Nothing,' I said. My Yellow-jersey and I showered and I said I'd see him on *lundi*. As I was talking to small Absolem and Mustapha on the boulevard, a Moroccan man passed and said to them, '*Hassissi*,' at which they looked sheepish. I suppose it's the equivalent of bum-boy. In a civilisation where homosexuality is frowned upon, whether active or passive, I can't think of an English equivalent of *luart*. Larbi frequently admits to *luart* but not *hass-hass*, though, in fact, I have been up him as he must very well know.

Met Paddington. He said he'd been smoking Kif. He walked with us for a little. He talked of sex. I spoke of vaseline, which he agreed was good as a hair tonic also. 'Spit,' he said 'is good with a boy, but sometimes the mouth is dry and it's impossible to make enough.' He then said, 'When I go into the country I usually take a piece of soap.' 'But isn't it painful?' 'Yes,' he admitted, 'it can be painful.' He said he was going to Spain in a few weeks. 'Many lovely boys there,' he said smiling. 'Seventeen, eighteen, I have fucked many Spanish boys.' Mohammed Khomsi turned up. I expressed considerable surprise that he hadn't

gone to Gibraltar. 'I go maybe tomorrow,' he said, 'there is trouble with money.'
We left Paddington who, having smoked Kif, wasn't in a mood to walk very far.
Nigel told me a most amusing limerick. 'It's an old army one,' he said. 'Surely
you've heard it?' He reported it in his clipped upper-class voice:

> The sexual urge of a camel
> Is greater than anyone thinks
> In moments of erotic excitement
> It frequently buggers the Sphinx.
> Now the Sphinx's posterior passage
> Is washed by the sands of the Nile
> Which explains both the hump on the camel
> And the Sphinx's inscrutable smile.

Went to dinner with Nigel. 'I was once very nearly married to a lesbian,' he
confessed over the meal, as we wearily waited for the menu. 'She turned me
down, fortunately.' He said that El Aïoun was the place for boys, 'and for tea
also, I believe,' he said. 'I like young boys.' 'How young?' I said. 'Oh very young,'
he said. 'But *how* young?' I pressed. 'Twelve?' 'Oh no,' he said. 'About fourteen.'
'Oh, perfectly natural,' I said. 'I think I have finally settled for fifteen. This is
because my Yellow-jersey is fifteen, though, mind you, I lust for Mustapha and
he can't be more than fourteen. I think it a little indiscreet to bring him back to
the house, so I shall have him in a cabin one day. If his prick is as undeveloped as
last year, I shall know that he is not fourteen.' 'What will you do then?' Nigel
said. 'I shall leave it for a year or two,' I said. 'Like the peaches on a sunny wall,'
Kenneth said. Nigel left to go to bed. 'I had a little something this afternoon,' he
said, 'and at my age (forty-five) and with the accumulated middle-class guilt of
four-and-a-half decades, I feel I must look for solace in sleep.'

Sunday 28 May

Weather (at ten o'clock) looks very dim, cloudy, threatening. Nigel gave me a
piece of ludicrous writing as advice to children written by Uncle Clap. Sent it to
Kenneth Williams (as from me of course). I altered Uncle Clap (which is a little
crude) to Uncle Whippity. Frank gave me a limerick today. I think he'd invented
it himself. He said it's to be credited to Professor Frank Holroyd.

> The King was in his counting house
> Counting out his money.
> The Queen was in the parlour
> Eating bread and honey.
> The maid was in the stable
> A-teaching of the groom

That the vagina, not the anus
Is the entrance to the womb.

Nasser arrived on time. He bought the hashish and this time he said we must bake it in the oven first. So whilst I lay sunbathing on the terrace, Kenneth lit the oven and Nasser spread the hash in a tray and roasted it in the oven. Halfway through the operation the gas ran out. I rang up the gas and after an interval of half an hour or so they arrived, changed the empty canister for a full one and then departed. The roasting of the hashish continued. I, who had taken a large piece of the previous cake, lay in a daydream in the sun. Before the cake was baked, Nigel turned up for tea and Nasser went. Kenneth said he wanted *l'amour* with me. But I was, by this time, in a pleasant stupor on the terrace in the sun. Nigel spoke for a time of the world situation which, for some curious reason, worries him. Apparently Nasser[1] (dictator of Egypt) has made provoking statements to Israel, and Russia supports Egypt. Could lead to an extremely grave situation. 'I hope it won't affect the Moroccan attitude towards the English,' I said.

Monday 29 May

Got up early. We found that the bus that leaves for Tetouan goes at 9.30. Larbi arrived at 8.30. He has a small overnight bag with him, much more elegant than Kenneth and me, who packed our things in the fisherman's satchel I use for the beach. We caught the bus to T. I saw Mohammed Yellow-jersey near the bus station on a bike, told him I was going to be away for a day or so and gave him a couple of dirs. Saw Mustapha also and resisted the temptation to give anything but a charming smile, which he returned.

The countryside was gold and green under a blazing sun. All over Morocco one suddenly comes upon ancient graveyards. The ruin of a hotel stands among mimosa. A great flight of steps leading up to a derelict building on a hillside. A place of some importance during colonial days, now abandoned, falling to pieces ransacked by the surrounding villages for building materials. The sadness of recent death. Empires nearer than the Roman. We arrived at the bus terminal at 11.30. I have always meant to stay at Tetouan. On the evidence of its bus terminal it seems to be a fascinating place. Around the walls, above the buses, are murals of Moroccan life and industry. Painted presumably, under the Spanish occupation. Peasants ploughing and sowing, reaping and hoeing. 'There's no pictorial image of a Moroccan prick, though,' George Greeves said, 'and that's a

---

1 Gamal Abdel Nasser (1918–1970). Egyptian political leader and president of the United Arab Republic. After the six day Arab–Israeli war in June 1967, heavy losses on the Arab side led to Nasser's resignation. But he was persuaded to withdraw it almost immediately.

grave omission. When I rule the world, I am going to have the prick enshrined in glory. Give the prick back its place in life.'[1]

We caught a bus. We climbed mountain roads into the heart of the *Desert Song*[2] country. 'There's no desert for 1,000 miles,' Kenneth said, 'but this is where Abdul-Karim and the Red Shadow had their Rif Wars.' We got to Chechaouen at about two o'clock. It's perhaps the most beautiful town I have ever seen. It's sprawled under high grey rocks. An important part of the town is a spring which gushed from the rock. 'Supposed to be where Moses struck water,' G.G. said. 'He was rather out of his way, wasn't he?' I said. 'The holy well, the spring of water gushing from the rock, very *Golden Bough*-ish,'[3] K.H. said. As we alighted from the bus we found a guide. He was a pleasant man of about thirty. 'We want to go to the Hotel Rif,' I said. We'd been to Chechaouen and stayed at the Rif before. It's a small hotel, full of Islamic things. There is never any hot water but I prefer it to the hotel known as the one with the swimming-pool, built by the Moroccan tourist board. 'I wish we'd chosen someone younger and prettier to guide us,' I said. 'I was trying to get you someone younger,' Kenneth said, 'but this big frump is obviously the senior one.' We arrived at the Rif. A double room was fourteen dirhams. Larbi put his bag with Kenneth's in the double room. 'There isn't going to be any pretence,' Kenneth said as the page led me to a single room (seven dirham). I washed my hands, had a piss, a lie down, and then we went to the dining-room. There were two Americans finishing their meal. Otherwise the place was deserted. One young, shy waiter served us. Larbi very subdued. Impressed by the hotel or tired by the journey. I couldn't tell. After a meal which was very good, we went out and were pleased to find that we'd lost our guide. Kenneth, who remembered the place vaguely from two years ago, led us upwards through a series of winding alleys, white painted houses with heavy blue doors, so perfect, so beautiful, an occasional splash of terracotta, and everywhere boys and young men sauntering around. V. Firbank.

1 In *What the Butler Saw*, Orton invoked the phallic intention of comedy when 'the missing part of Sir Winston Churchill' is held aloft at the penultimate moment and waved over the proceedings. Says Rance, with admiration: 'How much more inspiring if, in those dark days, we'd seen what we see now. Instead, we had to be content with a cigar – the symbol falling far short, as we all realize, of the object itself.'
  For detailed discussion of Orton's clowning and phallic fun see *Prick Up Your Ears*, pp. 113–115.
2 Popular operetta. Music by Sigmund Romberg. Book and lyrics by Oscar Hammerstein II and Otto Harbach. Filmed in 1929, 1943, 1952.
3 By Sir James Frazer (1854–1941), 1890. A pioneering volume of cultural anthropology whose accounts – based on secondary sources – of fertility rites, the sacrificial killing of kings, the dying god, the scapegoat, etc – had great literary influence on D. H. Lawrence, T. S. Eliot, Ezra Pound as well as Orton. 'You sound, at the end of your article on *Sloane*, as if you aren't at all convinced that *The Golden B[ough]* and *Northanger A[bbey]* could furnish me with inspiration,' Orton wrote Glenn Loney on 25 March 1966. 'I assure you that it is possible to draw poisoned water from the clearest of wells . . .'

Previous page: Orton, 1965
Above left: Orton on his Tangier patio terrace, 1967
Above right: Orton eating hash cake, 1967
Below: Orton and friend, 1965

Above:
Kenneth Halliwell,
1967

Right:
Orton, Kenneth
Williams and
Halliwell in Tangier,
1965

Left: Halliwell, 1967; Orton
sunbathes in background

Below: Halliwell and Orton go
native, 1965

Inset: Tangier

Above left:
Avril Elgar (Joyce) gives Michael Standing (Wilson) tea and sympathy in *The Ruffian on the Stair*, 1967

Above right:
Bill Fraser (McCorquodale) is discovered at the finale of *Funeral Games*, 1968

Left:
Sir Ralph Richardson (Dr. Rance) deals with Julia Foster (Geraldine Barclay) as the bemused Stanley Baxter (Dr. Prentice) looks on in the posthumous West End debut of *What the Butler Saw*, 1969

Right:
Orton, October 1966

Below:
25 Noel Road, 9 August 1967

After wandering about and taking a few photographs, we met a boy of about fifteen. He was dark and on his upper lips the first downy hairs of a schoolboy moustache. His name, inevitably, was Mohammed. He took us to the spring and we sat at a café among the trees. It was deserted except for a few Moroccans lying asleep on mats inside a kind of wicker cage roofed with leaves. We ordered mint tea and I said to Mohammed, 'When we were here before we smoked Kif.' He brightened visibly. 'You like Kif?' he said. 'Yes,' I said. He sent a small boy off for Kif (50 francs) and a pipe. When he returned, we smoked, with intervals, for a couple of hours. Very strong. I found it had a powerful effect, but I felt rather sick. As I don't normally smoke cigarettes this made it rather difficult. I had to inhale to gain anything from the drug, but when I inhaled the world swam and the trees became transparent, the sounds magnified and a feeling of nausea overcame me. When the sickness passed the effect was pleasant. Larbi brightened up considerably. Mohammed was suddenly very provocative and, as we left the café, plucked a sprig of jasmine from a nearby bush and presented it to me. We walked back to the hotel, met our former elderly guide, who, seeing Mohammed, stopped, chatted and smiled and parted in a most philosophic way.

We took the two boys into the swimming-pool hotel. Bought them coffee. Kenneth and I had Coca-Cola. Nobody about except four tight-arsed German queens. We told Mohammed to call for us at the hotel at nine. He said he'd take us to a café where Kif was smoked. Had dinner served by the waiter. The hotel desk clerk was a man in his twenties, the waiter maybe seventeen and the page fourteen, and another boy of twelve, all very friendly. Larbi, after the Kif, chatted a lot to the waiter. Drugs certainly oil the wheels of human intercourse though not, in my case, sexual. Mohammed turned up at nine. A disappointment, in a way, because the waiter said we could stay in the hotel and smoke Kif with him, the page and the desk clerk. A most interesting combination. Mohammed took us to a café where, as expected, we had to witness a dance by a Moroccan queer. He wriggled and jumped around to cymbal and drum, with bangles on his ankle. I was as always, when confronted with this spectacle, reminded of the Hebrew prophets and thought, not for the first time, how ancient Canaan must have been a little like this. I bought a postcard of the dancer and a small boy, also dressed as a girl. 'That boy is good for fuck,' Mohammed said pointing to the boy in the picture. 'Quel age?' I said. Mohammed shrugged his shoulders. 'Perhaps ten,' he said. He went on to say that the boy had been had by most of the male population in the town. 'You like this boy for *l'amour?*' Larbi said, nodding at Mohammed. 'OK', I said, feeling most unsexy and half asleep. Larbi spoke to Mohammed who said it wasn't possible for him to come to the hotel. The patron wouldn't let guests take boys back. However, he said, he'd be delighted to come to Tangier and sleep with me there. I told Larbi to explain that I was going on Sunday, and for Mohammed to come after I came back from London. 'OK, this boy say he come June 8th,' Larbi said. We went back to the hotel. The waiter and page had gone. We went to bed and fell asleep immediately. Kenneth told me later that he and Larbi had both found coming very difficult under Kif. It took about three quarters of an hour to come. Under those circumstances mutual masturbation is all that could reasonably be accomplished. The idea of fucking for three quarters of an hour solid is ridiculous, I said, unless you were a trained gymnast.

Tuesday 30 May

Woke at seven. Showered in cold water. Last night Larbi came up with the suggestion that instead of returning to Tangier via Tetouan we should take the bus to Ouezzane, get a second bus and visit his mother who, for some reason, was staying with his auntie in Ksar-el-Kebir. In a moment of rashness Kenneth and I agreed to this.

At 12.30 we arrived at Ksar-el-Kebir – the Leicester of Morocco, but once again interesting to see a Moorish town in 1967 ... The hot sun, the children playing, and always, everywhere, boys and young men. Not a sign very often of a woman, which pleased me greatly. The taxi had dropped us outside a small shop. Larbi took us inside and introduced us to a dour Moor, who didn't seem over-anxious to see us. 'Ma famille,' Larbi said with a genteel nod. We shook hands with the man who Larbi said was his uncle, and bought a packet of biscuits. Larbi bought a loaf and some horrible *beurre crale* which tasted like fermented camel-spew and indeed my guess might not have been wild. After saying something which didn't sound at all welcoming, the Moor shopkeeper bid us farewell.

We walked through some streets, across a railway line and up to a terrace house. We were welcomed by a young girl kissing our hands, and then a fat woman (Larbi's mother) appeared and, behind, an ugly woman (auntie) and a youngish woman (their Fatima) and a small child. During the next half hour or so the behaviour of the family (Larbi's cousin Mohammed of about twelve appeared, but an irresistibly ugly child) reminded me of O'Casey[1]. I was almost persuaded that I could understand Arabic. On the downstairs, the house consisted of two rooms. A passage led direct from the front door into the 'parlour'. Off this was another room where the cooking was done. In the parlour were low bundles of folded linen. In the other room was a double-bed behind a curtain. The furniture in the parlour consisted of one small circular table. The other room had a place for working. On the floor was a dish with several fish in it. Larbi's mother made us a cup of mint 'tay'. I wanted to piss and Larbi led me behind a curtain off the hall. I found the usual native-type lavatory. Two raised places for the feet and a hole in the floor for the shit to drop through. Absolutely no precautions were

1 Sean O'Casey (1880–1964). Irish playwright.

taken for the old and infirm in their toilet. As George Greeves once remarked, 'If I got my arse that low they'd have to bury me in that position.' We went onto the roof and took a number of photographs of the family. We then went on to the street and took some more. We left at two o'clock. The bus which left for Larache at 2.30 travelled through beautiful countryside, but what interested me was the Moroccan girl dressed in European dress and her girlfriend (in Moroccan dress). They were behaving exactly like English tarts in the forties. I thought they were probably called 'Rita' and 'Marlene'. Marlene was the quiet one who finally ended up in *The News of the World* giving evidence about a man who'd murdered and raped 'Rita' after asking her to go with him in his car . . . Their conversation, though it was in Arabic, I translated into the Good-Time-Girl type of film dialogue. I saw Jean Kent[1] playing 'Rita'. We changed buses and eventually went to Tangier. After a shower and a cup of tea, we went out to dinner. Met Nigel and agreed to him coming to tea tomorrow to taste our hashish cake. Larbi has got to go back to Ksar-el-Kebir to take money to his mother. I no longer ever try to understand.

Wednesday 31 May

A Tangier wind sprang up this morning. We tried to go down to the beach, but the gales and the mist of sand blown across the beach cafés defeated us. We went back and sat on the terrace which is sheltered from the wind and overlooks the garden. Nigel came round and borrowed *A Case of Human Bondage*. I haven't finished reading it yet. I find it a book, although difficult to put down, easy not to pick up. Nigel went at one-ish and promised to return about four, to sample what he called 'your rich mocca cake'. Mohammed Yellow-jersey was coming at two. When the time approached for the boy to come, I realised that the Fatima hadn't yet left and was showing no sign of leaving. She'd left her coat and kitchen shoes behind the door and gone downstairs to her mother. I couldn't lock the door leading downstairs because she wouldn't be able to get back. Yet, she could at any time appear in the apartment. All the elements of farce were present. It needed only for the boy to arrive, have to be concealed in the bedroom, the Fatima *and* her mother appear in the flat, Larbi and perhaps Nasser to turn up, plus the Baron to turn up with some complaint and then all it needed was a title. Fortunately the Fatima did go at 2.30 and Mohammed Yellow-jersey came at three and so it all worked perfectly. He arrived covered with sand. He went into the bathroom and washed his face. I suggested he wash his feet which were coated in sand. He did and we went into the bedroom where we had very exciting sex. Very goatish. He smelt like he needed a bath and I had been sunbathing all

1 Jean Kent (1921–   ). British leading lady of forties, formerly a Windmill Girl.

morning and was sweating. We both looked scruffy and our fucking matched our appearance.

Thursday 1 June

Wind all day. Made no attempt to go onto the beach. Stayed all morning on the terrace. Nigel popped in briefly and confessed to finding Beverley Nichols 'a silly wet queen'. Nasser came at one and we had a cup of tea. He ate some of the cake. We had very good sex. Larbi turned up with his cock swollen in an alarming manner. I first noticed it through his trousers and idly thought, his cock seems larger than it usually is. He finally flashed it and I was appalled at the curious nature of it. It was as though his cock had been blown up with air. He'd been to a doctor, I saw the card; it said, 'oedema of the penis'. Kenneth took him into the bedroom and I gather, though Larbi is still there and Kenneth said nothing, that Larbi couldn't come. What the nature of this is, is a mystery. He himself says it's a mosquito sting, but Kenneth said, 'Some queen, probably Dutch, has sucked him off too hard.' 'Nonsense,' I said, 'no amount of sucking can make a cock swell to twice its size. If any queen could do that she'd be in constant demand all over the world.' Larbi looked very attractive. He wandered around like a choirboy in Firbank who was like 'a killer that has seen a vision'. He'd had his hair cut. He wore a khaki shirt and a pair of trousers given him by Kenneth. He'd bought himself a red and black cheap yachting cap from some departmental store. He looked no more than his years. He came over and hugged me before he went. 'Goodbye Joo.' He kissed me and, rather brow-beaten, left. Kenneth came from the front door. 'He probably hasn't the sense to lay off the hashish whilst having his injections,' he said. Later he said that he thought Larbi had probably gone to a witch-doctor to have the size of his cock increased and, as with back-street abortions, the experiment had misfired. 'You may be right,' I said. 'It's perfectly normal for a male to wish to have a large cock and, of course, no one else's will do – it has to be your own.'

We went to dinner. Wind blowing violently even on the boulevard. Didn't bother attempting to have coffee at a café. Came straight home and went to bed. The effect of hashish made me suddenly sexy about an hour after going to bed and I tossed myself off imagining two soldiers, a schoolboy and a Greek fucking each other in the rain at the back of an army lorry.

Friday 2 June

Woke at 7.20. Sun shining. No wind at first but about nine it started up and it seemed to be going to be another windy day. 'It must be the longest blow job in the history of the world,' Nigel said later. I sunbathed on the terrace till twelve. We'd been invited to G. Greeve's at one for lunch. Left the house at 12.30. Found a strange old man sitting at the foot of the steps eating sardines out of a tin. He seemed surprised to find the door opening and two Europeans treading him down. He recovered his composure and held out his hand for money. 'Are we expected to pay to have these foul creatures foul our doorstep?' Kenneth asked as we ignored the pathetic whinings coming from under the soles of our feet and strolled down the alley towards the boulevard.

Went to G. Greeves. Found him amicable but in pain. His back was causing him trouble. 'I had some marvellous pills,' he said, 'and I lent them to Peter Churchill. Now, in my hour of need, I am without.' He staggered out of his bedroom, his enormous belly sagging over his pyjamas, his underwear dating him more than his birth certificate. 'Have you met this rich American queen?' he said, sitting in a basket chair. 'Miss Robinson' Raines, G.G.'s male nurse and companion ('my fucking grand-daughter you mean'), was as softly-spoken as any young lady in Harrods. 'She calls herself Gerda,' George said. 'But she's a rich American queen, and I find her a cunt, but not one to be sniffed at, as the soldier said of his mother's.'

He ladled out a kind of mutton broth and lentils. 'I have the Fatima piss in this,' he said, leering over the pot. The lunch consisted of the broth and salad and yoghurt. 'That's health food, better than all the spunk you've been swallowing.' During the meal he kept saying, 'Oh my fucking back, I'm probably going to give birth.' Then he said, 'Joe, when you're in London get me some stuff.' He gestured to a bottle of patent medicine. 'I'll give you the address of my doctor. A queer. Tell him your poor fucking auntie is passing out and come and save her.' He said he was going to a party at The Pergola and would ring and tell us whether it was worth attending. 'You can come down and join us there,' he said. We left at two. Kenneth was in sudden agony because the plaster had come off one of his boils and was hurting him. Met Rees-Davies. He told us that G. Greeves had been drunk two nights ago. 'That explains his sudden attack of backache,' he said, winking with his glass eye. 'I've been circumcised,' he said as we were leaving. 'I had it done as a gesture to the Arab race,' he said, laughing as we left him. 'Do you suppose he was sane when he said that,' Kenneth asked, grunting as his trouser leg caught at the boil. 'Rees-Davies used to be a missionary,' G.G. said on another occasion, 'and very pure. He was interested in finding a new bit of Africa hitherto known only to black men: well, Dai had this negro servant. Big boy he was. And he conceived a sudden foul craving for the arsehole of this Welsh God. Finally realising that perhaps God's sole purpose in creating the world was in order that Dai Rees-Davies should have a cock up his bum, he finally gave in and let the black savage fuck him. Oh, it was absolutely fucking lovely. In and out, in and out went the massive negro cock. When it was all over, the first words Dai said were, "Well M'sala, you have penetrated where no white man has ever been," and that's how Miss Rees-Davies (that was) was done for the first time.' It was with this thought that I left Rees-Davies smiling Welshly in the sunlight.

Kenneth had a bath when we got in at about 2.30. I lay on the terrace. Nigel called round. He's most worried about the Egypt/Israel situation. 'We'll be spat upon in the streets,' he said. 'These people can turn so quickly.' 'But Egypt is 1000 miles away,' I said. 'How could that affect the attitude of the Moroccans?' 'It'll be the British in Singapore all over again,' he said. 'Oh, why was Balfour[1] born with a tongue? If he'd been dumb the King David Hotel would never have been blown up, and we'd not be on the brink of a third World War.' '*The Daily Telegraph* says that Israel will have to take her chance,' Kenneth said. 'Britain is going under UN mandate.' 'I hope it isn't Poland,' Nigel said mournfully as we got into his car.

We met Frank later. 'There's to be a concentration camp for Europeans near Asilah,' he said, how seriously I wasn't certain. 'We'll be interred there.' 'Oh my goodness,' Nigel said, suddenly lisping, 'we'll be at the mercy of the brute commandants!' Frank seemed genuinely upset by the situation. 'It's very serious you know,' he said, as I laughed away some ridiculous suggestion that we'd all be butchered in our beds. 'I've seen it before,' he said. 'I know how it feels to be humiliated.' 'Was the Boxer Rebellion[2] as bad as one hears?' I asked. 'Shocking,' Frank said. 'We'll have to organise ourselves for the worst,' Nigel said. 'That's like as usual for me,' I said. Frank then said, 'I've been humiliated twice by that boy of Kevin's.' He stared around the table, his little moustache twitching, his old face looking hurt. 'I arranged to meet him and waited all afternoon. Then I saw him with some other man.' He shook his head. 'I've finished my papier-mâché mask. I wanted to show it to him today.' 'Well, of course, they have no artistic sense,' I said.

We left the restaurant. Nigel and Frank went for a paper and whilst I was waiting Paddington came up. After the evening's conversation, I expected him to have news of the King of Morocco's orders for the maltreatment of Europeans. Instead he greeted me with, 'That young boy, have you seen his cock?' 'Yes,' I said, 'it's very big, *malade*.' Paddington then went into great details of his sorrow for Larbi and the horror of any *malade* in any way connected with the cock. I gathered from Paddington's attitude that the *malade* of the cock was more important to him than Egypt attacking Israel.

1 James Balfour (1st Earl of Balfour) (1848–1930). Responsible for Balfour Declaration (1917) which promised Zionists a national home in Palestine.

2 Boxer Rebellion. An outbreak of anti-foreign violence in China in 1900. Takes its name from a secret organisation translated as 'The Society of Harmonious Fists', popularly called 'Boxers', who attacked converts to Christianity, missionaries, workers on foreign controlled railways.

Saturday 3 June

Day of wind and cloud. Went to the boulevard. Changed money with Blands. Sat on the Place de France. I had a coffee. Kenneth had a mint tea. Sat looking beyond the awning of the café at the grey sky that threatened rain. Felt though that, provided one spent the time drugged or drunk, the world was a fine place.[1] Bought a packet of soup. Ate soup and read the Baron's pornographic book, *The Strange Cult*. It is a 'period' piece, the whole thing, from the style of writing and illustrations being written and set circa 1924. It's American and mainly concerned with sucking off, mainly lesbian, and of the 'wild things' that the young set got up to in the day before yesterday. Only buggery is omitted from the list of sexual crimes it is possible to commit.

Larbi arrived at three. Yellow-jersey arrived and had tea. Yellow-jersey and I had it off in the bedroom. How incredible it is, I thought later as I watched him take a shower, to really see a nude fifteen-year-old. That small waist, sudden jutting of the bum; it wasn't just sex, it was an aesthetic experience. Sitting in the bath, he looked as if he were on canvas by a French impressionist – some painter of the stature of Renoir.[2] There was a faint flush of hair in the small of his back, spreading out to the top of the buttocks. He stood quite naturally and unselfconsciously towelling himself and I thought that nothing ages one more than the sight of one's juniors, if they're beautiful in the nude. I glanced into the mirror recognising at once that I was old enough to be the boy's father. Larbi and Yellow-jersey soon left after sex. Mohammed Khomsi rang the bell. I opened the door. 'Hallo,' he smiled. 'Are you going to Gibraltar?' I said. 'Maybe, I have no money.' 'Oh,' I said in a cold tone. 'You can't come in.' 'Is Kenneth's cock better?' he asked. 'It was never ill as far as I know,' I said. 'I see you tomorrow?' 'I'm going to London tomorrow,' I said. With this he pissed off.

Sunday 4 June

Woke up early. Not delighted by the prospect of having to fly back to London. Always hate travelling. The weather here, though, as Kenneth said, is encouraging for the traveller. It's rainy this morning. As I write this the cypresses are dripping and dank. The sky grey and overcast. Kenneth and I had breakfast and I read the final section of *The Strange Cult*. One or two moments of hilarity. The lines are worth preserving. 'Inez closed her eyes. Pete and the other fellows were the farthest from her thoughts. She could think of nothing but Lillian's tongue which glided madly in and out of her tingling cunt . . .'

1 Orton's stage direction at the finale of *What the Butler Saw* is an image of numbed transcendence: 'They pick up their clothes and weary, bleeding, drugged and drunk, climb the rope ladder into the blazing light.'

2 Auguste Renoir (1841–1919). French impressionist painter. Father of film-maker Jean Renoir (1894–1979).

Started packing and had a sudden panic that I'd lost my air-ticket. It wasn't with my passport. Oh God! I began running around the flat tearing open doors with Kenneth behind me saying, 'You really shouldn't take this hashish. You're bad enough without it. With it you're beyond a joke.' I found it at last tucked away in a drawer with some letters. I'm only taking home a tee-shirt, a bottle of librium tablets and some film to be developed. (*11.15*) Had a cup of coffee. The Fatima messing and fart-arsing about. The restlessness of the female. Busy, busy, always busy. And, often to no purpose. Let a woman into the house, even a servant, and before long you're forced to an odd corner, and beg her pardon as you disturb her at her work. Paddington said last night, 'How do you get your face to shine? I use Old Spice After Shave but my face won't shine like yours.' Didn't really know what to say except that I'd eaten a better quality of hashish than him.

Uneventful flight. Clouds across Spain. Nothing heard or overheard that was interesting. Clouds broken with a haze as we crossed the Bay of Biscay. Got to the Channel Islands and cloud thickened again and remained so until we got to London. Very grey evening in London. I got through the customs easily. I didn't have to wait for any case – took a satchel. Bought a carton of milk from a machine near Gloucester Road tube. Rang the Royal Court to ask about rehearsals. 'Don't come now,' they said after consulting Peter Gill. 'Come at ten o'clock for the run-through of the play.'

So I went home. Flat musty. Opened all the windows. Made an enormous pot of tea and, after a wash, sat down to open the letters which had piled up in my absence. A sinister one from the bank manager asking me to step in and see him as 'something irregular has happened with regard to the travellers' cheques issued to you on the 21 February.' One from Leonie saying she was in hospital awaiting the birth of a baby and not enjoying it much, and another one dated a fortnight later from Aunt Lucy asking if I'd heard the news of Leonie's daughter? Sent a telegram congratulating her – although weeks too late. Enormous picture of me in the *Sunday Times* for 28 May. (This was the edition banned in Morocco for political reasons.) Very good picture, the background is a tree in Cheyne Walk.

Went to the Court at nine. Found Peter rehearsing. Actors kept staggering out saying, 'When are we going to have a break?' In the downstairs bar were sandwiches and hard-boiled eggs. These were to feed the actors and technicians. Talked to Bill Gaskill. He says he likes *Erpingham Camp* very much – this is probably a bad omen. Hung about for the next few hours. Saw a copy of the programme. Another good picture. And a nude drawing by P. Procktor which has a definite charm. Drank several cartons of coffee from the automatic vending machines in the corner of the bar. At one, Peter began a run-through of *Erpingham*. It was brilliant but very ragged. Needs more rehearsals. He'd given the play more scenery than I'd asked for. Some of this was cumbersome. And

Bernard Gallagher, though a good actor giving a good performance, wasn't right as Erpingham. But certainly it ought, with more rehearsing, to be an interesting production. I got back at 2.30. Very exhausting day. Took two of Kenneth's secret 'suicide pills', Nembutal. Fell into a deep sleep.

Monday 5 June

Woke at eight. Felt drowsily benevolent for the rest of the day. Went to the hairdresser's. Then arrived at the Court. Saw run-through of *The Ruffian*[1]. Not as good as the original Sunday night performance. This due mainly to the fact that Kenneth Cranham is missing from the cast. Avril Elgar[2] is totally different from Sheila Ballantine, who played the part originally. I think Avril is a better actress, but she isn't funny. Went home. Dress rehearsal at seven. Before a sort of audience. Saw bank manager. The note proved to be very sinister. 'We issued the cheques, as you know, Mr Orton,' said the manager peering through his spectacles, 'for sterling areas only.' 'Yes,' I said. 'These cheques have been put through a bank in Spain!' he said turning the cheques over. 'And we have the same business with the cheques issued to Mr Halliwell,' he said. 'Have you been to Spain?' 'No,' I said. 'I gave these cheques to a man who I assumed would put them through an account in Gibraltar.' 'You were in Gibraltar?' 'Yes,' I said feeling immediately that I would regret this. 'Are you on business in Morocco?' he said. 'Yes,' I had the sense to say, 'I'm working on a film script. Mr Halliwell is my personal assistant.' The bank manager consulted with his assistant and came to the conclusion that as I was working I would be allowed expenses by the treasury and we might get away with it on that excuse. 'Bring your passport in,' the manager said, 'and if possible some proof of the authenticity of your statement.'

I went to see Peggy who, after admiring my tan, settled down to talk. I told her the currency problem. She promised to write a letter to the bank manager. Drafted one and said, 'He wants my passport to check whether or not I've been to Gibraltar.' 'You must say that you didn't go to Gibraltar,' Peggy said. 'Say you gave them to a man who was going for the day and you thought he would put them through the Barclay's branch of Gibraltar.'[3]

---

1 Peter Gill to Joe Orton, 3 June 1967, about *The Ruffian on the Stair*. 'I read the play first on the advice of Harold Pinter when I was looking for a play to complete a double-bill (which fell through). So then I asked to do it here. And here we are.'

2 Avril Elgar (1932–   ). Actress. Played Joyce in *The Ruffian on the Stair*.

3 Orton to Peggy Ramsay, 7 June 1967: 'This is the copy of the letter I wrote to the bank manager about my currency fracas. I wrote it *after* reading the notices of *Crimes of Passion*, hence the chastened mood. The story is that I gave them to a man who I knew was going to Gibraltar. I naturally assumed that he would cash them at Barclays in Gibraltar. I was too busy to go myself. It means slightly back-peddling on the fact that I told him I'd been in Gibraltar myself. But, with the pressure of work and a first night at the Royal Court approaching, an author is liable to be a little vague as to what exactly did happen. . . .'

The dress rehearsal, to which Peggy came, wasn't a phenomenal success. *Ruffian* very slow. *Erpingham* rather good though impossibly ragged and needed a lot of rehearsing. Peggy unenthusiastic on the whole. Think it isn't going to be a success. Had dinner with Bill Gaskill, Peggy and Oscar. 'It's quite an amusing evening,' Oscar said. Felt annoyed. *Erpingham* is the best (stage) play of mine performed so far. If only Arthur Lowe[1] were playing Erpingham, they'd all be raving. Oscar took me by car to Baker Street Station. Walked along Euston Road for quite a long way before I caught a taxi. Nearly one when I got in. Took two valium tablets and bed.

Tuesday 6 June

The big day. Whole day spent either at the Court or shopping for things promised to various people in Tangier. George Greeves wanted me to get him some tablets, which turned out to be on prescription. But I found a chemist behind the Piccadilly Theatre who sold them to me without a prescription – charging ten shillings more in the process. I got a copy of the *Satyricon*[2] for Nigel. Peter Gill spent most of the day tightening *Erpingham*, especially scene changes in the blackout. I had a cup of coffee with the girl who runs the box office. She'd just confessed to her husband that she's been having an affair with another man for eight years. 'We met on a cruise,' she said. 'I felt love at first sight. I've been having a sort of minor breakdown,' she said. 'That's why I fainted a few weeks ago.' 'You're not going to get a divorce?' I said. 'Oh no,' she said. 'You don't want to?' I asked. 'As long as your husband doesn't mind, why shouldn't you love two people at once?' She said I was the only person she knew who had taken this attitude. 'It's perfectly sensible,' I said. 'Why break up your marriage, have a lover. Just carry on as before.' We talked of the war. She is Jewish. 'It looks as though Nasser is finished,' I said. 'I'm very glad.' Although I like the Arabs, I don't like Nasser. I bought a record of the hit songs in 1967. Not the originals – faked-up ones to sound like the originals. But I bought it for Madame the Frenchwoman who runs the Alhambra in Tangier. I am sick of the records she plays when I go there to eat. Went home at four. Had a bath. Played a record or two. Wrote a few letters – one to Leonie – one to Kenneth Williams – then I just lay on the bed and thought a lot. I got to the Royal Court at seven. They were having difficulties with the programmes – only a few had arrived. I went to my seat and sat down. Saw Sheila Hancock[3] sitting with Oscar. She smiled and blew

1 Arthur Lowe (1915–1982). Actor. Both Orton and Gill wanted this resourceful comic actor for Erpingham.

2 *Satyricon.* By Petronius (1st cent. AD). A comic, often licentious romance.

3 Sheila Hancock (1933–   ). Actress. Played Kath in the Broadway production of *Entertaining Mr Sloane* (1965). Orton to Kenneth Halliwell, 2 October 1965: 'Sheila is amazing. The whole production (clearly) has been built around her ... Sheila has an enormous pregnant belly in Acts Two and Three and yet she still is "delicious" and funny ... Her clothes make her appear to be a gone-off Monroe. But I can't grumble because both she and Lee (Montague) are so terrific.'

a kiss. *Ruffian* began. It seemed slow at first. It was the best performance this cast had given of the play. The whole thing came over as a sad little play. Spoke to Sheila in the interval. She adored the play. 'I liked the bits about loneliness,' she said. 'Loneliness in the theatre is usually embarrassing, but this wasn't.' We talked about *Sloane*. 'I suggested Albie,' she said, 'for Eddie.' I'd already been asked by the Rediffusion casting woman if I thought Finney could play Eddie. 'It would be wonderful if he could, or if we could get him,' I said, and pushed the matter to the back of my mind, as one of those vain hopes. I saw the Egyptian journalist who'd interviewed me before I left for Morocco. 'I like the play very much,' he said. 'I will try – maybe it could be put on in Cairo – after the war,' he added, sadly. 'My wife is not with me,' he said. 'Where are you sitting?' I said. 'In the stalls,' he said, smiling and coming very close in that way no Englishman – except for Kenneth Cranham – would do. 'I can't sit in the stalls,' I said, wondering what he'd be like in bed and thinking I'd try. 'Ring me tomorrow,' I said, as he shook my hand warmly. I next spoke to Oscar, who is Jewish. 'That was an Egyptian,' I said. 'You see what a valuable addition I would be to the Diplomatic Service.'

The bell rang and we went back to the theatre for *Erpingham Camp* – the main part of the evening. It went extremely well. A great deal of enthusiasm from the audience. I was pleased that within the limits and bearing in mind the difficulty, it went so well. I admired Peter's production. It had style. Too much enthusiasm afterwards though. I feared when so many 'pros' were raving in the dressing-room after. 'This should be transferred,' someone said in a loud voice. 'We must wait until tomorrow for the verdict,' I said. 'Oh fuck the critics,' Peter Gill said. 'They don't matter.' This is bravado. Of course they matter. B. Gaskill seemed pleased and so did Oscar. Everybody enthusiastic. Had a drink in the club of the Court.

I left early as I wanted a bit of sex. Took two valium tablets and waited for the No.19 bus in Sloane Square. Got off at Piccadilly. Went to the Holloway Road. Went to the Gents lavatory. Nothing much in there. A man of about thirty. Then another man came in, in his twenties. He began to suck the first man off. The first man dropped his trousers and offered me his arse. I said it was too dangerous. This was immediately confirmed when three men came in and stood inside the doorway. The man doing the sucking left. I rather fancied him so I followed. 'Who was that fellow?' he said in a little Irish accent. 'I don't know,' I said. 'Have you got a place?' I said. 'Yes, at Highbury,' he said. He took me back to his furnished room. I took off my shirt. 'You've a lovely body,' he said running his hands over. 'And where did you get such a lovely tan?' 'I've had my holidays,' I said. 'I went to Torremolinos.' I chose this because it's quite a likely place for a working lad to go. The man dropped to his knees, undid my pants and pulled them down, I was going to get my cock out. Instead he nuzzled and sucked it through my underpants. After he'd done this for a bit, I pulled him up and stuck my tongue down his throat and pulled him to the bed. He took his clothes off and I got on top of him. 'Oh you've a grand cock,' he said, stroking it. I realised how much of sex was missed in Morocco by not being able to talk the language. I lifted his legs in the air, spat on my hand, wiped my cock, and got the end into his arse. 'Oh no,' he cried. 'No, no!' I stopped, and then realised that this was part of his personal kink. I gripped him hard. 'I'm going to fuck you,' I said. 'Keep quiet.' I pinned him to the bed with his legs up in the air and shoved my cock right up him. He gave a cry 'Oh my God. Oh you're hurting me.' I began to fuck him. It was a very good fuck. 'Let me see,' he said. 'I want to see your cock going in and out.' I had to lift myself up so that he could see my cock. He stroked my balls as I fucked him and I left my prick in after I'd come. 'Oh I needed that,' he said, 'I needed a good fucking, you certainly know how to fuck.' He then wanted me to lie on my belly. 'Oh you've lovely muscles,' he said stroking my back. 'I'd love a threesome with you and some other chap,' he said as a final shot. I got dressed after washing my cock and kissed him goodnight and went home. I had to walk all the way back. Very tired. Outside a newsagent I saw a placard about the cooling down of the Egypt/Israel situation. So I stole it. As a souvenir and a reminder that, whilst I was having a first night and fucking an Irishman (the second was more satisfactory than the first) The Third World War would have been averted. Got in at two and slept until 7.30.

Wednesday 7 June

Went out at eight. Got all the papers. Read them. Not good reviews. All lukewarm. Not a single review one could honestly say would do the box office good. Rang Peggy. She'd read *The Times*; *The Financial Times* was very cool; *The Guardian* had reverted to its original position on *Sloane*; *The Mirror* hostile, 'Double-bill that was almost a double-bore.' Oh well I did have a good fuck last night. I got something out of my return to London. Had an interview at ten with a woman from *The Evening News*. A telephone chat with someone from *The Evening Standard*, who had seen the plays at the dress rehearsal and liked them. The Egyptian rang and I had to ask him to ring later as I was being interviewed.

Went to the Court. Very downcast at the lack of enthusiasm for the plays. I had an interview for *Town and Around* in which they asked, rather aggressively, I thought, 'What the gimmick of having yourself drawn in the nude for the programme was.' I said, 'There are many people who might like a nude picture of me, I'm not unattractive, you know.' They said they wouldn't be using the interview today, perhaps sometime next week, which in polite terms, I suppose, means never. I was asked to be on *Late Night Line Up* with John Mortimer. We had to watch and discuss *A Flea In Her Ear*, the National Theatre production which was televised earlier in the evening. I hated it as much as I had done on seeing it in the theatre. I watched as I packed, drank up the milk that was left and took the rubbish to the bin. A taxi called at 9.20, took me to the studio at Shepherds Bush. In a special viewing room the play was still going on. It was directed and acted with great speed and no reality. I watched and all the time I wondered how the second night of *Crimes of Passion* was going. Rang Peter. He said it was going v. well. Harold Pinter was in front, as well as all the weekly critics. Pinter, I'm sure, won't like the way *Erpingham* is directed, or acted. He liked the much more naturalistic way it was done on telly. Said goodbye to Peter. Said I was sorry it hadn't been better received. He said that someone had said that Harold Hobson[1] liked the evening – don't entirely believe this. He was supposed to have liked *Loot* but gave it a very small notice. No hope there, I am afraid. Did the *Late Night Line Up*[2]. Expressed my views on *Flea* by saying that in farce everything (the externals) must be believed. The actors were dressed as though they were period equivalent of Mick Jagger.[3] Now it wouldn't be funny if Mick Jagger were caught in a brothel, but if Harold Wilson[4] were caught in a brothel it would be extremely funny. After the programme we talked a bit and then I was taken to the air terminal at Gloucester Road. I checked in.

Landed at Gibraltar. Had to wait nearly an hour for a plane to Tangier. Finally got in at about ten-ish. Instead of a taxi, I got the airport bus. This isn't a bus – it's no bigger than a landrover. I sat in it with a blond beatnik type. He said he'd been turned away the day before and told to get his hair cut. Apparently they said (in French) 'He's only here to smoke Kif.' His argument was that he could smoke Kif just as well with short hair. 'But you're talking western logic,' I said, 'and they're using Arab logic, which is that you may be smoking Kif but you don't look as if you do.' They don't mind what you do as long as you don't attract attention, and with long hair and a beard you do attract attention. We lapsed into silence. He said he thought he'd seen me before. 'Very likely,' I said dryly, 'there was a quarter-page picture of me in *The Sunday Times* last week.' 'You're Joe Orton,' he said. It's the first time I've been recognised.

1 Sir Harold Hobson (1904–   ). Then drama critic for *The Sunday Times*. Orton to Glenn Loney, 4 October 1966: 'In a week when *Loot* was the only new play, Hobson chose to come not on the first night, but the night before, and decided to review everything else in the English Theatre as well as *Loot*. If one wants to be charitable one could hope that he was intending to devote his whole column to the play when it transfers. I'm not, of course, charitable.'
2 Orton to Peggy Ramsay, 12 June 1967: '. . . I had a lovely time with John Mortimer on *Late Night Line Up*. Did you watch it? He told me they'd offered Kenneth Williams a part in the new Feydeau and he accepted imagining that the part offered was the jeune premier – of course, it isn't. And now Binkie has got to explain the mistake. It sounds like the beginning of a Feydeau . . .'
3 Mick Jagger (1943–   ). Rock star and lead singer of The Rolling Stones whose music, like Orton's plays, sounded a new note of mockery, sexual aggression and outrageousness in the 60s.
4 Sir Harold Wilson (1916–   ). British politician. Labour Prime Minister 1964–70; 1974–76. Attended same grammar school as Kenneth Halliwell.

Got home to be greeted by the Fatima, Kenneth, Larbi and the boy from Chechaouen (Mohammed Ali). Kenneth said that the town had been unnaturally quiet during the crisis. He said that the reviews he'd read were not bad. 'No,' I said, 'very lukewarm.' He said it was bound to happen after the rave notices for *Loot*. 'They were not going to give you *more* praise,' he said. He said that the interview in the programme was excellent, 'and you may get good notices from the Sundays.' Mohammed Ali had arrived a couple of days ago and Kenneth has started having him (on a purely wanking basis). 'He'd be no good for you,' Kenneth said, 'because he won't turn over.' 'How do you know,' I said. 'Well, Kevin said that none of them from there will turn over.' 'Kevin is a foolish queen and so are you,' I said, in sudden rage. I didn't want Mohammed Ali but it was tiresome to find Kenneth having him. 'I am not taking Larbi off your hands,' I said, 'I am not having any more of your poxy cast-offs like Mohammed.' 'Oh, about Mohammed Khomsi,' Kenneth said. 'He's a police informer. Don't have anything else to do with him. I am sure he told the police about Mustapha and Absolem last year.'

Went down to The Windmill. Had a meal. Showed *The Sunday Times* with my picture around and then went home to bed. Was woken up at 5.30 by Kenneth tripping in with Mohammed Ali. I was lying naked in bed and I suppose because of the nervous excitement of the last few days, and the plane journey, I suddenly felt very depressed. Was curt with Mohammed A. who started stroking me. 'Tell your stupid whore to leave me alone,' I said, sulking, to Kenneth. 'I don't want boys brought to me when I am lying naked and distraught.' Kenneth and the boy went away. Later in the day at the Alhambra we met Nigel and an American queen called David. Very depressed. Tired. Behaved rudely to Kenneth, who is getting on my nerves. Went home to bed.

Sunday 11 June

Spent the last few days recovering. All the English papers have been banned. So the progress of the war and the attitude of the Sunday critics are equally in doubt. Feeling has quietened down. Not that it ever ran high. Nigel took me up to his house in his car. On the way, a boy made an ambiguous gesture in my direction. 'Was he spitting at me?' I said recalling the political situation. 'No,' said Nigel, 'he was blowing you a kiss.' I'm glad things have returned to normal.

Nasser came this afternoon to bring the hashish, and to help Kenneth make another cake. I had already tried eating a little cake several times during the late morning and afternoon instead of a large slice all at once. It works much better. Yellow-jersey came. Smoked a cigarette. I'd bought him a pair of trousers at Marks and Sparks. He wasn't wearing them. I wanted to know why. He said they were in a cupboard at his house. I didn't believe him. He's probably sold them for five dirham when they cost thirty-five. I made him promise to come tomorrow and show me the trousers. I took his clothes off. And explored his body. I fingered his buttocks. He became very excited. The hashish had really worked rather well. Giving me incredible confidence. I turned him over, admired the shape of his back, the beautiful shape that you have to be fourteen to have. His buttocks, which weren't dark at all, but had a creamy look, rose very sharply from his waist. He lay his face on the pillow. I put my prick up as far as he would allow and fucked solidly for three quarters of an hour. Finally I came, shooting between his buttocks all over the bedspread. 'Fatima's come,' he said. We showered and I gave him five dirham and he asked for another one. 'No,' I said, 'you can have it when you show me the trousers.' He went off perfectly satisfied, and not for the first time I reflected that having had a boy of his age in England I'd spend the rest of my time in terror of his parents or the police. At one moment with my cock in his arse, the image was, and as I write still is, overpoweringly erotic, and I reflected that whatever the Sunday papers have said about *Crimes of Passion* was of little or no importance compared with this.

Monday 12 June

It rather looks as if there won't be any English papers, due to the political situation.[1] I shall have to write to Peggy and ask her to post the notices on.[2] Ironic to think that by the time I read them the play will be off. Saturday is the last night.

After debating whether or not to put our money in a bank in Tangier and deciding against it for the moment, we went down to The Windmill. I wanted to bathe, but a cold wind sprang up about midday and a thick mist covered the sun. Came home at two and, the mist having gone, lay on the terrace. Kenneth disappeared and five minutes later stood in the doorway and said, 'My case has been opened and some money is missing.' I got up and followed him. He counted the money and about £90 (in dirham) was missing. Kenneth had counted it this morning prior to putting it in a bank. We suspect the Fatima, probably in league with the gardener. Kenneth wanted to go down the Baron and have a scene forbidding the Fatima to enter the house. 'We've no proof that it's her,' I

---

1 Orton to Kenneth Williams, 16 June 1967: 'I'm certainly pooh-poohing the "trouble", though all the silly queens here can talk about now is "the dreadful political situation". They've transferred their allegiance from the circumcised penis to the Secretary General of the United Nations. Fickle in their emotions.'

2 Orton to Peggy Ramsay, 12 June 1967: '... Would you post out the Sunday reviews. Just the three. I'm expecting them to echo the dailies and so have resigned myself to lukewarmishness. Also any news of any kind about reactions to the plays (if any there be). I'm sorry Peter didn't get better reviews. I do admire him as a director. I can't see anyone else who I'd willingly let direct my next full length. It's ironic that by the time you've received this letter and replied and I've got the reviews the plays will be off. So it's all academic in a way. This is rather a dreary letter. I don't know why. I'm v. happy ...'

said. 'Who else is it then?' 'No one else,' I said, 'but she'll say we've had boys in. We know it can't be any of them, they'd never be able to get into the flat, and none of them are ever alone in the flat for any length of time. But we can't prove the Fatima did it. We must forget the whole business.' Kenneth agreed reluctantly.

Yellow-jersey turned up wearing the pair of trousers I had given him and wanted to see, a new pair of shoes, a new striped tee-shirt. He looked sheepish. I let him in, admired his clothes (a lot smarter than his working clothes) and he then gestured to the wardrobe. I opened it and he pointed to my blue coat. I said 'No possible,' and shut the door. I gave him two dirham and told him to come tomorrow at three. 'It might just be Larbi in league with the Fatima,' Kenneth said. (Later . . .) Larbi arrived and, not feeling like sex – the loss of a considerable amount of money is an anti-aphrodisiac – Kenneth told him to come tomorrow. The boy from Chechaouen had left this morning for the country with a raging toothache – 'Probably assumed for the occasion,' Kenneth said – and so we are both hashed up and quiet. Saw Hubert Pitman on the boulevard. He said, 'You were rather sent up in *The Sunday Times*.' 'What was the review like?' I said. 'Oh pretty good, it wasn't a slap on the back. Well you'd hardly expect it with your writing, would you?' He tittered to himself and promised to let me read the *ST*. Letter from Kenneth Williams in the post telling about an article in *The Evening News*[1] about me. Hope it's good for box office. About seven, the phone rang. It was Pitman. 'Shall I read the review to you, Joe?' he said. 'Yes,' I said. He then read Hobson's notice. It wasn't, or didn't seem, at all bad. Rather better than any of the dailies. Went out to dinner. Saw Mohammed Yellow-jersey on the boulevard about ten – got up in my trousers, I was glad to see, and his new tee-shirt and shoes. If there were any tourists he'd be an earner. I should think Frank Holroyd wants to make a papier-mâché mask of my face. I believe the process involves being coated with plaster of Paris. Feel it incumbent upon me to indulge an old man's whim.

Tuesday 13 June

Woke as usual and had tea. The Fatima came at nine – twenty minutes later than usual. Kenneth swears he detects signs of guilt. Certainly she is unusually silent.

---

1 'Money and Mr Orton' by Patricia Johnson, 9 June 1967: '. . . I got such marvellous reviews for *Loot*, I couldn't possibly follow it, no matter what I produced . . . No, I won't be writing in Morocco because I like it very much and I don't go to the touristy parts with snake charmers and dancing boys. I tried Libya once. I went because my father said he'd had a lovely time there. He forgot to tell me it was during the war . . . I hate possessions, but I really do think I'll have to get something larger soon, just to have a room to work in. I work better when there's someone else wandering around but it's not fair to the other person. They can't read, and if they want to type anything, the place sounds like a typing pool. Yes, I suppose I'll have to get a house . . . I always have to force myself to write, to work, but I don't even try on holiday. I think life's for living. Just walking, sitting in the sun. No one wrote anything in the Garden of Eden. . . .'

Stupid bitch. Can't even conceal guilt. The first principle of crime is an innocent-seeming manner after the event. 'It's typical of the ludicrousness of my life,' I said to Ken, 'that I come to a place where people are always being robbed by boys and am robbed by a girl.'

Went to dinner, met G. Greeves and Dai on the boulevard. Dai had *The Sunday Express*. Not a bad notice for *Crimes of Passion*. Thursday, G. Greeves coming to tea and promised to bring *The Observer* and *Telegraph*. Very good line George came out with at dinner: 'No good deed ever goes unpunished.'

Wednesday 14 June

Not very good weather. Cloudy and with a stiff breeze. Went to the Mamora. Saw Jimmy, who accepted a cheque for £100. He was full of the dark doings in Meknes. 'They're cutting their throats out there,' he said. Whose I didn't like to enquire. 'I wouldn't be a Jewish queen for all the tea in China,' he said. He spat out the names of Terence Craig-Cohen[1], Hubert Pitman and Ian with contempt. 'Tight-arsed bitches,' he said, and referred to the two Englishmen who had taken over The Windmill as 'a pair of boncy queens. They'll have their licence taken away after the first fucking week,' he said. 'There are only three known queens who haven't been had by the police,' he said, in a quiet voice. 'And everyone knows I am one of them. Old Pitman came up to me in the market one day and said, "Why Jimmy, look how you're dressed" – she was immaculate. "Piss off," I said as loud as I could, "you dirty mental queen." Oh, she couldn't get out of the place quick enough.'

I went down to The Windmill. Didn't bathe. Saw a very pretty boy of about eleven. He kept rolling over in the sand, showing first his cock and then his arse. But I had got Yellow-jersey coming at three. He arrived at 3.40. He lay on the

1 Orton to Kenneth Williams, 16 June 1967: '. . . Bill and Mike at the W. have your picture. It occupied pride of place on the bar for several days until replaced by a half empty Chianti bottle. I hope Fate has no crueller surprise in store for you on the roadway of Life. Peter at The Pergola had a spot of bother a few days ago – a bit of trade tried to cut his cock off. Succeeded in making a nasty gash in his stomach. He was poorly for a few days, but he's up and about now. Looking rather wan, I thought. Someone who calls himself Terence Craig-Cohen was fluttering about The Windmill like a fart in a bottle saying "Oh what a tragedy! What a dreadful thing to happen!" K.H. and I rounded upon him and blamed it on the political situation. "Oh I'm sure you're wrong!" C.C. fluted. "That's the trouble with you English upper classes," I said. "You don't know the world in which you live." "You're lost without your nannies," K.H. added, rather rudely, and in that rather high-handed manner of his. C.C. flew out of The Windmill in a huff. Certain it is that we're both persona non grata at the Craig-Cohen Lodge . . . I've not seen any papers except *The Sunday Express* which said of *Crimes of Passion*, "The play shows this author's well-known contempt for humanity to the full . . ." . . . We'll be back (Allah permitting) on July 2nd . . . Do you know I've lost over 2 inches on my waistline? But then, you see, this fucking is just the same as doing press-ups. My gym instructor in the nick had the trimmest figure. And I thought it was from using bar-bells.'

bed smiling, a ludicrous parody of sexual invitation. I locked the door of the bedroom and had a fleeting moment of indulging in illicit pleasures triggered off, I suppose, by the turning of the key in the lock. I picked up a towel and put it on the bedside table. 'La creme,' Yellow-jersey said, his eyes half-closed. I took the vaseline from the drawer and took his clothes off. I played with his cock, in order to excite myself, not him. He hugged me suddenly and said he'd been tossed off by an English tourist. 'Where?' I said. He looked puzzled. 'Un Anglais,' he made the gesture of masturbation – 'moi – la toilette.' 'La plage,' I said. He nodded, very pleased. 'Did he pay you dirham?' I said. 'Yes,' he said. He kissed me and we both laughed. I didn't ask how much the English tourist had paid him, because it was probably more than I do. 'Surely though,' Kenneth said later, 'it isn't necessary to have boys in lavatories in this country.' 'Perhaps some people being forced into the lavatories in England get to associate sexual pleasure with the smell of piss.' 'But that loo is next to the police station,' Kenneth said. 'It's madness.' Yellow-jersey and I were naked. I was fully awake. I turned him over, knelt above him, greased my cock with vaseline and spit, stroked his buttocks and wiped the residue of grease on my hand. Yellow-jersey, his face on the pillow, his eyes closed, gave a little moan. My cock was very hard. I fucked for about twenty minutes. Once I paused, took the towel and wiped the sweat from my chest and his back. I find that it makes a farting noise which is most unpleasant.

At the end of twenty minutes, I got up and had a piss. When I came back, Yellow-jersey was laying on his stomach with his arms spreadeagled like young Christ crucified seen from the back without his cross. I straddled the boy, put my cock in again and fucked him for another ten minutes or so – coming at last with enormous physical and mental pleasure. Yellow-jersey's cock was still hard as I reached round and felt it. He kissed my cheek. We lay like this for several minutes as my cock cooled off. After we'd wiped ourselves down and he'd said, 'No,' much to my relief, at my suggestion of tossing him off, he repeated, 'La toilette, Anglais.' I gave him a cigarette. He said his name was Mohammed, what was my name? 'Joe,' I said. He looked puzzled. 'Yusuf – Arab – Joe – Anglais.' He paused and reflectively stroked my cock. 'Hallo Joe,' he said. 'Hallo Mohammed,' I said. After half an hour we got up and had a shower. He said his underpants – which he also used for swimming – were no good. They were made of crêpe-de-chine and much too large for him. When we'd showered I gave him the pair of red jockey pants which I'd bought him at Marks and Sparks. He put them on and examined himself in the mirror – posed – admired – said 'very good,' and accepted them. He looked very pretty in them. He said he'd throw his old ones away. As he was leaving I told him to come on Friday. We are having G. Greeves here for tea tomorrow.

Went round to the Hotel Mamora. It used to be rendezvous for perverts of all kinds three years ago. Tiresome queens of all nations flocked there. It was then taken over by two English queers from Bournemouth who decided that the money lay with virtue and not vice. They now cater for 'trippers', coach loads of the buggers. Jimmy said, 'You've seen the big black thing at the reception desk, haven't you?' 'Yes,' I said. 'Well, when he first came here, I couldn't cotton on to his fucking name, so I called him Lucy. I did this for about a fortnight and then he suddenly comes to me and says, "No call me Lucy, Lucy no good." "Oh Christ," I thought, "some evil queen's told him that it's a girl's name." – "What shall I call you then?" "No Lucy, call me Rosie." So I do. I call him all the names you know.' A great hulking Moroccan passed carrying a dustbin full of waste. 'Mind where you're putting that, Fenella,' he shouted. The porter nodded and went through the kitchen. 'She'll tip that lot in the soup if I don't watch her,' he said. He suddenly kicked up his legs and began to sing: 'Fly me to the moon and let me play among the stars.'

Kenneth and I went up to the boulevard. My hash was working well. We met Frank. Had to put up with a typically professional pedantic argument on the exact meaning of the word 'naturalism' which Kenneth and I used as a term of abuse[1] and Frank used as high praise. He also has the odd impression that Pinter is a naturalistic writer. Under the influence of the hash, I became impatient at this twittering argument. 'I think Pinter is the best of the new young writers,' he said. 'Do you?' I said, but he wasn't aware of the irony in my voice.

We left Frank and went back to the Mamora. George had arrived with the money. Jimmy took us up to the salon and, dressed only in a pair of brown shorts, flopped onto the chaise-longue. 'Isn't it camp, dears?' he said, as a small dog leapt upon him, 'I love the south,' he said. 'I've got a small house in Agadir. You can have it anytime you want. Just ask. You can swim nude with the boys, and the seas are "limpid". You've been to Marrakesh?' 'No,' I said. 'Oh you must go,' he nodded, 'but the first time you go, you probably won't like it. We went last winter and were introduced to the waiter, and the next night (a Moroccan he was) he took us to a house and without a word of a lie, dear, there were twenty Moroccan boys there – none of them over twenty – all naked in a room, having one another – and they put the lights out. I was embarrassed at first, but I soon got into the swing of things. It was a party, you see, dears. All these young chaps having me and each other.' He paused and said, 'All it cost me was a crate of Coca-Cola. And there's cottage trade as well. Down south I was in the gents and this young Moroccan was sucking me off and the other, older Moroccan was stuffing her. Stuffing her, and I got frightened you know, because the older Moroccan

---

1 Joe Orton: 'I write in a certain way because I couldn't express [myself] in naturalistic terms. I think the whole naturalistic movement of the twenties and thirties you can't do anything in. You can't do anything except discuss Mavis's new hat, discuss the sort of teacup things, teacup drama. I mean, in naturalistic plays I couldn't make any comment on what kind of policeman Truscott is, or the law, or the big general things of the Establishment . . .'

suddenly pulled the kid away from my cock and start to suck me off himself.' 'It sounds as if Marrakesh isn't so very different from the Holloway Road,' Kenneth said wryly. 'Oh how can you say that?' Jimmy said.

Thursday 15 June

Woke to grey skies and rain. All morning it rained but brightened a little at about two. Spent the whole morning writing up this diary. Went to the bank at three in order to deposit the dirham obtained from Jimmy. Found that my sunglasses had disappeared. Although Kenneth said I may have left them at the Mamora, I am sure that the Fatima has pinched them. 'You're more annoyed about the sunglasses than you are about £100,' Kenneth said. 'Your sense of proportion is ridiculous.' 'The loss of £100 didn't inconvenience me in any way,' I said; 'the loss of my sunglasses does. I shall have to buy a new pair. And they only have awful ones here. So I shall have to throw them away when I get home.'

Kevin arrived at four. He had brought several books of nude photographs. He'd got them in New York. They were not pornographic – they showed the cocks but were ostensibly supposed to be "nudist" magazines. But why these magazines were devoted entirely to young men – often in pairs – was never really explained. I found most of them dull. So professional. Not erotic. One or two were rather good. Like all such magazines they were ultimately designed for masturbators. He also had an erotic novel from which he read passages. Not very well-written and so, for me, not sexually exciting. G. Greeves arrived later with Richard. Very merry party, due to the cake which proved a big success. George told his version of the story of Cain and Abel. 'It seems that Cain was having trouble with Abel and Abel threatened to tell his father. So Cain walloped the bastard. Quite right too. Cunt.' He beamed round. He took several photographs. Larbi arrived. Kenneth went off with him. 'Are those two having trade?' George said. 'I expect so,' I said. 'I had trade with a lad once,' said George, 'who was later struck by lightning.' I laughed. 'It's true,' George said. 'He was under a tree and he was struck by lightning.' He paused reflectively. 'Though as I recall, he liked women as well, so perhaps he was killed for that.' He laughed. 'Oh yes, the Prince of Darkness took him.' He shook his head sadly, 'He was a good little fuck though.'

Friday 16 June

Weather bright between sudden banks of haze. I went to the boulevard at ten. I posted a letter to Kenneth Williams. I went to Kents for a pair of sunglasses. They were too expensive for my tastes so I came home disgruntled. Later I phoned the Mamora and asked Jimmy if I'd left the sunglasses at the hotel. Jimmy said I had and so I found them. We had a brief panic an hour or so after the last incident, when Kenneth couldn't find my underpants. 'She's got *them* now,' he said as I realised that we were on the way to Fatimaphobia. I eventually found them in the airing cupboard (so called). Mohammed Ali turned up at eleven (the Fatima had left by then). I said 'Quel age?' He said, 'Dix-neuf.' 'Dix-fucking-neuf?' I shouted. 'Nineteen?' 'Oui,' he said, looking obviously no more than sixteen. 'You couldn't come to England anyway,' I said, 'because in England you have to be twenty-one.' He smiled, shook hands and said, 'Amigos,' in a hushed tone and lowered his eyes. 'You see, the whole point of my penis,' I said, 'is to look into your eyes and say you're mine.' This with a sort of casual, finishing-off-the-evening voice. 'That is good,' he said, 'to have amigos.' I eventually said, 'Wipe that silly grin off your face and put it on my arse.' 'Harse,' he said.

We had managed sardines and bread and tea – Kenneth took the pest's photographs. He looks like a pretty monkey. He borrowed my suntan oil and he spilt a great pool. He disappeared with Kenneth. At three Yellow-jersey arrived. 'Yellow-jersey?' I said through the bedroom door. 'Oui,' Kenneth said. There was an extraordinary pause. I had been eating the cake for two hours, during which time something looking like a lettuce buzzed past my ear. Kenneth said, 'Let him in then,' in an authoritative voice. I let Yellow-jersey in. He had to have a foot-bath because of his feet, covered with sand, 'as per usual,' my old mother would have retorted. I had to fuck on spit because the vaseline was in the other bedroom. After about twenty minutes or so I stopped, and seeing the red underpants still round his ankles, I pulled them up over the boy's knees so that if I lifted myself I could see my cock going in and out. I suddenly wanted to piss. I went into the bathroom. 'I demand that vaseline,' I said. 'I don't care who you are, you're to hand it over at once.' The door suddenly opened and Kenneth appeared. He said, 'You've been in there for an hour, and you're just asking for vaseline.' He handed me the jar. I closed the door. I found no difficulty whatsoever in getting a hard on. I pushed it in. I pulled the drawers up higher and, as I fucked him, my balls occasionally brushed against the material and I experienced great delight. Was this, I wondered, the result of my balls touching the material – i.e. purely physical, or was it – giving the whole idea a totally unexpected twist – the result of 'fetishist' touching, as with religious awe, the object of his adoring. 'Oh, Oh!' I cried. 'You come?' Yellow-jersey expressed considerable surprise. I kissed his back and neck and came my belly-full up his reeking arse. 'Oh, Oh!' I said. 'I'm inclined to favour the spiritual values nowadays when so many persons are queer.' 'Good fuck,' he said. I nodded. He wiped us down, he was now off-hard and didn't want to be tossed off – had it off in the loo, I expect. He hugged me and kissed my shoulders. After a while he got up and had a douche. Kenneth took photos of him in his red drawers. I told him to come again tomorrow. He nodded and beamingly said goodbye to Ken. I went on getting higher over the next hour or so. I sat on the terrace until the sun went behind a bank of cloud. I remember laughing at the idea of Michael Codron: instead of sending a telegram on the first night of *Crimes of Passion* saying, 'Good luck to the stuffed snakes,' he'd really cabled 'Good luck from two puff-adders.' I shall tell Kenneth Williams that that really happened.

Saturday 17 June

It's pouring with rain. Tropical. The cypresses in the garden are sighing. The water is sloshing over the terrace in bucketfuls. Curious morning. Kenneth knocked on the door and said, 'A telegram has arrived. The Fatima has brought it up from the Baron's kitchen.' It was from Peter Willes. It announced that *Sloane* had been cancelled indefinitely. He said he'd explain more fully when I came home. 'It was obvious that Rediffusion would get cold feet,' Kenneth said.[1]

'If the rain is coming down at this rate when Mohammed Jersey arrives,' I said, 'it will be my fantasies come true.' Kenneth stared blandly, the Kif working. 'You're well aware of my rain obsession,' I said. 'It's always in the rain that the soldier/engineer/apprentice/lorrydriver/master sergeant in the Marines fucks the schoolboy/errand boy or mentally defective farm labourer recently released from borstal.' 'Isn't it in the back of a lorry or in a shed though,' Kenneth said. 'Yes,' I said, 'but with a fifteen-year-old boy and the rain, two-thirds of the fantasy is reality, the setting is of minor importance.' Didn't take any cake today. It was pouring with rain at 2.30, when Yellow-jersey arrived.[2]

Sunday 18 June

Woke feeling a little better, though dazed. Rain has stopped. Sky still cloudy though. Fell asleep on the couch at ten-thirtyish and dimly heard the doorbell ring at eleven. It was Mohammed Ali (from Chechaouen). The Fatima let him in. He came over and kissed my cheek. I pretended to be asleep in order to avoid talking to him. Dozed off. At twelve, Kenneth woke me. 'Are you on Kif as well?'

---

1 Orton to Peggy Ramsay, 19 June 1967: '... P. Willes sent a v. melodramatic cable. I'd gathered that A.R. was collapsing anyway. So long as they do *Funeral Games* it's OK by me. They may pick up their pipes and be gone. Actually it saved me from a v. embarrassing position as I'd already *privately* decided to write no more television plays – they're so difficult to mount on stage after TV has deflowered them. If Willes had remained at A.R., I'd've felt inclined to write a TV play now and then to keep him happy ... And perhaps when we get a revival of *Sloane* it will be in a more interesting medium than television ...' [A.R. is Associated Rediffusion.]

2 Orton to Peggy Ramsay, 19 June 1967: '... It poured with rain here on Saturday night. Came down in torrents. Suddenly there was a terrific flash and every light in Tangier went out. The whole town was in darkness. I was in the flat. It was pitch black. No light at all. Then Kenneth remembered seeing half a candle in the cupboard. So we sat for about twenty minutes in the enormous room – with chandelier and "period" furniture. Kenneth said it was like a set for a Hammer film – Dr Terror's House of Horrors – then the lights went on again and it was confident in many breasts that God had decided not so to do with Tangier as with the Cities of the Plain.'

he asked. 'You're not spending the whole of the day in a coma, are you?' I got up. Shaved. Heard M. Ali rattling the door of the bathroom. Called, 'Goodbye, you tiresome bore,' in a loud merry voice. 'Goodbye bore,' he said, shuffling away. After I'd shaved, I went into the living-room. The Fatima had gone early. 'What a pest that boy is,' Kenneth said. 'It's God's judgement on you for treachery,' I said. 'If you hadn't had him whilst I was away, he would have come for me, and this would now have been my problem and not yours.' I sat down in the sun, which was shining hazily. 'What would you have done?' he said. 'I would have got rid of him by now,' I said. 'He's like Mohammed Goldtooth (Khomsi), boring the tits off everyone with his constant jibber.' Hubert Pitman rang shortly after this. 'I wonder, Joe,' he said, 'whether you'd like to come for a drive to Malabata? I have this young man staying with me. I thought it might amuse you.' 'I can't come today,' I said. 'I'm baking a cake.' There was a pause. 'Good heavens!' he said. 'What an extraordinary thing to do.' 'I bought the mixed fruit out from England,' I said. 'I've just put the oven on.' He rang off. Kenneth gave me instructions to take the cake out of the oven at 6.15, and then went into the bedroom. I sat reading Beatrix Potter until I heard Larbi talking in a loud voice. I went into the hall and saw him standing naked by the telephone. He was ringing his mother. 'Oui, Mama,' he said, twisting the telephone cord round his cock. I stood behind him and as he rang off, pulled the cord, which caught his cock. 'Hey, my cock!' he shouted, and laughed. He turned to Ken. 'I speak for my mama – Joe – he *comme ça* – my cock.' He looked very ravishing standing among the Baron's bric-a-brac. Nigel arrived. Later we went to dinner. And even later saw Hubert Pitman on the boulevard with an incredible ponce wearing green velvet and white satin. 'So *that's* his young man,' Kenneth said. 'He must want his eyes seeing to.'

Monday 19 June

The post this morning brought notices and news from London. Sunday notices fair – none of them glowing. I rather agree with what they say. It did need a star in *Erpingham*. B. Gallagher is a good actor – it needed that extra candle-power a star has.[1] Went to Mamora to fetch my sunglasses. Jimmy, George and a host of Moroccans were busy preparing a meal for a coach-load of people – from Lyons Tours. We decided to have lunch at The Windmill. As we got down on the road, Kenneth pulled me back. 'It's old Pitman,' he said cowering behind a tree. 'Don't let him see you.' So Hubert Pitman strode by. 'What a good job I saw him,' Kenneth said, as the titled gent disappeared round a corner. Lunched at The

---

1 Orton to Peggy Ramsay, 19 June 1967: 'Thanks for the notices. I thought they were very fair. Nothing one could seriously argue with. I feel the *Erpingham Camp* would've been differently reviewed if Arthur Lowe had played Erpingham. But no harm has been done. Nobody can call *Crimes of Passion* a failure. We've got a publisher – v. important. And I feel ready to come home and finish the third play . . .'

Windmill. After talking to Nigel, who referred to Israel as a 'ghetto' state, I went home. Mohammed (Chechaouen) came round at three. Kenneth got rid of him. Yellow-jersey came at 3.20. I had a shower, as I'd been sitting in the sun. He sat in the bedroom smoking. As I'd been eating bits of cake since one, I was feeling very good. The whole process of taking a shower, and later undressing Yellow-jersey, was very sensual. I fucked him twice today. Went to Florians for dinner with Frank and Nigel. Frank very cross because I didn't go to his house this morning in order to be sculpted. 'I had my materials all ready,' he complained. 'It was pouring with rain this morning,' I said, which was perfectly true. 'You could have got a taxi,' he wailed. 'I couldn't have got one back,' I said. 'You're not on the telephone, and I couldn't have been stuck in your place all day.' 'Well anyway, I didn't waste my materials,' he said. 'An old boy-friend rang and I made a perfectly splendid model of him.' Met a man called Desmond who said that 'England is America's poodle.' We all agreed.

Tuesday 21 June

Weather perfect today. Clear sky. No sign of rain. Or wind. Went to the beach early. Bathed. Sat outside The Windmill. At the back, facing the railway line. Nigel, Frank and Kenneth talked of nothing but the Middle East crisis. Endlessly chewing the situation backwards and forwards to entertain themselves. I hardly listened, let alone joined in. Frank, being over eighty finds it difficult to hear a statement like 'England is not a democracy'.[1] Left at 1.30 for home. On the way, we met Madame Jungles (the female impersonator). He's a bit of a bore, but after Frank's professional stiffness, I rather welcomed his camp. 'I'm never going to Nino's for dinner again,' he said, 'after that disgusting meal I was served the other night.' 'We're not going either,' said Kenneth. 'I had a perfect meal in Florian's yesterday,' he said, 'and why shouldn't I move around. I can afford to with my money. Nino begged me to give him a photograph of my act,' he said looking distressed. 'And now I don't eat there, he's torn it up. What a way to behave, isn't it? Childish cow. What a puerile thing to do. I can go anywhere with my money.'

The fiesta began last night and, throughout the night, guns were heard firing on two or three occasions. When I woke up I had a sudden nightmare of people battering at the front door, and woke up crying loudly, 'Stop it! Stop it!' 'It's the guns,' Kenneth cried rushing into the room. It was like a play about the French Revolution.

Wednesday 21 June

'Do you remember inventing a wildly funny joke?' Kenneth said. 'When?' I said. 'Last night while we were trying to get a meal.' 'Oh yes,' I said, 'about a vicar

1 Orton raised such mischievous notions in his plays. Says Truscott: 'You're at liberty to answer your own doorbell, miss. That is how we tell whether or not we live in a free country.'

with a large congregation, but a very small organ.' 'It was funnier last night,' Kenneth said. Boring Mohammed Ali turned up this morning before the Fatima. He spoke to Kenneth and, on being lent a pair of bathing trunks, went away. The Fatima arrived next. The last ring on the bell was Larbi. The Fatima let him in and he stayed till three. Most of the time he was asleep on the sofa. He said he'd spent the night at The Pergola beach café. 'No good,' he said, 'many mosquitoes'. He was very taken by my nude snaps. Kept shaking his head and laughing. He wants to have nude ones of himself. Ken and Larbi went to the bedroom. After a few seconds Kenneth reappeared. 'Where's that ring Kevin gave to you?' he said. 'I'm wearing it,' I said. 'Give it to me,' said K.[1] 'You're not going to teach that child your foul tricks?' I said with wonder in my voice, unlocking the band of twisted ebony. 'Oh it's a marvellous new discovery,' Kenneth said, taking the ring from me.

Kenneth says that Larbi, after viewing the strange ring with suspicion, consented to have it put on and be wanked. 'After two or three strokes he was squealing "good, good"'. He insisted that we buy three in London, one for Kenneth, one for me and one for himself. 'He's addicted to it,' Kenneth said.

Went to dinner. Boulevard very crowded. It's Mohammed's birthday, so Larbi says. Kenneth says to me that it's a pagan festival revamped, 'Same as Christmas,' he said. 'Islam chose to turn the midsummer festival into Mohammed's birthday exactly the same way as Christianity turned the mid-winter one into Christ's birthday. It's strange though, isn't it, how the midsummer festival in England remained firmly with the pagan Gods?' Had dinner. Saw George Greeves with two respectable looking Americans, a man and his wife. George was being respectable. Quite benign. Does he have a special selection of stories for respectable occasions, I wonder.

Friday 23 June

Kenneth's birthday today.[2] Weather windy, as usual, but clear skies and bright sun. In one week we must leave this apartment. We have to move into a hotel for a couple of nights until the 2 July. Went to Blands and discovered that there is an Air Maroc flight direct to London on Friday. The problem now is whether we can transfer to them from BEA and whether we want to. Decided finally that the idea of a hotel for two days (no sex possible) is too daunting, and that we'll take a risk with Air Maroc. 'Anyway,' Kenneth said, 'it's probably a subsidiary of Air France, like Ghana Airways is an offshoot of BOAC.' Larbi arrived at nine o'clock this morning. I said, 'This one small boy. You fuck him?' 'Yes,' Larbi said. 'Me

---

1 Orton had been given a ring 'which fitted round the cock, under the balls and is supposed to have a very sensual effect . . . It had no particular effect on me.'
2 Halliwell was forty-one.

fuck him right in,' I said. I demonstrated. 'You fuck him properly?' Larbi hesitated and said, 'No right in.' So the thirteen-year-old can't take it properly. 'You'd better be careful,' Kenneth said. 'You'll look fine if you hurt him and he's pouring with blood.' This later at The Windmill. 'I wish you wouldn't spread these rumours,' I said angrily. 'Anyone would think I made a habit of splitting young kids' arses. It's quite easy to tell when you're hurting a boy. They're not dumb, you know.'

Showed Pitman the Royal Court drawing by P. Procktor. 'With every programme we gave away a nude drawing of the author.' He stared, alarmed. 'Not like this one?' he said, looking at the drawing. 'Yes,' I said. 'Good heavens.' He looked shattered. 'What one can get away with nowadays.' He was looking very silly. He wore a flowered playsuit, and it didn't suit him. Frank Holroyd arrived back from a day trip to Gibraltar bubbling over with tales of a new Carnaby Street shop selling 'with-it' clothes. He had bought a shirt as a sample. It was an old type of Fred Perry shirt. On the back was a label saying 'Empire Made'. 'How incredible,' I said, 'to say "Empire Made". I'd no idea anybody did it now.' 'It must be made in Hong Kong,' Kenneth said, 'it's the only bit of the empire left.' I arranged to have a plaster cast of my face made this evening. Came home. M. (Chechaouen) arrived. Spent the next hour listening to his prattle. He is such a boring boy. Every sentence begins, 'How much cost this?' Simply because it is one of the few sentences he can speak. Mohammed Yellow-jersey arrived at 2.30. I sent him away for an hour. Nasser turned up at three. I gave him ten dirham. Five for some hashish and five for himself. He said he saw boy 'Yellow' waiting round the corner. 'He your friend?' he said. 'Yes,' I said. 'Me like boy. Very good harse.' A lot of laughing and then he went. M. Yellow rang about half an hour after. I'd taken some of the cake before. Yellow washed his feet which were covered in sand. Went to bed. I turned him over and put my prick in. It was like putting it into a sandpit. The little lad had an arsehole like a section of the Sahara. Looking very foolish, he got up and went to the bathroom to wash at the bidet. He came back. We began again. This time there was a violent ring at the door – very disturbing. Nobody answered it. Finally we had a very exhilarating session. I felt as though I were about to pass out. Yellow-jersey fell asleep (or appeared to do so) increasing to an alarming degree the fantasy of fucking him whilst he was unconscious against his will. After he'd gone, I settled down in the salon, nearly speechless with hash.

Larbi turned up at five. We took him to Frank's flat to watch my mask being made. An unnerving experience for me.[1] Under the influence of drugs the plaster

1 Orton to Peggy Ramsay, 19 June 1967: 'There's a rather strange old man out here called Professor Frank Holroyd. He wants to make a mask of my face. He does it in plaster – you know, like the death mask of Irving. I foolishly agreed and now I've been told he nearly killed his last victim by covering him with plaster of Paris until he couldn't breathe. So I view the whole episode with some trepidation.'

being put over my face didn't bother me much – though I had an overwhelming desire to laugh at the ridiculousness of it all – but when the time came to fill in my ear thus taking my *sound* as well as my vision by half, I found the whole thing got very frightening and sinister. Suddenly I wasn't in control anymore. I didn't know what was my invention and what was real. I had to insist on my ear not being blocked with plaster. Left Frank pottering around with the finished mould. Though, as Kenneth said, 'All the masks he ever does look the same, so what is the point of taking an impression of somebody's face?'

Saturday 24 June

We took the plunge today and changed our BEA tickets for Air Maroc. We fly back on Friday. Weather up till 11.30 not good. A little cloud. Have told Yellow-jersey, 'No milk today.' Letter from K. Williams. Olivier has prostate trouble. All this taking up fucking at such an advanced age, I expect. Went to The Windmill. A little depressing. The tourist season (such as there is) will be upon us shortly and an influx of limp queens has hit The Windmill. They all wander around wetly complaining of the 'trade' and their inability to prevent their skins from being burnt and their arses from being fucked. Unpleasant to hear them talking so loudly. Went down to The Pergola because Kevin Iver was there and I wanted to speak to him about the hashish cake. He has rather foolishly invited Larbi to his house. Idiotic creature. 'These things must be kept secret.' The whole trouble with Western Society today is the lack of anything worth concealing.

Larbi arrived at five-ish, making rather a nuisance of himself. He's just a high-spirited male prostitute really. An old man rang at the door asking for dirhams for the poor of Tangier. I had to sign a slip of paper to say how much I'd given. Larbi made his exit into the bedroom with Kenneth, saying to me, 'After, I fuck you, yes?' 'You and whose army?' I said. 'Yes, good,' he said. 'There's a lack of understanding between the East and the West which is truly frightening,' I said. 'You frightened,' he said, 'I take it with vaseline. Very good for you.' 'Piss off!' I said.

Went to Florian's for dinner. Have taken no hash cake today. Took two librium. Very pleasant quiet evening. Came home early and talked – me sitting on Kenneth's bed while he drank a cup of coffee. I was asleep by ten o'clock.

Sunday 25 June

It is half past nine and the Fatima hasn't arrived yet. Perhaps she isn't coming today. I hope not. Women are a terrible drag to have around. It's like a holiday when she isn't here. Although the last two months have been very enjoyable and a great success, neither Kenneth nor I will be sorry to leave on Friday. I feel the need to do something fresh. Not work – though undoubtedly I shall finish *What the Butler Saw* – just a change of scene. Even sex with a teenage boy becomes monotonous. Ecstasy is as liable to bore as boredom. I need the atmosphere of London for a month or two in order to stir me from the lethargy into which I am in danger of falling.

Sat on the terrace. The Fatima, who steals food at an alarming rate, yesterday gobbled a large slice of hashish cake left purposely in the cupboard. An hour or so later she fell silent and morose. Today she arrived two hours late and explained rather bleatingly that she'd been *malade*. 'That will teach you to eat my food you thieving bitch,' I said with a cordial smile. 'Oui monsieur,' she said slinking into the kitchen. Because she came two hours late, she appeared to imagine that she should stay till three instead of one. At 2.30 I said, 'Fatima, you may go.' I pointed to my watch. She didn't understand. M. Yellow-jersey turned up as she was leaving. She looked very disdainful. I see her as having a towny accent and looking askance at Yellow-jersey's countryfied manners.

Monday 26 June

Blue skies. No wind. A letter arrived from P. Willes. He said he'd been to see *Crimes of Passion*. He'd left at the interval. Hadn't seen *Erpingham*. Curious letter, full of his usual bitchiness.[1] 'He's in love with you,' Peggy once said. 'It's flirting in reverse.' Spent the whole day on the beach and bathing. Yellow-jersey came in the afternoon. Spent about an hour and a half in bed during which time we fell asleep, both during and after sex. I hadn't taken any hash. Larbi has invited Kenneth and I to have lunch with his family tomorrow. 'He wanted me to give him some money for the ingredients,' Kenneth said. 'It seems rather odd to invite someone to have a meal at your house and ask them to pay for the meal,' I said. 'Rather like Syrie Maugham[2] presenting her weekend guests with laundry bills.' Saw nobody in the evening. Went to bed early.

Tuesday 27 June

The weather again perfect. Blue skies. Hot. No wind. Spent the morning in The Windmill. Went to Larbi's house by taxi. He'd invited M. Ali (Chechaouen) to come along with us. The house was outside Tangier. In a sprawling suburb of Moorish houses. Half the place seemed to be ruined, the rest of the place partly

---

1 Peter Willes to Joe Orton, undated: '. . . Dorothy Dickson and I went to the last night of *Crimes of Passion* at the Royal Court. We did not stay for *The Erpingham Camp*. Harold had been earlier and had words with Gill. I would have shot him. Harold had been amused by a throwaway of you drawn naked in the programme but when we went there wasn't a throwaway only a photograph of you looking very smug . . . There was nothing to be smug about. I was very sad. It'll be nice to see you when you get back eventually. You are not interested in any news other than news about yourself so my love to yourself.'

2 Syrie Maugham. (1879–1955). Fashionable interior decorator; married to W. Somerset Maugham 1916–27.

built. Several houses had fallen down and been left. Children played among the rubble. Larbi's house was very similar to the house in Ksar-el-Kebir. All built on one floor – on the road were a few hens tethered by the leg. Larbi showed us his mother's room with a big double bed with brass bedknobs. Over the bed was a picture of King Mohammed V and his family, taken some years ago when the present sultan was a youth. He pointed out the various princes and princesses and showed us another picture of a Moroccan football team. Why this was in his mother's room he didn't explain. Perhaps it belonged to his father.

The house was lit by oil lamps – the cooking was done on an oil stove, yet on the wall there was a telephone and in the second bedroom was an extension. 'My brother, he *travail* on the *telegraphie*,' Larbi said by way of explanation. The bedroom with the telephone extension belonged to the brother. There were large framed photos of him on the wall. Larbi suddenly produced a gun and pointed it at me. I held up my hands. 'I kill you,' Larbi shouted wildly. We all laughed as he pulled the trigger. I had the feeling that no writer with an eye for the ironic could resist having the gun loaded and the playwright of promise falling dead beside the telephone extension. 'An Evelyn Waugh touch,' Kenneth said, as I told him after the gun had clicked harmlessly.

I lay on the terrace till six. Larbi and Kenneth went into the bedroom. I sat writing until seven when there was a ring at the door. Always in a panic when a doorbell goes, Kenneth rushed from the bedroom. 'See who it is,' he said to me. It was Nigel. 'Will you join us at Florian's tonight?' 'Yes,' I said. I noticed that Kenneth had given Larbi a pink shirt. He looked very good in it. 'You look very good in that,' I said. 'Kenneth bought it for me, but – ' 'How tactless you are,' Kenneth snapped suddenly angry. 'Why what's the matter?' I said. We went into the living-room. 'Telling him I bought it for you,' Kenneth said. 'It doesn't matter,' I said. 'It's an expensive shirt. He's lucky to have it.' Larbi, aware that Kenneth was angry, sat on the settee. 'There was an incredible scene at The Pergola today,' Nigel said. 'A fourteen-year-old blond English boy came in with four big Moroccans. He was holding court.' 'Fourteen?' I said. 'Yes,' Nigel said, 'I was told he was fourteen. He is here with his mother.' 'Are the Moroccans fucking him?' I said. 'Well, I don't know,' said Nigel. 'I suppose he will get fucked if he carries on like that.' Larbi left shortly after this conversation. Nigel expressed an interest in M. Ali (Chechaouen). Kenneth, anxious to sell his share of the boy, said, 'Yes he's very good in bed, and he'll do anything.' 'How do you know?' I said. 'You've only asked him to do so little.' Kenneth said, 'Oh, all the boys will do anything.' 'They won't,' I said. 'There's a lot of things they won't do.' It was very irritating to be told by someone who likes being masturbated that the boys 'will do anything.' 'You said yourself that he wouldn't take it. It was your excuse for having him in the first place.'

Kenneth became violently angry shortly after this and attacked me, hitting me about the head[1] and knocking my pen from my hand. He left the room and, a short time later, the house. I got back to the flat about 9.45. Kenneth was lying in his bed in a towel dressing-gown, looking tight-lipped. I realised that it was no good speaking to him, the 'sore' would come sooner or later. I'd just settled down for the night when the door opened and Kenneth entered. I was selfish, I couldn't bear not to be the centre of attention, I was continually sneering at him for only wishing to be masturbated while I was 'virile' in fucking boys. 'I saw you in Nigel's car,' he said, 'and I've never seen you at a distance before. I thought, What a long-nosed ponce.' The holiday had been too perfect. I was determined to spoil it somehow. 'And when we get back to London,' he said, 'we're finished. This is the end!' I had heard this so often. 'I wonder you didn't add "I'm going back to Mother",' I said wearily. 'That's the kind of line which makes your plays ultimately worthless,' he said. It went on and on until I put out the light. He slammed the door and went to bed.

Wednesday 28 June

Weather fine. A wind blowing though. Kenneth still in a sulk. 'What are we going to do about getting a strap for my case,' he said, petulant. 'I went to the boulevard last night – I can't find a place.'

I went up to the boulevard and for five dirham bought a strap. 'Life is difficult,' I said, 'but not altogether intolerable. The small things, like a strap for one's luggage, can be found quite easily.'

Kenneth was less tiresome after this. I spent the morning writing. The Fatima had arrived at 8.45. She sat for an hour staring at the wall in the kitchen and drinking a cup of tea. At 9.45 she unlocked the door into the garden and went down to chat to her mother and the gardener. She did a little work for the next two hours. At 12.30 she had vanished back into the garden leaving her yashmak and slippers upstairs. Kenneth, in a growing rage, said, 'I'm going to put her things outside and go down to The Pergola.' 'Why?' I said. 'I'm not leaving her in the house,' he said. 'When she's finished she should go.' 'It seems hardly worthwhile to bother since we're off to London on Friday,' I said. But Kenneth, angry and determined, put the Fatima's clothes on the bench on the terrace and

---

1 This was Halliwell's first attack on Orton's head, a foreshadowing of his murder. Halliwell's rage was inspired, significantly, by Orton's provocative statement which drew attention to Halliwell's inadequacy. Writes Alexander Lowe in *Narcissism: The Denial of Self*: 'Rage has an irrational quality ... Anger, in contrast, is a focused reaction; it is directed toward removing a force that is acting against it. When the force is removed or nullified, the anger subsides ... Rage, however, is not in line with the provocation; it continues until it is spent. And Rage is destructive rather than constructive ... Rage is tinged with murderous intent ... Recognising the murderous quality of all such reactions, we can postulate that the insult provoking the reaction must strike a vital chord ... Describing the rage as narcissistic tells us that the insult was to the person's sense of self, that it was a narcissistic injury. The experience was one of humiliation, of being powerless.'

locked the garden door. We went down to The Pergola. Nigel was sitting there. Kenneth, in a very loud voice, said, 'I've taught our Fatima a lesson.' He then told the whole story and ended saying, 'Joe wanted to ignore her, but she's got to be made to realise.' Nigel said, 'How right you are, dear, it takes a woman to deal with a woman.' 'If I'd said that,' I said, aside to Kenneth, 'you'd be on a charter flight back to London by now.'

The fourteen-year-old-boy appeared with a Moroccan. He wasn't good-looking. A little queen, in fact. I'd like to fuck him though, just because he's fourteen and blond. Kenneth began an argument. 'He's *awful*,' he said in loud irritating tones. 'I can't understand anyone going with him.' 'If he takes it and he's fourteen,' I said, 'I can see perfectly why the Moroccans are interested and I would be too.' An elderly queen leaned across and said, 'He's a raver. My Ali had him and said, "He has a prick *that* big" – he measured an impossible length (about two feet) on his arm. Ali said he got it right up.' There was a licking of lips all round. 'Well,' Kenneth said in a tight voice, 'all I'd like to do to the creature is whip him.' 'You're simply substituting violence for sex,' I said. 'Your psychological slip is showing. A whip is a phallic symbol. You're doing on a symbolic level exactly what I do in reality.'

We went to lunch. 'I've just enough energy to live without working,' Nigel said, flopping into a chair. 'Oh what will happen to exotic Tangier when I am dead and gone.' A terrible Moroccan queen sat at the bar. Someone called her a queen. 'I'm not a queen,' she said. 'I'm too young to be a queen.' And then later, contradicting herself, she said, 'I'm old enough to be a queen's mother.' 'I find Arab queers most offensive,' I said. 'Western society pushes people queer who wouldn't be so in the East. There are pressures to conform to the image of the "queer". The Arabs have all the benefits of homosexuality – ' 'With none of the doubts,' Nigel finished. 'Yes,' I said. 'As George Greeves always says,' Nigel remarked as the waiter brought the menu, 'if you can't keep a curved tongue up my arse, what can you do?'

Kenneth and I went to a flat in the rue Dante. We'd been invited for drinks by a woman called Edwina Morney-Brooks. Edwina is a little fat woman who dresses in a bathing costume and has a red wig for evening wear. When we got to her flat in the rue Dante we were greeted by Mr Brooks, who owns a factory in Coventry and is always drunk. 'Bon soir mon ami,' he said in a loud and cheerful voice, and he showed us into the comfortable lounge. 'You haven't met my daughter's friend have you?' Edwina said, looking forward with a charming smile at a fairly ugly girl in her twenties. 'Shareen is a very glamourous model girl,' Mr Brooks ventured. 'She's in drag for Bragg,' Kenneth said, referring to our mutual friend Bernadine Bragg who owns the draper's business that employs Shareen. 'It means beautiful lady in Persian,' Shareen said and we all guessed that she was talking about her name. Shareen went out into the streets looking for bottled or tinned orange, and an American woman who lives in Tangier and plays bridge in the afternoon entered by the main door complaining loudly about the lift. She was called Anna Bedles and she was old. 'I can't get to sleep at nights,' she remarked. 'Last night I tossed and turned and just couldn't get comfortable.' 'You should have got the Moroccan out of your bed,' I said. Everybody fell silent at the suggestion and Anna got up and made for the drinks table.

A lot of people came in later, including a woman who looked like an ant. She had on a pair of black and white check sunglasses and was obviously short-sighted. A lot of men sat between the women and twitched their moustaches. A dyed-blonde woman kept snorting into her drink and saying, 'Such a lot of people about on the boulevard.' Mr Brooks had fallen into an hysterical fit with the whiskey and launched into a story of a jealous woman's Arab lover who, though once rich and admired, was now hawking his penis about the streets. Edwina's face was a study. She got up quietly and said in tones of cold contempt, 'That'll *do*, Jack. We don't want this talk here.' She went away rather rapidly and returned with a glass of milk. 'Drink this,' she said to Mr Brooks, 'and don't talk so much.' Nothing else happened and we left at eight. We went to Le Claridge for dinner. Dai arrived at 8.30 and said that George would be late. He launched into a reminiscence of a member of the Royal Guard who'd once been 'a little playmate of mine.' He twinkled devilishly, his one eye winking like a warning beacon. At this moment a little boy, no more than nine, entered the restaurant and saluted Dai with 'Donne moi une cigarette.' Dai looked quickly around the restaurant and said, 'You shouldn't come here, you know.' He passed the boy a cigarette and he scampered away. 'They've never come in here before,' Dai said, shaking his head. 'He's very naughty.'

When George came in, we told him of the incident and Dai's evident discomfort. 'I've just been to the most shitty party,' George said, sitting down. 'Look round,' he said, addressing the restaurant in general, 'and see what shit-headed cunts people the earth.' He said he'd been having a long conversation with 'that queen who goes around in clerical drag calling herself Father Theodore. Though what fucking church she belongs to all fuck couldn't tell you,' George said, passing an eye down the menu. 'There's Dai's little cock-sucker,' he said, as a small boy passed the restaurant window. 'Now George,' Dai said primly, 'concentrate on the menu or we'll never get served.'

Thursday 29 June

Last day. Terrible wind. Went to the beach. Took photos of Hamid Yellow-jersey and Larbi on the beach. Had lunch at The Pergola. Omelette. Excellent. A man came up to me and told me he'd seen *Loot* last week. 'Marvellous,' he said. 'Coral Browne told me to go and see it. Splendid.' He said he had a house in

Marrakesh. 'Any time you come south,' he said, 'I'd be pleased to put you up.' At home at about three I photographed Hamid in the nude from the back. 'You can take it to Boots to be developed,' Kenneth said. Took Yellow-jersey into the bedroom. I'd taken too much cake and so the sex, though good, went on too long. I was fucking for an hour. Yellow-jersey very upset because I'm leaving. He doesn't believe I'll return. October seems so far off. Such a lot of things can happen.

Friday 30 June

Got up at 7.30. Packed. It is now 9.30. I'm going up to the boulevard to take money from the bank to pay the Fatima.

London
July–August 1967

Friday 30 June

Went to the bank. V. hot day. A little cloud. The sky not completely clear. After withdrawing 300 dirham, I went down to The Windmill. It was deserted as usual. Said goodbye to Mike and Bill. 'We shan't be here when you come in October,' Bill said, 'we've always tried to attract a special sort of clientele. I hope our successors will carry on with our policy.' He didn't sound very hopeful. Looking around at the deserted bar and sun-lounge, I thought it unlikely that anyone would wish to continue the policy of failure so lovingly nurtured by Bill and Mike. Nigel peeped in. 'I've come to have my cunny kissed,' he said. We went down to The Pergola. I said goodbye to Peter Pollack who said that Jayne Mansfield[1] had been killed in a car crash. 'Her head, apparently, was completely severed from her body,' Peter P. said, folding up a Spanish paper. 'It was found some distance away from the car.' 'How gruesome!' Nigel said, with a shudder. 'Why do they print such things?' 'I don't suppose they do in the English papers,' I said. 'It's the bloodthirsty Spaniards.' 'And what became of her great tits, d'you suppose?' Nigel said. 'Didn't they protect her?' He nodded to an old man who passed by swinging a beachbag. 'He looks as though his cunny has been well-kissed,' he said.

We looked into The Pergola sandpit. No friend caught our eye. 'I'll come and say bon voyage to Kenneth,' Nigel said, as we got into his car. Yellow-jersey and Larbi were sitting on the settee. Yellow-jersey was looking opulent: canvas shoes, white socks, sand-coloured trousers and brown shirt. We took a photograph of him and Larbi. For a while Nigel talked. I went to have a bath. When I got back Larbi was showing Yellow-jersey the drawings in *The Secret Cult*. The effect was electrifying. Neither Yellow-jersey nor Larbi are conscious of the out-of-date style of the drawings. Or the hairstyles on the men and women. Yellow-jersey began giggling hysterically and turning over the pages in a frantic desire to see the other pictures. He stared at each picture for a long time and made many comments in Arabic. Kenneth gave away the remains of the bathroom cupboard – shaving cream, after-shave and talcum powder to Larbi. I gave Yellow-jersey a bottle of vanilla essence. 'Perfume,' I said, and he sprinkled some on his chest.

1 Jayne Mansfield (1932–1967). Actress.

When M. Ali (Chechaouen) arrived, Kenneth gave him a nylon shirt. General hilarity. Nigel v. schoolboyish. His eyes shining. 'I'm going to make a pass at M. Ali (Chechaouen),' he said, 'he has a very pretty bottom.' I took Yellow-jersey into the bedroom and gave him a parting gift of fifteen dirham. 'I'll see you in September,' I said. He hugged me and I put my hand down his trousers and stroked his buttocks. He kissed my cheek.

Reginald Allen arrived with the car. Larbi wanted to come to the airport. 'No,' I said, 'if you come Hamid must come.' 'Why?' Larbi said. 'Because it isn't fair to take you and not Hamid,' I said. He only wanted to ride in the car to score off Hamid. To prove he had a closer relationship with us than Yellow-jersey. He's a great show-off, being a couple of years older. 'Say goodbye now. And leave the Fatima to work!'

We left the flat. The Fatima, v. glum at having received no tip, stared mournfully after us. 'The bitch has £100 of ours,' Kenneth said, 'not even God would tip so much.' Reginald Allen v. gleeful. Passing a policeman on traffic duty he said, 'That policeman has a very small prick. Very disappointing.' And a little later he approached another policeman and said, 'This one has eight children and takes absolutely no notice of me at all.' He leaned from the car and shouted, 'Bonjour!' The handsome policeman smiled. 'Have you tried offering him money?' I said. 'It's so difficult to get into conversation with him,' Allen said, 'it's always such a busy corner. I wish they'd put him in some more tranquil spot.' At the airport he looked like Billy Bunter. 'Write to me when you're coming again,' he said, in a jolly sort of way, 'and I'll come and pick you up.'

The Air Maroc flight was excellent. Good food. Not too many people on board. The flight was scheduled for two hours and forty minutes. It was overdue by a few minutes. We landed without mishap and, as I remarked to Kenneth, 'the party was over'.

No difficulty with the customs. I simply chose the customs officer that, in an emergency, I wouldn't mind sleeping with, and got through without having even to open my case. London hot, very little difference in actual temperature from Tangier. Muggy though. Not dry heat. 'How dead everyone looks,' Kenneth remarked as we arrived at Gloucester Road. We took a taxi home. Kenneth went for some milk. But the supermarket had closed down during our absence and we had to borrow a bottle of milk from the people next door. A great many letters. And press cuttings. Invitations to parties which I shall not accept. And an invitation to a private viewing at the Drian Galleries of some sculpture. I shall go to this because it might be good for Kenneth's collages. Mick Jagger has been arrested on a drugs charge. All a put-up job I should think.

Saturday 1 July

Warm, muggy day. Rang Peter Willes who had a scarifying tale to tell of back-biting and throat-cutting at Rediffusion. Heads rolling and resignations being accepted every day. They won't now do *Funeral Games* or, it seems, *Entertaining Mr Sloane* on television. I'm seeing him on Monday. *The Good and Faithful Servant* has been nominated as the ITV entry for the Italia Prize which, so P. Willes says, is quite important. 'We last won it with Harold's *The Lover*,'[1] he said. He also said that ITV were thinking originally of nominating Peggy Ashcroft[2] and Roy Dotrice[3] in *Dear Liar*[4], a sort of entertainment made up of bits and pieces from Shaw's correspondence with Mrs P. Campbell. 'Only they discovered that the prize was given for an original television play,' Willes said, 'and so they had the good sense to choose yours.' The whole day has been spent settling in. I've had to stick press cuttings of *Crimes of Passion* into a scrap book until I'm sweating with the work. Shall be pleased when I can begin to read *What the Butler Saw*. Tonight Kenneth and I are going to the Criterion to see the new McLeavy.

Sunday 2 July

Last night Kenneth and I saw the second performance of *Loot*. It was a very hot night. A very small audience. It was an excellent performance. The new man as McLeavy improved the play considerably. The opening scene with Fay, and the proposal scene, which had always dragged, were taken at a good lick. Not a brilliant McLeavy, but certainly up to Sheila and Simon Ward. *Not* up to Kenneth Cranham or Michael. Kenneth Cranham is in the film of *Oliver*. He is getting £50 a day. Michael Bates is also receiving rewards for his performance in the shape of film jobs. He appears to be specialising in brutal and venal policemen.

Today I read *What the Butler Saw* and was pleased with it. There are sections that have to be rewritten and others to be clarified. Not a lot of hard graft, though. I shall enjoy this part of the work. It's a final polishing.

Monday 3 July

Went to see Peter Willes. He was fully awake in his office. Moaned a good deal about Peter Gill's production of *The Ruffian on the Stair*. 'I simply couldn't believe that it could be a good play,' he said, 'and yet you know how I love it. Simply couldn't believe it was a good play. I must've been mistaken. Harold was so crawss with Gill. Oh, they had words.' He took exception to the fact that *The Ruffian* hadn't been given a naturalistic production. 'Where was the door?' he said. 'It was played on an empty stage – just furniture. Perfectly scandalous. Oh, shame on you for allowing such a thing!' I laughed. 'Don't sit there laughing,' he said, 'it's very serious.' I left him and went to see Peggy. I showed her my nude

1 By Harold Pinter, 1963.
2 Dame Peggy Ashcroft (1907–   ). Actress.
3 Roy Dotrice (1923–   ). Actor.
4 *Dear Liar* (1960). Adapted by Jerome Kilty.

photograph. 'What a pity we couldn't've had that in the programme,' she said. I said that in the new play there wasn't a single religious person. 'They're all atheists,' I said. 'How splendid!' she said, looking rather relieved. 'Though,' I said, 'I imagine we shall have to get rid of the Lord Chamberlain before the play can be put on.' 'How exciting,' she said.

Went to the Royal Court. Picked up my book of photographs. The two they'd included in the programme were missing. How typical. Helen Montagu[1] said she'd spoken to Arthur Lowe who was v. excited by my writing a part for him in the next play. 'He's looking forward to playing it,' she said. 'But he hasn't read it yet,' I said. 'It may not appeal to him.' 'Oh, I'm sure it will,' she said. 'Well, he must keep his fingers crossed,' I said. 'He may think it a horrible play. People often do with the things I write, you know.'

Went into the West End. Bought records of 'Peek-a-boo', 'Release Me' and 'I Was Kaiser Bill's Batman'. Saw the new Beatles LP but didn't buy it. Shall hear it first.

Waited at the Arts Theatre for Peter Gill. How stuffy and middle-class the Arts is. Not my cup of tea. Two old women were talking. One about seventy. 'You know May Hallet,' the woman behind the bar said to another old woman. The woman stared at May Hallet and said, 'May!' and then in a cheerful voice added, 'You know I'm nearly blind now?' 'No,' May Hallet said, 'I didn't. I'm nearly deaf myself.' 'I can hardly see anything,' the second woman said, 'and I'm worried for fear people imagine I'm cutting them.' 'You don't want that,' May Hallet said, gruffly. Although she was very old one could see she'd been a lesbian once. 'You must come and see my new flat,' the second woman said, 'I've got a cat. It's just like a dog. I've always had dogs and this is my first cat. And I'm so pleased that it's just like a dog.' 'Are you working?' May Hallet asked. 'No,' the second woman said, 'I'm looking for work. I haven't worked for nearly a month. I'll take anything – radio, television, films.' 'What about the theatre?' May Hallet said. 'Oh, the theatre too, but there's simply nothing for me.' 'You don't want to say that,' May Hallet said. 'Are you working?' the second woman asked her. 'I'm too old. Yes, I'm really too old,' May Hallet said. She had red carpet slippers on and had arthritis. It was a very sad scene because it was played in such a cheerful way. 'Now, May, don't forget to ring me. I shall look forward to seeing you and showing you my cat. His name is Michael.' She leaned on her stick and watched as May Hallet hobbled away.

Saw Peter Gill. Had a v. pleasant lunch. He's going to Canada. How awful for him. But it's only for a month or two.

Got back home. Did work on *What the Butler Saw*. Wrote in the scene with Nick and Mrs Prentice. The first scene. Pleased with it so far. Saw a

1 Helen Montagu (1934–). Theatrical producer.

dress rehearsal of *The Three Sisters*[1] at the National this evening. Plowright[2] excellent. Playing Masha as a sad, vulgar woman. Not a beauty. Just a fattish provincial woman. Excellent. When Vershinin said, 'You're beautiful, your eyes are shining and you're beautiful,' one knew that it wasn't true. He was saying she was beautiful because he was bored. He was bored with the dreadful, flat provincial life and he began to make love to her out of boredom. The set was entirely composed of bamboo slats. As though Grandpapa Prozorov had visited Nippon and fallen in love with a geisha. Olivier's production old-fashioned. I'm glad he's had something odd wrong with his prostate, though. Perhaps now he'll release Plowright from childbearing. She's going to be a great actress one day.

In the pub were several people from the National Theatre. I saw Robert Lang[3] lurking in the corner. As everyone drifted back after the interval, several policemen ran into the bar and surrounded two women. I couldn't understand what the fuss was about. One of the women was screaming, 'He wouldn't attack anybody! He's a pacifist!' Kenneth and I came home. We didn't wait for the second act.

Tuesday 4 July

Wrote *What the Butler Saw* from eleven. Sent a picture of Reggie Marsh[4] in *The Erpingham Camp* to Methuen. They were having a picture from *The Ruffian*. There were no suitable pictures of *Erpingham* at the Court. I feel that *Crimes of Passion* must have a picture from *Erpingham*. So it has to be of the television production. Saw Peggy. She's quite extraordinary. Being v. sophisticated about my taste 'for little boys'. Willes has told her this. 'Well, you're legal now,' she said, showing her ignorance. (The homosexual bill becomes law today.)[5] 'It's only legal over twenty-one,' I said, 'I like boys of fifteen.' She looked rather bright. Great attempts at modernity. I saw Peter Willes this evening for dinner. 'Most people are very shocked by paederasty,' he said. 'You mustn't let people know you fuck little boys.'

He said Coral Browne[6] had met Vivien Merchant and said, 'You're playing Lady M, aren't you dear? What are you going to do with the fucking candle? I wouldn't bring it on. I left it in a sconce offstage. I wouldn't bring it on.' And

---

1 By Anton Chekhov, 1901.
2 Joan Plowright (1929–). Actress.
3 Robert Lang (1934–). Actor and director.
4 Reginald Marsh (1926–). Actor.
5 The Homosexual Bill. Became law on 27 July, 1967, made sex in private between two consenting male adults no longer an illegal offence and fixed the age of adulthood at twenty-one.
6 Coral Browne (1913–). Actress.

Vivien had said, 'Peter wants me to play Lady M. in a grey wig with a grey face but I *don't* think it's quite right somehow.' 'I wouldn't play her in a fucking grey wig,' Coral Browne said, 'I played her as mature, but still very lovely.' 'I had such trouble with Macbeth,' she said, a little later, 'he was so jealous. I got all the notices, you see. And on one night he pulled my wig off. Threw it across the stage. You've really no idea how much trouble I had. It's the baby. That's the crux of the matter. I wanted to play her with a baby at her tit in the first scene. He wouldn't hear of it. Afraid I'd get the pathos, you see.' 'Coral is really wonderful,' Peter Willes said, 'she had her face lifted when she was forty. And that's the perfect age to have it done. It doesn't make you look any younger, but it makes you look *better*.' He brought me a book to read by Mrs Molesworth called *The Palace in the Garden*.

He said something quite extraordinary had happened when he visited H. Pinter and his wife on Sunday. 'Just as I was leaving,' he said, 'Harold drew me aside and said, "Would you read this? We've always disapproved of 'Crawfie' but it might interest you." Crawfie?' Willes thought, wondering how the Queen's nurse could be mixed up with H. Pinter. 'And when I read this manuscript he pressed into my hand I realised – it'd been written by the tutor Harold had engaged to look after his son Daniel. It was ridiculous. In America, of course, they're treating him like Jesus. It's frightening to think someone you engage as your cook-housekeeper might write an autobiographical novel based on her stay in the house. And the terrifying thing is,' P. Willes said, his eyes popping, 'were they flattered? If they were there's no hope for Harold. It's all over. He's confessed to having difficulty writing. "I can't write anymore," he said. I'm not surprised. That enormous house near Regent's Park. And the chandeliers.' Willes went away clucking over the whole situation.

Wednesday 5 July

Wrote solidly all day. Kenneth thinks, from the few lines he's read, that Arthur Lowe should play Dr Prentice. I want Pat Routledge to play Mrs Prentice. In the evening we went to dinner at Kenneth Williams. We arrived at his flat at six. His mother rang on the bell about five minutes later. 'I've brought this,' she said, handing him a letter. Kenneth glanced at it. 'It's a rates demand,' he said. His mother sat down and had a sherry. She said she'd had a letter from Kenneth's sister. 'She's touring,' Mrs Williams said. 'Getting all those big Greek sailors,' Kenneth said. Mrs Williams gave a squawk. 'I bet you wish you were there, don't you, Lou?' Kenneth said to his mother. 'No, I don't!' Mrs Williams said. 'She'll be getting the dick,' Kenneth said. He kept bringing the conversation round to fucking by the most unlikely methods. I was a little surprised to hear someone talk so freely in front of their mother.¹ I'm not altogether sure that I liked the way Kenneth 'got at' his mother via the conversation. I thought she'd've much sooner had a more conventional chat over a glass of sherry. Perhaps she normally had 'broadminded' conversation. I got the impression Kenneth was tearing into her, realising that, in front of me at least, she'd've appreciated a little modesty. I may be wrong.

A friend of Kenneth's from his army days arrived later, and his mother left. This man, once a lorry driver, now a second-hand clothes-merchant, was living with a young man called Syd. I'd met Syd² on a previous occasion. A nice young man. A bit effeminate, but good natured. The lorry driver said, 'Syd's gone up west with Harry.' Kenneth looked surprised, 'His previous affair,' he said to me. 'You're all one big happy family now,' he said. 'Yes,' the lorry driver said. 'Quite a harem you've got,' Kenneth said. We went out to dinner. Kenneth was looking tired. 'I have no sex, you know,' he said. 'It's love I want,' he said, later. P. Willes, who was sitting with someone else in the corner of the restaurant, suddenly sent a note to me by the waiter. It said, 'When *I* ask you to come to dinner with me you're too *tired*. Or too *bored*. Yet you run around all the time after Mr Williams. What is the matter with you?' I was contemplating sending a rude note back, but didn't. I asked Kenneth W. if he'd liked my letters from Tangier. 'Well, I simply love Edna,' he said, 'But Uncle Whippity³ is too rude for me.' 'Yes,' Kenneth Halliwell said when we got home, 'he can't take the other side of you can he?' We left Kenneth at 9.20. 'You ought to get some sleep,' I said. 'I do appreciate your coming round,' Kenneth said, as we left. 'Someone I know took an overdose when they realised that they had no friends. Isn't that awful?' I gave him the programme from the Royal Court. He was delighted when he saw a picture of himself in it. 'It's me!' he said, 'How nice!' The lorry driver dropped us at Euston. We walked the rest of the way home.

Thursday 6 July

Weather hot, muggy. Spent the whole day typing the first act of *What the Butler Saw*. P. Willes rang. 'Who was that other gentleman sitting with you and Kenneth Williams last night?' he said. 'A lorry driver,' I said. 'He didn't look like a lorry driver,' Willes said, tartly. 'No,' I said, 'he's given it up and has taken to selling second-hand clothes.' 'Are you ever going to wash that tee-shirt of yours?' Willes

---

1 Kenneth Williams: 'It's the pot calling the kettle black. Joe was just as shocking. He gave a detailed account of coupling in the alley of a Leicester council house with his bum exposed to the elements.' For Williams's diary account of the conversation see *Just Williams* (Dent, 1985), pp. 167–8.
2 His name was Stan. He didn't like Orton. According to Kenneth Williams's *Just Williams*, Stan said: '"He's so boring – always talking about himself" – but I pointed out it was a fascinating self to talk about.'
3 Uncle Whippity was just lewd, where Edna Welthorpe had some satiric and literary flair.

said. 'You've been wearing it for ages.' 'I let the sweat collect,' I said, 'and then when I pick someone up it gives them a kinky thrill.' Willes rang off after a chat. He seemed in a good mood. He's sent *Sloane* to the ITA. 'They'll probably ban it,' Willes said.

Henry Budgen rang. He said sex in Cyprus is difficult. 'It's difficult anywhere if your name is Henry Budgen,' K.H. said.

Friday 7 July

Began to type up the second act of *What the Butler Saw*. I'm not encountering any real difficulties so far. I'm just polishing, straightening. Weather hot, muggy, not very pleasant. The telephone has been cut off. I don't know why. It rang and fell silent. The newspapers are quite hysterical today over the knighting of Sir Francis Chichester[1] – an old man who has sailed round the Horn because he can't get one of his own. Headlines – SIR LONDON! – KNIGHT OF THE CHEERING RIVER! – A KNIGHT TO REMEMBER! – and KNIGHTING SEEN BY MILLIONS (at the Queen's request). The television news was obsessed by Wimbledon. Boring shots of people playing tennis. 'The only ball game worth playing is the kind one plays with one's own balls,' Kenneth Halliwell said. Douglas sent me some photographs and contacts of me and of *The Ruffian on the Stair*. Excellent. The National Theatre *Three Sisters* has had excellent notices. I still think it was bad. The critics have no discernment. We went down to the Cri tonight. Everybody fairly cheerful. Kenneth told the story of Bette Davis[2] on the set of her new film. A man came up to her and said, 'Well, Miss Davis, I'm glad to meet you. We haven't got much in the way of weather, but I'm sure you'll manage without it.' Bette Davis turned to her agent and said, 'Who is this creep?' 'He's your publicity man,' her agent said. 'Sack him,' Bette Davis said. 'I don't want any goddamn creep talking to me about the weather.' Came home. Kenneth is lying on the bed smoking a cigarette. It is very hot.

Saturday 8 July

Very hot day. Telephone off so nobody could contact me. Kenneth has bad hay fever. Did nothing at all except type *What the Butler Saw*.

Tuesday 11 July

The last few days have been hot, muggy, typical dreadful English weather. I've finished typing *What the Butler Saw*. Yesterday Kenneth read the script and was

---

1 Sir Francis Chichester (1901–72). Yachtsman. Knighted with Sir Francis Drake's sword for successful solo circumnavigation of the world (1966).
2 Bette Davis (1908–   ). Actress. From 1937–1947, the box office queen of Hollywood.

enthusiastic – he made several important suggestions which I'm carrying out.¹ He was impressed by the way in which, using the context of a farce, I'd managed to produce a *Golden Bough* subtext – even (he pointed out) the castration of Sir Winston Churchill (the father-figure) and the descent of the god at the end – Sergeant Match, drugged and dressed in a woman's gown. It was only to be expected that Kenneth would get these references to classical literature. Whether anyone else will spot them is another matter. 'You must get a director who, while making it funny, brings out the subtext,' Kenneth said. He suggests that the dress Match wears should be of something suggestive of leopard-skin – this would make it funny when Nick wears it and get the right 'image' for the Euripidean ending when Match wears it.

Today I started typing the copies to be given to Peggy. I went into the West End this morning and bought tickets for the matinee tomorrow of *The Desert Song*. It's a dreadful touring version that has come on at the Palace. 'Oh, it's very chic to go to it,' Peter Willes said when I told him. 'I'm sure you'll enjoy yourself enormously. Only please remember that when it was done originally it had 100 Rifs.' He doesn't like *Up Against It*. 'It's too mad,' he said, 'too ridiculous. I mean they leave the town and then there's the dark wood. And then that girl keeps turning up. Oh, I do like there to be a proper story.' I said there was a story. But all he kept saying was, 'It's all too mad.' 'What about *Alice Through the Looking Glass*?' I said. 'Precisely,' he said, 'I *hate* that.' He was just off to Nottingham to see Pinter's production of the Robert Shaw play with Donald Pleasence.²

Tonight I'm off to meet the Egyptian journalist who is going to translate *Loot* into Arabic. I like him v. much. Though, unless I go to bed with him, we haven't a lot in common.

I got to the South Kensington tube station at a quarter to eight. I had to meet Achmed Ossman at eight. Strange atmosphere. People wandering about. A hot, muggy night. Achmed arrived at eight. We went to a pub and talked. He, wary at first, with the present situation vis-à-vis the Arab/Israel conflict. I said I was pro-Arab and he brightened considerably. He is in favour of Nasser. He says he's liberalising Egypt. Though, to hear him talk, the liberalising seems to consist mainly of the Arab girls becoming freer sexually. I'm not in favour of this – the more girl-conscious they become out there the less boy-conscious. I received a distinct impression (Achmed being rather middle-class) that boys and hashish are distinctly out of fashion with the trendy Arabs. It's all whiskey and Western

---

1 Peter Wood: 'Joe acknowledged a tremendous debt to Halliwell. He struck one as having more confidence of Joe, of being Joe's mentor. I was struck by Halliwell's unselfishness. He'd wanted to write desperately and wanted to write well. He'd given so much time to Joe's writing. He was the first person to recognize that extraordinary style. It was a phenomenal notion, a revolutionary notion, that you should have a group of people on the stage speaking this mandarin language . . .'

2 *The Man in the Glass Booth.*

thought. He's a nice man, though. He said he'd read *Sloane*. Very enthusiastic. He said he'd like to get *Loot* put on first because, for the Arabs, *Loot* is less shocking than *Sloane*. 'It's the sexual subjects which are most difficult, you see,' he said. We talked of Pinter. His work isn't known in Egypt. Not surprisingly Harold being Jewish. He asked if *Entertaining Mr Sloane* was on before *The Homecoming*. 'Oh, yes,' I said. 'Two years before.' 'The similarities are overwhelming,' he said. He thought perhaps Harold had seen *Sloane* and been influenced by it in the second act of *The Homecoming*. 'I'm sure he did,' I said. '*The Homecoming* couldn't have been written without *Sloane*. And, you know, in a way the second act – although I admire it very much – isn't true. Harold, I'm sure, would never share anyone sexually. I would. And so *Sloane* springs from the way I think. *The Homecoming* doesn't spring from the way Harold thinks.'

He asked if I'd like to go to his house. I agreed. He went and rang his wife. She was tidying the place. We went round after drinking another beer and he introduced me to his wife (an Egyptian girl) and a Jordanian man and a Syrian woman. The man and woman (friends of theirs) were both drunk. The woman was a bore. She was drinking whiskey and sherry mixed. She tried to persuade me to drink the same. I had a whiskey. Hate the stuff but I didn't want to offend any ancient Arab custom. Later she put sherry in it. And later than this attempted to give me more whiskey. When I again refused she became tiresome – asking why? And behaving in a generally disagreeable manner. Finally Achmed said something to her in Arabic and she became petulant. I got up and said I must go. Achmed accompanied me, a little tight, to the tube station. 'I'm very sorry for her behaviour,' he said. 'She doesn't realise that when Englishmen say "No" they mean "No".' 'Don't Arab men mean "No" when they say so?' I asked. 'Not at all,' he said, with a smile, 'they like to be persuaded.' If this is true it sheds a new light on the Arab male psychology. I said he wasn't to worry. I'd already forgotten the Syrian woman (though she was so ugly that forgetting her was a pleasure). Left him and took the tube to Holloway Road hoping to find a bit of sex. I was tight and a little sleepy. Met a young boy (about seventeen I'd judge). He was rather effeminate. I said, 'Do you take it?' He said, 'No.' I got him in the doorway of a lavatory. He looked out – seeing if anyone was coming. I held him from behind and tried to fuck him. It was impossible, though. So many people kept coming in. I took him for a short walk, looking for a spot where I could have him. Impossible. Gave up at last and said, 'Goodnight.' He lived with his parents in Stamford Hill. I caught the bus home. Kenneth wasn't asleep. We talked for a long time. I made a cup of tea. Didn't sleep till about two. Wretched whiskey made me feel sick.

Wednesday 12 July

Spent the whole morning typing up *What the Butler Saw*. Kenneth is rereading the second half of the play. He's suggested one or two cuts. I shall take his advice. The play is long enough for me to be able to cut anything that isn't a good line or necessary for the understanding of the play. He said he watched a programme last night in which Alastair Sim[1] starred. Kenneth says that Sim would be ideal for Dr Rance. Agree with him. And Arthur Lowe as Dr Prentice. Kenneth also says that we should offer Mrs Prentice to Coral Browne. She would be rather good – though I doubt whether she'd accept. In the afternoon we went to the Palace Theatre with Sheila Ballantine and Kenneth Cranham[2] to scc *The Desert Song*, the old musical revived. It was a touring version which has been brought into the Palace because the modern American musical *110 in the Shade*[3] flopped so rapidly. It's difficult to judge *The Desert Song* on this production. It was clearly written for great stars of the old type. Very funny. We all laughed at the ridiculous lines – though v. discreetly because most of the audience (of old ladies) were taking it seriously and enjoying it. Kenneth Halliwell said that a lot of it reminded him of my writing. Not surprising really since my writing is a deliberate satire on bad theatre. The plot gave me the idea for my next play. In the interval we had tea and cakes. There was an ashtray that I'd've loved to pinch. It had on it 'The property of Emile Littler'. Emile Littler is the prudish impresario who came out strongly a couple of years ago in favour of the old type of theatre.[4] *The Desert Song* has wonderful numbers. High romance. Very moving in spite of their silliness. It could've been a much better show. Only then, I suppose, the old ladies wouldn't've liked it so much. We went to Lyons for tea afterwards. Kenneth Halliwell had the photographs we'd taken in Morocco including the naked ones of Hamid and me. We passed them across the table to Kenneth Cranham and Sheila as they ate their toasted tea cakes. We talked of the pictures of the Queen and the Duke of Edinburgh in the foyer of the Palace Theatre. Ridiculously glamorous paintings making them look as though they'd just ascended into heaven. The Queen seemed to be surrounded entirely by negroes. What the significance of this was we didn't understand.

After tea we sat by the fountain in Piccadilly Circus. There seemed to be a lot of beautiful, blonde, clean young men and women sitting around. I couldn't understand what they were doing there. 'Being beautiful,' Sheila Ballantine said. 'They're the beautiful people'. From what I could see they also seemed to be lacking sexually. Kenneth Cranham spoke to one girl who was nice and smiled a lot. He didn't look as though he was ever going to fuck her, though. And all the

1 Alastair Sim (1900–76). Superb English character actor.
2 Kenneth Cranham: 'It was quite hard to see Joe because you always risked incurring Kenneth's wrath. Kenneth was very verbal, very daunting.'
3 *110 in the Shade*. Adaptation of N. Richard Nash's *The Rainmaker*. Music by Harvey Schmidt; Lyrics by Tom Jones (US performances, 350; UK, 52).
4 Sir Emile Littler (1901–1973). Theatre impresario. He began the controversy by contending that 'some of the plays in in the West End at present are absolutely filthy and unnecessary.'

boys didn't look anti-homo – just nothing – like beautiful dolls just waiting to be taken out of their cellophane wrappers. The fact that many of them were Americans (including the girl Ken spoke to) confirmed what I'd already suspected – they're the young rich – beautiful, sexless little bores. As bad as the chinless wonders from our noble houses. Kenneth and I came home after I'd stolen a poster near Piccadilly Circus which said 'Cannibals Eat Congo Whites'. Rang Achmed who invited me to have a meal with his wife tomorrow. I invited Kenneth H. who refused, saying that he'd be interested in hashish, but not a lot of boring middle-class Egyptians.

Thursday 13 July

All day typing *What the Butler Saw*. Weather stifling. No sign of rain. 'I wish I'd stayed in Morocco,' Kenneth moaned. 'Oh, this terrible city!'

In the evening, about seven, I went to South Kensington. The tube was crowded, stuffy, dusty. In the lift two young men dressed in red shoes, bright green velvet trousers, flowered shirts and white canvas coats were arguing with the lift-woman – a negress – over the price of the ticket. Holding everyone up. Suddenly I was anti-beautiful people. And then I had second thoughts. Met Achmed and his wife. We went to a restaurant with candles on the tables and roughly painted walls. I had veal. And a water-ice. We talked about cockroaches. In Arabic they're called 'sosarr' or that is what it sounds like. I can't spell it. Then we talked about Shakespeare. And then drunken women. It was a pleasant evening. We went to another place for coffee, only I didn't have coffee. I had an orange juice. I left them at ten and thought of picking someone up. I dropped off at the Holloway Road tube. Wandered about. In a lavatory in a back street I met a middle-aged man with a cropped haircut. Not very attractive. He said he lived in a council flat. 'I'm waiting to go back to sea,' he said. We walked for about a hundred yards and he said, 'You don't want it stuck up your arse, do you?' I said I wasn't keen. 'And you're not going to suck me off, are you?' he said. 'No,' I said. 'You just want to shoot your gun,' he said, 'like me.' He turned round. 'We'd better go back,' he said. 'You can pick up a queer in that toilet. They've got cars. And houses. The best time is dinner-time. They've got cars most of them. I've fucked their arses in their rooms,' he said, lighting a cigarette. 'I expect you have too.' We went into the lavatory. Only one man there. I stood next to him. The man with the cropped hair went away. The man I stood next to was a Greek Cypriot. He wasn't very young. About thirty-five. Very stupid-looking. 'Come to the park,' he said, in an ice-cream seller's accent, 'I'll shag you.' I thought it was a stupid idea. And when we got to the park it seemed as though I'd met a maniac. 'See over there,' he said, 'two men. They shag. And over there,' he pointed to a courting couple, 'a man and a girl. They shag, perhaps. I've come here. Everybody shags.' We wandered around for a time. 'Over here,' he said, pointing to a clump of trees that were perhaps three feet away from a well-lighted pavement. 'Please let me shag you,' he said, 'I'll be quick.' 'But we're in the light!' I said, 'we can be seen.' 'Naw,' he said, 'nobody notice.' Up against a tree, I dropped my trousers and he fucked me. He was quick. Afterwards he tossed me off. As we were walking away he said, 'I shag a boy last week. I pay him £2. You don't want money do you?' 'No,' I said, 'I've plenty of money.' He laughed at this and said, 'Me too. I've plenty of money. Too many people shag here,' he said, ambling off across the dark ground, 'maybe next time we shag in a room. Maybe next time you shag me as well.' I said that it would be a pleasure and left him. When I got home Kenneth told me of a play he'd seen with an actor in it called Alexis Kanner.[1] 'You ought to think of him for Sergeant Match,' he said. We talked for a long time. I fell asleep at last about one o'clock. It was a hot night.

Friday 14 July

Again typed *What the Butler Saw*. Again hot weather. Kenneth is feeling ill with hay fever. Went down to the Criterion. Sheila Ballantine has forgotten to bring her Beatles record *Sergeant Pepper's Lonely Hearts' Club Band*. Talked about Americans. Who are mad. Simon Ward said, 'Out of their minds.' 'Do you think perhaps that they're creatures from another planet?' I said. 'Their divorce laws are disturbing,' Simon said. 'Will they ever found a serious school of philosophy?' I said. 'Have any of you heard of Cecil Tennant[2]?' Michael Bates asked, looking round the door. 'I've heard of Margot Tennant,' I said, standing up to go. 'Oh, no,' Michael said, 'he's a different chap all together. Cecil Tennant has been killed in a car crash on the way back from Vivien Leigh's funeral.' 'Poor Vivien Leigh,' Sheila said, 'I did admire her.' 'She made a courageous stand for the old St James's Theatre,' Michael said, 'I admired her for it. Well, she's dead now.' He went off to change. 'When Charles Marowitz had a cold once,' Simon said, 'Michael, in all seriousness, took me aside and told me it was "one of the symptoms of syphilis".' 'Americans can't understand our sense of humour,' Kenneth Cranham said, taking off his tee-shirt. 'Look,' he said, 'an English tan.' Took a walk. Nobody around to pick up. Only a lot of disgusting old men. I shall be a disgusting old man myself one day, I thought, mournfully. Only I have high hopes of dying in my prime.

Saturday 15 July

Hot weather. Typed *What the Butler Saw*. I've got well on into the second act – to the part where Mrs Prentice is flung onto the bowl of roses. P. Willes rang this

1 Alexis Kanner (1942–). Actor.
2 Cecil Tennant (1932–1967). Managing Director of MCA in England and Laurence Olivier's production company.

evening. He said, 'I don't mind hearing your sexual experiences at first hand, but I do object to having them repeated across a crowded restaurant.' 'Who by?' I said. 'Kenneth Williams was in Biagi's and he was talking about Morocco and somebody who, surely, must be you. The gentleman he was with kept saying "Oh, my goodness!" and laughing. And Kenneth Williams kept fluttering his eyelashes and camping loudly and offensively.' 'Well, I've no control over him,' I said. 'Tell me about Vivien Leigh.' 'Oh, my dear, I was distraught,' P. Willes said. 'You see she was drugged by the doctors – some crash cure for TB. And she must've just died in her sleep. Dorothy D. went round the day before and said that Vivien was sitting up in bed surrounded by people and flowers and looking radiant, only she couldn't talk. Some wretched drug or other. And Dorothy received a strange letter from her written in wobbly writing. Oh, it's too much. You see she was exactly *my* generation and when someone who was so glittery and wonderful dies and it's your *own* period it's terribly upsetting.' He said he'd wandered around television house 'like a lost soul wailing to myself,' and it was 'dreadful to be working in a medium that cared so little for really wonderful people dying.'

Sunday 16 July

Last night it rained. But today the weather was still hot and close. I finished typing up *What the Butler Saw*. I added very little on this version (just incorporated Kenneth's suggestions which were excellent), except the description of the light from the garden when the lights in the room go out. And stressed the leopard-spotted dress for Match. The Euripidean ending works, surprisingly, as 'all is forgiven' – just as in the later Shakespeare plays. Listened to the *Top of the Pops*. Mostly rubbish. Though I like 'Alternative Title' – the Monkees whom I loathe. And 'A Whiter Shade of Pale'. One line from a pop song struck me as being good: 'The old fortune-teller lies dead on the floor, nobody wants their fortunes told anymore.' Great relief to have finished *The Butler*. I can now give my mind full rein for the historical farce set on the eve of Edward VII's coronation in 1902 and called (at the moment) *Prick Up Your Ears*[1]. I hope I can write a play worthy of one of Kenneth Halliwell's most brilliant titles. I've already got a quotation

---

1 Joe Orton: 'I think one should have tradition ... You can't reject tradition completely ... I've written the first draft of a third play [*What the Butler Saw*] which will be a conventional form, but the ideas I've got for a fourth play won't be conventional form at all. So you see I'm not even committed to the conventional theatre. But I think that one should prove that one can do it, like Picasso proved that he could paint perfectly recognisable people in his early period and then he went on to do much more experimental things. But what does irritate me is the kind of artist and the kind of writer where you know perfectly well the artist can't paint a nude woman if he tried or the writer can't construct a play if he tried. I think one should prove that one could do it, and if one then doesn't chose to do it, that's all right.'

from *The Critic*[1] for the play: 'Where history gives you a good heroic outline for a play, you may fill up with a little love at your own discretion: in doing which, nine times out of ten, you only make up a deficiency in the private history of the times.'

Monday 17 July

Kenneth v. irritating today. Weather hot again. Blue skies. Kenneth's nerves are on edge. Hay fever. He had a row this morning. Trembling with rage. About my nastiness when I said, 'Are you going to stand in front of the mirror all day?' He said, 'I've been washing your fucking underpants! That's why I've been at the sink!' He shouted it out loudly and I said, 'Please, don't let the whole neighbourhood know you're a queen.' 'You know I have hay fever and you deliberately get on my nerves,' he said. 'I'm going out today,' I said, 'I can't stand much more of it.' 'Go out then,' he said, 'I don't want you in here.'[2] I went to Boots for the enlargements of the holiday snaps. They'd merely duplicated them, not enlarged them. So I had to take them back. Long face from Kenneth. 'I should've taken them myself,' he said, 'and why did you pay for them?' I took *What the Butler Saw* to Peggy. She looked at the title and said, 'Oh! It's just like the title of an old farce!' The thing she was most taken with was the quotation from Tourneur.[3] I'll be interested to know what her reactions are. She said, 'Bill Gaskill's lover has left him. He's gone off with a photographer. And Bill was in a terrible state. But he's got over it now. He's going to throw himself into the Court. They're not doing any more revivals. Just new plays. He wants to do *Dingo*[4] by Charles Wood.' I said I read the play last night and thought it excellent. (I didn't say that I thought it excellent only within the limits of Charles's style.) 'It's splendid, isn't it?' she said. We talked a bit and I went away. I decided to get a bit of sex. I went to the lavatory under the bridge in the Hornsey Road. I picked up a negro about twenty-five years of age. We went back to his room in Harringay. He said he was frightened of fucking young boys (he thought I was twenty.) He told me of his friend, a coloured man, who fucked teenage boys. 'I'd be too scared,' he said. He sat on the bed in his underwear for a while talking of a white man he knew who was married and a scoutmaster. 'He's always got kids at his house,' he said, his

---

1 By Richard Brinsley Sheridan, 1779.
2 Miss Boynes: 'Late at night, John would scream "Leave me alone!" and so on. I didn't hear all the words because my hearing wasn't good and I used ear-plugs ... There might have been fear in Ken that John was getting away from him. John was obviously doing well and getting to know so many other people, and so often Ken was on his own, which was unusual because in the beginning they were always together. Never apart ...'
3 Cyril Tourneur (c1575–1626). 'Surely we're all made people, and they/Whom we think are, are not.' *Revenger's Tragedy* (c1606).
4 By Charles Wood (1932–). Playwright.

eyes popping. 'And he fucks them. I'd be too worried.' We lay on the bed. He had a fair body. Going to fat about the stomach. 'I drink too much beer,' he said. He fucked me and came very quickly. He had a bucket of water and put Dettol in it. We washed. Then I lay on the bed with him and I fucked him. It was a bit difficult getting my prick in because he had such a big arse. 'I haven't taken it for five months,' he said, as I put my clothes on. 'I like fucking or being fucked,' he said, 'I've no use for wanking or being sucked off, you know. Come again,' he said, as I left, 'on Wednesday.' Came home. Did nothing all afternoon. Hot and unpleasant. Wish I was in Morocco. I keep thinking of Hamid and, occasionally, of Mustapha. I really must have it up Mustapha in the autumn.

Tuesday 18 July

It was hot again. Not sunny. Sun between cloud. I went to the Garden Restaurant in Henrietta Street at 12.30. I had to meet a man from the BBC. I forget his name. It's something with a 'Y' on the end. He had with him a woman from Rumania. She's seen *Loot* and hopes to get it put on in Rumania. The man with the name I forget has told her to read *Sloane*. She says she will. Adding, as I told her a little of the plot, that if 'sex' came into it then she doubted whether it would be possible to stage the play. She'd been given ten years hard labour for political offences in Rumania and had actually served three. It sounds a depressing place to be in. I wouldn't like to be found dead (or alive) in an Iron Curtain country. She said how one of her greatest friends had been arrested by 'the moral police' for homosexuality. He'd said he was having an affair with her. 'And I had to go to the police headquarters and explain the most intimate details of the affair – which had never happened, of course,' she said. 'Didn't they try to trap you?' I said. 'Oh, yes,' she said, 'sometimes they asked questions which were most difficult.' 'Like was he circumcised or not?' I said. 'Well,' she laughed a little hysterically, 'not quite like that, you know.' She said the man finally hanged himself. 'Not because of this case,' she said, 'but another one. A political case.' A depressing sort of country and one which, I'm sure, wouldn't welcome my plays. I went on to a house in Aubrey Walk N8 to be photographed for *Queen* magazine. It was all very bright. A lot of clever and attractive young people. A young man said, 'We're doing the "goodies" today.' 'What do you mean?' I said. He showed me a photograph to be included in the same issue as ours. It was of a group of about eight people – including Nicholas Tomalin[1] and Kathy McGowran[2]. 'They're the baddies,' he said. 'That'll be on the opposite page to yours.' They're going to contrast various sets of people. The rest of my group were soon assembled –

1 Nicholas Tomalin (1931–1973). Journalist.
2 Cathy McGowan (1944–). TV personality on popular 60s show, *Ready Steady Go*.

Tom Courtenay, Lucy Fleming[1], Susannah York[2] and a chinese girl, and a young man wearing a gold coat and a male mini-skirt. 'Do you go around in that all the time?' I said. 'No,' he said, 'I changed upstairs.' After the photographs were taken we sat in a rather nice room. I drank lemonade. And then I went home. The issue of *Queen* magazine with the photographs is out on 2 August. I can't quite see what the text will be like.

Wednesday 19 July

I went to the negro's room again today. He told me his mother died of cancer. 'Of the womb,' he said, 'and that's a terrible thing, you know.' He said, 'If it's the breast then they can cut them off. Only it doesn't always work. I know a woman who had her breast off and now she's dead. Oh, man, that cancer is a terrible thing. Most people don't live, you know that.' He said his father died when he was seventeen. He had several sisters and brothers in England and in America. 'Mostly their marriages are failures,' he said, 'they don't seem to get on. And they separate. I don't know what you feel about this. I feel pretty bad.' He said, 'I've a West Indian paper here. I just bought it. I'm looking for a job.' We took off our clothes and I let him fuck me. Then, after he'd listened to the one o'clock news on a portable wireless – 'the news is bad all over the world. My God! I don't know a single spot where the news is good' – I fucked him. I took a lot longer in fucking him. 'I come off too quick, man,' he said morosely as I got up off him. 'If I could pick up a gay doctor I'd ask him about that.' I went home and had bacon sandwiches and talked to Kenneth who was playing *Pal Joey*[3] on the record player. I had a bath later on. I meant to write a few letters. But time slipped away. In the evening we went to the Comedy Theatre to see a preview of a new play called *A Day in the Death of Joe Egg*.[4] We met Christine Grant (the girl from the National Theatre box office) and Achmed and his wife. We talked a bit. Mark Linford, smiling in the foyer, told me that *Loot* had had a very good house last night. The play was à comedy about a man and woman whose baby was a spastic – little more than a vegetable. It wasn't well written. Facetious. It should've been cruel and funny. It was simply flippant and sentimental. Characters kept talking to the audience. A lot of 'music-hall' overtones. The characters 'acted' a good deal in funny voices 'being' doctors and BBC announcers. 'I can't stand this,' Kenneth Halliwell said to me in an undertone, 'let's go now.' 'No,' I said, 'we must wait till the interval.' The play rambled on for about an hour and then we escaped, taking Christine with us. Achmed and his wife opted to stay. For no

1 Lucy Fleming (1947–). Actress.
2 Susannah York (1941–). Actress.
3 Adapted from his short stories by John O'Hara. Music by Richard Rodgers. Lyrics by Lorenz Hart, 1940.
4 By Peter Nichols (1927–), 1967.

very good reason as far as I could see except that they obviously considered walking out of theatres not done. Christine said she felt guilty. I said, 'Why should we stay and endure another hour? I'd be so fed up by the end.'

We walked round to the Criterion. The first act curtain was falling when we arrived in Sheila's dressing-room. We talked a lot. Michael Bates said his wife had been to see *Joe Egg* and hated it. He told me a joke about a priest who suggested at a Roman Catholic synod that the clergy should wear bathing trunks in their baths 'in order not to look down on the unemployed'. Sheila had her copy of *Sergeant Pepper's Lonely Hearts' Club Band*. Kenneth said he'd like to watch the second act of *Loot*. So K., Christine and I all went upstairs and sat in the circle. It was a very good audience. Mostly young people. Pretty full house. It went better than I've seen it for a long time. Seeming extra-brilliant after the first act of *Joe Egg*. Went home on the bus.

Thursday 20 July

Weather warm. Got up early. Played Sheila's copy of *Sergeant Pepper*. It's very good. Some numbers I like more than others. 'With a Little Help From My Friends', and 'When I'm Sixty-Four' and 'A Day in the Life'. Certainly the most brilliant of the Beatles records. They get better all the time. Did very little all day. Went down to the record shop in Sicilian Arcade and bought a copy of the LP. Kenneth bought an old Etonian tie. He thinks it's funny but, as I pointed out, he's come full-circle and the tie is most conventional. Unless you know it's an old Etonian it isn't funny. Still it looks a nice plain tie anyway. Went off at sixish to the Court. I was invited out to dinner by B. Gaskill. He took me to a restaurant – a Greek one – in Charlotte Street. We talked. Of nothing really. I found it difficult. I had to be so active. He seemed to have no real conversation. If I hadn't wracked my brains desperately for something to say, the evening would've wilted. I left him early. Took a tube to Holloway Road. Scouted around. Nothing worth fucking. As I was leaving a toilet, a young kid came in dressed in a motor-cyclist's outfit – boots, leather trousers, leather jacket and crash helmet – it was a warm evening and this seemed odd. I was just zipping up my fly as he came in. I waited a little. Tucked my vest into my pants – it had come loose. The motor-cyclist looked over his shoulder and stared. I walked away. He followed me outside. But seemed undecided. I walked away from the bridge to the bus stop. When I looked back, the cyclist was standing staring after me. A middle-aged man, who'd been in the lavatory and had come to the bus-stop, said to me, 'What do you make of him then?' 'He doesn't seem to have a bike, does he?' I said. 'He's not the law, is he?' the man said. 'Shouldn't think so,' I said. 'Where's his bike then?' the man repeated. 'He may not have one,' I said. The man looked very worried. 'I don't like that sort of thing,' he said. 'You don't know where you are with it, do you?' As we watched, the young man walked towards us. And then

I noticed that a little further away from us, down the road, was a motor-bike. On it sat another figure dressed in leather. It was clear that the young man was a pillion passenger on the bike. He walked on. Still staring at me. He got on the bike and his companion drove away. 'You can get some queer bastards around these toilets,' the middle-aged man said. 'He may've been prepared for a threesome,' I said. 'You mean he had somewhere to go?' 'Probably,' I said, 'but he should've said.'

I caught a bus and went home. When I told Kenneth, he said that the young man was probably a sado-masochist. 'He behaved in a very odd way,' I said. We talked for a while. I made a cup of tea. We talked of the *As You Like It* which the National are doing in October with men playing the girls' parts. Gaskill told me that the man playing Celia is thirty-five. 'Ridiculous waste of time,' Kenneth said, 'the usual compromise. Do it. But don't let it be a success. Let's have all the old men in the company with credentials – wives and children – playing parts which were written for boys. Ugh! I don't want to hear anymore about it.' We put in our ear-plugs (a noisy television) and went to sleep.

Friday 21 July

Went to see the cast. Oscar rang in the afternoon. *Loot* is coming off in August. Told the cast this. Oscar said he'd given *Up Against It* to Dick Lester who liked it but thought it should be directed by a younger Dick Lester. He's going to try Karel Reisz. Dick Lester is now off on some pretentious bandwaggon. Not seeing that comedy is a valid criticism of society, farce a valid comment on life. Kenneth has bought himself a safari outfit from a firm of tropical-kit tailors. He put the whole thing on to go down to the Criterion. He looked as though he was going to do a number called *Jungle Drums*. He was v. cross because I told him. A man who raped two nine-year-old girls has just been sentenced to life. V. sexy photograph of him in *The Evening Standard*. I said, to Sheila, 'I'd like a copy of that photograph. Do you think if I asked the *Standard* for one they'd think I was kinky?' 'I should think they might,' she said. I read out a line from the judge's summing up, 'This man was highly-sexed and perverted.' I folded up the paper. 'It sounds like me,' I said. 'You're not highly-sexed,' Kenneth said. 'What a thing to say to a friend,' Sheila said. I was angry and sat glumly looking out of the window all the way home. Watched an excerpt from *Relatively Speaking* by Alan Ayckbourn[1]. A nice light situation comedy. It's on at the Duke of York's theatre. Gives no offence. The reactionaries are cooing with delight over it. Not a bad play, though. Just not well-written enough. I thought I'd use the Mrs Warren cliché as one of the plots of *Prick Up Your Ears*.

1 By Alan Ayckbourn (1939–   ), 1967.

Saturday 22 July

Went to Peter Willes's for dinner. When we got there he stared at Kenneth in horror. 'That's an old Etonian tie!' he screeched. 'Yes,' Kenneth said. 'It's a joke.' Willes looked staggered and wrinkled up his face in an evil sort of way. 'Well, I'm afraid it's a joke against you then. People will imagine you're passing yourself off as an old Etonian. They'll laugh at you.' 'I'm sending up Eton,' Kenneth said. 'Oh, no!' Willes cackled with a sort of eldritch shriek. 'You're just pathetic! I mean it's disgraceful wearing that tie.' 'It's a joke!' Kenneth said, looking tight-lipped, a little embarrassed and angry. 'People will know.' 'Not the people I meet,' Kenneth said, 'they'll think it's funny.' 'You're making people angry,' Willes said. 'I don't care,' Kenneth said, laughing a little too readily, 'I want to make them angry.' 'But why?' Willes said, as we sat down. 'People dislike you enough already. Why make them more angry? I mean – it's permissible, although silly, as a foible of youth, but you – a middle-aged nonentity – it's sad and pathetic!' I could see that the conversation had become impossible and that unless something were done the evening would begin in ruins. 'Now stop this both of you!' I said, in a commanding voice, 'It's ridiculous to carry on in this way over a wretched tie!' After an uneasy silence a sort of rapprochement was restored. I gave Willes my new play. 'You'll hate it,' Kenneth said. 'Why do you say that?' Willes said, quickly. Kenneth laughed. The conversation drifted on in a desultory way, meandering through insults and bubbling over with recrimination, until Kenneth exploded, 'All you people that are mad on Joe[1] really have no idea what he's like.' Willes paled. 'I'm not mad on Joe! Whatever do you mean?' Fortunately before Kenneth could answer this question (and rend our relationship with Peter Willes to shreds), the doorbell rang. Peter W. came back into the room with a plump, not unattractive, middle-aged man. 'This is Allan Davis[2]. He directed *Spring and Port Wine*.' Willes sullenly went and poured out iced sherry. 'I thought you were a blond,' Allan Davis said to me. 'Why?' I said. 'You look like a blond on the drawing in the Royal Court programme.' Rather a silly reason for thinking someone is blond – especially when there was a photograph showing clearly that I was dark. 'Peggy Ramsay says he dyes his hair.' Willes said. 'Oh, Peggy always has extraordinary ideas,' I said, crossly. 'When I was dark-haired, she thought I was blond. When I came back from Morocco with blond hairs where the sun had bleached them, she thought I'd been touching them up. I offered to show her my pubic hair to prove that I've always had dark hair. Only she looked odd at the suggestion.' 'I should think so too!' Willes said, pursing his lips. 'You really are ridiculous. Fancy exposing your cock to your agent. Really!'

1 Sir Terence Rattigan: 'I'd have liked to go on seeing Joe, but if I was going to have to see Halliwell, too, no, that was too much.'
2 Allan Davis (1913–   ). Director.

The doorbell rang and Lady Glasgow[1] came in. 'I've travelled all the way down from Scotland by bus,' she said. 'My maid has broken a piece of Sèvres china and I must have it mended.' 'Why did you travel by bus?' I asked. 'It's so much quicker by train.' 'But the *expense!*' Vanda, Lady Glasgow said. I thought that these rich people are off their chumps. Moaning about the difference between bus and rail fares and yet spending pounds on having bits of dinner plates fitted together after some clumsy domestic has fallen down the kitchen steps. Lady G. was quite gay. A lady novelist called Theodora something or other made her entrance later. 'She was a great drug addict in the twenties,' Willes whispered to me as she was in the lavatory. 'Couldn't get her off the things. I don't know what it was. She's retired now.'

We went out to dinner later. Theodora smiling a lot. Lady Glasgow and Peter Willes discussing the merits or demerits of Kenneth's joke against Eton. 'I always say that my son goes to Slough Grammar school,' Lady G. said. I'd taken two librium tablets. Lady G. gave two more to me. Producing them gaily from her handbag. 'I have to take tranquillisers when my husband is driving,' she said. 'I simply cannot stand the nervous strain of having him behind the wheel. And prayers are of no avail. It's medical science that calms me down.' She paused after eating raspberries. 'We were simply inundated with priests last week,' she said. 'Did you try Domestos?' I said. 'It kills all known germs.' Vanda, Lady Glasgow laughed and we all went back to Willes's flat. After a short discussion on the customs of the English gentry towards the end of the nineteenth century apropos of Willes producing *Lady Windermere's Fan*[2] for television, Kenneth and I trooped off. 'If only my old aunt were alive,' Vanda, Lady Glasgow said, with a shake of her head, 'she could really have told us whether or not the footmen would've worn gloves.' Kenneth H. said, outside on the pavement, 'Willes's production of *Lady Windermere's Fan* is likely to be so atrocious that nobody will notice the fact that the footmen have trousers. Let alone gloves. It will be switch-off time that night!' He was still smarting from the 'middle-aged nonentity' line. And quite right too. Kenneth has more talent, although it's hidden, than P. Willes can flash if he had the reflector from Mount Palomar to do it with.

Sunday 23 July

Yesterday morning Peggy rang me. Quite early. She'd read *What the Butler Saw* in a hotel room in York late on Thursday night. 'People must've thought I was mad,' she said. 'I simply had hysterics. It's the very best thing you've done so far. And technically in advance of *Loot*.' She had one or two reservations. The Lord

1 Hon. Ursula Vanda Maud (Dowager Countess of Glasgow) (1912–84).
2 By Oscar Wilde, 1892.

Chamberlain, she said, 'isn't going to allow you to show Churchill's prick on the stage.' 'I thought of altering it to President Kennedy's[1],' I said. 'Oh, but that's much, *much* worse!' Peggy said. 'He's a martyr. You'd never get away with that. And the other thing is the incest. I simply don't know whether all that fucking of parents and children will be allowed.' She said, 'The play is bound to be a scandal. And that would be a pity. It'd be a pity,' she said, 'if your considerable talent were to always be associated with subjects of scandal and concern.' She went on to suggest that the fourth play should perhaps be a little more conventional. I told Kenneth this, who laughed, drinking a cup of tea and reading a letter. 'Well, the title alone isn't going to reassure her,' he said. And, when I think of it, *Prick Up Your Ears* couldn't possibly be the title of a conventional play. Oscar, to whom Peggy had given the script, rang this morning. He's delighted. He's going to get the typed version to the Lord Chamberlain omitting only the stage direction about the contraceptive. He doesn't see much that the Lord Chamberlain could object to. Apart, of course, from the showing of the prick. 'If he insists on too many cuts we'll have to think of putting it on at the Royal Court.' I'm not keen on this. I think a short tour and straight into the West End. Oscar has invited Kenneth and I down to Brighton for a long weekend next week. We're going to discuss more then. Willes rang this afternoon. Full of the most fervent praise of *What the Butler Saw*. 'Oh,' he said, 'it's so exciting. It's like a Palais Royale farce. It's simply splendid. And it must be done exquisitely.' 'He only likes it because I said he wouldn't,' Kenneth said, bitterly. 'And because its set's middle-class and French windowy,' I said. 'It has such wit and style and the theatrical technique is stunning!' Willes crowed down the line. He had to ring off because guests were at his door. He's arranging some kind of old lags get-together or something.

Kenneth Williams rang. He's feeling low and depressed. I invited him round for a cup of tea. He accepted with a touching gratitude. I met him at the bus-stop in Upper Street. We walked down Essex Road to put a note in the door of a block of flats where Stan (the old-clothes man/lorry driver) lived. Coming back I told Kenneth of the leather job the other night and, while I remembered the incident, of a boy whose mother was Armenian, his father was Greek and he was born in Egypt. 'I met him in the Holloway Road last November,' I said, 'shortly before I began keeping my diary. It was very foggy and we had nowhere to go. We went along some back street and came into a cul-de-sac. He started to feel my prick. I got very excited. He wanted me to put it up his arse. I took him into a doorway. But it wasn't deep enough. We walked back a bit down the cul-de-sac

---

1 John F. Kennedy (1917–63). American politician and president. The 'missing part' might have been more apt for Kennedy. 'The sheer pace of Kennedy's sex life, its serial and simultaneous variety, awed his friends and competitors,' writes Gary Wills in *The Kennedys*.

and he said, 'Fuck me', in very urgent tones, 'I want you to fuck me.' And, although it was in the street, he dropped his trousers and bent over. I got my cock up him and, quicker than I've ever done before, fucked away like mad. He took it right up and kept moaning as I stuffed him. 'Have you seen him again since?' Kenneth said. 'No,' I said, 'I've never met him again. I'd've liked to. He was a good fuck.' Kenneth viewed the story with that strange mixture of excitement and disapproval that marks his character. We had a pleasant stroll round. Went back to the flat and had a cup of tea.[1]

Later on I walked him to King's Cross where he caught a bus home. On the way we talked about sex. 'You must do whatever you like,' I said, 'as long as you enjoy it and don't hurt anyone else, that's all that matters.' 'I'm basically guilty about being a homosexual you see,' he said. 'Then you shouldn't be,' I said. 'Get yourself fucked if you want to. Get yourself anything you like. Reject all the values of society.[2] And enjoy sex. When you're dead you'll regret not having fun with your genital organs.' He told me how he'd visited an East End pub. 'And all these young chaps were crowding round. One of them said to me, 'Kaw! Ken, it's legal now, you know. And he started to pull his trousers down. And the landlady said, "Ernie! Now then! We'll have none of that." "But he's a celebrity, we've got to put on a show," Ernie said. "Not that kind of a show," the landlady said. She was the disapproving type,' Kenneth said. 'And what happened?' I said. 'Oh, nothing. We went back about a week later and the pub was empty.' 'You should've seized your chance,' I said. 'I know,' Kenneth said, 'I just feel so guilty about it all.' 'Fucking Judeo-Christian civilisation!' I said, in a furious voice, startling a passing pedestrian. We parted and I hope I'd done him a bit of good. At least I'd told him not to feel guilty. It isn't as simple as that, but at least I've tried to help him.[3]

---

1 In *Just Williams*, Kenneth Williams recounts the conversation from his diary notes of the meeting: 'Then we fell to discussing relationships. "Sharing of any kind means an invasion of privacy," I said. Joe talked about his horror of involvement: "I need to be utterly free." I quoted Camus' line, "All freedom is a threat to someone," whereupon K.H. declared, "Love is involvement, you can't live without love." "There are many definitions of love," said Joe, "it depends on your point of view. You can love your work and be entirely committed to the pursuit of perfection." "Sexual promiscuity," he said, now provided him with material for his writing; "I need to be the fly on the wall". But Kenneth Halliwell disagreed: "It's all right letting off steam on holiday but a home life should have the stability of a loyal relationship." "You sound like a heterosexual," Joe countered, but Halliwell stuck to his guns and said that promiscuity led to wasted aims: "You can only live properly if it's for a person or for God."'

2 In *What the Butler Saw*, Orton makes the point in comic terms: 'Reject all para-normal phenomena. It's the only way to remain sane.'

3 Orton to Kenneth Williams, 1 August 1967: 'I'm glad I was able to be of assistance to you. Anytime you feel "blue" . . . don't hesitate to ring. I can't promise to be as therapeutic as Sheldon was, but I've a big heart and my penis isn't to be sniffed at either . . .'

Monday 24 July

I went to Rediffusion this morning to collect the script of *What the Butler Saw* from P. Willes. 'Come in, you clever little thing,' he said, appearing in the doorway of his office. 'Now,' he said, 'you simply *must* get things right. It would be too awful if anything went wrong. And, really, after that night at the Royal Court I honestly turn very odd at the thought of what you'll let some fool do. But, there it is, all on paper. A realistic set – I wonder if Patrick Cargill[1] and Dilys[2] Laye would be able to play Mr and Mrs Prentice?' 'I want Arthur Lowe,' I said. 'I saw Patrick Cargill, you know,' he said, shaking his gory locks. I didn't agree. I don't think he has a lot of idea on how my plays should be acted. His casting is always so naturalistic. I left with the script and went to Curzon Street. Left the script with Liz (Oscar's secretary) who said she was going to retype the page with the stage direction, 'Dr Prentice takes a contraceptive from the desk.' 'In order not to annoy the Lord Chamberlain too much.' Willes doesn't think we'll have trouble with the Lord Chamberlain. This makes me tremble. It probably means the play will be banned outright.

At five-thirty we met Christine outside the cinema in the Haymarket where the film *A Man For All Seasons* is playing. Christine knows the woman in the box office. We had three free seats. The film itself had won seven Oscars. It was a straight-forward second-rate historical film with affectations. Not as silly as Hollywood histories in the thirties and forties – at least not overtly as silly – not as brilliant as *Ivan the Terrible*. Pretentious. All the performances were 'actorish'. Not a breath of life – any life in any century – from beginning to end of the two-hour traffic. The dialogue (which had pretentions to the brilliant, epigrammatic debate) was banal and flat to the point of parody. The politics of the period were missing. A yawn. The advertisements before the film were more worthy of praise.

We went to Lyons Corner House in Coventry Street afterwards and had a meal. It came to £19 6s. for three. Very good value. Afterwards we went to the Criterion for the interval. Had a word with M. Bates and Sheila. Then we strolled down Lower Regent Street past the statues, looking strange and beautiful in the dusk, into St James's Park. We walked all the way to Whitehall Palace. Lit with spotlights. Just lit, though. A really expert lighting consultant is needed to bring out the wonders of architecture by night. The guards on duty had a uniform I'd never seen before. Black boots, white trousers, a black tunic and a helmet with a red plume. If I have the character of a guardsman in *Prick Up Your Ears* I shall have that uniform. I must find out what regiment it is. Walked to Waterloo across Hungerford Bridge. Waited for Christine's train to Datchet.

1 Patrick Cargill (1918–). Actor.
2 Dilys Laye (1934–). Actress.

Drank orange squash from plastic containers. Was approached by a methylated-spirits drinker for money. Said 'No'. There seemed to be quite a large number of derelicts in the station. Got home at eleven. Went to bed.

Tuesday 25 July

Grey day. Nothing much happened. Detroit is torn by riot and rapine. There is an empty church round the corner from Noel Road which was burned to the ground last night. Loot and the sack of empires is in the air. DETROIT BURNING! was one headline. Science fictionville. Willes rang to say that the ITA would allow *Sloane* to be performed on telly. 'I feel it's dated!' Willes said. I rang Clive at five o'clock. Talked for a bit. He's the young man I was introduced to by K. Williams. Spoke about Morocco. He was off-putting about having dinner. Came to the real point of the telephone call: 'How about me coming up to your place about five tomorrow for a cup of tea?' He went strange. 'I've got to go to the doctor's tomorrow. It's awkward, see.' 'I'll ring you sometime then,' I said, putting the phone down. 'Another one crossed off the list,' I said to Kenneth H. Kenneth shrugged. 'I don't know why you bothered ringing.' 'Well,' I said, 'I wouldn't've minded fucking him. He has a nice body. But if sex is out, he can get stuffed. I'm not interested in him for any other reason.'

Wednesday 26 July

Perfect weather. London, of course, isn't the ideal place to enjoy it. Letter from Peggy to say that *Loot* has been banned in South Africa. Went into the West End this afternoon. Saw a poster on a bus for *The News of the World* – THE GESTAPO'S BLUEPRINT FOR HELL – BY THOSE WHO LIVED THROUGH IT. A new stamp has been issued to commemorate Sir Francis Chichester's historic journey round the Horn. Kenneth and I went into Lillywhites in the Haymarket. We were just too late to miss a man who'd decided to commit suicide by jumping from the window of New Zealand House. They caught him unfortunately. Wandered round Lillywhites. I bought a blue vest in their sports department. Went to John Michael's in Regent Street. I bought a pair of blue jeans made of cotton. Kenneth bought a black shirt. I saw a pair of trousers made of white towelling but decided against buying them. The colour mainly. We went to take our negatives to Wallace Heaton for enlarging. I especially want the one of Hamid naked showing his bum. We walked to Baker Street. Arguing about a polaroid camera. Kenneth says it's a waste of money. I want one. Conspicuous wealth, I suppose. Oscar rang when we got home. I'm arranging to meet him tomorrow at Victoria. He's invited K. and I down to Brighton for the weekend. He said he'd spotted a mistake in *The Butler*. He said that in the first scene Geraldine explains that 'her mother' has been blown to bits by a statue. 'Shouldn't it be her step-mother?' Oscar asked. This evening I retyped two pages of the first act to make the thing more logical. Kenneth too says he spotted another mistake. When asked, in the first scene, Geraldine says she can't type. Yet in the last act she feels that her experiences have affected her typing speed. I've promised to alter it to shorthand speed.

Thursday 27 July

Peter Willes rang early this morning. 'I've just had a letter from Hermione Baddeley in America,' he said. 'She says that your agent wrote a most rude letter to one of the brightest directors in New York. He's "most highly thought of".' 'I'm not responsible for what my agent does,' I said. Willes brushed this aside and began to talk of the production of *Lady Windermere's Fan*. 'I've been speaking to Oscar Wilde's son. I asked if his father had ever explained how Mrs Erlynne got into Lord Darlington's rooms? I'm having him give her the key. You see, its so ridiculous – she simply breaks into a man's apartment in the middle of the night. It's a wonder she wasn't arrested as a burglar. And I've decided that at the ball they'll dance to "Ta-ra-a-boom-de-ay". I know that Lady Windermere would never tolerate the music hall. And I simply said to the music director, "Well, whilst Lady Windermere was trulling around, an impudent young man went up to the leader of the band and asked for "Ta-ra-a-boom-de-ay". When Lady Windermere got back there they all were – doing the gallop – she was simply furious, but there wasn't anything she could do.' 'I hope some television executive doesn't ask my sons in sixty years time what exactly I meant by my plays,' I said. 'The way you carry on it'd be something of a miracle if you produced a son,' P. Willes said. I talked for a bit and went down to Knightsbridge to have my hair cut. 'All these Indians and Chinese,' Mr Nicko, my hairdresser said, 'swarms of them. The whole street behind my flat is taken over by the Yellow Peril.' He seemed to be in a nervy state. 'These riots in America will happen over here,' he said, handing me over to the shampoo girl. When I'd had my hair washed, he hurried forward, razor in hand, and slashing at my hair, complained of the violence in foreign parts. I took Kenneth's case – the one broken open by the Fatima in Morocco – to a shop to be mended. Then I went to John Michael in Regent Street to collect my blue jeans which had been shortened. In the shop was a young woman and her father. The father, moustached, bespectacled, was trying on a suit. 'Oh, Daddy!' the girl said, 'you look perfectly frightful. Give him something else,' she said to the assistant. The assistant gave the man another coat. The girl said, 'The double-vent is most unflattering to him, isn't it?' The assistant measured the man's waist. 'Thirty-seven, you know, sir. And it'd be more comfortable with thirty-eight.' The man looked depressed, v. down in the mouth. 'You should try and take something off your waistline, Daddy,' the girl said. 'I'd like something different,' the man said, handing the suit back to the assistant. 'Give him a grey!' the girl said, giving an imperious toss of her head. 'I'd like a blue,' the man said. 'Don't give him a blue. He has any number of blue suits.' There was a short argument between the old man and the girl and she suddenly said, 'Very well! I wash my hands of you!' and began to read a magazine. The assistant looked perplexed. I went into a changing booth and changed my trousers. When I came out the old man was posturing in front of the mirror with a blue suit coat on. The girl, looking up from her magazine, said 'Excellent. You could walk out in that. You look most smart.'

I took the thirty-eight bus home. It had an advertisement for *The News of the World* on it which said: HOW SAFE IS YOUR COACH HOLIDAY? Peggy rang. She said she's 'fixing up' Enid Bagnold[1] – an authoress and playwright of the last generation. 'She's writing her autobiography,' Peggy said, 'and really she's been fucked by some fascinating people – H. G. Wells[2], Frank Harris[3] – she's living in Kipling's house[4]. 'Was she fucked by him as well?' I said. 'Almost certainly,' Peggy said, 'though all these dead people are so boring. And Enid won't tell the truth about them.' 'No,' I said, 'it's extraordinary how, as people grow older and they have less to lose by telling the truth, they grow more discreet, not less.' 'If only,' Peggy said, 'she'd tell us that H.G. Wells couldn't get it in. Or wore women's knickers or had a fear of pubic hair. That would add to our knowledge of the man and his works. As it is she'll certainly only dither around the subject.' 'A lot of verbal asterisks,' I said. 'Exactly,' Peggy said.

Kenneth and I left shortly after this conversation for Victoria Station. We'd arranged to meet Oscar Lewenstein at ten minutes to seven. The bus was full. A rather fat girl (blind to everyone but her own breasts) wearing a mini-skirt got on and had to stand next to me. She kept rubbing up against my leg. I got a hard on. It showed through the jeans I was wearing. I asked Kenneth as we got off the bus if he'd noticed the girl. 'Yes,' he said, 'the man next to me was getting v. excited.' 'You mean me?' I gasped. 'No,' Kenneth said, 'the other side.' 'I was getting excited too,' I said, blushing and feeling foolish. 'She was rubbing her thighs up and down in a v. bold way. What d'you suppose would've happened if I'd followed her off the bus?' 'She'd've charged you three quid, I expect.' Kenneth said, in a cold manner. 'I've never seen a more obvious pro on a number 19 bus before.'

We went to the station buffet and had a cup of tea. Met Oscar later. On the way down to Brighton (we had bacon and eggs) Oscar outlined his plans for *What the Butler Saw*. 'Do you want it produced at the Court?' he said. 'I don't think it's

1 Enid Bagnold (1889–1981). Novelist and playwright. Author of *National Velvet* and *The Chalk Garden*.
2 H.G. Wells (1866–1946). Influential English novelist. Popularised political and scientific ideas with such works as *A Short History of the World, The Time Machine, The War of the Worlds*.
3 Frank Harris (1856–1936). Flamboyant editor and author of *My Life and Loves*.
4 Rudyard Kipling (1865–1936). Novelist. Won Nobel Prize for Literature in 1907.

a Court play,' I said. 'Frankly, neither do I,' Oscar said. 'And what I propose is this – we've sent it to the Lord Chamberlain;¹ now if it comes back with minor requirements – I mean, for instance, he almost certainly won't allow the references to Mr Churchill, will he?' 'It's only a statue,' I said. 'He won't be too pleased,' Oscar said, 'and what about the laws of libel?' 'What am I saying about Churchill, though?' I said. 'You're saying he had a big prick,' Oscar said. 'That isn't libellous, surely?' I said. 'I wouldn't sue anybody for saying I had a big prick. No man would. In fact I might pay them to do that.' Oscar snuffled for a minute and said, 'Well, friend, supposing Churchill has to go – would it make the play impossible to perform?' 'You could alter it to somebody else,' Kenneth said (he was eating Welsh rarebit). 'A local worthy,' I said. 'Like Councillor Albert Parker in *When We Are Married*².' 'And what about the incest?' Oscar said. 'I couldn't change that,' I said, 'and even changing Churchill would be a blow.' 'If the Lord Chamberlain is too ruthless we'll have to go on at the Court in a club theatre production,' Oscar said. 'On the other hand, if we get away with it, I have a mad idea of doing it with somebody like Binkie and trying to get the Haymarket.' 'That'd be wonderul,' I said, 'it'd be a sort of joke even putting *What The Butler Saw* on at the Haymarket – Theatre of Perfection.'³ We discussed the set. 'It should be beautiful. Nothing extraordinary. A lovely set. When the curtain goes up one should feel that we're right back in the old theatre of reassurance – roses, French windows, middle-class characters.' Oscar thought of Ralph Richardson⁴

1 In the end, it was not the Lord Chamberlain who refused to allow Sir Winston's 'missing part' to be flourished on stage, but Sir Ralph Richardson.

2 By J.P. Priestley (1894–1983), 1938.

3 When *What the Butler Saw* opened in 1969, Binkie Beaumont was co-producer and the play was staged at the Queen's Theatre. As early as 14 February 1967, Beaumont had written Orton: 'The object of my note is to say that if you ever felt in the mood, or had an idea of a play which might embrace Ralph Richardson's talents, I am sure it could be a thrilling experience.' Thrilling was not the word. Stanley Baxter, who played Prentice, recalls: 'After the first ten minutes of the second act, the barracking started, which meant that very few lines were heard completely. "Take it off", "Rubbish", "Filth", "Shame". First time it ever had happened to me. I was getting a guilty sense of exhilaration in fighting them. They really wanted to jump on the stage and kill us all. There was the exhilaration of a fight. The auditorium was divided. The "gods" hating us and the rest of the auditorium on our side. The "gods" making enough noise to destroy'.

Oscar Lewenstein to Ronald Bryden, 11 March 1969: 'In your review of *What the Butler Saw*, you, in common with most critics, mentioned the disturbances from the gallery (in fact the upper circle at the Queen's Theatre) and I think gave the impression that some sort of spontaneous revulsion at the play swept the gallery. In this you and your colleagues are mistaken. The whole affair was organised and carried through by about six people who were heard to plan it in the pub during the interval. "We will do Joe Orton" were the words they are reported to have said. In fact, the same small group wrecked the first night of *Spitting Image* a few months ago . . .'

4 Sir Ralph Richardson (1902–1983). Pre-eminent English actor. Richardson did play Dr Rance in the disastrous premier production of *What the Butler Saw*. Coral Browne, who played Mrs Prentice, recalls: 'Originally Ralph turned it down. He changed his mind. We played in Brighton a week before we came to town. I've never seen anything like it. He was attacked. People were writing him

as Dr Rance. I'm not too sure. Although I admire Richardson, I'd say he was a good ten years too old for the part. And he isn't primarily noted for his comic acting. 'I'd like Alastair Sim,' I said. Oscar wasn't too keen. Both Kenneth and I thought Oscar misguided in suggesting Richardson. But I didn't feel inclined to argue until later.

At Brighton Station (where a light rain was falling) we were met by Oscar's wife, Eileen[2]. She drove us to the house which is in Shoreham. A large Edwardian pile not a hundred yards from the gas-works – 'We get smells sometimes' – glass, white walls and a terrace overlooking and, at times, seeming almost to be part of, a row of breakwaters. A sullen, grey sea heaved audibly outside the sitting-room windows. We met Oscar's mother, a small, withered Jewess, and his children, Mark (14)[3] and Peter (11)[4]. Both were middle-class children. Brought up in a liberal atmosphere. Oscar, during the evening, talked of 'homosexuality', 'abortion' and 'disarmament' in front of the two boys. Neither child was sexually attractive. Mark wore spectacles. Even when he removed them he wasn't erotic. He was thin, studious, red-haired. I was perfectly safe from his charms for he had none. He was interested in 'all kinds of sport' but 'mainly cricket'. He watched this continually during the hours ahead. Peter was younger. He was depressingly unsexual. Although, as it later turned out, this was something of a relief. For, when the boredom set in, rape would've been a pleasant alternative. We talked until nearly midnight. Both Kenneth and I did our party pieces and then staggered into the bedroom to flop exhausted upon the pillows. 'What about a game?' I heard Mark saying, presumably meaning billiards for there was a table in the glass conservatory-like annexe to the bedrooms. 'Not tonight, darling,' Eileen said, 'we have guests.' This was close on midnight. 'Imagine playing any game – let alone billiards – at nearly twelve o'clock,' Kenneth said. The family trooped downstairs. The children to their rooms and Oscar and his wife to their lounge. Kenneth and I sat talking for five minutes or so and went to bed.

July 28 Friday

Got up early. Before eight. Nobody stirring. Kenneth and I shaved and went down to the kitchen. A fat Italian woman was fiddling about at the stove. 'Justa minute!' she said, vaguely putting cups onto a tray, 'I'm busy. I'm getting the toast.' She left the kitchen with a tray. Kenneth and I sat miserably on a couchette at the end of the kitchen staring through vast glass windows – the

---

letters. Ralph got terribly depressed, terribly down thinking he'd made a mistake. Taking a part in a "dirty" play. He replied to every one of those letters. Attack. Attack. Attack. The front of house manager was attacked. Well, he just left town. I think by this time Ralph had given up the ghost.'
2 Eileen Lewenstein (1925–   ). Potter and co-editor of *Ceramic Review*.
3 Mark Lewenstein (1953–   ). Computer programmer.
4 Peter Lewenstein (1956–   ). Journalist.

whole house was like a place for forcing cucumbers – and listened to the sea moaning to itself. With a swoosh the rain pattered across the panes of glass. The Italian woman returned. 'Whatta you want?' she said. 'Could we have poached egg on toast?' I said, clearing my throat. 'And for me,' Kenneth said. 'For you?' the woman said, smashing open an egg and putting it into the poacher, 'Whatta you want? An egg?' 'Please,' Kenneth said. We both ate poached eggs and toast and honey. It was a pleasant kitchen. A little too modern: ceramic tiles, unpolished wood, large working surfaces. The chairs were cheap, but expensive-looking. Comfortable until they fell to pieces. The rain poured down onto a grey, uninviting sea. We went upstairs. I took off my clothes. Lay on the bed suddenly overcome by lethargy. I forced myself to do my exercises. Depressing atmosphere. I wished it was Saturday. Not Friday. We couldn't escape until Monday. When I'd finished the exercises Kenneth opened the door and we went into the sitting-room. Only one chair was really comfortable. A large red leather egg-like thing. One of the children was sitting on it reading a newspaper. Oscar and his wife were lying on canvas deckchair-loungettes in the glass-covered annexe. The older boy, Mark, was reading *The Sun*. Oscar was scanning *The Times*. A copy of the local Brighton paper was on the table. Eileen was reading *The Morning Star*. Kenneth looked up after a while – he'd picked up a newspaper – and read out a line: 'You don't need drugs to love people. Love is far older than drugs. It goes right back to Jesus. I'm a believer.' This was said by pop star Lulu[1] in a discussion on drug-taking. Dame Alice Baker[2], the Minister of Health, had confessed to being horrified by an article in a magazine in which the Beatles had said they took LSD and marijuana. A long and pointless conversation for a few minutes. Communism, the position of Israel, drugs and drug-takers and the concentration camps were briefly touched upon. Old Mrs Lewenstein groped her way into the room and sat on a couch leafing through a paper. Kenneth picked up a copy of W.H. Auden's poems and started to read it. I went and had a shit. In the lavatory I thought how bleak the house was. When I flushed the toilet I knocked the toilet roll onto the floor and the paper unfolded. I had to spend ten minutes rolling it up again. When I got back to the sitting room I found that coffee had been served. The coffee cups (v. small) were full of hardly-warm coffee, and some really quite nice biscuits were handed round. Appalled by the prospect of sitting with my thumbs up my arse until lunchtime, I dragged Kenneth out for a walk. 'We both look dreadful in those mirrors,' Kenneth said resentfully as we tramped over the shingle in the direction of a power station. 'It's the white walls,' I said, 'all our Moroccan sunburn vanishes in a flash of light.'

It was an uncomfortable walk. The shingle was hard on the feet. It began to

1 Lulu (Marie Laurie Frieda) (1948–   ). Singer.
2 Dame Alice Bacon. Labour MP. Minister of State; Home Office (1964–67). Life Baronness, 1970.

spit with rain. Kenneth grumbled. He said we'd get wet. 'And we haven't a change of clothes,' he said. 'Why did you come out?' I said, 'I couldn't face sitting in there all day!' It was a thoroughly unpleasant walk. We had to clamber over inumberable breakwaters which were thick with slime and grime. As we approached the power station our nostrils were assailed by a terrible stench. The sea frothed and bubbled with the rain and an overpowering smell of chemicals, rotting seaweed and the dung of countless birds met us. 'This is a terrible way to spend our leisure,' Kenneth said. We turned back, sweating in the muggy heat. I saw a path leading between two wire fences. We took it and found ourselves on a road. Lorries thundered past. 'We'd do ourselves more good walking through Piccadilly Circus,' Kenneth commented sourly.

When we got back Oscar said, 'Eileen and I are leaving you for an hour or so this afternoon. We're visiting Cecil Tennant's widow.' I was rather relieved. It meant that at last Kenneth and I could have a quiet afternoon without feeling that we were expected to talk. Lunch was spaghetti. Not v. good. OK. 'I thought these weekends were famous for their food jaunts,' I said to Kenneth later. 'Perhaps we'll have something nice for dinner.' I went to bed. Slept for an hour or so. Got up and found Kenneth reading Auden. The old lady was tatting or fiddling with herself or something. The two boys were downstairs watching cricket. 'It's stopped raining,' I said, 'let's get out of here!' This time we walked in the direction of Brighton – along the front. We walked solidly for over an hour. Although the sun had come out it was not a warm afternoon. In spite of this, large numbers of holiday-makers were bathing and sitting on the cold, lank sands. Here and there were numbers of nearly-naked young boys. This made me unhappy. After passing a fifteen-year-old youth lying face-downward, wearing red bathing-drawers, I said, in a rage, 'England is intolerable. I'd be able to fuck that in an Arab country. I could take him home and stick my cock up him!' 'This is verbal exhibitionism!' Kenneth said, glancing at a number of evil-faced old women in a shelter. 'Look at them – crouching like Norns or the spirit of fucking British civilisation,' I said. 'I hate this tight-arsed civilisation.' We walked, both cross and not enjoying it, till we passed the Palace Pier. 'We'd better go back,' Kenneth said, wearily. 'It'll be time for dinner.' On the way back we tried to avoid looking at boys and talked about Tangier. 'We must get back there as soon as poss. Let's take a flat, unfurnished,' Kenneth said. 'We could be there now. Instead of this wilderness.'

'Did you have a nice walk?' old Mrs L. said, looking up from watching something nauseating on television. 'Yes,' Kenneth said. Somehow or other old Mrs L. got onto the subject of the concentration camps (probably because K. and I were feverish with thoughts of Arab boys). 'I can never stand in a lift, you know, without thinking of the gas chambers.' I wondered idly what would happen if I interfered with one of Oscar's children. 'And people sometimes ask,' old Mrs L.

wheezed, 'why the Jews went to their deaths without complaining.' It began to rain. 'And people say it's the Zionists,' Mrs L. said, 'only I can't be too sure.' Mark and Peter came bounding in: dull eyes and jaundice, spectacles and sharp voices. They said England or Pakistan had won something or other. 'Why are the Egyptians against Israel?' Mrs L. asked, 'I mean – surely its wrong?' I thought about the little boy on the beach and felt sick. 'They've worked so hard cultivating the desert. It was barren, you know. Just a patch of scrub. And now, they tell me, it's so wonderful.' 'All green fields,' Kenneth said, picking up Auden's poetry. 'All green and fertile,' old Mrs Lewenstein said. And not one of them bends over, I thought – while just across the border there's poverty and bum-fucking. 'I shall go and put on my blue vest,' I said, leaving the room.

Oscar said, half a decade later, his hair blown about like a bird's ruff of feathers, 'Mrs Tennant was more than pleased to see us. She was waiting for her husband to return. And when he didn't she went to meet him. At the top of the hill she found a wrecked car and her children bleeding. Cecil was dead.' 'Was he drunk?' old Mrs Lewenstein queried. 'No,' Oscar said, 'and nothing was wrong with the car. It's a complete mystery.' 'Like the Marie Celeste,' Kenneth said. A silence fell, broken only by the rustling of the rain on the glass roof and walls of the annexe in which we were sitting.

We had lamb (tough) and cheese and coffee. The rest of the evening passed. Kenneth and I stumbled into bed. We were both numb. 'What gets me,' Kenneth said, 'is that you can't get a cup of tea!' He sat on my bed. 'And Oscar is a millionaire, isn't he?' 'He's rich,' I said. 'I really resent not being able to have a cup of tea at bedtime,' Kenneth said.

Saturday 29 July

On Saturday I did my exercises and went for a long walk. I got wet. The spray, blown by the wind, made me damp. I couldn't persuade Kenneth to come with me. I tramped to the West Pier. Brighton has a number of monuments – Queen Victoria, Peace and a man blowing a bugle. People were crowding round the pier and the monuments. I heard a woman say, 'I said, "Do you want a cup of tea, Daddy?" And he said, 'No, Joyce, but what I would like is a nice ice-cream.' I walked back to Oscar's house from the West Pier in half an hour. 'Isn't it disappointing weather?' an elderly woman shrieked from a shelter as I passed. She was calling to a man in a trilby hat. He ignored her completely. I saw a young boy, blond and v. healthy-looking, filling a bucket with water on the promenade. As he turned the tap off he looked up. Our eyes met. A great spasm of rage overtook me. I find lust an emotion indistinguishable from anger. Or, at least, anger predominates when I see something I can't have. I feel I may run mad one day and commit rape. Arriving back at the glass booth I found Kenneth sitting reading. 'Why not come for a walk?' I said. 'I can't,' he said, morosely. 'It's raining.' 'No, it isn't,' I said, 'it's just spray.' 'We went for a little walk,' Oscar said, 'just down the prom.' After lunch of chicken (tough), 'Our Italian lady isn't in today,' Eileen said. Probably just as well, I thought, ungratefully, or we'd be chewing on spaghetti again. In the afternoon a Mr and Mrs Cotton (friends of Oscar's) arrived. He was jolly and hearty. She was an ex-Scandinavian woman. Large and blondish. I could imagine her stripping off and being handy with birch twigs. They were the parents of a talented young actor called Oliver Cotton[1]. 'Our children don't like Brighton,' Mrs Cotton said. We talked for a while, more or less intelligently. I don't think anyone said anything that didn't make sense. I went for a swim in the sea. It wasn't as cold as it looked. I swam for about half an hour. Came back. Dried myself. Mr and Mrs Cotton were just leaving. 'We were supposed to see a play by a friend of ours,' Mrs C. said, 'only I simply can't face it.' We talked about the Arab/Israel conflict. And concentration camps. Kenneth brought that up. He's rather tiresome about them. And we touched briefly on world hunger. 'Nobody is starving in China today,' Oscar said. Only the place is like a madhouse, I thought. 'One can't approve,' Oscar said, 'but nobody goes hungry.' Just mad, I thought.

Peggy arrived about eight. It was raining. 'Darling!' she said, 'I'm going to take you to a Chinese restaurant.' How I loathe Chinky food, I thought – and said – 'Oh, that'll be nice. I've always liked Chinese cooking.' We went to Peggy's house. She drove Kenneth and I and one of Oscar's children to her 'little place'. It was a nice old house in a back street. Built mid-nineteenth century. Peggy had filled it with bric-a-brac. All of it interesting but really there was too much. 'This is my ibis,' she said, producing something from a cupboard. 'Isn't it rather sweet? It's from a tomb. It's over three thousand years old. Noël Willman[2] said it's simply bound to be an ibis if it's an Egyptian bird.' 'It's not an ibis,' I said, tiresomely, 'an ibis is a wading bird.' Peggy passed the bird (clearly a falcon or horus – if it was genuine which I doubted)[3] around and everybody examined it. 'They used to have them on tombs. To take away the soul to heaven or something. Isn't it quaint? Only Joe says it isn't an ibis.' She showed us a pair of Chinese dragon-like creatures made of china and painted to look like metal. 'One's a boy and one's a girl,' she said, 'you can see.' She turned the creatures over and showed us. Then she passed me a weird kind of object like a telescope. On looking through it one saw the whole room reduced and duplicated about a dozen times. 'Like being a bee,' Peggy said, 'or an ant. Don't you think it's fascinating?' She took me downstairs and showed me the garden. There was a

---

1 Oliver Cotton (1944–   ). Actor.
2 Noël Willman (1918–   ). Actor and director.
3 Peggy Ramsay: 'Joe sneered at the horus. It was a genuine wood-carved Egyptian bird placed on graves and intended to take souls to heaven. It's a form of Egyptian god. One is either superstitious or one isn't. I didn't think he should have laughed at it. Joe died within two weeks of that.'

large number of shrubs, dripping in the rain, and a lilac tree. I liked the garden. Cluttered gardens are fun. Cluttered houses I'm not fond of. 'Look at this,' Peggy said, rummaging in a drawer and bringing out a piece of pottery, 'it's oriental. Of unknown origin.' We had orange juice to drink. Old Mrs Lewenstein hobbled downstairs to pee. Eileen sat smiling in a mystic sort of way. 'She's kept Oscar because she doesn't try to assert herself,' Peggy whispered as we went down the stairs. Halfway down she turned and said, 'No! I meant to show you upstairs, didn't I?' So we went upstairs and she opened up the bedrooms which were rather nice. Though full of wall-plates (given to her by Robert Bolt). 'And this picture,' she said, pointing to a startling portrait on the wall, 'is a great favourite with a friend of mine who likes little boys.' 'It isn't a little boy,' I said. 'No,' Peggy said, 'it's rather original, though, don't you think so?' We went in Peggy's car to a Chinese restaurant. It was pouring with rain. Peggy said, 'You get out and I'll find somewhere to park the car.' Kenneth and Peter and I got out and went into the restaurant. It was half-dark. 'Miss Ramsay's party are upstairs,' said the sinister oriental manager of the restaurant – the second-best one in Brighton. Upstairs were Oscar, old Mrs Lewenstein and Mark. 'We're waiting for Eileen,' Oscar said, 'she's gone to park the car.' 'So has Peggy,' Kenneth said.

We waited for about twenty minutes. Eileen returned. Ten minutes after this Peggy came in. 'Did you find somewhere to park?' I said, 'Yes,' she said, 'I went home and parked outside my house. I think it's much simpler, don't you?' Peggy ordered a ridiculous meal. She kept insisting that there wasn't enough. 'Bring another bowl of rice,' she said to the moon-faced waiter. 'No! Two bowls of rice.' She then turned and scanned the menu and ordered a waiter with long moustachios to bring us all savoury pancakes. They tasted like shoe-leather dipped in something a hyena might be expected to pass after eating a purgative root. 'Ugh!' I heard Kenneth groan as he tried eating one. 'There's not enough of these!' Peggy said, tearing at a waiter's sleeve. 'I've had quite enough to eat,' everybody chorused at once. 'These pancakes are horrible,' Peter piped. This was the signal for us all to admit that well, perhaps, they weren't as tasty as might have been hoped. We had lychees and ice-cream and ginger. After this we had green tea. 'Isn't it delicious?' Peggy beamed as we imbibed the scented filth.

Sleep that night was untroubled. And I woke up at eight the next morning to find Kenneth leafing through a copy of *The Sun* for yesterday. 'Another day,' he said, 'and we'll be free!'

Sunday 30 July

Oscar has been sent two new plays by John Osborne. 'He's written a trilogy this time,' Oscar said. 'He wants them put on all at once.' 'What are they like?' I said. 'There's a portrait of Vanessa Redgrave in the first play which I think is probably libellous.' He put the play down and stretched out in his deckchair-loungette under the glass roof. 'Vanessa discovered, when she was twenty years old, that her father was a homosexual.' 'He must've been bi-sexual,' I said, 'or she wouldn't be alive today.' 'He hasn't had any heterosexual relations since the birth of his last child.' 'No,' I said, 'but he has several children. He must've at least shown willing. He can't be called a homosexual.' 'Well,' Oscar said, rather tetchily, I thought, 'Vanessa didn't find out about him until she was twenty. And there's a rather cruel reference to this in John's play.' 'What's the other play about?' Kenneth said. 'It's about a lot of people in a hotel in Amsterdam. And the presence of Tony Richardson is felt throughout the play.' 'Does Tony Richardson appear in the play?' I said. 'No,' Oscar said. 'And does the play make sense if you don't know that these characters are Vanessa Redgrave and Tony Richardson?' There was a long pause. 'I'm not sure,' Oscar said. He turned to Eileen who was sitting listening intently to what was being said. 'What do you think of them, my love?' 'I thought they were frankly boring,' Eileen said. We were interrupted by the entrance of Georgie. Georgie is the son of the Italian woman who cooks and cleans the house. He is three years old. The woman's father turned her out of her house in Naples when the child was expected. Somehow she got to England. She's now married to an Englishman who won't work. He lives off her. The child is v. attractive. V. sexy. Even at the age of three. He suddenly came and flung himself into my arms. I wasn't sure whether it was a blessing or not that he wasn't ten years older. 'Zhivana wants to go back to Naples,' Eileen said. 'Yes,' I said, 'Naples is certainly the place for Georgie.' I disentangled myself from him. He started to fight me. I became sexually excited. 'Was it an Italian made her pregnant?' I said. 'Yes,' old Mrs Lewenstein said, 'and she had to leave Italy. It was a disgraceful thing to happen.' 'I don't know whether it's the heredity or what,' Kenneth said later, 'but Georgie is alive, sexual and human. Those Lewenstein children should arouse one more, shouldn't they? I mean – Mark and Peter are both a lot older than Georgie.' 'It's the fucking middle classes,' I said, falling back, when in doubt, upon class hatred, 'I've never got a hard on over a middle-class kid yet.' I went out for a walk. To Brighton and back. We had lunch at one o'clock. Melon and cold meat and cheese. Oscar talked about *What the Butler Saw*. His ideas seem OK. I'm not too happy about Richardson (Ralph) but we can come to that later. There was a great discussion about Israel. Oscar says he doesn't like Israel. This surprised me. 'I thought Israel was left-wing?' I said. Oscar says it isn't. I can't understand politics. I went to bed for an hour or so. When I woke up Kenneth and Oscar were watching an old film on the television. It was *Love Me Tonight* with Jeannette MacDonald[1] and Maurice Chevalier[2].

1 Jeanette MacDonald (1902–65). American concert singer and leading lady, fondly remembered for a series of operettas with Nelson Eddy.
2 Maurice Chevalier (1888–1972). French singer and entertainer.

Music by Rodgers[1] and Hart[2]. Impoverished tailor (Maurice) went to the chatêau of the Duc de Something to collect his money. Here he was mistaken for a baron and introduced to the duke's lovely sex-hungry niece Jeannette. She imagines him to be a scion of a noble house. He falls hopelessly in love with the proud aristocrat. His love is returned. But disaster ensues when the beautiful Jeannette discovers him to be a humble tailor. Love, as always, triumphs in the end. Jeannette on a thoroughbred horse pursues the train taking her plebian lover away from her forever. They are united when she stands in the middle of the tracks and dares the train to run her down. '*Up Against It* should be directed like that,' I said, as, with a soaring of violins, the film came to an end. Oscar then told me that Dick Lester had more or less turned down the film. And, that morning, so had Karel Reisz. 'Karel feels it's too mad for him,' Oscar said. He's now sent the script to United Artists to see what ludicrous objections they have to it.

In the evening, braving the rain in a mac borrowed from Oscar, we all went into Brighton. Our intention was to see the new James Bond film – *You Only Live Twice*. We couldn't get in. The others, including Kenneth, decided to see *In Like Flint*. I couldn't face the idea. I said I'd go for a walk and then go home. Eileen gave me the keys of the house. I was surprised that they only seemed to possess one set. I left them going into the box office and trudged through the drizzle about the town. After walking for a long while I found a gent's lavatory on a patch of grass near a church. I went in. It was v. dark. There was a man in there. Tall, grand and smiling. In the gloom he looked aristocratic. When the lights were turned on (after about five minutes) I could see that he was stupid, smiling and bank-clerkish. He showed his cock. I let him feel mine. 'Oo!' he gasped, not noticing the sinister sore that he had developed on the end over the last week or so. 'Oo!' I asked if he had anywhere to go back to. 'No,' he said, 'I don't have the choice of my neighbours, you see. They're down on me and I couldn't take the risk.' He nodded to a dwarf skulking in the corner of the lavatory. 'He'll suck you off, though. I've seen him do it.' He made a motion to the dwarfish creature, rather as someone would call a taxi. The dwarf sucked me off while the other man smiled benevolently and then, I suppose, went back to his neighbours refreshed.

I walked about Brighton. I had a cup of tea at the station. I thought a lot about *Prick Up Your Ears*. And things in general. Then I walked on and found myself, inexplicably, in Old Steine. I hit the Royal Pavilion at one point, got back to the front, found I was walking in the wrong direction, trudged three quarters of the way back to Shoreham and then managed to catch a bus. When I got in, Oscar

---

1 Richard Rodgers (1902–79). American composer who, with Lorenz Hart and Oscar Hammerstein II, created some of the greatest American musicals.
2 Lorenz Hart (1895–1943). Lyricist.

and his family were sitting about talking and reading. 'It wasn't a bad film,' Kenneth said. When we were in the bedroom, he said, 'We were waiting outside the house like lemons.' He seemed v. cross, 'Peter had to climb into the house.' 'Weren't there any keys?' I said. 'No,' Kenneth said. He began to undress. 'And when we got in, there was absolutely no suggestion of a cup of tea. I've never been in such an extraordinary house.'

Monday 31 July

After breakfast and exercises and a swim, Kenneth and I were driven to the station. As the train moved away from Brighton, I experienced a feeling of relief. A waiter came round with a menu which he flung on our table. He returned with a card which said, THIS TABLE IS FOR THE CONVENIENCE OF PATRONS WISHING TO TAKE REFRESHMENTS. Kenneth and I scanned the menu and decided to have coffee and bacon and eggs. We waited and waited. No attendant came round. Not even with coffee. At last, halfway through the journey, I got up and went into the buffet car and bought two coffees and brought them back to our seat. We drank. When we got out of the train at Victoria Kenneth said, 'What was the point of the elaborate menu and the card if no meal was served?' Neither of us understood this BR ritual. We caught a 19 bus home. We didn't do much for the rest of the day. Remembering that I'd invited Achmed Ossman down to Leicester, I rang his number to confirm the date. A woman answered and when I asked for Mr Ossman she said, 'They've gone away.' When I asked if they'd left a telephone number she said, 'No! I've no forwarding address and no telephone number!' She sounded upset. We went to bed early. Kenneth was looking wan.

Tuesday 1 August

Said goodbye to Kenneth this morning. He seemed odd. On the spur of the moment I asked if he wanted to come home to Leicester[1] with me. He looked surprised and said, 'No.'[2]

---

1 Orton was returning to Leicester to see a production of *Entertaining Mr Sloane* at the Phoenix Theatre, which had asked him originally to direct it. Orton to Peggy Ramsay, 26 May 1967: 'I certainly will not discuss *Sloane* or anything else for their club members . . . I will though be in Leicester to see my family about that time and so I don't mind agreeing to seeing a performance.' He did attend a performance. According to the Nottingham *Guardian-Journal*, 2 August 1967, Orton 'was introduced to the cast of the Phoenix. Later he said: "This is a great thrill for me. I often come to Leicester from London where I live, to see my father, and I have close associations with the city."'

2 Sheila Ballantine: 'Kenneth came to see me about a week before he killed Joe. They'd been to Oscar's and they were rather miserable. Then Joe went to Leicester and while he was gone, Ken came down to the theatre. I got to the theatre and he'd been there an hour, sitting on the steps. He brought me a book, *The Thirties*, by Malcolm Muggeridge. "I brought that book you wanted", he

said. I thought to myself I'd never discussed wanting it. But I thought he wanted to talk. So we went into my dressing-room. He sat there while I made up. He started telling me how ill he was, how he was going to have a nervous breakdown. And how awful he felt. He was a bit strange. He'd rung the Samaritans and gone there. He said that was no good, they just make cups of tea. He got up and walked out. I asked if he'd been to the doctor's. He said, "Yes, and I've got these purple hearts . . ." Kenneth Cranham and I took Halliwell for a drink.'

Kenneth Cranham: 'We'd never seen Kenneth on his own, and upset. He was upset about Willes's statement. "It was me that thought of the title of *Loot*. It was me that got Joe to write." All he talked about was Joe and Joe's play *What the Butler Saw*. He had the manuscript with him.'

Sheila Ballantine: 'He told us about the new play *What the Butler Saw*, as if it was a bit of a secret he was letting us in on. It was a bit sad because he was rather suggesting how important he was in the decisions that were made. He was making a lot of that. I knew that he was disturbed. I said, "Do come and stay with me." "No," he said, "Joe's coming back tomorrow." They came in on the Friday after Joe was back. They came to the dressing-room, and by that time Kenneth was very much stranger. He had that funny shut-off thing that people do. Joe was being hilarious, describing Kath and how she was overdoing her sexual advances to the boy (in the Leicester production of *Sloane*). I was being the boy and he was being Kath. And he was groping me in front of Kenneth. I thought, he obviously doesn't know how ill Kenneth is, or he wouldn't be mucking about in front of him. Right in the middle of this, Kenneth started talking about himself. ". . . And I went to the Samaritans, and I. . . ." I said, "Yes, I know." Joe said, "Oh, you told her that, did you?" And then he went on with his description. And I thought, my God, he can't see. He hasn't noticed.'

Orton and Halliwell died in the early hours of 9 August 1967. The right side of Orton's head had been staved in with a hammer which lay on Orton's counterpane. His cranium carried the mark of nine hammer blows which, to the coronor, suggested a frenzy. Brain tissue and blood were at the head of the bed, the side of the bedding and on the ceiling. There were no marks on Orton's hands or arms.

Halliwell lay nude in the middle of the bedroom. He'd removed his soiled pyjama top which was lying across the desk chair. The top of his chest and head were splattered with blood. Near him on the floor was a glass and a can of grapefruit juice with which he'd swallowed twenty-two Nembutals. Halliwell died first. When they were discovered, rigor mortis had set into all but Halliwell's arms; Orton's sheets were still warm.

On the desk, police found a note:

> If you read his diary all will be explained.
> K.H.
> P.S. Especially the latter part.

Appendices

THE CORRESPONDENCE OF EDNA WELTHORPE & OTHERS

'Edna Welthorpe' is the pseudonym Orton invented in the mid-50s to tease suburban dottiness and also to create mischief. 'Edna' is the precursor of the trickster temperament Orton's plays made sensational. Watchdog of public morals and daft egotist, 'Edna' berates the world and provokes its credulity and outrageousness. In later years, with success, Orton called 'Edna' into service to create controversy over himself and his work; and, in his high spirits, to relish the fluting looniness of her voice.

Edna's first recorded prank was an attempt to get 78 tickets to the Institutional Fashion Fair.

THE NATIONAL TRADE PRESS LTD

TLB/YC

29th October, 1958.

Mrs E. Welthorpe,
1a Regent Lodge,
161 West End Lane,
London N.W.6.

Dear Madam,

We have received your request for 78 admission tickets for the International Trade Fashion Fair, but as this Exhibition is intended for Trade Buyers only we would appreciate it if you will kindly let us know your connection in this request. We will then give your request our further consideration.

Yours faithfully,

S.W. BUNCE.
Circulation Manager.

Edna replied:

3rd November, 1958.

Dear Mr Bunce,

I am at a loss to understand your communication of the 29th October, ref: TLB./YC. I did not request 78 admission tickets for the International Trade Fashion Fair, the idea is absurd! I merely asked for seven or eight. I am well aware that the Exhibition is intended for Trade Buyers only, and I consider your request to know what my connection is in this respect both rude and uncalled for.

It is a matter of supreme indifference to myself or to the firm I represent whether or not I come to the International Trade Fashion Fair. But since I was sent your postcard I assumed that my custom would be desired. If the contrary is the case then I certainly do not wish to attend.

Will you kindly let me know in due course what your opinion is upon the subject.

I am,

Yours faithfully,

(Edna Welthorpe – Mrs)

THE NATIONAL TRADE PRESS LTD

SWB/YC

4th November, 1958.

Mrs E. Welthorpe,
1a Regent Lodge,
161 West End Lane,
London N.W.6.

Dear Madam,

We thank you for your letter of the 3rd instant, in reference to your request for tickets for the International Trade Fashion Fair, and regret that there has been some misunderstanding in regard to this. We of course, will be delighted to welcome you to this Fair and the only reason we raised the question of the number of tickets required is that we interpreted your request as a requirement of 78 tickets, which was a rather unusual request to receive from what appears to be a private address, bearing in mind that the Fair is intended for Trade Buyers.

We trust that this explanation explains our intention in the previous letter, and have pleasure in enclosing 8 tickets with this letter.

Yours faithfully,

S.W. BUNCE.
Circulation Manager.

'Edna' always showed an interest in theatre. At first, she attempted to pioneer a debate on sexual matters; but with age, she was forthright in her condemnation of violence and sexuality on the stage, or anywhere else for that matter. 'Edna Welthorpe writes,' Orton confided to Kenneth Williams from Tangier: '"The people here leave a lot to be desired and flaunt their preferences for what they cryptically call 'bits of the other' at every cafe. I might have been assaulted through the ears on many occasions – by words only," she adds.'

2nd November, 1958.

Dear Sir,

Your name has kindly been given to me in connection
with the availability of the Heath Street Baptist Church
Hall. If it is at all possible, I should like to begin rehearsals
there during the next few weeks, and later to present for
three performances, 'The Pansy', a play which pleads for
greater tolerance on the subject of homosexuality.

It is with the utmost hesitance that I approach a
minister upon so controversial a topic; but the attitude
of enlightened Churchmen seems to have undergone a
favourable revolution during the past decade. It is with
this thought in mind that I decided to contact you.

I am told that you forbid dancing in your hall. This is a
difficulty, as there is a certain amount of dancing in several
scenes. However, if you too strongly object I could cut these
as, at the request of certain members of the cast, I have
already expurgated the scenes which were to have taken
place in the Kilburn Branch Library in Cotleigh Road.

Trusting to have your reply in due course, I am,

Yours faithfully,

Edna Welthorpe, (Mrs)

A fortnight later she tried again:

15th November 1958.

Dear Sir,

Re: Hiring of Heath Street Baptist Hall.

I wrote to you a fortnight ago with regard to the above
matter. I have received no reply. I would have thought
that to answer such an urgent communication would
have been only common courtesy. All I requested was
permission to stage a play in your hall. If this was not

possible or desireable a simple Yes or No would have been all the acknowledgement I require.

I and my company are anxious to secure somewhere to present an extremely interesting play. I stated in my last letter to you the reasons why I preferred a Church Hall. If you feel that it is too controversial a subject please let me know. But I would like a straight Yes or No.

Awaiting your reply,

Yours sincerely,

Edna Welthorpe (Mrs)

17 November 1958

Dear Mrs Welthorpe,

Thank you for your two letters, In your first you ended: 'Trusting to have your reply in due course'. Now it so happens that we meet for business monthly and tomorrow, Tuesday 18th November is the time for the November meeting, and it will be at that meeting that your request will be considered, together with any others there may be – there is one other at least – and then you will hear, as you requested, 'in due course'. My Church officers are busy people and have all sorts of other things to do so that special meetings are not much in favour.

I would assure you that your request has scarcely been out of mind since you sent it. If it were left to me personally I should not be able to agree to it, but in so responsible a matter I feel that only the fullest consideration by all concerned would be just.

I hope these considerations will help you to feel ashamed of your strictures. I might add that it is the custom among us, when we write desiring replies, to enclose a stamped and addressed envelope, which you did not do. However, you may count on a reply as soon as I know the answer of my Church Officers.

Yours sincerely,
Rev. G. W. Sterry

Orton wrote to Rev. Sterry declaring Edna Welthorpe dead. He got the following reply.

8 December 1958

Dear Madam,

Thank you for your very kind letter. I am sorry you have not received my other letter. I wrote the next day after our meeting, so that your niece might know our decision as soon as possible. I am afraid that we felt that we had to say No. Because I thought she might feel we had been merely obscurantist and awkward I explained to her that our Lecture Hall is not suitable as it has no stage or means of entrance or exit to or from where a stage would be. Our only other hall is so dilapidated as not to be fit for use.

I was shocked to learn that your niece had died, and I wish to say how sorry I am and would offer you my sincerest condolences on this unfortunate event. It is very sad to think that one's last contacts with anyone had been on the level that mine were with her, but you, if I may say so, have lifted the whole business on to an entirely different level, and I am grateful.

With every good wish,
Yours sincerely,

Rev. G. W. Sterry

Meanwhile, Edna had turned her wrath on Littlewoods, the mail order firm.

15th November 1958.

Dear Sirs,

I am puzzled by several letters I have received from you. Apparently you are under the impression that I am organising something for you, or at least that someone in this flat is. I assure you that there is no one called Mr Orton living here. I am a widow and dwell alone.

You state that catalogues are expensive. I have no doubt that they are, but what, may I ask, has that to do with me. You surely cannot imagine that I have stolen your catalogue. And as for *selling* anything which your firm makes . . . Please believe me if I arrived at the New Acol Bridge Club with a catalogue under my arm and explained to my friends that all goods were at cash prices, yet payable by small weekly instalments, why I think they would laugh at me.

Will you please stop sending letters to me, or I shall seriously have to consider putting the affair into the hands of my solicitor.

Yours faithfully,

Edna Welthorope. (Mrs)

MMC/AI/505.   21st November 1958.

Mrs E. Welthorpe,
Flat 3,
Regent Lodge,
161 West End Lane,
London N.W.6.

Dear Mrs Welthorpe,

Thank you for your letter.

We are so sorry to learn that you are being troubled with correspondence regarding a 'Home-Shopping' service, and do apologise for any annoyance caused. You may rest assured however, that an application was received by us and naturally we took it to be authentic.

To avoid further correspondence being sent, could you possibly let us have any letter or pamphlet received recently, or let us have the organiser's number which will begin with c. 1, 2, 3, 4 or 5. All our records are compiled numerically and your co-operation will be much appreciated.

Please use the back of this letter for your reply, also the accompanying prepaid envelope.

With best wishes.

Yours faithfully,
LITTLEWOODS MAIL ORDER STORES LTD.

ENC.P.P.E.

Orton replied, adopting a new identity.

7th December, 1958.

Dear Sirs,

Regarding your letter of 21st November, reference: MMC/A/505.

The above letter was written to a Mrs Edna Welthorpe. It appears to be about a correspondence regarding a Home-Shopping service. I have just taken over this flat from a disgusting black woman who left the place in utter confusion. In the cupboard under the stairs was an enormous amount of literature from various firms. All the letters were addressed to different people.

I do not know what you required from her but as I have burnt the whole lot with a lot of rubbish, I should think that it is extremely unlikely that you will receive the information. However, if you will tell me what it is that you wanted so urgently I will endeavour to do my best.

Yours faithfully,

Donald H. Hartley

Edna, the outraged consumer, also wrote to the food concern, Smedleys:

Flat 4,
25, Noel Road,
London, N.1.

30th April 1965.

Dear Sir,

I recently purchased a tin of Morton's blackcurrant pie filling. It was delicious. Choc-full of rich fruit. Then, wishing to try another variety, I came upon Smedley's raspberry pie filling. And I tried that. And really! How can you call such stuff pie filling? There wasn't a raspberry in it. I was very disappointed after trying Morton's blackcurrant.

Please try to do better in future. And what on earth is 'EDIBLE STARCH' and 'LOCUST BEAN GUM'? If that is what you put into your pie fillings I'm not surprised at the result.

I shan't try any more of your pie fillings until the fruit content is considerably higher. My stomach really turned at what I saw when I opened the tin.

Yours sincerely,

Edna Welthorpe (Mrs)

SMEDLEY'S LIMITED

HG/RH   3rd May, 1965.

Mrs E. Welthorpe,
Flat 4,
25, Noel Road,
London N.1.

Dear Madam,

We acknowledge with thanks your letter and are concerned to receive your report of Smedley's canned raspberry pie filling.

The most modern methods of production are employed in Smedley factories and at every state the strictest super-vision is exercised to ensure that quality is maintained at the very highest level. Your helpful co-operation in writing to us is greatly appreciated and you have our assurance that the matter will be referred to our Technical Department for investigation.

In accordance with our guarantee, we have pleasure in enclosing postal order value 2/- to refund the purchase price and postage, with our sincere apologies for the inconvenience which you have been caused.

Yours faithfully,
SMEDLEY'S LIMITED.

Customer Service Dept.

And, as an outraged viewer, Edna wrote to Kenneth Williams:

3 April 1966

Dear Mr Williams,

I must take up cudgels with you over your recent appearance on *Juke Box Jury*. I regretted many of your remarks which, in my opinion, were quite uncalled-for and tasteless in the extreme.

Especially offensive to me as a nursing mother was your attack on infants and their ways. My own baby, born recently, cried throughout the programme. Which, I feel, more than proves my point.

More serious was your veiled threat to wear plastic earrings. This greatly disturbed me and my whole family. We were not alone in our fright. The usually irrepressible 'Millie' Martin seemed quite put out by your vile decision to flout convention. For the rest of the evening – long after you had left our screen – the idea was discussed among my family circle.

I cannot condemn too strongly the whole sorry business,

made especially more deplorable for me as I thoroughly enjoyed many of the records which found no favour with you.

These 'kinky' comments and 'lurid', 'off-colour' 'gags' must be ejected from our TV screen. Saturday night viewers must be protected from people like you.

Yours faithfully,

Edna Welthorpe (Mrs)

Edna wrote to the Ritz:

Flat 4
25, Noel Road,
London, N.1.

Tuesday 14th February 1967.

The Manager
The Ritz Hotel,
Piccadilly,
London, W.1.

Dear Sir,

I'm writing to ask a question which, as a hotelier, I'm sure you'll be eager to answer. A month ago I visited the Ritz in company with Mrs Sally Warren – a tall grey-haired lady. During our brief stay at your hotel I lost a brown Morocco handbag with the initials E.W. stamped on the flap. The contents of the bag weren't valuable – they consisted of a purse containing a few loose coins, a Boots folder with snapshots of members of my family and a pair of gloves made of some hairy material.

I wonder if you, or any of your staff, have come across my handbag? If you can give me any assistance, in its recovery I'd be most grateful.

There is no value attached to the bag or the contents. If

it has been thrown away you needn't be afraid to tell me. I shan't be angry. It would be a relief in many ways to know what has happened to my purse.

And may I take this opportunity of saying that, in my opinion, the Ritz is unbeatable? I was staggered by the splendour of it all.

Yours faithfully,

(E. Welthorpe – Mrs)

Ritz Hotel,
London, W.1.

15th February, 1967.

Mrs Edna Welthorpe,
Flat 4,
25, Noel Road,
London, N.1.

Dear Madam,

We are in receipt of your letter of the 14th February, the contents of which we have noted, and for which we thank you.

We very much regret to inform you, however, that no handbag, as described in your letter, has been found and none of our staff remember seeing it.

Trusting that you will ultimately recover your handbag, and assuring you of our best attention,

We remain,

Yours faithfully,
FOR THE RITZ HOTEL

E. Schwenter
General Manager

ES/SS

Orton contributed to the furore over *Entertaining Mr Sloane* under various *noms de plume*. 'Peter Pinnell' opened the attack in the pages of *The Daily Telegraph*.

'MR SLOANE'

Sir – In finding so much to praise in 'Entertaining Mr Sloane', which seems to be nothing more than a highly sensationalised, lurid, crude and over-dramatised picture of life at its lowest, surely your dramatic critic has taken leave of his senses.

The effect this nauseating work had on me was to make me want to fill my lungs with some fresh, wholesome Leicester Square air. A distinguished critic, if I quote him correctly, felt the sensation of snakes swarming around his ankles while watching it.

Yours truly,

Peter Pinnell

'Edna Welthorpe' soon picked up his theme in a diatribe against Orton and his kind.

NAUSEATED

Sir – As a playgoer of forty years standing, may I say that I heartily agree with Peter Pinnell in his condemnation of 'Entertaining Mr Sloane'.

I myself was nauseated by this endless parade of mental and physical perversion. And to be told that such a disgusting piece of filth now passes for humour!

Today's young playwrights take it upon themselves to flaunt their contempt for ordinary decent people. I hope that the ordinary decent people of this country will shortly strike back!

Yours truly,

Edna Welthorpe (Mrs)

Orton let 'John Carlsen' answer Edna's' criticism of life and art.

ARISING FROM 'MR SLOANE'

Sir – Two points arise from Mrs Edna Welthorpe's letter regarding 'Entertaining Mr Sloane'.

One is that everyone is perfectly entitled to like or dislike a play – on any subject – according to personal taste, which is why there is such a wide range of theatrical fare available in London at the moment – everything from opera to 'One for the Pot'. Some people are, however, more fortunate than others in their ability to enjoy a wider field of subjects, and is surely not for the more 'blinkered' citizens to censure them for that.

Secondly, I cannot recall a successful play – from, say, 'Othello' to 'St. Joan' from 'Tamburlaine' to 'Look Back in Anger' which concerned itself with 'ordinary decent people'! One agrees that ordinary, decent people are the salt of the earth and the backbone of the country – but they do not make subjects for exciting, stimulating, controversial drama.

Yours faithfully,

John. A. Carlsen

Orton kept his pseudonyms alive with yet another letter about *Entertaining Mr Sloane* disagreeing with *all* of them.

OTHELLO, JOAN and MR SLOANE

Sir – I feel I must take up cudgels with Mr Carlsen on behalf of Mrs Welthorpe and Mr Pinnell. I myself was neither nauseated by 'Entertaining Mr Sloane' nor did I feel as if snakes had been crawling around my ankles and I hope I am not blinkered, but Mr Carlsen's suggestion that Othello (the noble Moor!) and St Joan (belatedly

canonised) are not decent people or the 'salt of the earth',
I find more than controversial.

I find it completely unacceptable!

These fine plays, together with 'Mrs Warren's Profession' and 'Ghosts' were not, I repeat NOT, intended
at their original productions to be funny, as I gather
'Entertaining Mr Sloane' is.

Yours in fair play.

Jay Chakiris

When *Entertaining Mr Sloane* transferred to the West End, Orton had 'Donald
Hartley' rave about the play in its old and new venue.

SEEING IT AGAIN

Sir – I saw 'Entertaining Mr Sloane' twice at the New
Arts. I shall see it again at Wyndham's.

God knows the theatre is dreary enough at the present
time. Any oasis in the wasteland is welcome. And 'Entertaining Mr Sloane' is not a mirage which disappears when
the thirsty traveller approaches. The water is there, the
exotic landscape is real. And if we find the customs of the
country differ from our own – what else is foreign travel
for?

Donald H. Hartley

Orton's *Entertaining Mr Sloane* correspondence ends with a hymn to its quality by
another invented Orton character.

Sir – What, not one word in *favour* of poor 'Mr Sloane'?
Well, here goes: I myself consider – a) the dialogue
brilliant; b) the comedy breath-taking; c) the drama
satisfying; d) the play as a whole well-written if not
profound; e) let us, however, exhort Mr Orton to turn his

gaze higher. As Oscar Wilde said in another context, 'Some of us are walking in the gutter, but we can look at the stars!'

Yours faithfully,

Alan Crosby

With *Loot*, Orton's theatrical gaze was pitched higher toward farce. When one writer in *Plays and Players* criticised the magazine's choice of *Loot* as best play of 1966, Orton summoned 'Donald H. Hartley' to savage the man, and 'Edna Welthorpe' to praise him for dismissing Orton's dubious talents.

February 17th 1967.

Dear Sir,

I take great exception to the Green Room piece in *Plays and Players* (March issue). Mr David Benedictus, in my opinion, shows a lamentable want of tact in suggesting that Joe Orton's *Loot* was not the best play of 1967. I'm sure that the London Critics who gave Mr Orton the awards (both the *Evening Standard* and the *Plays and Players* accolade) were perfectly sincere in their nomination.

It was perfectly foolish of Mr Benedictus to give as his award a television play. And it is really no come-back to say that *Loot* was seen publicly in a previous year. *Loot* was first presented to the London critics in 1966. And they judged it the best play of that year. We should accept their judgement without carping.

Really, if every pip-squeak circus pony were to give awards for the horse of the year goodness knows where we should be!

Yrs.

Donald H. Hartley

19 February 1967

May I add my thoughts to those of David Benedictus on the subject of those 'much-talked-of' awards?

I agree that no one should seriously nominate as the play of the year a piece of indecent tomfoolery like *Loot*. Drama should be uplifting. The plays of Joe Orton have a most unpleasant effect on me. I was plunged into the dumps for weeks after seeing his *Entertaining Mr Sloane*. I saw *Loot* with my young niece; we both fled from the theatre in horror and amazement well before the end. I could see no humour in it. Yet it is widely advertised as a rib-tickler. Surely this is wrong?

These plays do nothing but harm to our image abroad, presenting us as the slaves of sensation and unnatural practice. Mr Benedictus does well to point out the inadequacies of our present honours system!

Edna Welthorpe

But, if 'Edna' had nothing nice to say about Orton, she was full of obtuse praise in her fan letter to Kenneth Williams.

25 February 1967

Dear Mr Williams

Bravo for your splendid performance in the panel game *Watch My Bluff* (Friday).

I was enthralled at your masterful control of what could, and I'm sure on many occasions was, a tense and difficult situation.

The way you held your team was brilliant. I'm sure Miss Maxine Audrey and Mr Joe Horton must've taken some handling. But you showed you were a past master of the art of diplomacy.

Let us see more of you on television in the future! And here's power to your elbow.

Yours sincerely,

Edna Welthorpe (Mrs)

The management of the Criterion Theatre forwarded this letter to Orton . . .

9 April 1967

Dear Sir,

On Saturday I went with my family to see *Loot* at your theatre, and feel compelled to express to you our disgust at the contents of the play. As Christians, we were naturally dismayed to see the Roman Catholic Church abused, but even were I not a Christian I should have been ashamed to take my mother and sister to hear the accompanying filth. I am in consequence writing to the Lord Chamberlain, suggesting that the play should be reviewed yet again, and at the least severely edited.

May I suggest that your advertisements should indicate to the public the immoral tone of the play. This would have spared us the annoyance and embarrassment of buying tickets for a play we felt forced to leave at the interval.

Yours faithfully,

J. P. H. Joy

. . . who put 'Edna' on their case.

Flat 4,
25, Noel Road
London, N.1.

14th April 1967.

Dear J. P. H. Joy,

Please let me say at once that I am conscious of a great feeling of uneasiness at writing to you. I must write, however, to tell you that you are not alone in disliking the play *Loot*. I myself consider it to be the most loathsome play on in London at the present moment. 'Bestial' is how I described it to an acquaintance the other day. When I tell you that in the second act (which you had the good fortune to miss) there was a discussion upon the raping of children with Mars bars with other filthy details of a sexual and psychopathic nature I'm sure you'll pardon my writing.

Please, please, as a fellow Christian, let me applaud your design in writing to the Lord Chamberlain. I myself have written several letters to the papers (none alas published) and am trying to contact my MP at the moment. I took an elderly aunt of mine to see the play and really I had to go round to the manager afterwards and demand an apology. This truly horrible play shouldn't contaminate our streets.

It was most wrong of me to write to you, I'm sure. Your letter was passed to me for filing. I do hope you will respect my confidence in this. It has received the most respectful attention here. Naturally I cannot express any but my own opinion. And that you have fully.

I am trying, in a solo capacity, to arrange a meeting with the Lord Chamberlain to protest against plays in general and this travesty of the free-society *Loot* in particular. I wonder if you'd like to be included in our mission?

Yours, in great sympathy,

Edna Welthorpe (Mrs).

Chronology

1933
Born John Kingsley Orton on the Saffron Lane Estates, Leicester

1944
Fails 11+ Exams.

1944–7
Attends Clark's College, Leicester.

1949
Joins Leicester Drama Society, Bats Players, Vaughan Players.

1951
May: Begins at Royal Academy of Dramatic Art (RADA), London. Meets Kenneth Leith Halliwell.
June: Moves into Halliwell's flat at 161 West End Lane, London NW6.

1953
Assistant Stage Manager at Ipswich Rep. Billed as 'John K. Orton'.
Begins literary collaboration with Halliwell. They write *The Silver Bucket* (unpublished).

1955
They write *The Mechanical Womb* (a sci-fi spoof, unpublished); *The Last Days of Sodom* (unpublished).

1956
They write *The Boy Hairdresser* (a satire in blank verse, unpublished).

1957
Orton begins writing independently of Halliwell.
Writes *Between Us Girls* (unpublished).

1958
Orton begins 'Edna Welthorpe' letters.

1959
Halliwell buys them a new flat at 25 Noel Rd., Islington, London N1.
They begin stealing and defacing public library books in satirical ways.

1960
Orton and Halliwell collaborate on the novel, *The Boy Hairdresser* (unpublished).

1961
Orton writes *The Vision of Gombold Proval* (posthumously published as *Head to Toe*). Submits *The Visit* to the Royal Court Theatre London.

1962
Orton and Halliwell arrested for stealing 72 library books and 'wilfully' damaging the books including the removal of 1,653 plates from art books.
Orton sent to H M Prison East Church at Sheerness, Kent; Halliwell sent to H M Prison Ford at Arundel, Sussex.

1963
August: *The Ruffian on the Stair* (originally titled *The Boy Hairdresser*) sold to the BBC Third Programme (Broadcast 31 August 1964).
September–December: Writes *Entertaining Mr Sloane*.
December: Orton acquires a literary agent: Margaret Ramsay.

1964
May: *Entertaining Mr Sloane* produced at the Arts Theatre Club, London (6 May).
June: Completes *The Good and Faithful Servant* (produced by Rediffusion Television, 6 April 1967). *Entertaining Mr Sloane* transfers to Wyndham's Theatre, London, 29 June.
June–October: Writes *Loot*.

1965
February–March: *Loot* produced. Closes in Wimbledon, 20 March.
April: *Loot* produced at the University Theatre, Manchester, 11–23 April.
May–July: First visit to Tangier.
July–September: Writes *The Erpingham Camp* (produced in early version by Rediffusion Television, 27 June 1966).
October: *Entertaining Mr Sloane* opens on Broadway.

1966
May–July: Second visit to Tangier.
September: *Loot* produced successfully in London.
November: Completes *Funeral Games* (produced by Yorkshire Television, 25 August 1966); *Loot* transfers to the Criterion Theatre, London, 1 November 1966.
December: Begins *Diaries*. Starts *What the Butler Saw*.

1967
January: Wins *Evening Standard Award* and *Plays and Players Award* for Best Play of 1966. Begins screenplay for the Beatles, *Up Against It*.

March: Finishes *Up Against It*.

April: Rewrites *The Ruffian on the Stair* and *The Erpingham Camp* for the stage double-bill *Crimes of Passion*. *Up Against It* rejected by the Beatles. Oscar Lewenstein picks up the film option.

May–July: Third visit to Tangier.

June: *Crimes of Passion* opens at the Royal Court Theatre, London.

July: Completes *What the Butler Saw*.

August: Murdered on 9 August by Kenneth Halliwell who takes his own life with an overdose of sleeping pills.

List of Published Work

All Orton's stage and television plays are collected in one paperback volume, *Orton: the Complete Plays* (Methuen, World Dramatists, 1976) which also contains a useful introduction by John Lahr. The plays, with the dates of their first publication, are:

The Ruffian on the Stair (1966 radio version; revised 1967)
Entertaining Mr Sloane (1964)
The Good and Faithful Servant (1970)
Loot (1967)
The Erpingham Camp (1967)
Funeral Games (1970)
What the Butler Saw (1969)

Orton's screenplay, *Up Against It*, is published in paperback by Methuen (1979). His novel, originally entitled *The Vision of Gombold Proval*, was published posthumously in 1971 under the title *Head to Toe* by Anthony Blond and appeared in a Panther paperback edition. It was re-issued by Methuen in 1986.

Orton's biography is John Lahr's *Prick Up Your Ears* (Penguin).

Index

Collins
Guide to
ROSES

BERTRAM
PARK

PLANTING
CULTIVATION
PRUNING

—

1350 ROSES
DESCRIBED

—

80 PAGES OF
ILLUSTRATIONS

635
·93
ROS

COLLINS

Collins Guide to

ROSES

by
BERTRAM
PARK